A WAR OF INDIVIDUALS

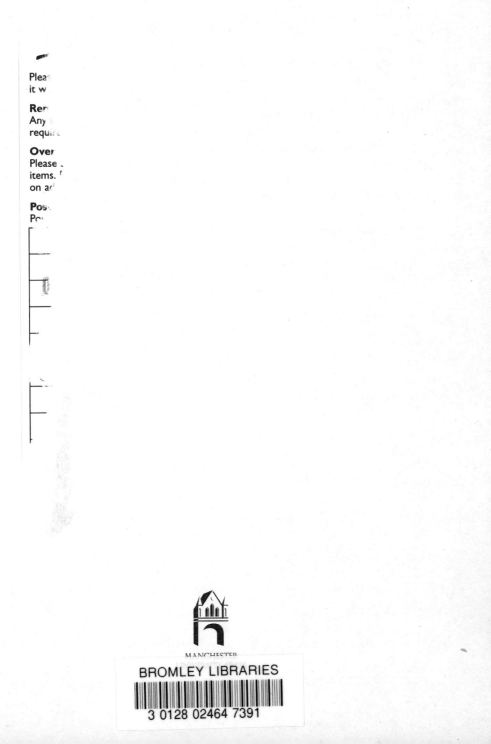

A WAR OF INDIVIDUALS

Bloomsbury attitudes to the Great War

JONATHAN ATKIN

Manchester University Press

Manchester and New York

distributed exclusively in the USA by Palgrave

Published by Manchester University Press
Oxford Road, Manchester M13 9NR, UK
and Room 400, 175 Fifth Avenue, New York, NY 10010, USA
www.manchesteruniversitypress.co.uk

Distributed exclusively in the USA by
Palgrave, 175 Fifth Avenue, New York,
NY 10010, USA

Distributed exclusively in Canada by
UBC Press, University of British Columbia, 2029 West Mall,
Vancouver, BC, Canada V6T 1Z2

British Library Cataloguing-in-Publication Data
A catalogue record for this book is available from the British Library

Library of Congress Cataloging-in-Publication Data applied for

ISBN 0 7190 6070 2 *hardback*
ISBN 0 7190 6071 0 *paperback*

First published 2002
10 09 08 07 06 05 04 03 02   10 9 8 7 6 5 4 3 2 1

Typeset by Freelance Publishing Services, Brinscall, Lancs.
www.freelancepublishingservices.co.uk
Printed in Great Britain
by Bookcraft (Bath) Ltd, Midsomer Norton

Contents

Acknowledgements and abbreviations

I would like to thank my tutors at the University of Leeds, Dr Hugh Cecil and Dr Richard Whiting, for their continued advice, support and generosity when completing my initial PhD.

I would also like to thank the staff at all the archives and libraries I visited during the course of my research, particularly Peter Liddle and his staff at the Liddle Collection in Leeds for putting up with me, and the staff at the William Ready Division of Archives and Research Collection at McMaster University, Hamilton, Ontario for making me feel welcome when I was far from home.

And last, but certainly not least, I would like to thank my parents for their unwavering support over the years.

This book is dedicated to Frances Partridge, who kindly took the time to recall friends, places and incidents from her remarkable life.

BL,MC	British Library, Manuscripts Collection
IWM	Imperial War Museum
McM,BRP	McMaster University, Hamilton, Ontario, Canada, William Ready Division of Archives and Research Collection
TGA,CTP	Tate Gallery Archive, Charleston Trust Papers
UL,LC	University of Leeds, Liddle Collection
UV,DC	University of Victoria, British Columbia, Canada, Doyle Collection

Introduction

The Great War still haunts us. During the first few weeks of 1998, various British national broadsheets carried articles on recently released War Office papers dating back over eighty years and relating to the case of the celebrated First World War poet, Siegfried Sassoon. Although at times a fearless and sometimes reckless warrior, known to the men who served under him as 'Mad Jack', Sassoon had also written powerful anti-war poetry and, though decorated for his bravery on the Western Front, had thrown his Military Cross into the river Mersey whilst on leave.

According to his hitherto confidential army file, now released by the Public Records Office, the War Office had considered him 'a lunatic'. The *Independent* carried with its article, which was entitled 'Siegfried Sassoon – mad, sad or heroically confused?', a large black and white photograph of Sassoon in his uniform. The soldier-poet stares out of the picture, as if into the future. One cannot tell from his expression whether he is about to frown or smile. Will he proffer the hand of friendship or the bayonet of hate? This was the paradox of Sassoon: that a brave, military man should write the verse that he did and also compose his famous 'Soldier's Declaration' against the conduct of the war (which was printed in *The Times* in July 1916) but should then return to the trenches afterwards, to live or die. *Was* he mad? The authorities naturally thought so. Not only mad, but dangerously so – liable to influence others with his proclamations on the conflict and its conduct. Anti-war reaction was expected from 'conchies' and Bohemian types, perhaps, but most definitely not from serving officers in His Majesty's Forces.

As well as the extraordinariness of his character, it was this apparent paradox which lay within Sassoon and, I began to realise, many others, which I wanted to explore when I began the research that forms the basis for this book. My earlier undergraduate research on the attitude of the Bloomsbury Group to the Great War had told me that, far from all opposing the conflict as one, as generally believed, the individuals who constituted this most famous circle of friends reacted in many *different* ways to the coming of war. Some of the younger 'members', such as the artist Duncan Grant, even *supported* the war during the initial rush of popular enthusiasm during the hot August and September of 1914.

Other members of the group, like the influential economist John Maynard Keynes, actually worked for the war effort at the heart of government. In fact, each invididual took their own line, though they were in general agreement over the wrongness of the Great War and, most particularly, the barriers that the war imposed between the personal ideals of truth and beauty on the one hand and the active pursuit of these by individuals, on the other. The years of the Great War were the formative ones that helped to mould the group into the image that would be recast by the public imagination in succeeding generations. But why had they reacted in the ways they did? I found I wanted to explore deeper – into both the past itself and the personalities of bohemian Bloomsbury.

I learnt that the older members of Bloomsbury had been taught to revere the appreciation of beauty, art and friendship by their mentor, the kindly yet intense philosopher G.E. Moore, in the intellectual ferment of the Cambridge of the 1880s. Beauty and its appreciation were to be seen as an absolute good and hence one of the driving aims of life itself, if that life were to be lived to its maximum emotional potential. Despite their varying attitudes to war and the Great War in particular, it was this process of aesthetic fulfilment which Bloomsbury felt the war disrupted or stunted in a dramatic manner. For too long this awareness had been credited only to those 'celebrities' of Bloomsbury whose profile was dramatic enough to warrant investigation by writers and journalists. Now the time had come for a re-evaluation of the scope of this searchingly individual form of anti-war feeling. Crucially, did its beam cast itself wider than the rarefied air of Ottoline Morrell of Garsington Manor or aesthetic work-ethic of Vanessa Bell's Charleston farmhouse? This book will investigate its extent and also the themes that were its means of expression in the numerous diaries, articles and letters that formed a part of the vast literary legacy of the epoch.

The Great War of 1914 to 1918 was the first 'modern' war, both in reality and in the popular imagination. It involved more spheres of human experience than perhaps any previous conflict. Whole populations were caught up in it and exhibited myriad shades of reaction to it – including, naturally, opposition. This book concentrates on those individualistic British citizens whose motivation for opposition in thought or deed was grounded upon moral, humanistic or aesthetic precepts. There have been previous studies based around specific British religious or political conscientious objection to the war but none concentrating on any existing moral, humanistic or aesthetic anti-war feeling – reactions that, as we will see, were as valid and real as any of a religious or political nature. I felt it was time to set the record straight.

Very occasionally, this humanistic anti-war feeling has been noted in 'official' studies. In his *Pacifism in Britain 1914–1945: The Defining of a Faith*, the historian Martin Ceadel singles out what he terms 'humanitarian pacifism' as a valid form of anti-war feeling, stating that it is 'no less a dogma' than religious or political pacifism. However, in Ceadel's book, humanitarian pacifism is classed

as 'all absolute objections to war based on its consequences for human existence',[1] a categorisation that is at once too narrow (with its use of the term
'absolute objection') and too wide. Ceadel also describes 'humanitarian pacifism' as, 'the major pacifist innovation of the *inter-war period*' (my italics).[2]
While this may be true in terms of strict pacifism, my study champions a clearly
identifiable 'humanitarian' anti-war feeling during the Great War itself – in all
its humanistic, aesthetic and moral contexts: not simply the cases of individuals
who believed all war to be wrong, but also – using a term Martin Ceadel em-
ploys – amongst *pacificists*, such as the celebrated philosopher Bertrand Russell,
who regarded *some* wars as justifiable.

Crucially, aesthetic opposition to the conflict was identified as such at the
time. Howard Marten, chairman of the Harrow branch of the anti call-up No
Conscription Fellowship and a conscientious objector,[3] noted that, in his view,
the individuals who opposed the war were, 'men from every conceivable angle
of life ... a sort of cross-section of every type'. In addition to members of the
established churches or smaller religious groups and those from a political background such as the Independent Labour Party, Marten also observed:

> a very curious group of what I used to call artistically-minded. There were a lot of
> men who were not in any way organised or attached, but I should call them the
> aesthetic group: artists, musicians and all that. There were quite a considerable num-
> ber of them ... They had a terrific repugnance at war which could only express itself
> individually ... They're not group-minded. They're individuals to the core; so that
> naturally they would, almost inevitably, take a very personal attitude to that sort of
> thing.[4]

So – who *were* these curious people? This book will comprehensively docu-
ment the breadth and precise nature of these (to quote W.H. Auden on a later
war) 'affirming flames' of individual yet linked aesthetic reaction, as and when
they occurred in people of all types and locations. The book's trajectory will take
us from the core friendships of the Bloomsbury group upwards and outwards
into a society at once activated and traumatised by war. We shall move through
the shifting boundaries of Bloomsbury, to friends and mentors, such as Bertrand
Russell and Ottoline Morrell and on to encompass other well-known figures of
the period; artists, poets and writers such as Sassoon and Owen, Nash and Gurney
and explore their aesthetic links to Bloomsbury war attitudes through their own
contact with the conflict, whether at home or at the front. Then our search will
take us to obscurer figures, male and female, some of whom achieved brief notoriety during the war and inter-war period, but who are largely forgotten now,
such as the extraordinary Mabel St Clair Stobart. Finally, in order to show that
Bloomsbury attitudes existed (consciously or unconsciously) farther away still
from the scribbled thoughts of Virginia Woolf, Lytton Strachey and their friends,
we will meet individuals who now live only in the memories of descendants or in
bundles of papers and battered leather diaries stored carefully in archives around
the world.

To accomplish this scope of research, a wide range of source materials were consulted. These included published memoirs and accounts of personal experience, public statements and articles from newspapers and journals and private comments from letters and diaries found in archives such as the Liddle Collection at the University of Leeds and the files of the Imperial War Museum (from which Howard Marten's earlier identification of aesthetic and individualistic opposition to the war was taken). With a few important exceptions, all the evidence presented in this book will be centred around personal letters, diaries, memoirs and factual articles, as these generally present a more direct and certainly more individual reflection of the thoughts and feelings of the people involved, even when some hindsight was involved. Partly due to the limitations of time and space, there is much less focus on artistic material in the form of poems, novels and fictionalised representation which was, to a much greater extent, shaped with public awareness always in mind and, therefore, needed to be treated quite differently.

In January 1915, the obscure poet Max Plowman, on his way to Dorking to be billeted in the 4th Field Ambulance (but later to resign from the army), wrote to his brother that, 'War is ultimately an affair of individuals – and as such is insane and unmitigated filth'. This was due, Plowman thought, due to the damage inflicted by the conflict upon individual souls. His only hope for his army career was that, 'I meet someone fit to speak to'.[5] Max Plowman is cited by historian Keith Robbins in his *The Abolition of War* as an individual for whom *direct* contact with the war served to convince him that it was unjustifiable. Robbins also acknowledges the diversity of reasons leading to an individual conscientious objection. Just as Plowman saw that war 'was an affair of individuals', Robbins writes that the diversity of reaction should occasion no surprise to those looking back on the war because, as he writes, 'in a sense, "individuality" lay at the heart of the conscientious objector's argument. Whatever the precise nature of the case being articulated, it was intensely individual'.[6] The notion of a person standing apart from the war and feeling an aesthetic or humanistic reaction against it lies at the heart of my book. 'Humanistic' here not only stands for kindliness and a belief in mercy and friendship over difference but also in its more formal meaning, that of Classical studies and literary culture and an intellectual order that placed the mind of man and human interests first. It was a fear for the survival of this culture and of aestheticism, seen as a linear progression from the ancient Greeks and Romans via the Renaissance, that inspired many to oppose the destructive forces of the war. A humanistic response to the conflict usually emphasised the observation of an individual's feelings and reactions as a basis for a greater understanding of the self.

The hesitant Max Plowman represents the sensitive individual soul, for whom pacifism would hopefully be 'friendship in action', reacting to the bruteness – both physical and moral – of the war. The use of his words for the title of this book is an indicator that the viewpoint here will be a *personal* one using the thoughts and feelings of those who experienced the war and expressed themselves in a variety of forms, in both public and private. This book will show that Plowman's case was by no means atypical and that people with similar views or reactions to the war were not, as is commonly perceived, all isolated bohemian Bloomsbury-types turning their backs to the conflict by painting or writing in the country as the war drifted past them, largely unnoticed.

Martin Ceadel refers to Bloomsbury's opposition to the war as 'quasi-pacifism', a reaction he describes as 'numerically insignificant' and 'elitist' simply because they were *pacificists* (that is, some did not regard war as *always* wrong) and because the individuals involved were peculiarly articulate and achieved a prominence due to their artistic reputations. He states that the reactions of individuals of 'this type' can be categorised merely by their superficiality and that pacifism amongst them rarely existed in 'pure form'.[7]

However, this study will show that reactions very similar to those of the individuals who constituted Bloomsbury, whether in Ceadel's 'pure form' or not, existed through a wider spectrum of differing social backgrounds and contacts. Although this book will initially single out the better known, it will also include the much less celebrated – individuals such as Bernard Adams (whose memoirs are long out of print), as well as those whose identity rests only in fading sepia photographs – their letters and diaries having found their way into various archives scattered across Britain.

This book, then, will provide evidence that humanistic, aesthetic or moral anti-war reaction existed (having been previously comparatively little documented) and, crucially, show for the first time that it existed through a far more widespread variety of individual experience than was generally assumed to be the case.

These numerous anti-war reactions manifested themselves in a variety of forms. Martin Ceadel states: 'It must be admitted that a truly conscientious humanitarian pacifism and mere quasi-pacifism based on one's own particular qualities and sensitivity to civilised values are easier to distinguish in theory than in practice'.[8] In full awareness of this problem, this book will gradually draw out common themes of humanistic response linking the individuals involved across barriers of intellectual capacity, geographical location and time. Themes such as the war's perceived threat to individual liberty; its threat to personal and collective morals; its coarsening effect upon personality and on the capacity to appreciate ideals of beauty and art; and its detrimental effect upon the linear progression of civilisation and associated value systems, thus providing a valuable commentary, by those who felt themselves to be adversely affected, on the war's effect upon society and culture.

It would be rash to speak of a 'typical' anti-war response to the Great War. Although the humanistic/aesthetic response already outlined can be clearly distinguished from, for example, the equally identifiable responses of the Quakers, the Independent Labour Party or the Union of Democratic Control – there were obviously overlapping cases.[9] For example, a humanistic approach to the war sometimes involved a person affiliating him or herself to a political or religious group, but this need to associate with others with similar general aims did not necessarily lessen the original nature of the personal reaction. The individual could also move from an affiliation with a recognised anti-war group to a more personal style of reaction to the war – as will be shown in the case of mathematician and philosopher Bertrand Russell – owing to disaffection with the nature and style of 'organised protest'. Thus the edges of the fields of response and reaction were blurred in some cases; hardly surprising when a conflict on such an unprecedented scale as the Great War presented such 'myriad faces' to the individual.

An attempt to describe these 'myriad faces' was made by an ordinary soldier, Bernard Adams, who initially spent eight months at the front with the Royal Welch Fusiliers before returning to fight and die in February 1917.

> I have not yet found a perfect simile for this war, but the nearest I can think of is that of a pack of cards. Life in this war is a series of events so utterly different and disconnected, that the effect upon the actor in the midst of them is like receiving a hand of cards from an invisible dealer. There are four suits in the pack. Spades represent the dullness, mud, weariness, and sordidness. Clubs stand for another side, the humour, the cheerfulness, the jollity, the good-fellowship. In diamonds I see the glitter of excitement and adventure. Hearts are a tragic suit of agony, horror and death. And to each man the invisible dealer gives a succession of cards; sometimes they seem all black; sometimes they are red and black alternately; and at times they come red, red, red; and at the end is the ace of hearts.[10]

In addition, Adams echoed fellow soldier Max Plowman in one of the last things he ever wrote, 'War is evil. Justice is stronger than Force. Yet was there need of all this bloodshed to prove this? For this war is not as past wars; this is everyman's war, a war of civilians, a war of men who hate war, of men who fight for a cause, who are compelled to kill and hate it.'[11] This statement embodies an apparent contradiction which occurs again and again at various points during this study: the fact that many whose sensibilities were naturally inclined against the values seen to be underlying the conflict still felt the need to be a part of the direct experience. Men who abhorred war could at the same time be seen to be fighting for some sort of cause – 'the war to end all wars' and the 'fight for freedom' for example. Noble and peaceful ideals underpinned many a decision to join up. Men of fine-tuned sentiment still allowed themselves to be compelled to kill for many personal reasons, such as duty, fear or comradeship. A small number, of course, refused to be compelled, even after the introduction of conscription in 1916. The history of these conscientious objectors, some of them 'absolutists', has been chronicled in detail elsewhere (both individual accounts and collectively). In the case of such active forms of protest in appearing before a public, decision-making tribunal and becoming a conscientious objector, research has indicated that the majority of documented objectors backed up their stated objection with either specific religious or political motives – for example, out of a total of 3,964 conscientious objectors referred to the Pelham Committee (established in June 1916 to advise the local Tribunals on alternative work for those conscientious objectors who would accept it), 1,716 alone declared themselves to be religious Christadelphians.[12]

The seeming contradiction in wanting to take some part in a war the motives behind which one disagreed with, is highlighted by historian Brian Bond in his 'British "Anti-War" Writers and their Critics',[13] in which he states that some of the best 'anti-war satirists' were not actually pacifists or conscientious objectors but 'brave and even zealous subalterns', and that, though discontented with the 'justice' of the war, they returned to the front.[14] However, Bond then takes the same line as Adrian Caesar's *Taking It Like a Man*, in which Caesar attributes these individuals' attitudes to the war to their 'personal hang-ups'; for example, sexual problems deriving from repressive social and educational backgrounds. According to Bond and Caesar, the war provided for them an opportunity to 'obtain personal freedom' and a chance to 'seek love and consolation through suffering'.[15] In fact, as will be demonstrated, the reverse seems as often as not true, and the conflict was, in fact, in the opinion of those who showed humanistic opposition to it, a barrier to personal freedom and, perceived as such, was itself often a reason for the formation of an anti-war stance. However, Bond, in stating that, 'These famous "anti-war" writers … believed that protest against the war depended upon participation in it',[16] *is* right to identify this apparent contradiction (which applied in some, but not all, cases). He correctly asserts that some attitudes crushed under the weight of an 'anti-war' label could be 'ambivalent if not actually supportive' towards the conflict.[17]

One such attitude, which Brian Bond examines, is that of Siegfried Sassoon, mentioned at the start of this Introduction. Though Bond identifies Sassoon's high concerns with unit pride and comradeship, he simplifies Sassoon's spectrum of response in suggesting that his anti-war writing merely refers to an 'antagonism and mutual lack of empathy between home and military fronts',[18] while Martin Ceadel attributes Sassoon's 'conversion' merely to 'the unsettling experience of convalescence in Britain'.[19] Bond also over-simplifies the response to Sassoon's protest by saying that his front-line colleagues deplored his actions. This was not the whole case and this book will explore the need for direct experience of the war that underlay the anti-war stance of Siegfried Sassoon (and others like him) and his decision to return to the front. As already stated, Keith Robbins has identified soldier Max Plowman (later well-known for his inter-war pacifist stance) as an individual for whom direct experience of the war was crucial both to his understanding of it and in the formation of his anti-war position. This book will show that this *need* for experience was to be the case for other individuals besides Plowman and Sassoon.

This study concentrates chiefly on humanistic/aesthetic anti-war responses during the conflict itself and in the early inter-war period. Although various memoirs which will be cited appeared considerably later than this, in general these later writings have been used only as a source of judgements where they are particularly significant to the principal themes of the book, or where they quote material from diaries, letters or jottings made at the time of the war.

The war proved a testing ground for previously held convictions, beliefs or concepts – such as those of the philosopher G.E. Moore and late-Victorian Cambridge.[20] Moore's absolute ideals of beauty, truth and goodness were later to be exemplified by the pursuits and life-goals of the Bloomsbury Group. The war tested such ideals as it affected those who most valued them; disparate individuals interconnected by their approaches to a war which pushed ideas concerning the liberty and duty of an individual to the fore, especially in the minds of those who already supported, or now found themselves championing, the ideal of 'the self'.

Notes

1 Martin Ceadel, *Pacifism in Great Britain 1914–1945: The Defining of a Faith* (Oxford, 1980), p. 12.
2 *Ibid.,* p. 81.
3 The No Conscription Fellowship was established by journalist Fenner Brockway of the *Labour Leader* in November 1914 as a movement to provide support for those who would refuse to enlist, if called. The NCF headquarters was established off Fleet Street in spring 1915 and the first National Convention was held in November of that year.
4 Imperial War Museum, Sound Archive, file of H.C. Marten, 383/6, p. 9.
5 *Bridge Into the Future: Letters of Max Plowman*, ed. D.L. Plowman (London, 1944), p. 29.
6 Keith Robbins, 'The British Experience of Conscientious Objection' in Hugh Cecil and Peter Liddle (eds), *Facing Armageddon – The First World War Experienced* (London, 1996), pp. 695–6.
7 Ceadel, *Pacifism.* p. 44.
8 *Ibid.,* pp. 44–5.
9 The Union of Democratic Control was formed in September 1914 by Charles Trevelyan, E.D. Morel, Norman Angell and J.R. MacDonald and, although concerned with possible 'Prussianism' resulting from the Defence of the Realm Act, its main aims were to press for greater public accountability in foreign affairs (an end to secret diplomacy), improved international understanding and a fair peace settlement. The first meeting of its General Council was held on 17 November 1914. The UDC and its approach were not based upon an individualistic, aesthetic opposition to the existence of the war; neither was the ILP. By contrast, the spiritual opposition of the Quakers to the conflict was centred around inner personal conviction. For more background on 'organised' opposition to the war, see Keith Robbins, *The Abolition of War* (Cardiff, 1976).
10 Bernard Adams, *Nothing of Importance* (Stevenage, 1988), pp. xxvii–xxviii.
11 *Ibid.,* p. 303.
12 See John Rae, *Conscience and Politics* (Oxford, 1970), pp. 250–1. The Christadelphians were one of the larger non-combatant religious sects. In February 1915 they petitioned Parliament to grant them legal exemption from military service (on similar grounds to the Quakers) if conscription became law. The Pelham Committee was established by the Board of Trade and named after its first chairman, H.W. Pelham. T. Edmund Harvey, the MP responsible

for the amendment allowing work of national importance, was also a member.

Of around 16,000 conscientious objectors in total, over 6,000 conscientious objectors went to prison at least once and there were approximately 1,500 'absolutists' who refused to assist the war effort via any alternative work or Government scheme – see Arthur Marwick, *The Deluge* (London, 6th edn 1986), pp. 81–2.

13 Brian Bond, 'British "Anti-War" Writers and their Critics' in Cecil and Liddle (eds), *Facing Armageddon*.

14 *Ibid.*, p. 817.

15 *Ibid.*, p. 817. Adrian Caesar writes, 'Any potential critique of the politics of the war is subordinated to the personal, emotional and erotic implications of suffering'. Adrian Caesar, *Taking it Like a Man:: Suffering, Sexuality and the War-Poets* (Manchester, 1993), p. 97.

16 Bond, 'British "Anti-War" Writers', p. 818.

17 *Ibid.*, p. 829.

18 *Ibid.*, p. 819.

19 Ceadel, *Pacifism*, p. 56.

20 For a detailed background to the aesthetics of Bloomsbury see Paul Levy, *G.E. Moore and the Cambridge Apostles* (Oxford, 1981), Gertrude Himmelfarb, 'A Genealogy of Morals: From Clapham to Bloomsbury', in Himmelfarb, *Marriage and Morals Amongst the Victorians – Essays* (London, 1986) and J.K. Johnstone, 'The Philosophic Background and Works of Art of the Group known as Bloomsbury', PhD thesis (University of Leeds, 1952).

'Recognised' forms of opposition

Opposition to the Great War took many forms. This was perhaps not surprising, given its scale. It was a unique occasion for Great Britain. Never before had the whole, industrialised nation been mobilised for war on this scale. In medieval times, men who worked on the land had, in times of threat, left their harvests and gone to war as part of the agreement between landowner and serf. Much later, with the establishment of a regular army and navy, there was little need of binding agreements. As often as not, men joined up out of sheer patriotism or desire to repel foreign invaders. The more unfortunate were simply press-ganged, even in times of peace. Now, with the coming of the first 'total war', and an initial rush to answer the nation's call to arms; the government was able to boast by September 1915 that almost three million men had volunteered for armed service. This was not deemed ultimately sufficient and, for the first time, everyone – from humble clerks to country squires – was forced to bear arms from 1916.

Such a call-up was bound to find disfavour and foster discontent. The majority of those who declared an opposition towards compulsory enlistment (or the war as a whole) did so in the name of Christ. As outlined in the Introduction, of a wartime total of 3,964 conscientious objectors referred to the adjudicating Pelham Committee by local tribunals, 1,716 declared themselves Christadelphians and hence possessed of a religious objection to the war. There existed, of course, other denominations of religious opposition within the almost 4,000 declared conscientious objectors – in particular the Quakers. However, out of this total, 240 men declined to state a specific denomination and instead declared a *personal* objection of a religious nature. More crucially, although forty-two men stated their objection to be of a specific political nature, almost five times as many declared their objection to be a *moral* objection to the conflict whilst over a quarter of all the men referred did not state (or were not able to state) the nature of their objection.[1] If these figures are taken as representative of overall proportions of categories of opposition to the war then it is clear that there was a significant proportion of individuals who did not base their opposition to the war on specifically religious or political grounds. This book aims to fill some of the gaps in these statistics.

Firstly, however, it is worth pointing out how even within the 'organised' forms of anti-war protest there was a great variety of personal response. This diversity was observed by a range of contemporary observers – from leaders or commentators such as Clifford Allen, the young chairman of the No Conscription Fellowship (NCF), and the Quaker J.W. Graham, the author of *Conscription and Conscience* (1922), to individuals such as the conscientious objector Howard Marten, mentioned in the Introduction. Crucially, these observations included (as will be seen) some evidence of *contemporary* recognition of aesthetic, humanistic and moral objections.

While religion of all denominations played a large part in determining responses to the war, both for and against, in many cases the boundaries between 'recognised' opposition and humanistic anti-war reaction could become blurred. Strong religious beliefs served to keep many individuals from extreme doubt concerning their place in the war or their response to it and yet, perhaps not uncommonly, as in the case of Kenneth Campbell which follows, we observe an individual for whom the conflict's effect was to take the edge off their religious way of life.

Many of the generally unwavering convictions concerning the war, whether for or against, were centred on a personal religious faith that had guided the individual before the war and was now brought to bear directly upon the conflict. The religious were encouraged by sermons, flags and parades at their local churches to 'fight the good fight', whether at home or abroad, whilst men of a Quaker background were some of the first to have their consciences officially recognised by the tribunals established to deal with cases of conscientious objection after the implementation of the Military Service Act of January 1916 (which, incidentally, exempted ministers of religion from military service). Sometimes, previously firm religious feelings could be adversely affected by exposure to the reality of the war at the front.

For 2nd Lt. Kenneth Campbell of the 9th Argyll and Sutherland Highlanders, although the war was a physical game with a 'tremendous moral backing', it represented neither a strengthening nor coarsening of character but instead led to a slackening of religious devotion. 'When one is taken from the props of congenial friends', he wrote to his friend A.V. Murray, 'one should all the more feel the personality of Christ and the real oneness of the Church which transcends time and place'. However, on active service the reality was different, as Campbell admitted; 'To put it crudely one feels much inclined after a heavy day to have a "blow out" than say one's prayers. In fact my feelings in Church now are what they were at school'. Life at the front contained no real pain or joy for Campbell, only a constant struggle of 'moral choice'.[2]

As one would expect and as apparent in the categories of objection brought before the Pelham Committee, religious individuals made up a significant proportion of one of the main sources of strong and generally unfaltering critical opinion (and action) against the war. The Quakers and other smaller denominations were actively involved alongside the other diverse elements that made up the composition of the 'organised' peace movement in Britain. For example, in July 1915 a Joint Advisory Council was established linking the work of the No Conscription Fellowship to that of two specifically religious anti-war organisations, the Fellowship of Reconciliation and the Young Men's Service Committee of the Society of Friends.[3] Despite occasional tension between the religious and political 'wings' of the growing alliance of 'organised' groups, they all generally threw their weight behind the cases of conscientious objection that sprang up following the implementation of the Military Service Act in early 1916, whether these, on an individual basis, were of an 'absolutist' or 'alternativist' nature.[4]

Aside from the purely religious element, which tended to be centred upon the bedrock of specific concerns and structures, whether of the Church of England, nonconformity or Quakerism, evidence also exists of individuals who exhibited a drier, more 'rational' and (especially) moral stance in relation to the war. In his 1922 study of the experiences of the conscientious objectors and the wartime struggles of organisations such as the NCF, John W. Graham acknowledged the multiplicity of motives among those who protested against the war and, in some cases, refused military service. 'Many and various', he wrote, 'were the origins and upbringing of the men who banded themselves together to resist conscription, and many and various in consequence their beliefs'. He then recognised that the commonality of fellowship of these protestors, 'was the belief in the sacredness of human life as the vehicle of personality'.[5] Their protest had been aimed at a war the purpose of which had been, 'to destroy the garnered wealth of the world ... to ruin every lovely and cherished possession, to put death and destruction everywhere for life and growth, to baffle the march of beneficent evolution'.[6]

The kernel of the war's negative impact as far as the NCF was concerned was the compulsion of conscience issue, which Graham described simply as an attack upon the soul; to deny conscience on an individualistic basis was, as Kenneth Campbell had found, to 'deprive a man of his moral personality' and to force him to commit 'moral suicide'. The dignity of the human personality was sacred in itself and came above all else, and a world in which this was not recognised was a world in which no political and religious creeds could ever bring happiness. However, the championing of the freedom of personality:

> is not merely individualistic concern for a man's own purity or the salvation of his own soul, but a compulsion to champion a truth which seems to him vital to the soul of the nation and of mankind. To stand by such a truth so far as he sees it is a binding duty, and the only line of truly patriotic conduct. To betray it is to be false to one's self, one's nation and humanity.[7]

Like Graham, for whose book he provided the Preface, Clifford Allen saw the commonality of purpose of those involved in the peace movement and, specifically, the NCF. Reacting to the threat of conscription at the national convention of the NCF in November 1915, he had declared that, 'the right of private judgement ... must be left to the individual, since human personality is a thing which must be held as sacred'.[8] In his speech at the concluding convention in November 1919 he described pacifism as a philosophy of the sanctity of life set against a war which was evil because, 'it depends for its process and very existence upon a fundamentally wrong conception of the relationships of human beings to each other'.[9] He also analysed the make-up of the differing personal motivations that made up the body of the NCF, declaring that, hitherto, it had been generally assumed that a personal conscientious objection to war sprang from a religious belief of some kind, the Quakers being the most well-known. However, as he pointed out in his essay 'The Faith of the N.C.F.' (part of a No Conscription Fellowship souvenir pamphlet, published in 1919) religious objectors only formed a part of the visible spectrum of anti-war response; the rest he labelled under headings such as Socialists, political objectors and 'followers of Tolstoy'.

Allen had stated in his Presidential address to the NCF convention of 1915 that the organisation was built on a moral as well as a religious basis and later, in his 'The Faith of the N.C.F.' essay he pointed out that, in fact, it had been the largest category of objectors who had, 'advanced what was known as a Moral objection'. 'By this', Allen continued, 'they meant that they entertained fundamental beliefs either about the value of human personality, or about the relationship of human beings to each other. Each precluded them from engaging in war. Conscience related man to man'.[10] That there was a moral choice to be made and one not necessarily linked to a religious persuasion was also recognised in the *Absolutists' Objection to Conscription*, a 'statement and an appeal' issued by the Quaker Friends Service Committee which argued, 'We still believe that the man who regards military service as contrary to his deepest religious or moral conviction – a service which denies his sense of personal responsibility – is right in refusing obedience to the state'.[11] Individual choice was paramount. The statement did not claim that all objectors were right and soldiers wrong; it pointed out that, in all the nations at war, 'sincere' men had been drawn to fight through 'their own call' but, 'if the individual is not infallible', the statement declared, 'neither is the State, nor any religious organisation, nor newspapers, nor public opinion, especially in war-time'.[12]

The Manifesto issued by the NCF in September 1915 distinguished between and drew together the differing categories of objection and united them under the cause of the threat to the sacredness of the human personality. 'First and foremost', the pamphlet declared, 'our decision rests on the ground of the serious violation of moral and religious convictions which a system of compulsion must involve',[13] while another NCF pamphlet, *Compulsory Military and Alternative Services and the Conscientious Objector* (1916), pointed out that taking the Military Oath was the moral equivalent of handing one's conscience to another and that, as a body, it was not possible for all the shades of objection to define exactly what they were *not* prepared to do, concluding that conscience was, above all, an 'individual matter'.

These examples show that the existence of a *moral* element to objection to war and military compulsion was not only documented in post-war studies but also in contemporary publications. Those of a moral or aesthetic objection to war or sympathetic to this view also recorded or witnessed individual experiences themselves. Frank Shackleton, a company accountant and worker for the Adult School Movement, had always held firm views on the immorality of war and he perceived the folly of fighting Prussian militarism with the same instruments that it made use of – such as compulsion. Shackleton was soon alienated by the 'artificiality' of the orthodox churches' pro-war attitude to the conflict and was persuaded to declare for peace after attending a public meeting chaired by Clifford Allen. He had always felt that 'non-violence was in itself an individual matter' and at his local tribunal in March 1916 he declared his objection to be, 'as much a moral as a religious one' and that the individual alone had to be the arbiter in matters of conscience. Hence there existed the possibility of separately defined categories of opposition within the individual (in addition to the blurring of categories in the cases of people such as Kenneth Campbell), as Shackleton clearly possessed some religious inclination in addition to his personal moral code.[14]

His local tribunal turned Shackleton's case down and he refused non-combatant service when offered it by the appeal tribunal. After being arrested and detained at Felixstowe military camp, he was forcibly sent to France where he came into contact with some German prisoners at Le Havre. 'The safety of my loved ones', he mused, 'would, I felt, be surer in my practical belief in the inherent goodness in these young men, rather in their acceptance of orders from a brutal command'. He found the circumstances of men from all countries, some with university degrees, trapped in improvised shelters in France, Palestine or wherever the misfortunes of war had sent them, to be 'instances of prostitution of the mind beyond my comprehension'.[15]

Shackleton was an embarrassment to the authorities and, as such, was shunted around – from Rouen to the Calais Base Hospital and finally back to Britain, whilst being subjected to three courts martial and an eventual sentence of ten years penal servitude. He remained defiant, if weary, and later wrote, 'It seemed ludicrous to me to affirm my belief in the sacredness of human life, before men who had become inured to the sight of death, and to whom the value of a human life lay not in its sacredness but in its strategic worth'.[16] He was sent to Winchester Gaol where he accepted 'alternative' work offered under a Home Office scheme to make some practical use of conscientious objectors and was then transferred to road-making facilities, firstly at Dyce Quarry and then Longside. It was while he was involved in road-making that he observed the different categories of objectors working in his group, such as the Christadelphians and the 'Peculiar People' (faith healers). 'The rest of the party was made up of members of the better known religious denominations, agnostics, socialists and what were generally classified as "moralists".'[17]

Another individual who experienced Dyce Quarry under the Home Office scheme was Howard Marten (discussed in the Introduction) who was sentenced to death in France on 15 June 1916, following a court martial for refusing to drill. Stunned, he then found his sentence commuted to ten years penal servitude. Marten had always inclined to pacifist views and opposed martial violence. He joined the Harrow NCF and later became its chairman. It was in this unenviable position that he sometimes found it difficult to mediate between the differing opinions that were strongly expressed during the sometimes stormy meetings. 'They were some of the most argumentative people', he remembered to an interviewer, 'You found so many different points of view; it seemed inherent among pacifists ... they're men of strong individuality, and when you get that clash of personality coming along you almost inevitably strike strong differences of opinion'.[18] When he appeared before his local tribunal he declared himself an absolutist. 'I think it was more than just an objection to fighting', he recalled, 'It was an objection to having one's labour directed by an authority. We didn't feel anyone had the right to direct one's personal life in that way ... it was an objection to having one's life directed by an outside authority'.[19] Marten remembered the whole process of objection as being 'intensely personal' and we have seen in the Introduction his recognition of the differing elements that made up his local branch of the NCF, in particular his identification of an element which he labelled 'artistically-minded' and who were, 'individualists to the core'.[20] But who precisely *were* these people and what motivated them?

Notes

1 Rae, *Conscience and Politics*, pp. 250–1. For analysis of the religious element of opposition to the war, including the Quakers, see John W. Graham, *Conscription and Conscience* (London, 1922). Graham was himself a Quaker.

2 University of Leeds, Liddle Collection (UL,LC hereafter), file of A.V. Murray, letters dated 21 Dec. 1914 and 23 March 1915. For further examples of individuals of a religious persuasion and wrestling with moral concerns see C.G. Raven and Stephen Bowen, dicussed in Chapter 7.

3 The Fellowship of Reconciliation had been launched in Cambridge in December 1914 and was a union of Christian pacifists of all denominations who shared the Quaker view of war (it had 8,000 members by 1918). The Young Men's Service Committee of the Society of Friends consisted of Quakers of military age who individually rejected military service, in common with long-standing Society beliefs. Other anti-war organizations included the Stop The War Committee, run by J. Scott Duckers (see his account, *Handed Over* (London, 1917)) and the National Council Against Conscription (later the National Council for Civil Liberties) which acted as an auxiliary body to some of the larger groups – the NCF in particular – producing leaflets and assisting appellants before their tribunals. The Council was described by J.W. Graham as, 'a watchdog for liberty against D.O.R.A. [The Defense of the Realm Act] and the bureaucracy of war'.

4 'Absolutists' were those conscientious objectors who would not accept any 'alternative' to

military service, such as service in a Non-Combatant Corps, work 'of national importance' or work offered specifically to them under an official Home Office Scheme.

5 Graham, *Conscription and Conscience*, pp. 35–6.

6 *Ibid.*, p. 31.

7 *Ibid.*, p. 39.

8 Clifford Allen, 'Conscription and Conscience', Presidential address to the National Convention of the No Conscription Fellowship, 27 November 1915 (London, 1916), p. 7.

9 See Clifford Allen's speech of 30 Nov. 1919, cited in Graham, *Conscription and Conscience*, pp. 334–5.

10 Clifford Allen, 'The Faith of the N.C.F.' in *The No Conscription Fellowship Souvenir – The N.C.F. 1914–1919* (London, 1919). See UL,LC, file of S. White, CO/FAU Section.

11 Society of Friends – Friends Service Committee, *The Absolutists' Objection to Conscription – A Statement and an Appeal to the Conscience of the Nation* (London, 1917). See UL,LC, file of J. Sadler, CO/FAU Section.

12 *Ibid.*

13 *Manifesto of the N.C.F.* (London, 1915). See UL,LC, file of J. Sadler, CO/FAU section.

14 UL,LC, file of Frank Shackleton, 'All My Tomorrows' (manuscript of unpublished autobiographical novel), p. 81.

15 *Ibid.*, Shackleton, 'Tomorrows', p. 145.

16 *Ibid.*, p. 154.

17 *Ibid.*, pp. 207–8.

18 Imperial War Museum, Sound Archive, file of H.C. Marten, 383/6, p. 31.

19 *Ibid.*, pp. 2–3.

20 Marten also identified this 'artistic' element in his description of the various categories of objector that he had witnessed at a prison/work centre at Princetown on Dartmoor, supplied to J.W. Graham for Graham's study *Conscription and Conscience*. At the camp, Marten noted how, 'Many of the political and agnostic objectors, together with those belonging to *a not inconsiderable "Artistic" group* [my italics] were usually ranged in general policy alongside Friends, Tolstoyans and members of the F.O.R. [Fellowship of Reconciliation]'. See Graham, *Conscription and Conscience*, p. 235.

2

Bloomsbury

What *were* the anti-war feelings chiefly expressed *outside* 'organised' protest and not under political or religious banners – those attitudes which form the *raison d'être* for this study? As the Great War becomes more distant in time, certain actions and individuals become greyer and more obscure whilst others seem to become clearer and imbued with a dash of colour amid the sepia. One thinks particularly of the so-called Bloomsbury Group.[1] Any overview of 'alternative' attitudes to the war must consider the responses of Bloomsbury to the shadows of doubt and uncertainty thrown across page and canvas by the conflict. Despite their notoriety, the reactions of the Bloomsbury individuals are important both in their own right and as a mirror to the similar reactions of obscurer individuals from differing circumstances and backgrounds.

In the origins of Bloomsbury – well known as one of the foremost cultural groups of the late Victorian and Edwardian periods – is to be found the moral and aesthetic core for some of the most significant humanistic reactions to the war. The small circle of Cambridge undergraduates whose mutual appreciation of the thoughts and teachings of the academic and philosopher G.E. Moore led them to form lasting friendships, became the kernel of what would become labelled 'the Bloomsbury Group'. It was, as one academic described, 'a nucleus from which civilisation has spread outwards'.[2] This rippling effect, though temporarily dammed by the keenly-felt constrictions of the war, would continue to flow outwards through the twentieth century, inspiring, as is well known, much analysis and interpretation along the way.

The emotions of Bloomsbury mirrored to a large extent those of its mentors. For one of the 'fathers' of Bloomsbury, the older Cambridge academic and humanist Goldsworthy Lowes Dickinson,[3] the coming of war was disastrous. For him, as Bloomsbury patroness Lady Ottoline Morrell noted in 1916, the war came, 'like a battering ram, bruising him and knocking him permanently over ... he felt the Nation's calamities more poignantly and devastatingly than any private calamity of his own'.[4] Dickinson had himself referred to the time (in August 1914) when the war 'burst upon the world' in his published essay 'The Basis of a Permanent Peace'. Dickinson wrote that the effect of the war upon those who had not followed foreign affairs, and, by implication, were busy with their own lives, was one of incredulity followed by a feeling that it must never happen again. However, peaceful intentions then became 'submerged' beneath hopes of victory and fears of defeat. During the waging of the war, 'the purpose of it is in danger of being forgotten', he warned, pointing out that soldiers did not possess normal freedoms of choice; 'Those at the front have not the opportunity to consider the conditions of such a peace'. Hence, he concluded, it was the business of those at home to do so.[5]

Dickinson had gone up to Cambridge in 1881 from Charterhouse and had come, via a 'Shelleyan religion of humanity', into the orbit of the academic and thinker J.E. McTaggart and his philosophy of loving personal relationships linked to an absolute theoretical truth. Dickinson, though an atheist, had come from a background of Christian Socialism and, in common with much of the resultant Bloomsbury attitude toward the Great War, 'the dissent which they articulated shared certain Christian and Socialist presuppositions, but neither Christianity nor Socialism was the substance of their pacifism'.[6] From an early age, 'his desire to serve humanity was strong', E.M. Forster declared in his 1934 biography of Dickinson, though pointing out, in a statement tinged with Forster's own post-war regret, that 'love of humanity' did not now (in the 1930s) carry with it the same promise that it had done in the previous century. In 1887, three years after obtaining a First in Classics, Dickinson was elected to a Fellowship at King's College, his official subject being Political Science in which he lectured from 1896 to 1920.

With the dawn of a new century the concerns of the wider world now occupied more of Dickinson's time: for example, his involvement in the founding of the journal *Independent Review* in 1903 to help combat a policy of aggressive imperialism. As Forster put it, Dickinson's philosophy was that, 'We must first get the house straight then fill it with beautiful things ... though he [Dickinson] was sensible enough to know that unless we have a certain amount of beautiful things lying about we shall not think it worth while to get the house straight'.[7] Dickinson never lost his appreciation of beauty, especially that of the countryside of England. As he wrote in his 1901 volume *Letters from John Chinaman and other Essays*, 'To feel, and in order to feel to express, or at least to understand the expression of all that is lovely in Nature, of all that is poignant and sensitive in man is to us in itself a sufficient end'.[8] Dickinson's *The Meaning of Good* of 1901 (some of which was written whilst staying with artist and Bloomsbury 'member' Roger Fry) had been largely inspired by the ethics of Dickinson's rejected Christian background and the philosophy of McTaggart, though Dickinson was ultimately more affected by G.E. Moore's *Principia Ethica*, which appeared in 1903.

Dickinson was fifty-two in 1914 and following the outbreak of war he, like Bertrand Russell (see Chapter 3), wrote numerous articles on the war. He and Russell both joined the Union of Democratic Control and the No Conscription Fellowship, with Dickinson becoming President of the Cambridge branch of the UDC. In his writings, Dickinson apportioned blame to no single country for the conflict; rather, he argued, it was the fault of the secret diplomacy of the international diplomatic system, a system which, according to Dickinson, had to be altered by the implementation of some form of general alliance in order to prevent future conflicts from escalating. He became a leading figure in the League of Nations Society and grew, like Russell, impatient with the UDC which did not accept the wider concept of a league as an integral part of its policy.

Both Dickinson and Russell, according to the academic M.R. Pollock, shared the 'uncompromising individualism' of the conscientious objectors (whom they both supported in the Liberal press) and were engaged upon a crusade for moral principles, their ideals being those of the Cambridge Apostles: beauty, friendship, love, reason, individualism and private conscience. 'Passion is needed', wrote Dickinson in the *Nation*, 'for the real things, for good instead of evil, for truth instead of lies, for love instead of hate. To turn it into those channels, the friends of reason are always working'.[9] This focus on the channelling of human energies had much in common with the ideas of Bertrand Russell. Dickinson's pacifism, like that of Russell's, 'was couched primarily in rational and ethical terms rather than in political or economic terms',[10] as Forster later pointed out.

Though Dickinson perhaps placed too much faith in human rationality and tended, unlike Russell, to ignore the 'primitive and pre-logical' element that survived in 'civilised' modern man, both men agreed that the role of the pacifist was 'to create life' and that war was the enemy of 'the passion of love, the perception of beauty, the contemplation of truth'. During war, man's sensibilities were affected by a 'blind intoxication', and he became divorced from a peacetime existence of 'impassioned reason'.[11] Pacifists supported the concept of 'a free friendship where men co-operate or compete as independent individuals not as passive creatures of a man movement ... to be swept away on a torrent of corporate passion is to them not an ideal at all. On the contrary, it is the negation of all they value'.[12]

Just as Russell's later dismissal from Trinity College (see Chapter 3) seemed to 'snap one's last link with Cambridge', as Dickinson put it in a letter to his fellow academic, the war's effect had brought to Dickinson's Cambridge existence what he later described as a 'sense of alienation from common opinion' due to his own attitude and those of others towards him, in particular the patriotic McTaggart. Most of his former pupils were serving at the front, and his classes were now full of women. E.M. Forster proclaimed that Dickinson's 'greatest disillusionment' was with the attitudes of the leading academic institutions; 'those who should have been the leaders followed the crowd down a steep place' and the students, whom he expected to 'keep the light of truth burning in a storm', Dickinson found to be 'blindly patriotic', false or plain fearful when confronted with the tide of public opinion. 'All discussion, all pursuit of truth ceased in a moment', Dickinson later recalled, 'To win the war or to hide safely among the winners became the only preoccupation. Abroad

was heard only the sound of guns, at home only the ceaseless patter of a propaganda utterly indifferent to truth.'[13]

The war affected Dickinson profoundly; he often referred to a 'gulf' between
his remembered pre-war life and existence against the backdrop of war. In an
article entitled 'The Holy War', written for the *Nation*, he highlighted, 'the gulf
between nature, the past, all beautiful true and gracious things and beliefs, and
this black horror of inconceivability'.[14] In a letter of November 1914, included
by Forster in his biography, Dickinson wrote sadly that, 'if one's whole life has
been given up trying to establish reason and suddenly the gulf opens and one
finds that world is ruled by force and wishes to be so, one feels forlorn indeed
and more than forlorn'.[15]

Although he turned his back on his former academic world, shutting himself
up in his rooms, as he later described, with only his books, lamp and flickering
fire, in reality Dickinson continued to battle, in Forster's words, for 'the spirit
of reason'. In addition to his work with the Bryce Group,[16] the Society for a
Durable Peace and the League of Nations Society (later the League of Nations
Union), articles, pamphlets and publications poured out at a rate only perhaps
matched by Russell.[17] He wrote mainly for the readership of the *Manchester
Guardian*, the *Nation*, the *Cambridge Magazine*, *War and Peace* (later the *International Review*) as well as (again in common with Russell) for several journals in the United States. Forster describes him as being driven by his sense of
moral earnestness and the drive of his intellect, an intellect which, 'forbade him
to seek the solace either or patriotism, anti-patriotism or religion'. He was 'condemned' to follow this intellect, 'in a world which had become emotional'. In
1917, Dickinson cemented his alliance with Bloombury by visiting Leonard
and Virginia Woolf. Virginia, worried at his state, described him thus: 'This
war seems to possess him to leave little over. In fact he looked shrunk and
worn'.[18]

Despite resigning his lectureship in 1920, disillusioned and worn out by his
experiences during the war, Dickinson continued his literary campaign against
conflict in the following years, writing in 1923 that 'War, it is often said by its
apologists, is not the greatest of evils. To me, on the contrary, it appears to be
precisely that, if only because, in addition to its own evil, it includes and brings
with it others.' In addition, while citing personal accounts of 'pure affection',
comradeship and a sense of identity at the front as 'records of genuine experience
which it is no part of my case to belittle or deny', he maintained that both the
writers and readers of such accounts, 'would not suppose that such experiences justify war. They are only something to be set against its evils', it being to
Dickinson's mind 'a plain truth' that war and civilisation remained 'incompatible'.[19]

The war shattered Dickinson's pre-war optimism; the 'gulf' that he described
having opened up between the old world and the new was too great to bridge.
The conflict also dulled the optimism of the younger generation (the 'core' of

Bloomsbury) that, like Dickinson himself, had passed through Cambridge and shared many of the values that Dickinson held dear, values that derived from the university's apostolic notions of an individual's right to intellectual integrity, truth and the pursuit of love, friendship and beauty. When the war came, wrote one commentator:

> The Cambridge–Bloomsbury vision of civilisation progressing triumphantly towards a new golden age receded before the spectre of a civilisation hastening towards its own ruin. The confident expectation that Cambridge values would spread outward was belied by a world tragedy which appeared to threaten the very survival of these values.[20]

However, this fear was not immediately apparent during the final days of peace. There was generally no conception of the extent to which the conflict would threaten the civilised values that Bloomsbury held so dear. Lady Ottoline Morrell described her Bloomsbury friends descending en masse on her London home at the end of July 1914, 'all of them desperately jingo, longing to rush into the war at *once*'. She herself did not need actual experience of war to convince her of its wrongness. 'It seems absolute madness to me', she wrote to Bertrand Russell, adding that, 'They attacked Philip [her husband and an MP] violently because he was in favour of keeping out of it. They seem to utterly ignore the appalling horrors of war. The ruin and suffering and devastation of it.'[21]

In time her friends began to match Lady Ottoline's reaction; 'It was the progress of the war itself that changed attitudes', states Robert Skidelsky, the biographer of John Maynard Keynes – one of the first of Bloomsbury to find their initial view of the war altered but who, due to his association with the government via his work for the Treasury, was viewed by his friends as perhaps not sufficiently anti-war. However, as early as November 1914, Lady Ottoline recorded that:

> Duncan Grant brought Keynes last night who says he has only *begun* to realise the horror of the war during the last two weeks and he was evidently miserable and feeling it intensely and was ever so nice – quite different to what he was. He said his soul seems to have been laid bare to it and that before he had a cataract over it.[22]

Quentin Bell, the nephew of Virginia Woolf, stated in his lecture 'Recollections and Reflections on Maynard Keynes' that although Keynes was prepared, in metaphorical terms to shoulder a musket, he and Bloomsbury were in fact united during the war, 'by a determination to keep their heads in the maelstrom; whatever else they might do they would not accept the prevailing religion of hatred'.[23] Although Bell describes Keynes as 'morally committed' to the war because of his work for the War Office, he also states that Keynes was 'entirely in sympathy' with his friends, a point borne out by Ottoline Morrell's observation of November 1914. It seemed that Keynes was as deeply affected as his friends (and perhaps more so) by the war's pressure on their sense of self. This was not surprising given Keynes' shared Apostolic background and beliefs.

Keynes described the early influence of G.E. Moore on himself as having been, 'exciting, exhilarating, the beginning of a renaissance, the opening of a new heaven on a new earth'. He and his friends were 'the forerunners of a new dispensation', especially since they were able, as Keynes described, to accept Moore's 'religion' and discard the 'morals' contained in Moore's chapter in *Principia Ethica* on 'Ethics in Relation to Conduct'. Keynes described himself and his friends as being in one sense 'immoralists' in that they repudiated conventional wisdom and morality and recognised no moral obligation on them to conform or obey; 'Before heaven we claimed to be our own judge in our own case'.[24] While being concerned with 'the salvation of our own souls' through the practice of passionate contemplation of love, truth and beauty and enjoyment of aesthetic experience, this philosophy could be extended to cover whole societies: 'the supreme value of the civilised individuals, whose pluralisation, as more and more civilised individuals, was itself the only acceptable social form'.[25] It was the hope contained in this concept of society that the Great War began to stifle.

Keynes' initial reaction to the war was one of surprise and, as we have seen, it took a while for its full impact to sink in. Hence in August 1914 he had written to his father that, 'I am only gloomy in fits and starts' and that he found that he was 'beginning to get very well used to the situation'.[26] By the time he was taken by Duncan Grant to visit Lady Ottoline three months later, however, he was writing to Lytton Strachey from Cambridge that he was, 'absolutely and completely desolated. It is utterly unbearable to see day by day the youths going away, first to boredom and discomfort, and then to slaughter.'[27] He pointed to the fact that five undergraduates of King's College had already been killed. As the casualties mounted, so did the tension within Keynes' increasingly troubled mind. On the one hand was his concern for his friends – on the other, his role as an economist. The public servant in him believed that the war would soon be over and kept him too busy to get involved in organisations such as the Union of Democratic Control, whereas the humanistic element within him attempted to dissuade both his brother Geoffrey and his Hungarian friend Ferenc Bekassy from enlisting – he was unsuccessful in both cases.

As friends and undergraduates failed to return from the front, Keynes admitted to Duncan Grant that he found his subconscious feelings were muted and 'deeply depressed' by the pressure of the war and that he longed for the war to be over 'on almost any terms'. In April 1915, at the news of the deaths of Rupert Brooke and two more King's undergraduates, he described the war to Grant, as 'a nightmare to be stopt [sic] anyhow', praying that, 'May no other generation live under the cloud we live under'. At this point, Keynes was a busy government official with access to the Prime Minister in matters related to supplies and prices of foodstuffs. By May 1915, Keynes was deeply involved in the overall financial direction of the war as part of the Treasury's No. 1 Division. One side of him was attempting, unsuccessfully, to conceal the other; as Bertrand Russell commented to Lady Ottoline, he was 'using his intellect to hide the torment in his soul'.[28] One of his biographers has pointed out:

> Keynes' life was balanced between two sets of moral claims. His duty as an individual was to achieve good states of mind for himself and for those he was directly concerned with; his duty as a citizen was to help achieve a happy state of affairs for society. The two claims he thought of as logically independent of each other. He attached greater priority to the first than to the second, except when he thought the state was in danger.[29]

At no time was this more true than when embodied in his response to the public and personal claims to the Great War.

Keynes became increasingly busy at the Treasury throughout the war, causing his friends, and in particular Virginia Woolf, to worry that he would be 'lost' to humanity. However, despite a whirl of conferences, parties and being made Companion of the Bath (Third Class) in 1917, Keynes still spent weekends at the Charleston farmhouse of Bloomsbury artists Vanessa Bell and Duncan Grant. In addition, Keynes supported both Grant and his friend David Garnett in their claims for exemption from military service. Indeed, Keynes succeeded in obtaining commissions for Grant and other artists via Lord Beaverbrook, the Minister of Information, under that Ministry's War Artists Scheme. More prosaically, Keynes also provided Garnett with financial help for his bee-keeping.

On the more crucial issue of his own attitude to military service, Keynes did not make use of his certificate of exemption from military service on grounds of work of national importance supplied by Sir Thomas Heath, joint Permanent Secretary to the Treasury, in February 1916. Instead, he wrote out an application to the Holborn local tribunal for exemption on grounds of conscientious objection. In it, he stated that:

> I have a conscientious objection to surrendering my liberty of judgement ... My objection to submit to authority in this matter is truly conscientious. I am not prepared on such an issue as this to surrender my right of decision, as to what is or is not my duty, to any other person, and I should think it morally wrong to do so.[30]

Although there is no certainty that this actual statement was sent to the Holborn tribunal, the existence of a summons from the Clerk of the Tribunal for 28 March 1916 and a reply from Keynes stating that he was too busy at the Treasury to attend this date provide proof that Keynes must have made an initial application for exemption to the local authorities.

Keynes never appeared before the tribunal because the Treasury exempted him above his head, firstly for a six-month period and then later, in August 1916, with no time limit attached. However, Keynes' non-appearance at his exemption hearing coupled to the fact that he did not attempt to withdraw his application (despite the Treasury exemption) or try to get the date of the hearing changed (which would have been relatively simple, given his position within the Government) all point to the clear possibility, as Robert Skidelsky has pointed out, that Keynes was thinking of resigning from the Treasury over the conduct and continuance of the war and, in particular, the issue of conscription. Crucially, he applied for exemption on 23 February 1916, although by the date of the proposed hearing in late March he had decided to remain with the Government.

This gave him no pleasure. 'I work for a government I despise for ends I think criminal',[31] he wrote to Duncan Grant during the final year of the war, though he derived a 'moral justification', in the words of his biographer, in staying put at the Treasury and using his position to help friends such as Grant, David Garnett, Gerald Shove and others with their applications for exemption on grounds of conscience. The irony of this situation lay in the fact that his friends, particularly Garnett and Lytton Strachey, had pressured him to stop working for the Government and hence the war effort. Yet he was able to be of most practical help 'from within' and, in any case, 'he was as far from surrendering his conscience even to his friends as from surrendering it to the dictates of the state'.[32] An example of Keynes working from within was his influence on the original Military Service Bill. As Vanessa Bell reported to Roger Fry in early January 1916:

> Maynard came for the weekend … He held out hopes of a conscience clause. The bill had first been drafted without one then Reginald McKenna [the Chancellor of the Exchequer] put one in but Maynard thought that it would only do for Quakers and made him change it.[33]

To a certain extent, Keynes also remained at the Treasury in the hope and expectation that the war would soon be over, particularly after President Wilson's envoys visited Britain in early 1916 and the President's appeal of January 1917 for a negotiated peace. This was soon followed by the Russian Revolution and eventual withdrawal of that nation from the conflict. However, peace did not come as expected, and Keynes' pessimism took over once more and, 'reached its peak at the end of 1917 and continued until the end of the war',[34] spilling over into his account of the peace negotiations contained within *The Economic Consequences of the Peace* (1919). As he wrote to his mother in April 1918:

> Politics and war are just as depressing or even more so than they seem to be. If this Government were to beat the Germans, I should lose all faith for the future in the efficacy of intellectual processes; but there doesn't seem much risk of it. Everything is always decided for some reason other than the real merits of the case in the sphere with which I have contact. And I have no doubt that it is just the same with everything else.[35]

Lytton Strachey, sometimes described as Bloomsbury's most prominent conscientious objector, famously placed a catty note on Keynes' dinner plate in February 1916 (significantly, perhaps, a week before Keynes applied for exemption from military service on grounds of conscience) which read, 'Dear

Maynard, Why are you still at the Treasury? yours, Lytton'. Strachey shared Keynes' early Apostolistic background and admiration for G.E. Moore and was perhaps more responsive from the first to the changing circumstances of a nation at war and his part in it. Virginia Woolf noted that, 'He is one of the most supple of our friends ... the person whose mind seems softest to impressions, least starched by any formality or impediment'.[36]

As early as mid-August 1914, Strachey wrote to his brother James that:

> I think it's very important that people should be stirred up about Peace ... Any straw seems worth clutching at when such things are at stake. I'm sure the essential thing is to institute a Stop the War party in the Cabinet, backed by public opinion. It's no good wasting energies over blaming E. Grey [the Foreign Secretary] ... I haven't seen anyone who hasn't agreed in the main lines eg. that we should take nothing for ourselves and insist on ending it at the earliest possible moment. But perhaps by now there has been a German victory.[37]

He wisely suggested that appearing pro-German at the present time would have no beneficial effect, and the optimum position to adopt was anti-German and pro-peace.

Strachey thus exhibited knowledge, like Vanessa Bell, as discussed in Chapter 6, of the practical side of protest and an awareness of the plausibility of public opinion. As he wrote to his friend Dorothy Bussy a few days later:

> So far as I can make out there isn't the slightest enthusiasm for the war. I think the public are partly feeling simple horror and partly that it's a dreadful necessity. But I think there will be a change when the casualties begin – both in the direction of greater hostility to the Germans and also more active disgust at the whole thing. Though of course a great deal will depend on the actual turn of events.

On the Foreign Secretary, Grey and the political dimension Strachey commented, 'It's like a puppet show, with the poor little official dolls dancing and squeaking their official phrases, while the strings are being pulled by some devilish Unseen Power. One naturally wants to blame somebody – the Kaiser for choice – but the tragic irony, it seems to me, really is that everyone was helpless'. He concluded that 'The real horror is that Europe is not yet half civilised',[38] and echoed in his thoughts Bertrand Russell's public theories of the destructive emotions of mankind being allowed to run amok in a European situation that Russell, Strachey and the rest of Bloomsbury recognised as a return to barbarism. International culture that had bound mankind together was now threatened; when an outraged James Strachey pointed out to his brother the plans to leave German composers out of the Promenade Concerts and his letters of protest to the manager and press on the subject, Lytton replied, 'Let us leave this planet – hurriedly, hurriedly'.[39] He commented how he could now understand how people's personal feelings could be overcome by popular emotion. 'And at any rate one would not have to think any more',[40] he concluded, noting the perceived deadening effect of an existence under military control.

While his brother James was planning to produce a pamphlet entitled 'Why I shall not Join Lord Kitchener's Army – By a Fellow of Trinity', which he believed would have 'immense sale' in intellectual circles, Strachey was equally practical, knitting mufflers for soldiers, learning German and considering the position of intellectuals in the war, concluding that 'We're all far too weak physically to be of any use at all. If we weren't we'd still be too intelligent to be thrown away in some really not essential expedition.'[41] The natural place for intellectuals, thought Strachey – if they must be incorporated into the war-state – was, perhaps not surprisingly, in the National Reserve, this idea being partly prompted by the fact that he had just heard of his friend Duncan Grant's plans to join that body. Another option was for intellectuals to leave the country, either for the United States or, as Strachey stated in a later letter, for France, where the waters of conscience were (in September 1914) less muddied, and the intellectual could provide solid help in preventing that country's demise (this being the primary goal of enlisting; Strachey stated that he didn't care about a *British* victory, 'apart from personal questions'). Whatever option one chose, it was no use the intellectual pretending that he was not 'a special case' and, at the end of all things, 'one must resist if it comes to a push'.[42]

Strachey was appalled by the treatment of civilians of German extraction, and the Byronic death of handsome poet Rupert Brooke in the spring of 1915 seemed to symbolise the 'muddle and futility' of fate. Life under war had become merely a 'confused tale' and one that for some was 'just beginning and then broken off for no reason, and for ever'. In a letter to his friend Francis Birrell in August 1915, he described himself as resembling a desert cactus, dried-up and solitary, 'alone – desolate and destitute – in a country of overhanging thunder clouds and heavy emptiness'.[43] As Strachey's biographer Michael Holroyd has stated, 'He [Strachey] saw everything in terms of the individual and felt that he was growing increasingly sensitive'.[44] During the same month as his confession to Birrell, Strachey was approached by a schoolmaster at 'The Lacket', his country home near Marlborough, and, to his surprise, handed a Registration paper:

> As a method of getting hold of shirkers it seems to me strangely inefficient. Who on earth is 'skilled in any work other than that in which he is engaged?' Most strange! Perhaps I might put 'addressing envelopes' – but I can't think of anything else, except buggery, and I'm not very skilful at that ... At any rate, all one can do is put 'no' and then I suppose they mean to worry one with security agents.[45]

The following month, perhaps realising that the war had discovered him even at his present rural location, Strachey moved back to London, which was scarcely an improvement. He described the capital thus:

> The fog has descended in force and the shadow of Death reigns ... very nearly all the lights were out, which combined with the fog, produced complete darkness. In the streets of Soho one might have been on a Yorkshire moor for all one could see to the

contrary. How the human spirit manages to flicker even as faintly as it does is a mystery … it is solid, damp and heavy with the depression of war.[46]

After a 'dreary' Christmas spent at Lady Ottoline's often freezing Garsington Manor, the introduction of the Conscription Bill after months of speculation served to lift Strachey out of his malaise, and January 1916 found him energised, exclaiming to his brother James, 'isn't it still possible that something should be done? Surely there ought to be a continual stream of leaflets and pamphlets. Also, if possible, meetings all over the country and signatures collected against the Bill.'[47] Strachey joined the NCF and the National Council Against Conscription, the offices of which were now a frequent haunt of his brother, who had parted journalistic ways with the largely 'pro-war' *Spectator*. Strachey helped to draft 'Leaflet No. 3', which criticised the government for its conscription policy in that this would help to transform Britain into a police state (rather in the same vein as Bertrand Russell's later article which led to his personal prosecution, discussed in Chapter 3). The leaflet was suppressed by H.W. Massingham at the *Nation* but not before 500,000 copies had been distributed and it had been quoted in the *Morning Post*. In his article for the journal *War and Peace* entitled 'The Claims of Patriotism', Strachey called for common sense and a little scepticism while warning that, 'Amid the bigotry and hysteria of war, people on both sides too easily relinquish their individuality and with it their humanity'.[48]

This was also the time of Strachey's criticism of Keynes for working for a government that was seeking more and more to meet militarism with militarism. Both Strachey and his brother considered their futures under the new Military Service Act; James Strachey sent in his application for exemption early on. 'I went in only for conscience', he wrote, 'just said I thought the war wrong and wouldn't do anything of any kind to help in it and added "as evidence that I genuinely hold this view" the fact of my leaving the Spec.[*Spectator*]'.

The outlook was not promising; 'I now think that all is lost', continued James Strachey:

it looks to me as thought the Tribunals were absolutely refusing (illegally?) to exempt anyone on medical grounds. That's to say they prefer to leave the decision to the military authorities. In that case, you'd be called up and examined *after* you'd been 'deemed'. This complicates things extremely, especially in connection with conscience.[49]

James advised his brother to prepare some kind of statement, which Lytton did.[50] Lytton replied that, although he had many feelings against joining the army that were not of a conscientious nature, even if he found himself doing clerical work in the lowly Class IVb he would feel this expense of energy towards the war to be wrong and was prepared, as he told his brother, to go to prison rather than do work of even that sort. Both brothers recognised that the Military Service Act did not provide for exemption on grounds of objection to the specifics of the current war, but only to war in general. The words of the Act gave no guidance as to the motive of the objection to service, 'whether it's due to a general regard for the sanctity of human life, or to more particular objections to combatant service at the present moment – so long as the motive is conscientious. That word gives opportunities for endless argument'.[51] This and the 'intense' nervous strain of waiting for a tribunal was all part of the 'appalling and senseless misery' generated by the Act.

James Strachey's solution was to highlight one's objection to the present war and one's pro-Germanism, which he thought would infuriate the tribunals to such an extent that they would immediately reject those individuals for inclusion within the ranks of the military. His brother, who wrote to Virginia Woolf that he couldn't 'lie still' under the threat of the 'horrors of the outer world' (i.e. the tribunals) beginning to assert themselves, now placed his hope in 'the extremity of extremism' and found a new regard for Clifford Allen and the activities of the NCF in their refusal to compromise ('Britain's One Hope', as he described them to Vanessa Bell). He felt that once conscientious objectors placed themselves in occupations found for them by the authorities, 'they are done for'.

Lytton Strachey himself appeared as a claimant for exemption before a local Advisory Commitee (which would recommend a course of action to the tribunal) on 2 March 1916, at which he stated his conscientious objection was not based on religious grounds, but upon 'moral considerations' and although he could not say that *all* wars were wrong, his objection, he stated, was directed 'not simply against the present war'. He concluded that he would not act against his personal convictions, 'whatever the consequences may be'. When he finally appeared before the Hampstead Tribunal, with MP Philip Morrell as his character witness, his application for exemption was adjourned pending a medical which took place a few days later and resulted in him being rejected for any form of military service.

However, Strachey was unsatisfied with the tribunal's decision to grant him exemption from combatant service only and not the *absolute* exemption that he requested. He drafted an appeal statement which he sent to his brother and which read, 'Since my objection ... rested upon an objection to taking any part, direct or indirect, in the present war, the only exemption which could reasonably have been granted was an absolute one'. His objection also rested on the fact that the tribunal had provided him with no reason for its decision and that it had refused to let him question the Military Representative, whose objection to Strachey's claim was that it was not a 'conscientious' nature within the meaning of the Act. Strachey pointed out that the tribunal, in granting him partial exemption, had recognised that his claim was a 'conscientious' one and hence it had been 'unreasonable' of the tribunal, 'to withhold from me the only form of exemption which would appropriately meet my objection'.[52]

Although he was now technically 'safe' from the military, Strachey was prepared to help agitate for better treatment of conscientious objectors, if a deputation to the Prime Minister (organised by the Morrells and including the

Bishop of Oxford) failed to produce any improvement in the situation. In the meantime, in addition to visiting the Woolfs and braving Garsington once again, he settled back into work on his *Eminent Victorians* after his nerve-wracking brush with the authorities. However, the authorities were not to leave him in peace; in July 1916 he received a letter from the War Office stating that he had to present himself for another medical inspection before 30 September, and he took great exception to the fact that the order described him as, 'a man who offered himself for enlistment and was rejected since August 1915'. In the early summer of 1917 Strachey had to re-establish his case for conscientious objection. Philip Morrell was not allowed to testify, and a counsel was hired to represent him. A decision based upon an objection on grounds of conscience was adjourned pending yet another medical; this time Strachey was graded C4, placed in the reserve and ordered to re-appear every six months for further examinations unless he continued with his specifically 'conscientious' objection. On this occasion, with an apparently more serious chance of call-up, he was inclined 'to letting sleeping dogs lie'.

During the autumn of 1917, with work on *Eminent Victorians* almost completed and the numbers of German air-raids on London growing in number ('the horrors steadily increase', he wrote to Clive Bell),[53] Strachey and his companion, the artist Dora Carrington, moved to 'The Mill House' at Tidmarsh in Berkshire. He was restless with the uncertainty of the war and had written to his brother that, 'I wake up in the night and feel civilisation rocking', while at the same time had commented to Carrington that, 'the slowness of things is tiresome. The excitement seems to come in wads, with spaces of nothingness in between – no nice orderly crescendos. However, it's something to be able to reflect upon the excitements of the past during the nothingness of the present.'[54] He tried to keep the war at a distance by correcting the proofs for his book and writing reviews and articles for the journal *War and Peace* attacking the 'theology of militarism'.

However, the war constantly intruded upon his life. In March 1918 he was summoned for yet another medical examination, though on this occasion it was conducted by civil rather than military authorities, and he was declared permanently unfit for all forms of military service. During the previous month he had attended Bertand Russell's trial at Bow Street magistrates' Court (see Chapter 3), the proceedings of which he described to Lady Ottoline as, 'unjust, gross and generally wicked and disgusting … It makes one abandon hope that such monstrosities should occur, openly, and be accepted by very nearly everybody as a matter of course'. Strachey and his brother stepped out of the court, 'with our teeth chattering in fury'.[55]

Eminent Victorians was finally published in May 1918 and from then on Stachey's literary star was in the ascendant. However, at times when there were few distractions, the war still impinged upon his thoughts. In the final months of the conflict and with Carrington on holiday in Scotland, he wrote to her that, 'The worst of it is, as one sits in solitude, the war surges up and adds to one's depression – useless, quite useless to think of it, but one can't help it at times.'[56] Yet, throughout the war, he never quite gave up hope completely. He was able to employ his creative gifts and his intelligence in a practical way as weapons to disarm the stultifying effects of the conflict with a success that sometimes caught him unawares. As he commented to Lady Ottoline, 'At moments, I'm quite surprised how, with all these horrors around one, one goes on living as one does – and one even manages to execute an occasional pirouette on the edge of the precipice!'[57]

Strachey's war-life was intimately bound up with those of his friends to whom he was always ready to offer help and advice; the month of the long-awaited publication of *Eminent Victorians* found him warning Duncan Grant (who had been offered a job as an official War Artist) that the Central Tribunal could easily overturn their original decision and announce, '"If his conscience allows him to commemorate the war by his painting, why shouldn't it allow him to take part in it? We will therefore withdraw our exemption." They're such beasts…'[58] However, as we have seen, Strachey's friends did not all follow the same course of response, even if a similar philosophy of moral and aesthetic values linked and supported them all. Some, such as Clive Bell and Duncan Grant, as Ottoline Morrell noted with alarm, thought of enlisting in the early days of the war. David Garnett and Francis Birrell went to France as part of the Friends War Victims Relief Mission. However, when Duncan Grant was later deported as a 'pacifist anarchist'[59] while merely attempting to design costumes and scenery for a production of the opera *Pelleas et Melisande* in Paris, Garnett found that his enthusiasm had waned dramatically, writing to Strachey that:

> The whole business has shattered my vitality … Really it is awful being anywhere nowadays. I cannot earn a living anywhere without killing or being killed. I have much more sympathy than ever before with those Christians whose only profession in Rome was being thrown to lions.[60]

Garnett later recalled that, from the commencement of hostilities, 'I had had thoughts of enlisting – not from patriotic motives, but because I felt that the war was a great human experience which I ought not to miss',[61] and his work for the Mission was his method of fulfilling this common linking motivation – the need for experience. Even Leonard Woolf later admitted that if he had not been married or had not had to care for his wife during her periods of mental illness, 'I should have joined up, because, though I hated the war, I felt and still feel an irresistible desire to experience everything'.[62] As with others, Garnett's experience turned his thoughts against war. He had observed the displaced and bitter people of France and how the country itself was being 'bled white'. As discussed in Chapter 4 in the case of Siegfried Sassoon, Garnett, through his experience in France, came to see that Government and military policies were misplaced and resulted only in the suffering of innocents, which made him full of 'contempt and hatred for all systems of Government and Tyranny', as he explained to Lytton Strachey. A negotiated peace was essential if European civilisation (and civilised values) was to be saved from ruin. Hence his decision to take no further part in the war effort. 'I believed it was wrong to delegate one's right of private judgement and therefore it was impossible for me to be a solider', Garnett wrote in his memoirs.[63]

Like Lytton Strachey, Garnett had found that it was impossible not to 'brood continually' on the war. Garnett and Duncan Grant became fruit-farmers in the Suffolk countryside following their eventual exemption from military service by the tribunal system. Just as Garnett had considered and tested his options until he arrived by experience at the correct one, Grant's response was also based *initially* on a need for experience, although he eventually took a more instinctive route and found, together with his companion and fellow artist Vanessa Bell, that the best way to face the war was simply to continue painting. As Bell described their philosophy to Lytton Strachey, 'it seems the only thing to enjoy the present and the only way of cheating one's fate'.[64]

During the first weeks of war, Grant had been buoyed with an optimism that never fully left him, while at the same time appreciating the 'horrors' contained in the necessity for 'altering one's bearing', as he commented to Strachey in the first week of September 1914 (as he was considering joining the Reserve):

> I feel sure that one ought to give way to depression. But it's jolly difficult. I don't mean that one ought not to think that war was inevitable or wrong or the countless things that Bertie [Russell] or Maynard [Keynes] may think – so be depressed – but that one ought to plunge into the horror ... and then one rises to the surface cheerful.[65]

Grant relied on his painting, personal relationships and friends in high places to sustain him; Keynes brought his official weight to bear at tribunals; Clive Bell's father's position as a Lord High Sheriff warded off a threatened 'spy search' in May 1915, and in June of the following year Lytton Strachey complied with Grant's request for a written reference for the tribunal, declaring formally that, 'I entertain no doubt that his opinions with regard to war are and have been for the last 7 or 8 years [a length of time actually suggested by Grant] such as he states', and then on a more personal note (and with evident truth), 'He is a man of transparent honesty and I know of no one less likely to be influenced, either in his views or his conduct by considerations of a personal or selfish kind.'[66] In May 1918 Grant was also grateful for Strachey's warning about accepting work as an official War Artist and the chance of thus being called to the colours, though he replied that 'Neither I nor Nessa [Vanessa Bell] think there is any danger in accepting the work. I refused to join the army nominally as was first suggested and I do not cease in any way to be a C.O.' He hoped the work would take at least eight months, and there existed an inducement at the end of it that he found he could not ignore; 'I shall be only paid a living wage so that I see no reason why I should not take as long over it as I like.

And then the freedom! I shall be able to do my own work.'[67] So, with heavy irony, Grant ended the war an official War Artist.

Unlike Duncan Grant and David Garnett, the writer Clive Bell was less hampered by tribunals and the machinery of authority and hence able to have more freedom to undertake his own work during the war due to a medical complaint (an 'unhealed rupture') that rendered him unfit for military service. However, until the necessities of the Military Service Act brought his medical history to the fore, he existed 'in a world of agitation and uneasiness which is not at all what I like', as he described to his wife Vanessa. He was unsure about 'venturing out' and hesitant about his future position after the Act became fully effective as he certainly classed himself as a conscientious objector and included himself in the group of his friends that he expected might end up in the army or jail before long. 'I suppose we shall be conscripted in a few weeks', he wrote to Vanessa in spring 1916, 'and I dare say I shall be in jail before Duncan or Bunny [Garnett]'.[68] Early 1916 found Bell considering announcing that he had volunteered for agricultural work at Garsington ('and so avoid all bother', especially with his patriotic family) though by the middle of that year his attitude had stiffened, despite being, as he put it, 'more and more in the councils of high liberalism … if I chose to eat humble pie I could doubtless make my own position secure, but I don't choose to do anything of the sort'.[69]

Like Garnett and others at the start of the war, Bell had felt a need for experience of it and was keen to become involved. He described the prospect of war to Strachey as like being a compulsory spectator at a university match – a match which was expected to last for three years. The only way of mitigating the boredom was to come down from the terraces and 'take a hand in the game'. He explained to Strachey about his medical disqualification from military service, though he admitted that this was 'pure red-tape', as he had suffered from this condition for years, and it had not prevented him shooting and big-game hunting in Alaska and elsewhere; he then asked Strachey how one applied for a possible job in the Army Medical or Service Corps.

However, Bell's initial enthusiasm for taking part in 'the game' soon waned as the reality of the war sunk in – to be replaced by work on his pamphlet *Peace at Once*, which appeared in 1915 and which Bell used to warn its potential readership of the dangers of championing war through to total victory. This course of action could only lead to harmful effects upon the whole of civilisation and hence an inconclusive and early peace settlement was preferable to the total destruction of Germany (and civilisation with it). War was simply 'purposeless horror', and its effects were likened to the outbreak and spread of a particularly virulent disease bringing untimely death and terror in its wake, he argued. Bell also sought to define what made a nation, and he concluded that a country had 'no reality' apart from the individuals comprising it. Each of these individuals had, or should have, an existence 'of his or her own' and, 'since a nation consists of individuals, and since it can be shown that the sooner this war ends the better it will be for the majority of these individuals, it seems to me the part of a true patriot to agitate for immediate peace'.[70]

The ethics of jingoistic patriotism were incompatible with civilised values, a theme that he later explored further in his *Civilization* (1928), in which the concept of civilisation was defined as a sense of values combined with reason providing a setting where, 'the intellect must be free to deal as it pleases with whatever comes its way, it must be free to choose its own terms, phrases and images, and to play with all things what tricks it will'. Set against this was military despotism of the war years when:

> Under the Military Service Acts we saw men in thousands taken from their homes, their work, their amusements, and driven to a life they detested to be followed shortly by a death they feared. They entered the Army for precisely the same reason that sheep enter the slaughterhouse. They obeyed because they were afraid to disobey. It was the same in all belligerent countries where conscription obtained ... By 1917, at any rate, the issues at stake meant nothing to the ordinary conscript. If, instead of being told to march against the enemy, he had been told to march into the flames of Moloch's sacred furnace, it had been all one to him ... Now when a central government, depending frankly on a controlled press, courts martial, and the peculiar horror inspired by the process of trial and execution, has the power to make men do this, it has power to make them do anything.[71]

Bell's 1915 call for agitation for peace had been no mere journalistic outburst; a few months after the introduction of conscription he was still to be found writing to his friends that, 'we must keep the agitation up – in the house, in the country, on individuals – do impress that on all your friends. Give them a moment's peace and they will fall asleep and we shall have to begin all over again.'[72] He referred to a letter of his to the *Daily News* that was designed to wake up a government that had 'gone to sleep'. Bell never regarded his exemption certificate as a reason for inaction in regard to the conflict. In fact he was never quite sure if his status would be altered by the authorities; in August 1916, he reported to his wife that he was having trouble with the military who, he wrote, were trying to take advantage of the 'ambiguous wording' of his certificate to attempt to re-class his status to that of non-combatant from the existing one of total exemption from all service, military or otherwise.

After the appearance of his *Peace at Once*, Bell was a marked man. The pamphlet was as unpopular with the authorities as it was popular with his friends and opponents of the war. Francis Birrell had written from Sommeille (while working for the Friends War Victims Relief Mission) to Lytton Strachey that:

> We have all been reading Clive's pamphlet and following his persecution and he is now the hero of the Society of Friends, a strange destiny for him to attain, but the whole affair is too perfectly monstrous. I thought the pamphlet very bright indeed. England seems pretty bloody just now. One's well out of it.[73]

Like Bell, Birrell worried over the war's effect on the course of civilisation. Previously, he told Strachey, the world had the makings of a 'charming place' but now something had 'gone wrong with the machinery' throwing up a need for some form of 'divine mechanic' to set the world to rights; only, 'he never will come'. Despite his work for the Relief Committee, Birrell still found time to dispatch an appeal from France in February 1916 to his local tribunal in Chelsea. He was on the register of eligible males and fully expected to be summoned back to England at some point during the summer. 'I am sure I shan't get off', he commented to Strachey on his appeal, 'as God wasn't mentioned and he is the only person or thing the Tribunals are frightened of except Zeppelins'.[74]

Like Francis Birrell, E.M. Forster chose humanitarian work abroad as a non-combatant and yet sought permission to have his case heard by a tribunal back in England. He had gone to Alexandria at the end of October 1915 as a Red Cross 'searcher', attempting to obtain information on missing soldiers from the wounded in hospitals. The following year, the Red Cross decided to release its able-bodied men for active service. Forster was told to undergo a medical on the understanding that he would 'attest' if passed fit for active duty. Although he was declared fit, he wrote a letter to Sir Courtold Thomson, the Chief Red Cross Commissioner, requesting to be excused from attesting on grounds of conscience. Eventually an interview was granted at which Forster declared his objection to be one of instinct and not of religious persuasion. He was given permission to return to England to state his case before a tribunal. However, Forster's friends exerted pressure on high-ranking military acquaintances, and Thomson was informed that the army did not require Forster amongst its ranks. Forster wrote to his mother that he was 'quite shameless over this wire-pulling. If I can't keep out of the army by fair means then hey for foul!'[75] Forster had no desire to return to an England that he described as 'hag-ridden' by the war. Like Birrell and Bell, he worried over the effect of the conflict on civilisation; 'It is a damned bore, with a stalemate as the most possible outcome', he predicted in November 1914, 'But one has to see it through, and see it through with the knowledge that whichever side wins, civilization in Europe will be pipped for the next 30 years.'[76]

To Forster, the real war was a war of 'Authoritarians v. Libertarians' (as he later described it to his friend Siegfried Sassoon) and he had found his response to the war to be at first inadequate, confiding to his diary in August 1914 that, 'Civilisation as it topples carries my brain with it'.[77] He was profoundly irritated at first by his relation to a war the parameters of which he could not encompass in his mind, let alone in reality, and he felt he was confined to a 'narrowing circle of light'[78] as progress was turned back on itself. The war also meant, as it did for others, a drying up of creativity and, according to Forster's biographer, the conflict was a sign that he had to (temporarily, at least) 'give up all hope of creation'.[79] He began to struggle with his fiction, the deliberately unpublishable *Maurice* being his only work-in-progress of the war period. Forster acknowledged the root of his inability to write (even letters) as, 'the cause of all that is evil – ie. this war which saps away one's spirit',[80] and he was perturbed by the prospect of 'organisation and dehumanisation' enveloping all streams of life. 'Will the war leave nothing in the world but a card index?' he asked a friend in 1918.[81] By this time, however, he had come into a belief that, as defined to Siegfried Sassoon, due to Forster's own anti-war sentiments, 'one's at war with the world', and he was involved in a form of 'defensive warfare' on a personal level which had come to mean 'Violent individualism. Conscious shirking'.[82]

Forster's 'inmost recesses' had been invaded by 'the cosmology of strife', and he had been altered by the experience. He was aware of (and did not attempt to deny) the likely effect on the individual of the experience of the war, whether of a direct or indirect nature and, like others, part of him wanted from the start to be involved in some way. In August 1914, considering hospital work, he had felt as if, 'the war exists on my account. If I died it would stop, but it is here to give me experiences if I choose to receive them.'[83] On the death of Rupert Brooke, Forster had commented that Brooke's '1914' sonnets had been inspired by his romantic thoughts about war and not by his knowledge of it. If he had been spared to gain this knowledge, argued Forster, he would have expressed his thoughts with much greater 'grim and grotesque realism'. As he wrote to his friend Malcolm Darling, 'This war's like the bible – we're all going to take out of it what we bring to it', adding that, 'I, who never saw much purpose in the Universe, now see less'.[84]

In 1917 Forster wrote to Goldsworthy Lowes Dickinson including a copy of his essay 'Human Nature under War Conditions' (in which he argued that men were now functioning merely under the twin stimuli of fear or sorrow) and commenting that the motivations towards experience were clear: 'To merge myself. To test myself. To do my bit. To suffer what other soldiers suffer, that I may understand them. There – apart from compulsion – are the motives that send men to fight'. Forster pointed out that motivations of justice and honour were not enough: 'They were good enough trimmings for peacetime, but the supreme need now is the preservation of life. Let us look after the bodies that there may be a next generation which may have the right to look after the soul.'[85]

The war, comments one of Virginia Woolf's biographers, 'overshadows Virginia Woolf's work ... Her books are full of images of war: armies, guns, bombs, air-raids, battleships, shell-shock victims, war reports, photographs of war-victims, voices of dictators'.[86] Despite this, Woolf herself did not care for the war in contemporary fiction; she thought the war poetry of Siegfried Sassoon to be too close to the reality, just as she flinched at the sound of the guns in France in March 1918, clearly audible at her Sussex home, Asheham House, as the Germans pushed the Allies back towards Amiens. She wrote that the events across the Channel were 'towering over us too closely and too tremendously' to be fictionalised without a 'powerful jolt in the perspective' occurring.[87] Patriotism in literature she described as 'insidious poison'. Woolf assimilated the war only after the event and then only with a subtle tone. Another of her biographers has pointed out how the character of Jacob in *Jacob's Room* was based in part on her idolised brother Thoby, and the novel is partly a structure to join Thoby's death in 1906 with the Great War, 'an attempt to link her own personal sense of loss to the pervasive feeling of loss and disintegration which impinged on everyone in England in the early 1920s'.[88]

It had only been when her sister Vanessa Bell left London in March 1916, to keep house for Duncan Grant and David Garnett who were fruit farming to strengthen their claims for exemption from military service at Wissett Lodge in Suffolk, that Virginia Woolf admitted to her friend Ka Cox that Bloomsbury, in its London incarnation, seemed to have vanished into thin air 'like the morning mist'.[89] This could be seen to be representative of the differing responses of the group of friends to the war; some, like Keynes, burrowed further into the capital – to the very heart of Whitehall, while others, like Vanessa Bell, moved away from a London dominated by war to the relative peace of the country. Bell's country life and her perceived inactivity in response to the war has perhaps been taken for indifference by some, but, like her sister, her anti-war feeling lay in her repudiation of the importance given to the war by those 'in favour' of it and, far from being inactive, right from the start she possessed a keen appreciation of the war's effect upon her world of friendships and beyond, writing to Roger Fry during the first few days of war that, 'We have been in such a state of gloom about the war that it's difficult to think of anything else'.[90]

In mid-August 1914, Fry read to Vanessa the Foreign Office White Paper concerning Britain's involvement in the European war, and admitted to her husband Clive that she found it complicated and would have to read it again to herself to fully understand its implications, though she reported that, 'It has led to a great deal of argument here'. Also at that time, she persuaded her brother Adrian to delay his decision to volunteer for the armed forces: 'I told him I thought it very foolish', she reported to her husband, whom she encouraged in his anti-war writing (*Peace at Once*), while commenting sadly that, 'evidently the world is so mad that no-one will take it [her husband's pamphlet] seriously'.[91]

Vanessa Bell's initial response to the war was to travel to her sister Virginia at Asheham House where she and Grant painted furiously. As she wrote to Fry:

> If one simply waited for news one would rapidly get into a state of melancholia ... One can do no good, unluckily, by thinking of the horrors going on and though you know I don't ignore them, it seems to me now the only thing we can do is to go on keeping some kind of decent existence going.[92]

She deplored the fact that the only option open to people was to fight and if a person attempted to do something else, they were immediately accused of 'making a muddle'. She comprehended the 'awful' pressure on people such as her brother and Grant to enlist, and she supported Grant in his attempt to resist the 'moral pressure' to fight, believing that for Britain to become involved in the conflict was 'perfectly absurd' while some sort of stand against a huge army being sent abroad was 'most necessary'. When she saw that the newspapers were encouraging a long war resulting in total defeat of Germany, she thought it 'quite wrong' and complained that she felt it 'difficult to concentrate one's mind' amid the rumours and counter-rumours of the escalating conflict. 'One must simply work and try to find out what is permanent', she concluded.

By the high-watermark of the death of Rupert Brooke in April 1915, Vanessa Bell had moved to Eleanor House on the Sussex coast. She found all the talk about Brooke largely pointless just as she found talk of the war liable to 'put a stop' to other, creative thoughts, and she thought it most vital that these creative thoughts 'shouldn't be killed'. Hence she deliberately resisted returning to London. 'How idiotic to go home and listen to talk about the war and Rupert', she wrote to her husband, with Brooke's death symbolising the war itself and consequently her desire to be apart from it. However, the war's effects reached out to her through its influence upon her friends as they made plans to resist being forced to fight. When she finally returned to London, she found only a 'state of general gloom' which seemed to have taken the place of the social life she had formerly known; she deplored the fact that, 'no-one can now lead their normal lives'. 'How damnable it is', she exclaimed to Fry, 'that people with ideas utterly different from one's own should have so much power over one's life'.[93]

The advent of conscription in 1916 and its meaning with regard to her friends finally 'shattered Vanessa's carapace of ignorance', according to her biographer.[94] She had never been knowingly ignorant but had constructed an artificial shell of unthinking around herself for protection against the war's malign pressure upon her creative life. There occurred a closing of ranks at Asheham House in January 1916 when Vanessa and the Woolfs were joined by Clive Bell, Grant, Garnett, Keynes and Lytton Strachey amid much debate, with Vanessa reporting to Fry that, 'Duncan and Bunny [Garnett] and Lytton are all agreed that they would sooner go to prison than be forced to become soldiers', while she feared that the war's effect upon the normal course of existence would render life in England after the war's end 'impossible'. To her, the lack of conscription was the one thing that made England better than other countries, 'in spite of all … but if that goes I don't see any reason for bringing up one's children to be English'.[95] This perhaps helps to explain one side of her desire to bring up her boys in the country during the war where they would not be exposed to the conflict to the same extent as in London. However, such was her anger and frustration at the loss of personal freedom that the introduction of conscription would entail, that she admitted to Fry that, for once, she felt a desire to involve herself in public affairs and, although she felt that she lacked the appropriate background and necessary skills to do so, she did agree to undertake office work on a voluntary basis for the National Council for Civil Liberties.

By the time of Grant and Garnett's appearance before the Blything tribunal in May 1916, another move – to Wissett Lodge – had occurred, and Vanessa Bell and her children were now firmly planted in the country.[96] 'It is difficult to think freely of all kinds of other things with this uncertainty hanging over one', she wrote to Fry, '… we're not just leading a perfectly happy and contented life in the country because it has gone on so long'. She admitted, however, that it was much better to be painting in the country than in London, 'and if one only knew this [i.e. the resolution of Grant and Garnett's case] were going on, one could work hard'. The continuance of the state of affairs brought about by the war was beginning to trouble her more deeply:

> all these months of never being able to look ahead at all do make one long for some settlement and I had begun to hope it was settled. I think it gets on one's nerves at last – everything depending on letters and committees etc. One tries not to speculate as to what will happen but one can't help it and then one gets into a horrid state of mind.

Vanessa Bell perceived how the war, in addition to disrupting the production of the art of both herself and Grant, was also adversely affecting the creative processes of her friends; for example, she thought Fry's ideas to be expressed in too 'fragmentary' a fashion, and she encouraged him in particular to produce a solid piece of work as soon as the war was over, 'to start us all off again'.[97] While Grant tried to paint what he viewed as possibly his final pictures before the commencement of his land work, the Central Committee having granted himself and Garnett alternative agricultural employment, Bell travelled to Lewes and actually secured the work from a farmer, although they all still had to contend with an unfavourable report concerning suspect activities at Wissett Lodge which was sent to the War Agricultural Committee on the probable prompting of suspicious local residents. Partly in response to this, in October 1916, the whole group moved to Charleston, the farmhouse near Firle, which was to be Vanessa's home for the next three years (and in which she would eventually die, forty-five years later).

Vanessa Bell spent the remainder of the war bringing up her children, looking after Grant (who came close to a breakdown, due to anxiety and overwork) and painting, although she was still aware of the consequences of outside events prompted by the war, such as the Manpower Bill of April 1918 (the time of the great German offensive on the Western Front). This Bill, in addition to raising the age of conscription to cover those in the category of forty-one to fifty years (prompting her to fear whether Fry might be affected) also, she noted with alarm, proposed to give the authorities new powers to call up previously exempted men working on the land. 'One can only hope they won't think it worthwhile to do so', she wrote to Fry anxiously, 'but as things are at present [i.e. the German offensive] that seems rather a forlorn hope'. Her only hope this time was that Grant would be rejected on medical grounds, 'but meanwhile all is uncertain again which is horrid after thinking it was settled'.[98] Bell was not able to feel totally free of the war's interference until its actual end when she acknowledged to Fry that, although things had finally become calmer in her and Grant's country existence, 'I think the relief now is simply in thinking that the horror has stopped'.[99]

The physical self-removal from the war of Vanessa Bell was echoed to a certain extent in mental terms by her sister Virginia. Right at the start of the conflict, during the first hours of war, Virginia Woolf had merely noted the extra trains being run to and from the coast to transport people fleeing the Continent to London and beyond. However, after leaving Asheham House, which Virginia described to Ka Cox as being 'practically under martial law', the Woolfs went to London where Virginia was immediately struck by the conversation of her friends such as Lady Ottoline and Clive Bell, 'they talked and talked, and said it was the end of civilisation, and the rest of our lives are worthless'.[100] During the next few months, the Woolfs busied themselves with looking for alternative accommodation, eventually finding Hogarth House in Richmond at Christmas 1914. They were also immersed in their respective writing, Woolf working on her second novel, *Night and Day*. She remained telescopic in her view of the war and the world outside her window, believing, as she wrote in her diary, that the human race seemed to have no character or any real goals and fought only from 'a dreary sense of duty', though she appeared to take the same line as Bertrand Russell when she wrote to Duncan Grant describing her distress at what she saw as an 'evolution' in attitudes to life, brought on by the war. In peacetime, she had regarded her compatriots as essentially harmless, if stupid; 'but now they have been roused they seem full of the most violent and filthy passions'.[101]

Woolf was unimpressed by organised peace movements and found no inspiration at a Fabian meeting on 'The Conditions of Peace' at the end of January 1915, describing those attending as appearing 'singular and impotent'. Her insular reaction was given full reign by the onset of her mental breakdown in the spring of 1915 from which she did not recover until the end of that year. Virginia suffered from recurring mental difficulties all her life, though at this particular time she was perhaps more prone to attack due to possible tension between her inner, creative life and the outside war-life of the nation and her friends. The solitude of illness enabled her to establish a domestic routine that would assist her throughout the remainder of the war. By the time of her thirty-fourth birthday in January 1916, Woolf had settled into a routine of writing in the morning, walking in the afternoon and reading with her husband in the evening, although life and opinions did not remain so sedate for long. She wrote to her friend Margaret Llewelyn Davies that, due to the effect of the war, which she described as 'this preposterous masculine fiction', she felt herself becoming 'steadily more feminist'.[102] Under the influence of Llewelyn Davies, Woolf later chaired meetings of the Richmond branch of the Women's Co-operative Guild at Hogarth House, also the base of the Hogarth Press, the first publication of which appeared in July 1917.

Virginia Woolf's practical activities also extended to appealing to Lady Robert Cecil on behalf of Duncan Grant and his appeal to the Central Tribunal (the Chairman of which was Lord Salisbury, Lady Cecil's brother-in-law) regarding alternative employment; 'The first tribunal was so prejudiced against some that one felt it was rather hopeless to expect a fair hearing', she wrote, 'The war is a nightmare isn't it – two cousins of mine were killed this last week, and I suppose in other families it's much worse'.[103]

In May 1916, Leonard Woolf was awarded exemption from military service due to his trembling hands, and his wife had confided to her sister that she herself was still mentally 'in a very shaky state' and would probably succumb to a complete breakdown 'if they took him'. Although she observed to Ka Cox that, 'the whole of our world does nothing but talk about conscription', and regarded the summer of 1917 as a period when the rest of the human race had sunk to new depths ('how little one believes what anyone says now', she commented to Margaret Llewelyn Davies) it was no coincidence that the Hogarth Press sprang into life during the same period – an individual expression of productive creativity to counterbalance the muffling effect of both the war and her own mental instability.

Woolf's response to the conflict was, in her own words, to repudiate the importance attached to it by a violent world, although, with the guns audible from the garden at Asheham in which she was reading Wordsworth in the spring of 1918, Virginia could not help but admit to her diary that there was an 'odd pallor in those particular days of sunshine'. After a visit to see her brother-in-law Philip who had been wounded in action and was now in the Fishmonger's Hall in London (transformed into a temporary hospital), Woolf was struck by 'a feeling of the uselessness of it all, breaking these people and mending them again', a typical example of her ability to always see 'the skull beneath the skin' regarding the human condition. She later reasoned that the ability of a person to kill another human being (and by implication her *inability*, and that of her friends) was that, 'one's imagination is too sluggish to conceive what his life means to him – the infinite possibilities of a succession of days which are furled in him, and have already been spent'.[104]

In the days following the Armistice, Virginia felt that she had experienced such a change of perspective due to the war that she saw no meaning to the 'gossip of parties' that now abounded and nothing to celebrate in the wet feathers, languishing flags and 'sordid' crowds of a rainy London. The only positive thing to come out of the war, she reflected, was the fact that, for some, it had been an opportunity to stretch their minds in order to consider something universal, although now, 'we contract them at once to the squabbles of Lloyd George and a General Election'. From a situation of many minds concentrated, rightly or wrongly, willing or not, upon a single point, 'one feels now that the whole bunch has burst asunder and flown off with the utmost vigour in different directions. We are once more a nation of individuals'.[105]

Although Virginia Woolf had found the extremes of the Garsington Manor of Ottoline and Philip Morrell a little heavy on the senses ('too many scents and silks ... at moments the sense of it seemed to flag') she had comprehended its value as a haven to the threatened anti-war artistic community; 'I think Ott. deserves some credit for keeping her ship in full sail, as she certainly does ... O. and P. and Garsington House provide a good deal', and, despite her rather deprecatory comments about Lady Ottoline made to friends, she confided to her diary after her first visit in November 1917 that, 'On the whole I like Ottoline better than her friends have prepared one for liking her. Her vitality seemed to me a credit to her, and in private talk her vapours give way to some quite clear bursts of shrewdness'.[106] At their first meeting in 1909, Lady Ottoline had 'swooped down' on Woolf at 46 Gordon Square to issue her with an invitation to one of her celebrated 'Thursday nights'. Woolf had accepted and had taken Rupert Brooke with her to be introduced to their hostess, whom she described at the time as being regarded (even then) as a 'disembodied spirit' amongst her artists and writers. Both women were outsiders, propelled by their acute individual sensibilities to an observational position from without rather than within. The coming of the war and their views on it served to exaggerate this sense of 'otherness', though resulting in different approaches; Lady Ottoline, like Bertrand Russell, translating thoughts into deeds whilst Woolf, characteristically, transcribed them into the art of words, written and spoken.

Just as Bertrand Russell could be said to have both thought and operated outside of the intimate circle of his Bloomsbury friends in his response to the war, so too did his sometime mistress and friend, Lady Ottoline. Though described by some as the patroness of Bloomsbury, she had in fact a much wider circle of acquaintances and activities and was never regarded as such by Bloomsbury themselves, though they appreciated shared aesthetic goals, such as the genuine quality of Lady Ottoline's passionate support for a life lived in pursuit of truth and beauty and her deeply-held anti-war sentiments. It was not only Bloomsbury and her 'soul-mate' Russell that perceived her acute anti-war feeling; 'Lady Ottoline', remembered the anti-war writer Mary Agnes Hamilton, 'had a great deal to do with holding the pacifist movement together and keeping it warm'. Although Russell's intellect was the dominant one and his voice 'was the voice we followed, it was Ottoline who held us together'.[107] From the final days of peace in 1914, when many of her friends were by no means anti-war, Lady Ottoline and her husband had viewed the whole business as 'absolute madness', Philip Morrell being one of the few Members of Parliament to speak out continuously against the conflict from the first. At the end of July, with the war fast approaching, Lady Ottoline could only see 'the ruin and suffering and devastation of it ... simply to erect a sort of snobbish Pride into a Deity'.[108]

For Ottoline Morrell, the motives behind the war were based from the start on a distortion of the moral lodestar of friendship and creative co-operation, and she deplored the abounding desire to crush a fellow civilised nation. On August 9th 1914 she wrote in her journal:

> It amazes me how without any compunction the whole of Europe throws aside the moral and humane code that has been built up by years of civilised life. They all seem swallowed up in an earthquake, and out of chaos has come a lurid light that glorifies brutality and savagery, casting upon it a theatrical, rosy, false light which turns its real grinning, hideous face into that of some divine goddess.[109]

In this, she echoed Mary Agnes Hamilton's similar sense of a 'theatrical transformation scene' being enacted by the authorities in the first months of war (see Chapter 6).

Philip Morrell spoke out against the folly of the war in the Commons on 3 August 1914, standing alone with nearly all the House violently waving their order papers and calling on him to 'Sit down!' While Lady Ottoline and her husband hosted a meeting of the fledgling Union of Democratic Control in the drawing room of 44 Bedford Square, the house was also used to shelter Belgian refugees. The Morrell's popular Thursday parties began to be held again from December 1914 and former guests who were now 'pro-war' were not invited. However, Lady Ottoline's reaction to the war, like that of her lover, Bertrand Russell, also had a practical side; she worked for the Friends of Foreigners organisation, providing comfort where possible to the families of interned German fathers or husbands. She shared with Russell an intense sadness at seeing young men, 'full of new thought and life', sent abroad to probable death, and she continually urged him to harness his intellectual ability to his loathing of the war in order to convince others of their point of view through his writing and practical efforts ('Why don't you go and see Grey [the Foreign Secretary]', she urged him at one point), while herself feeling the war ever more keenly. By the end of 1914 she wrote to Russell that the depression she experienced, 'eats into one and seems to deaden everything'.[110]

It was in spring 1915 that the Morrells moved to their new home in Oxfordshire, Garsington Manor, which became a pilgrim's rest for individuals seeking escape from the war. At first, Lady Ottoline was relieved to be more isolated from the 'torrent of life' that had existed in London. The capital, she felt, had become entirely changed by the war. 'There seemed no spot that one touched that didn't fly open and show some picture of suffering, some macabre dance of death', she recalled:

> I felt very strange and out of tune with everything there ... overcome by the loneliness ... the sense of isolation of individuals; millions of people rushing about, so separate from each other and so alone. The war absorbs all attention and leaves London a chaos.[111]

At Garsington, it was hoped, these people would have an opportunity to think and talk in freedom. The house was to be 'a harbour, a refuge in the storm', for those tossed about helplessly on the waves of war, for, as she saw it:

The destructive torrent is so strong that it sweeps everyone with it ... Any delicate creative effort is blasted and seems trivial, for the war is so real and terrible, it blots out anything else and makes other work seem valueless, except that of passionate resistance, and that at times seems quixotic and futile.[112]

One such individual to be given refuge and support was Siegfried Sassoon whose poems Lady Ottoline had liked and responded to by letter. Whilst convalescing at Somerville College, Oxford in August 1916, and through the introduction of Oscar Wilde's tireless promoter Robbie Ross, Sassoon visited Garsington unannounced and was invited to spend a week there the following month, during which time Lady Ottoline inscribed in a book for Sassoon her conception of the purpose of life at Garsington – a world apart from the war's destructive influence. 'Come then', she wrote:

gather here – all who have passion and who desire to create new conditions of life – new visions of art and literature and new magic worlds of poetry and music. If I could but feel that days at Garsington had strengthened your efforts to live the noble life: to live freely, recklessly, with clear Reason released from convention – no longer absorbed in small personal events but valuing personal affairs as part of a grand whole – above all to live with passionate desire for Truth and Love and Understanding and Imagination.[113]

A deep mutual appreciation followed, with Lady Ottoline respecting Sassoon's ability to see and feel the war as a poet and artist and his 'woodland wildness' (compared with most intellectuals who, she wrote, 'walk along half-blind'). When Sassoon came to make his public protest against the war in 1917, it was Lady Ottoline whom he consulted first and she who encouraged him and introduced him to Bertrand Russell for advice on the wording of the Soldier's Declaration, writing to Russell that, 'I do wish he could join onto you, for I think he might find an outlet for his energies in that way'.[114] Other guests were not treated with as much sympathy; both the Bishop of Oxford and Asquith himself were lectured on the issue of compulsion and the treatment of conscientious objectors when they came to visit, with the Prime Minister being first separated from the other guests and marched up to Ottoline's bedroom ('I was very clear and forcible!' she recalled).

In Lady Ottoline's response to the war we find echoed many of the familiar themes of reaction we have already observed in association with male writers and artists: a championing of the individual and personal consciousness, an awareness of a diminishment of creative capacity, the blunting of individual sensibility and a fear for the wreckage of civilisation. She wrote to Russell in the summer of 1917 that she felt that the pressures of the war 'have worn us thin – worn away all feeling. I feel as empty as a drum, without any thoughts or ideas – one feels as if one had gone soft inside.'[115] In January 1918 she confided to her journal that 'This cataclysm sweeps away all individuality and forms like a flood of horror over the world, crushing, overwhelming all design, all form ...'[116] Her driving motivation was to champion common humanity and an acute concern over 'the wrecking of the fine eye of civilisation' and a 'breaking down of much that was fine and harmonious'. She saw that she was largely isolated in her opinions and motivations: 'What a different world mine is to my sister-in-law [the Duchess of Portland]'; she wrote to Russell:

> She would hate and loathe a thinker or artist and all my thoughts of love and sympathy go out to them and keeping these fragile things alive now. Ideas, art, poetry. The passion for work – 'war work' – kills these lovely creations. It seems like a corrugated iron shed put up on top of a heavenly garden.[117]

Isolated she might be in her views on the war, but those views were firmly held and her themes, as we can see, are familiar. As she once wrote in her journal:

> Nothing can convert me to feel that war is right. It is so obviously a violation of all civilisation and of the natural growth and development of man that comes from contact and understanding between people and nations ... It is surely essential that individuals should be treated as sacred until they have proved themselves pernicious. In war, all reason, all right intelligence, is thrown overboard, or forced to serve brutality and destruction. And men relapse into animals – to fight, men must become brutes. No-one who had not become so could go out deliberately to maim and inflict torture and death on other men or to destroy ruthlessly beautiful buildings and land.[118]

Although it was not until the 1920s that Frances Partridge (then Frances Marshall) came into the orbit of Ottoline Morrell, Virginia Woolf and the rest of Bloomsbury, her attitude to the war had been of a similar kind. A lifelong pacifist, she dates her anti-war feeling from the middle of the war when she was sixteen: 'I am more a pacifist than a devotee of any other -ism ... and I would call it moralistic or ethically based'.[119] Her future husband, Ralph Partridge, fought in the war and became a Major in his early twenties but resigned his commission as soon as the war ended, having been convinced on moral grounds that the pacifist argument was 'overwhelming', as he stated to the Appeal Tribunal for Conscientious Objectors during the Second World War in 1943. During the earlier war, 'All civilized values had disappeared' and both Frances Marshall and Ralph Partridge saw their country dominated by 'fear, hatred, anger and revenge'. The Marshall family had always approved of a love of nature and free expression, and the heroes of Frances' father had been Darwin, Ruskin, Tennyson and Leslie Stephen, also a family friend (and father of Vanessa Bell and Virginia Woolf).

In her memoirs, Partridge recalled the failure of communication between the young men returning from the front and those at home who 'lacked the imagination to bridge the gap'. In 1918 she went up to Newnham College, Cambridge, where J.E. McTaggart was lecturing, and G.E. Moore could still be encountered, his eyes usually buried in a book. Her brother had been on holiday in Germany when war was declared, and was interned. When he was finally released, he had been transformed from a lively and boisterous undergraduate of nineteen into a shy young man with a voice kept lowered, 'as if he didn't want to be heard'. Partridge felt that experiencing the war was akin to living a kind of sleeping life: 'You're practically under an anaesthetic.'[120]

Normal life was also disrupted to a large extent on the Home Front as everyone, including older people and women, was sucked into the war effort:

> They somehow had no *time*, everybody was put to it, in a way, to do something which would concern the war and it was thought awful that they shouldn't do that by the supporters of the war, who after all were the majority. But there were also unthinking people who really hadn't thought it out.

Partridge, emboldened by her upbringing with its lack of strict convention and her strong but threatened sense of individuality, enjoyed encountering these stray 'unthinking' people on the train to London and engaging them in conversation:

> because everybody talked to each other more in the war, – perhaps some village woman – I would try to make her understand how the German soldiers were really people like her sons ... individuals ... they [the people she talked to] kept reacting very quickly during anything like that – anything that was human.[121]

In examining the cases of these women associated with Bloomsbury we observe women for whom the war was instinctively wrong. Woolf and Bell had grown up in an intellectual atmosphere and had been left free by the death of their father to absorb the ethos of their brother's Bloomsbury friends. Partridge had been raised in a liberal, free-thinking family and had experienced the independence of Newnham College, Cambridge and a room and allowance of her own with which to cultivate her ideas. With her aristocratic upbringing, Lady Ottoline had also had time and leisure in which to develop her very particular aesthetic sensibilities. These women all reacted instinctively against the war due to a potent combination of aesthetic and humanistic concerns. The war drew forth these similar concerns, even if they found expression in different forms: Bell's self-imposed isolation and Woolf's mental echoing of this, Lady Ottoline's practical involvement with other aesthetic anti-war reaction and Partridge's formation of an intellectual, humanistic view on war that would influence her whole life.

E.M. Forster's earlier concerns about the war's effects neatly summarise the general views of the friends who constituted the Bloomsbury Group and its immediate circle. Forster's belief that civilisation would be 'pipped' whichever side won was shared by Lytton Strachey and Clive Bell, with Bell's *Peace at Once* a clarion call for early negotiations in order to preserve what was still left of a civilisation which had been about to fulfil its potential, but which was now being sent into reverse by the destructive energies unleashed by the war. This recognition of the destructive capacity of mankind was apparent in the writings of Goldsworthy Lowes Dickinson, one of the 'mentors' of Bloomsbury (and repeated in the thoughts and writings of Bertrand Russell, discussed in Chapter

3). Dickinson championed a life lived for 'impassioned reason' and hence the immense shock of the plunge into war.. To 'friends of reason', such as Bertrand Russell and himself, the war, with its submersion of peaceful creativity, could not be anything but a crushing blow, both intellectually and emotionally.

Though the conflict crushed Dickinson utterly, the younger individuals of Bloomsbury attempted to 'keep their heads' while the war raged around them. G.E. Moore had taught the Bloomsbury Group an awareness of the concept of intrinsic good, and that attaching this concept to things in isolation allowed for relative degrees of value to be decided upon and hence a moral value system could be established, allowing a more truthful view of the world: a system that appealed to intuition, reason and reflective judgement.

Moore had had little time for public virtues, believing that the only rules to which the individual should conform were those widely approved by common sense. In all other situations the individual should decide what positive good they could effect from each separate case directed by a knowledge of the intrinsic goodness and badness of things. Hence the individual who possessed a sound perception of these intrinsic values should be left free to make his or her own decisions as to the right or wrong of a particular issue. This particularly applied at a time when the Government seemed, more than ever, to be taking decisions on behalf of the people – decisions which seemed to threaten their individuality. A person's conduct would look after itself and be correct if it were guided by an awareness of intrinsic good – this was Bloomsbury's belief.

J.M. Keynes later commented that he and his friends, 'repudiated entirely customary morals, conventions and traditional wisdom. We were .... immoralists ... we recognised no moral obligation on us, no inner sanction, to conform or to obey'. Also, as well as being their own judges, 'we claimed the right to judge every individual case on its merits', as well as the self-control and wisdom to judge successfully.[122] According to Keynes, when the Bloomsbury Group became 'immoralists', they also rejected some of Moore's moral philosophy (in particular, his chapter in *Principia Ethica*, 'Ethics in Relation to Conduct') while accepting his basic 'religion' of an awareness of intrinsic goods (including beauty and friendship). Rejecting some of Moore's doctrine allowed Bloomsbury to further repudiate conventional moralistic obligations. Hence they were able, in one sense, to be their own judges and claim – as Keynes and Strachey did – a moral objection to surrendering their right of decision and becoming part of the military machine.

As we have seen, some of the Bloomsbury Group had been tempted to enlist during the first weeks of the war – not from a rush of patriotic fervour but, as David Garnett explained, more in order that they might share in what was clearly a great 'human experience'. In order to somehow test himself, E.M. Forster expressed a desire to 'merge' himself with the war; Bloomsbury had always regarded the 'passionate contemplation' of life, people and events as not only morally worthwhile but necessary. This desire to experience the war in a direct manner – despite a moral, humanistic or aesthetic opposition to it – was to be replicated, not only in the cases of Siegfried Sassoon and Wilfrid Owen but also among the more obscure, as discussed in Chapter 7. The themes of humanistic, aesthetic and moral reaction exhibited by Bloomsbury to the war – such as the submersion of individual sensibilities, the threat to the progress of civilisation and the drying up or diverting of creative energies – were to be perceived and echoed by other people, and in one particular individual – Bertrand Russell – they coalesced completely.

Notes

1 The Bloomsbury Group grew out of intellectual friendships forged in undergraduate Cambridge during the 1880s and 1890s. Although Thoby Stephen did not live long into the twentieth century, it was his siblings, Adrian, Vanessa and Virginia, who, freed by the death of their strict father, formed the nucleus of what became the Bloomsbury Group. The 'members' of the group often had difficulty in naming the entire fellowship, with characters seeming to drift in and out at will. In later years, some even denied the existence of any such group at all. The 'core' individuals included the economist John Maynard Keynes; the art critic and essayist Clive Bell and his wife Vanessa, the artist; the formidable writing and publishing team of Leonard and Virginia Woolf; Virginia's brother Adrian Stephen; the artist Duncan Grant (sometime lover of Vanessa) and the literary biographer Lytton Strachey. Others such as the writers David Garnett and E.M. Forster and friends and mentors such as Francis Birrell, Bertrand Russell, Ottoline Morrell and the art critic Roger Fry seemed to hover on the edges, sometimes precariously.

2 J.K. Johnstone, 'The Philosophic Background and Works of Art of the Group known as Bloomsbury', PhD. thesis (University of Leeds, 1952), p. 2.

3 Dickinson belonged to the older generation of Cambridge Apostles (including J.E. McTaggart, Nathaniel Wedd and Roger Fry) whose spiritual humanism had a profound effect on G.E. Moore, Bertrand Russell and, subsequently, the members of Bloomsbury themselves. J.K. Johnstone points out that, 'Even more important to Bloomsbury than Moore's philosophy was the Cambridge Humanism which is behind that philosophy'. *Ibid.*, p. 444. For more on the influence upon Bloomsbury of the older Apostles and 'Cambridge Humanism' see J.K. Johnstone, *The Bloomsbury Group* (London, 1954) and Paul Levy, *G.E. Moore and the Cambridge Apostles* (Oxford, 1981).

4 Ottoline Morrell, Journal, June 1916, cited in *Ottoline at Garsington – Memoirs of Lady Ottoline Morrell 1915–1918*, ed. R. Gathorne-Hardy (London, 1974), p. 117.

5 Goldsworthy Lowes Dickinson, 'The Basis of a Permanent Peace' in C.R. Buxton (ed.), *Towards a Lasting Settlement* (London, 1915), p. 11.

6 M.R. Pollock, 'British Pacifism during the First World War – the Cambridge–Bloomsbury contribution', PhD thesis (Columbia University, 1971, University Microfilms, Ann Arbor, MI), p. 1.

7 E.M. Forster, *Goldsworthy Lowes Dickinson* (London, 1934), p. 114.

8 Goldsworthy Lowes Dickinson, *Letters From John Chinaman and Other Essays* (London, 1901), p. 27.

9 Goldsworthy Lowes Dickinson, 'The Holy War', the *Nation*, 8 Aug. 1914, cited in Pollock, 'British Pacifism', p. 132.

10 Pollock, 'British Pacifism', p. 135.

11 Goldsworthy Lowes Dickinson, *After the War* (London, 1915), pp. 17–18.

12 Goldsworthy Lowes Dickinson, *The Choice Before Us*. (New York, 1919), p. 53. First published

London, 1917.

13 Cited in Forster, *Dickinson*, p. 162.

14 Goldsworthy Lowes Dickinson, 'The Holy War', the *Nation*, vol. 15, no. 19, 8 Aug. 1914.

15 Goldsworthy Lowes Dickinson [Letter to Mrs. Ashbee, 11 Nov. 1914], cited in Forster, *Dickinson*, p. 158.

16 The Bryce Group was so known simply because two early meetings were attended by Lord Bryce. It was a group, established by Dickinson, of interested persons who met to discuss and research the possibility of a future League of Nations. It was on behalf of this group that Dickinson went to the Hague in 1915 to meet with international pacifists, at which meeting the Society for a Durable Peace was formed. As a result of affiliating with other like-minded groups, the Bryce Group became the League of Nations Society in May 1915, which subsequently became the League of Nations Union in October 1918.

17 Publications included: *The War and the Way Out* (1914); *After the War* (1915); *The European Anarchy* (1916); *The Choice Before Us* (1917) and *Problems of International Settlement* (1918).

18 *The Diary of Virginia Woolf, Volume One*, ed. A.O. Bell (London, 1977), 21 Oct. 1917, p. 64.

19 G.L. Dickinson, *War: Its Nature, Cause and Cure* (London, 1923), pp. 6–7, 44.

20 Pollock, 'British Pacifism', p. 10.

21 McMaster University, Hamilton, Ontario, Canada, William Ready Division of Archives and Research Collection, Bertrand Russell, Papers, (McM,BRP), Ottoline Morrell to Bertrand Russell, 710 082299, 31 July 1914.

22 McM,BRP, Ottoline Morrell to Bertrand Russell, 710 082363, 11 Nov. 1914.

23 Quentin Bell, 'Recollections and Reflections on Maynard Keynes', Lecture 3, *Keynes and the Bloomsbury Group – the Fourth Keynes Seminar, University of Kent, 1978*, ed. D. Crabtree and A.P. Thirlwall (London, 1980), pp. 75–6.

24 J.M. Keynes, 'My Early Beliefs' (first read to the Bloomsbury Memoir Club in September 1938) *Collected Writings of J.M. Keynes, Volume X: Essays in Biography*, ed. Elizabeth Johnson (London, 1972), pp. 435, 446.

25 Raymond Williams, 'Bloomsbury as a Social and Cultural Group', Lecture 2, *Keynes and the Bloomsbury Group*, p. 62.

26 J.M. Keynes to N. Keynes, 14 Aug. 1914, cited in Sally Weston, 'Bertrand Russell, Leonard Woolf and John Maynard Keynes – A Biographical Examination of the Influences Established before 1914, which Dictated their Reaction to the First World War', MA thesis, University of Kent, 1992, p. 90.

27 J.M. Keynes to G.L. Strachey, 27 Nov. 1914, cited in Roy F. Harrod, *The Life of John Maynard Keynes* (London, 1951), p. 200.

28 Bertrand Russell to Ottoline Morrell, cited in Ronald W. Clark, *The Life of Bertrand Russell* (London, 1975), pp. 260–1.

29 Robert Skidelsky, *John Maynard Keynes – Volume One: Hopes Betrayed* (London, 1983), p. 157.

30 Cited in Elizabeth Johnson, 'Keynes' Attitude to Compulsory Military Service – A Comment', *Economic Journal*, ed. R. Harrod and R.A.G. Robinson, vol LXX, no. 277, March 1960, pp. 160–5.

31 Cited in Skidelsky, *Keynes*, p. 345.

32 Austin Robinson, 'A Personal View', in *Essays on Maynard Keynes*, ed. Milo Keynes (Cambridge, 1975), p. 16.

33 Tate Gallery Archive, Charleston Trust Papers (TGA,CTP hereafter), 8010.8.193, Vanessa Bell to Roger Fry, 4 Jan. 1916.

34 Weston, 'Russell, Woolf and Keynes – A Biographical Examination', p. 99.

35 J.M. Keynes to Mrs Keynes, 14 April 1918, cited in Harrod, *Keynes*, p. 226.

36 *The Diary of Virginia Woolf: Volume One – 1915–1919*, ed. Anne Olivier Bell (London,

1977), 12 Dec. 1917, p. 89.

37 British Library Manuscript Collection (BL,MC hereafter), Add MSS 60710.101, Lytton Strachey to James Strachey, 16 Aug. 1914.

38 Lytton Strachey to Dorothy Bussy, 21 Aug. 1914, cited in Michael Holroyd, *Lytton Strachey – the New Biography* (London, 1994), pp. 309, 311.

39 BL,MC, Add MSS 60710.105, Lytton Strachey to James Strachey, 18 Aug. 1914.

40 *Ibid.*

41 BL,MC, Add MSS 60710.141, L. Strachey to J. Strachey, 9 Sept. 1914.

42 *Ibid.*

43 Cited in Holyrod, *Strachey*, p. 323.

44 *Ibid.*

45 BL,MC, Add MSS, 60710.214, L. Strachey to J. Strachey, 11 Aug. 1915.

46 BL,MC, Add MSS, 60710.237, L. Strachey to J. Strachey, 30 Oct. 1915.

47 BL,MC, Add MSS, 60711.2, L. Strachey to J. Strachey, 14 Jan. 1916.

48 Lytton Strachey, 'The Claims of Patriotism', *War and Peace*, cited in Holroyd, *Strachey*, p. 341.

49 BL,MC, Add MSS 60711.7, J. Strachey to L. Strachey, 24 Feb. 1916.

50 'With the war, the supreme importance of international questions has been forced upon my attention. My opinions have for many years been strongly critical of the whole structure of society; and after a study of the diplomatic situation, and of the literature, both controversial and philosophic, arising out of the war, they developed naturally into those I now hold'. Cited in Holroyd, *Strachey*, p. 340.

51 BL,MC, Add MSS 60711.20, J. Strachey to L. Strachey, 1 March 1916.

52 BL,MC, Add MSS 60711.66, L. Strachey to J. Strachey; draft statement for appeal, undated.

53 BL,MC, Add MSS 71104.86, L. Strachey to Clive Bell, 20 Oct. 1917.

54 BL,MC, Add MSS 62888, L. Strachey to Carrington, 23 March 1917.

55 L. Strachey to Ottoline Morrell, 3 March 1918, cited in Holroyd, *Strachey*, pp. 411–12.

56 BL,MC, Add MSS 62889, L. Strachey to Dora Carrington, 9 July 1918.

57 L. Stachey to Ottoline Morrell, 16 Feb. 1916, cited in Holroyd, *Strachey*, p. 345.

58 BL,MC, Add MSS 59732.256, L. Strachey to Duncan Grant, 22 May 1918.

59 Grant had accompanied Garnett to France at the end of the latter's leave in November 1915, but had only got as far as Dieppe, where he aroused suspicion by being out of uniform and gave unsatisfactory answers when questioned: 'His manner was so strange and sentiments so unEnglish', as H.C. Wallis, the British Vice Consul in Dieppe described the circumstances of Grant's deportation later to Grant's aunt. Cited in Frances Spalding, *Duncan Grant* (London, 1997), p. 179.

60 BL,MC, Add MSS 6066.8788, David Garnett to L. Strachey, 6 Nov. 1915.

61 David Garnett, *Great Friends* (London, 1979), p. 134.

62 Leonard Woolf, *Beginning Again* (London, 1964), p. 177.

63 David Garnett, *Flowers of the Forest* (London, 1955), p. 123.

64 BL,MC, Add MSS 60659.199–200, Vanessa Bell to L. Strachey, 27 April [1916].

65 BL,MC, Add MSS 57933.122, D. Grant to L. Strachey [8 Sept. 1914].

66 BL,MC, Add MSS 59732.253, L. Strachey to D. Grant, undated.

67 BL,MC, Add MSS 57933.136, D. Grant to L. Strachey, 20 May 1918.

68 TGA,CTP, 8010.5.5, Clive Bell to Vanessa Bell, undated [Spring 1916].

69 TGA,CTP, 8010.5.12, C. Bell to V. Bell, [Spring 1916]. During the course of the conflict Bell breakfasted with Lloyd George and wrote a memorandum on the treatment of conscientious objectors for Asquith. Although Bell did not attain Keynes' heights of influence, his movements were viewed with suspicion in some quarters, not least by his own friends. Lytton Strachey reported to his brother in May 1916 that although Bertrand Russell and Clifford Allen (with Allen, at least, the 'recognized' side of conscientious objection) supported Bell in his views, they 'did not want it to be supposed that he [Bell] represented anything', – the anti-

war MP Philip Morrell having to explain this to Gilbert Murray, the sympathetic Regius Professor of Greek at Oxford. BL,MC, Add MSS 60711.41, L. Strachey to J. Strachey, 6 May 1916.

70 Clive Bell, *Peace at Once*, (London, 1915), p. 40.

71 Clive Bell, *Civilization and Old Friends* (Chicago, 1973), pp. 101, 158. *Civilization* originally published London, 1928.

72 TGA,CTP, 8010.5.9, C. Bell to V. Bell (Spring 1916).

73 BL,MC, Add MSS 60660.59, Francis Birrell to L. Strachey, 24 Sept. [1915].

74 BL,MC, Add MSS 60660.64, F. Birrell to L. Strachey, 1 March 1916.

75 Forster to his mother, 10 July 1916, cited in P.N. Furbank, *E.M. Forster – A Life, Volume Two* (London, 1978), p. 27.

76 Forster to Malcolm Darling, 6 Nov. 1914, *Selected Letters of E.M. Forster, Volume One*, ed. Mary Lago and P.N. Furbank (London 1983), no. 136, p. 214.

77 Forster, Diary, Aug. 1914, cited in P.N. Furbank, *E.M. Forster – A Life, Volume One* (London, 1977), p. 259.

78 *Ibid.*, Diary entry, 3 Aug. 1914, p. 259.

79 *Ibid.*, p. 259.

80 E.M. Forster to S.R. Masood, 8 Sep. 1917, *Selected Letters*, ed. Lago and Furbank, no. 175, p. 269.

81 E.M. Forster to F. Barger, 23 March 1918, *Selected Letters*, ed. Lago and Furbank, no. 187, p. 288.

82 E.M. Forster to Siegfried Sassoon, 2 May 1918, *Selected Letters*, ed. Lago and Furbank, no. 188, p. 289.

83 E.M. Forster, Diary, 4 Aug. 1914, cited in Furbank, *Forster – A Life, Volume One*, p. 259.

84 E.M. Forster to Malcolm Darling, 6 Nov. 1914, *Selected Letters*, ed. Lago and Furbank, no. 136, p. 214.

85 E.M. Forster to Goldsworthy Lowes Dickinson, 5 May 1917, *Selected Letters*, ed. Lago and Furbank, no. 165, pp. 251–3.

86 Hermoine Lee, *Virginia Woolf* (London, 1996), p. 341.

87 *The Essays of Virginia Woolf – Volume Two*, ed. Andrew McNellie (London, 1986), March 1917, p. 87.

88 James King, *Virginia Woolf* (London, 1994), p. 285.

89 Virginia Woolf to Ka Cox, 19 March 1916, 'The Question of Things Happening' – The Letters of Virginia Woolf – Volume Two, 1912–1922, ed. Nigel Nicholson (London, 1976), no. 746, p. 83.

90 TGA,CTP 8010.8.135, Vanessa Bell to Roger Fry, Aug. 1914.

91 TGA, CTP 8010.2.149, V. Bell to R. Fry, 17 June 1915.

92 TGA, CTP 8010.8.137, V. Bell to R. Fry, 25 Aug. 1914.

93 TGA, CTP 8010.8.166, V. Bell to R. Fry, 21 May 1915.

94 Frances Spalding, *Vanessa Bell* (London, 1983), p. 149.

95 TGA, CTP 8010.8.192, V. Bell to R. Fry, 1 Jan. 1916.

96 Despite testimonies from Philip Morrell, Vanessa Bell's brother Adrian Stephen and J.M. Keynes, the appeal of Grant and Garnett was rejected, with Vanessa Bell viewing the occasion as a 'complete farce' and commenting that the authorities had been 'so stupid that it was quite hopeless from the beginning and nothing made any impression on them' – even Keynes' dramatic revelation that Garnett's mother, Constance, who had been the translator of Tolstoy had elicited no response from the tribunal panel. Bell fully expected the two men to be sent to prison and her only hope was that they would be released as soon as possible. 'One's hopes go up and down', she wrote, 'and I expect it would be best, if one could, to take things as they come and not look ahead'. Further anxious days were spent waiting to hear the decision of the Central Tribunal regarding alternative employment, after the Appeal Tribunal at Ipswich had exempted both men from active service. This uncertainty occasioned an

appeal, made by Virginia Woolf but prompted by her sister, to Lady Robert Cecil on behalf of the two conscientious objectors. Bell feared that a delay in the decision-making process could mean that a new scheme for objectors was in preparation – one which would involve some kind of organised work which could mean, to Bell's intense concern, that 'they [Grant and Garnett] wouldn't be allowed to go on here' (i.e. continue with their normal lives – painting, in Grant's case).

97 TGA, CTP 8010.8.203, 8010.8.208, 8010.8.209, V. Bell to R. Fry, 22 June 1916; then un-dated (July/August 1916).
98 TGA, CTP 8010.8.266, V. Bell to R. Fry, 12 April 1918.
99 TGA, CTP 8010.8.277, V. Bell to R. Fry, 11 Nov. 1918.
100 V. Woolf to Ka Cox, 12 Aug. 1914, *Question of Things Happening* ed. Nicholson, no. 709, p. 51.
101 *Ibid.*, V. Woolf to Duncan Grant, no. 736, 15 Nov. 1915, p. 71.
102 *Ibid.*, V. Woolf to Margaret Llewlyn Davies, No. 740, 23 Jan. 1916, p. 76.
103 *Ibid.*, V. Woolf to Lady Robert Cecil, no. 767, 16 Jun. 1916, p. 100.
104 *The Diary of Virginia Woolf,* ed. Bell, 27 Aug. 1918, p. 186.
105 *Ibid.*, 15 Nov. 1918, p. 217.
106 *Ibid.*, 19 Nov. 1917, p. 79.
107 Mary Agnes Hamilton, *Remembering My Good Friends* (London, 1944), pp. 74, 76.
108 McM,BRP 710.082299, Lady Ottoline to Bertrand Russell, 31 July 1914.
109 Ottoline Morrell, 9 Aug. 1914, cited in *The Early Memoirs of Lady Ottoline Morrell*, ed. R. Gathorne-Hardy (London, 1963), p. 262.
110 McM,BRP 710.082345, Lady Ottoline to B. Russell, 14 Oct. 1914.
111 *Ottoline at Garsington – Memoirs of Lady Ottoline Morrell 1915–1918*, ed. R. Gathorne Hardy (London, 1974), pp. 31, 162.
112 Ottoline Morrell, Journal, cited in *Ottoline at Garsington*, ed. Gathorne-Hardy, p. 35.
113 Siegfried Sassoon, *Siegfried's Journey* (London, 1946), p. 23.
114 McM,BRP 710.082633, Lady Ottoline to B. Russell, 15 June 1917.
115 McM,BRP 710.082636, Lady Ottoline to B. Russell, 9 July 1917.
116 Ottoline Morrell, Journal, Jan. 1918, cited in *Ottoline at Garsington*, ed. Gathorne-Hardy, p. 233.
117 McM,BRP 710.082681, Lady Ottoline to B. Russell, 2 Sept. 1918.
118 Ottoline Morrell, Journal, cited in *Ottoline at Garsington*, ed. Gathorne-Hardy, pp. 83–4.
119 Frances Partridge, letter to J.P. Atkin, 18 Nov. 1994.
120 Interview between Frances Partridge and J.P. Atkin, 18 Jan. 1995.
121 *Ibid.*
122 J.M. Keynes, *Two Memoirs* (London, 1949), pp. 97–8.

3

Academics at war – Bertrand Russell
and Cambridge

The University and the outbreak of war

The thoughts and actions of the Cambridge mathematician and philosopher Bertrand Russell are central to this book. Russell was able to articulate with extraordinary clarity a fully humanistic opposition to the Great War and his ideas on war and the prevention of it directly affected the thinking of other individuals through his books, articles and speeches. On occasion, Russell's concepts were echoed spontaneously by other like-minded people – often from dissimilar backgrounds or situations. Although Russell enjoyed personal involvement with Bloomsbury (prompted by their Cambridge links and common aesthetics), he was able and willing to strike out intellectually and practically where most others faltered. At times during the war's course, Russell was truly a man alone, despite his seemingly secure position in 1914 amidst the Cambridge University establishment. It is interesting, then, to observe how that academic establishment reacted to the arrival of war.

On 1 August 1914 the *Cambridge Daily News* carried several comments by J.J. Thomson, the acute Master of Trinity College and future President of the Royal Society. He warned that 'War upon [Germany] in the interests of Serbia and Russia will be a sin against civilisation', while accurately predicting that, 'if by reason of honourable obligations we be unhappily involved in war, patriotism might still our mouths'.[1] This comment was a fair representation of the view of the academic establishment towards the possibility of armed conflict dominating Europe. To one side of this view was the opinion that war was morally wrong and would slow down dramatically the natural processes of learning (and even perhaps reverse this process) while creating barriers against international academic research and cooperation. On the other side was trepidation about the effect of the war on domestic affairs and in particular the smooth running of the country's principal centres of knowledge and learning.

An early indication of fears of increased militarism was the public debate over military training at Cambridge University in the late spring of 1914. The respected Cambridge academic A.C. Benson wrote to *The Times* criticising a proposal of compulsory military training at national level. Despite years of pressure from various interest groups and powerful figures, most notably the aged Field Marshal, Lord Roberts, the country had never accepted the practice of compulsory military service. Benson attacked the proposed (compulsory) military training as being an interference with liberty and was in turn attacked in print by the Master of Jesus College for taking this line. Benson then replied to his critic in an article in the *Cambridge Magazine* stating:

> The Master says, a little crudely, that perhaps I shall be ready to shout with the crowd, when the crowd is large enough. May this indicate an uneasy suspicion in his mind that the crowd in whose interest I am already feebly bleating, may turn out to be the larger after all?

Benson also criticised the University for using its authority to attempt to impose a private, internal scheme of compulsion, a matter which Benson felt was outside the natural province of the institution. He accepted that the country as a whole could impose such a scheme on the University but not the other way around. It was 'a wholly undesirable precedent', he felt, that a minority of residents could use the University Senate to impose such a scheme on the majority, most of whom, Benson predicted, would regard it with disfavour. He added that any such scheme, were it to be introduced, would be unworkable and bristling with not only administrative difficulties but also those of a more political nature.

The debate over personal freedoms in Cambridge did not die down with the coming of the war. By October 1914 there was great concern that undue pressure was being put upon Freshmen to join the Officer Training Corps (OTC). Apart from the fact that such pressure on those forced to act against real inclination would produce sub-standard officers, any such inducement was anyway 'illegal and unjustifiable' in the eyes of some.[3] The war's immediate effect seemed to be that of galvanising formerly latent energies whilst subtly cutting away at personal liberty of choice, a fact that took some time to be fully appreciated in the dramatic pace of the opening weeks of war. 'We are no longer half of us half-asleep', proclaimed the University-linked *Cambridge Magazine* at the start of the autumn term, 'We no longer read only the sporting news or no news at all. We have become interested in the present, and to some extent in the past, and some of us are already preparing to speculate on the future ...'[4] Meanwhile, the slogan of the University OTC programme had become 'No compulsion: No slackers', a compromise which seemed to suit the mood of the moment. The only reported problem of recruitment and training was a fear that a sense of the incongruous would overcome 'stolid and sober' patriotism. It was felt that some would be adversely affected when ordered about by those who were perceived as mentally inferior.

The *Cambridge Magazine* appealed for an overview of the situation; 'We officers are dealing not with a raw troop of Walworth mechanicals but a volunteer corps of University gentlemen – mutual sympathy and compromise should be the word for all'. More effective training would be achieved by an officer or undergraduate non-commissioned officer than by a drill sergeant who was likely to be either too good-natured or pusillanimous. 'After all', the magazine stated, a touch reluctantly, 'in war it is the man of action and not the man of intellect who assumes the lead'.[5] In tandem with the debate on the problems of training, the controversy over the question of compulsory OTC units at the University also continued, with more letters appearing in *The Times* and an article in *The Sportsman* warning that any compulsion of academia would be illegal without the consent of Parliament and that, 'The business of the country will come to a standstill if every young man who cannot limp or blink is to be frightened out of going on with his normal career because others say, "That fellow ought to be forming fours".'[6]

This line of argument was later picked up and amplified by the *Cambridge Magazine*, which was rapidly assuming the mantle of principal commentator and, in some cases, adjudicator in debates and controversy arising from a University attempting on the one hand to continue its academic life and on the other being 'at war'. In the confusion and uncertainty of the first few months of the conflict, the *Cambridge Magazine* stood largely for a calm and fair view of events, allowing as far as possible both sides of any debate arising out of these events to have their say, in contrast with most of the national press. Unlike many university journals, it was serious in tone, and this was reflected by the scarcity of pictures, photographs or cartoons appearing in its pages. The editor was the mercurial C.K. Ogden – described as 'an ugly little man, clever and quite interested in philosophy'[7] – and a steady khaki stream of uniformed ex-students made their way up to his office while back on leave with pieces that he had persuaded them to write for him about the war. Ogden was careful to print both sides of experience in the field.

The first article written from direct knowledge of the Western Front, by W.G. Gabain, was breathlessly excited and patriotic in tone; however the second, 'From Mons to the Marne on a Motor Bike' by J.K. Stevens of St John's College, was more reflective, even at this early stage of events. 'War is indeed, an education in itself', reported Stevens:

> and the facts which it teaches remain indelible and can never be forgotten. At times, however, it seems as if I had passed through a bad dream and often I can still see before me the ghastly work done by shrapnel and bullet, and ask myself the question, 'what have these men done to deserve such a death?' Perhaps diplomatists will answer.[8]

The *Cambridge Magazine* also commented on the odd contemporary cultural event – the autumn exhibition of the International Society of Sculptors, Painters and Gravers at the Grosvenor Gallery, which was described as a 'gladdening ray of sunshine' penetrating the prevailing 'gloom' of the general situation and was hailed as proof that not all current creative inspiration was the product of the 'sad and stirring' backdrop of war.

More importantly, Ogden tried to keep abreast of the full range of contemporary views on the conflict by commissioning articles from and about the stance of prominent intellectuals in relation to the war, such as one in response to the well-known pacifist Norman Angell's pamphlet for the Union of Democratic Control, *Shall this War End German Militarism?* The article in the *Cambridge Magazine*, 'What Norman Angell Thinks Now', bewailed the fact that it was only after the outbreak of war that people had begun to appreciate what Angell had been saying for the three years previously: namely, that war was an anachronism and evil in itself. The author of the article then followed this with his own warning that, far from ending militarism abroad – 'misled by the catchword that we must "smash" Germany' – Britain, in the midst of war-fever, was in danger of frustrating her aims and actually creating militarism, both at home and abroad. This cautionary note, written less than three months after the commencement of hostilities, was a typical example of the general level-headedness and foresight of the tone of the *Cambridge Magazine* during the months of conflict.

Another article in the national press under analysis and hence given extra prominence by the *Magazine* in the first few weeks of the war was one from the *Labour Leader* which had been written by the Honorary Treasurer of the *Cambridge Magazine* Shilling Fund for Belgian Refugee Students, Bertrand Russell.[9] In his article, 'War: the Cause and Cure', Russell had highlighted the fact that in the 'sudden vertigo' of war normal values became twisted or inverted. Any form of reason had come to be seen as treachery while mercy was now regarded by most as a strain of weakness. He looked ahead to the situation after the war when, in order to maximise the chances of a secure and lasting peace, the light of democracy had to be 'insistent' coupled with a lessening of the fear and jealousy which in the pre-war world had seemed to be the only common threads linking the Great Powers.

The coverage given to Russell's ideas elicited a swift response. A week later, W.E. Heitland agreed that, 'International relations will no doubt need to be placed on a better footing, if a way can be found, when this gruesome war is over', but, he continued, so difficult and widespread was the problem of democracy and international relations, that 'it will require gradual moral change far beyond the power of any constitutional reforms to being'.[10] There would be no straight and easy road towards changing the habits and spirits of nations. If this far-sighted warning had appeared in the national press (which was unlikely, since the national press tended to pounce on the day-to-day events of the conflict at this early stage, expecting a short war) the general reader would probably would have assumed the author was referring to Germany and to a lesser extent her allies in effecting a change of moral climate in the post-war world (after Germany had been defeated, of course). Heitland, however, did not point the finger of blame solely at Germany; his foresight was also fair. He merely pointed out that the international treaty system had ultimately brought about only distrust and other base emotions amongst all nations, not just the Central Powers.

In his reply to Heitland, Russell emphasised that it was the negative emotion of fear which had been brought forth by the bristling of international relations in the years before 1914. 'The sacrifices demanded from individuals', Russell wrote, 'in Germany and Austria, just as much as here, are so great that they cannot be attributed wholly to desire for conquest; and I think fear is the principle motive with ordinary citizens, though, of course, not the sole motive'.[11]

This calm, intellectual debate on the emotional causes of the war and speculation as to the moral tone of the post-war world occurred in October 1914, the same month that British troops were still arriving on the continent both from Britain and around the world – such as the 7th Division, made up of regular soldiers pulled back from stations around the Empire. With the war of movement by now largely at an end and the First Battle of Ypres raging, the chance of it all being over by Christmas had lessened considerably. While the media whipped up a storm of patriotic energy, a correspondent from the Union Society, signing himself only 'Depressed', wrote to the *Cambridge Magazine* supporting Russell (and the Cambridge branch of the Union of Democratic Control) with a suggestion that the foreign policy of nations be put under the control of the majority of the people constituting these nations, who would naturally, after the experiences of the war, oppose conflict and maintain future peace. Furthermore, he foresaw that, 'a time will shortly come when anyone who has anything constructive to say and can rise above the blustering ferocity which is so much in evidence just now, will be sure of a ready hearing in Cambridge'.[12]

Bertrand Russell – the trials of an individual philosophy

Many years later, in his autobiography, Bertrand Russell compared his pre-war academic life with his experiences after 1914 and commented that the two halves of the same life were as sharply divided as Faust's before and after his meeting with Mephistopheles. The war turned him – an aristocratic academic fast approaching middle age – into a whirlwind of activity and 'the most eloquent moral spokesman of his day'.[13] His life changed suddenly. In June 1914 he had returned from a visit to America, and he spent most of July in a Cambridge rife with talk of possible war. During the final days of peace Russell collected the signatures of over sixty Professors and Fellows in Cambridge for a statement supporting British neutrality in the coming hostilities. This he sent off to the *Manchester Guardian*, though, ironically, the effect of the statement was lessened considerably when most of the signatories changed their minds once Britain had actually declared war.[14]

To Russell, armed conflict was, 'so irrational as to be literally unthinkable'.[15] Although later in the war he might rethink and reshape his particular pacifism and his views on the pacifism of those around him, Russell's basic opposition to the war from the outbreak of hostilities was fundamental and stemmed directly from deep personal conviction. He had inherited from his liberal, aristocratic background strong beliefs in progress, toleration and fair play as well as a heightened regard for the values of civilisation and the power of reason. Civilisation was necessary to provide the cultural springboard whereby an individual might reach his or her full potential, and reason was the tool by which people could be convinced of the rightness of this and other concepts. Linked to the individual's chance for betterment was a belief in the sanctity of personal liberty within the State; states which, if they were civilised, would rely on negotiation rather than force to provide solutions to disputes between countries. Most of Russell's beliefs rested on a bedrock of assumed peace. For any advancement to occur, in anything from the individual condition to international relations, a background of peace was 'a precondition, as well as good in itself'.[16]

Russell suffered mental stress not only due to the onset of war itself but also because he felt so isolated in his opposition to it. 'I was living at the highest possible emotional tension', he later remembered, 'The prospect [of war] filled me with horror, but what filled me with even more horror was the fact that the anticipation of carnage was delightful to something like ninety per-cent of the population. I had to revise my views on human nature'.[17] This new, personal analysis of social interactivity would become his *Principles of Social Reconstruction*, and its genesis occurred very shortly after the start of the war, a period of loneliness for Russell and, as he remarked to his friend Lucy Donnelly, moral upheaval. He commented to her in August 1914 that, 'Events of a month ago seem to belong to a previous experience. All our hopes and faiths and foolish confidences are gone flaming down into hell ... Hardly anyone seems to remember common humanity'.[18] The terror of this spurred Russell to action. At the time he was writing to Lucy Donnelly, he was also outlining to Lady Ottoline Morrell his plans. 'It seems to me', he wrote, 'the only thing one can do now is to think how wars come and how they might be avoided, and then, after the peace, do all one can to bring other people round'. Thinking for the future was vital now that the present seemed a time 'in which we are powerless'.[19]

As Cambridge turned into a wartime community with two thousand troops rapidly arriving to be stationed in former students' lodgings, Russell's sense of disorientation was increased when he was put out of his rooms to make way for medical facilities in Neville's Court, and he lamented the war's probing intrusion into his life: 'having that beautiful place filled with the horror of war'.[20] All he could do after the failure of his petition to the *Manchester Guardian* was send a letter to the radical *Nation* which the editor, H.W. Massingham, printed reluctantly under the heading 'The Rights Of War'. In this article, using language the strength of which had previously been alien to him, Russell declared, 'Against the vast majority of my countrymen, even at this moment, in the name of humanity and civilisation, I protest against our share in the destruction of Germany'. He warned that the population had, in only a few days, been hurled 'down the steep slope to primitive barbarism, letting loose ... the instincts of hatred and blood-lust against which the whole fabric of society has been raised'.

While 'reason and mercy are swept away in one great flood of hatred', innocent young men of all nationalities, 'blindly obedient to the word of command', were being mown down by machine-gun fire. For only 'dim abstractions' concealed the fact that, 'the enemy are men, like ourselves, neither better nor worse – men who love their homes and the sunshine and all the simple pleasures of common lives'. Yet all clear-sightedness and reasoning was consumed in the 'flaming death of our civilisation and our hopes' brought about by emotions of greed and hatred fanned to white heat by politicians and press.[21]

Russell watched the undergraduates, now in uniform, undergoing their training and lamented that, 'it is so dreadful that such a force of idealism and self-sacrifice should go into such a channel'.[22] The conflict, to Russell, was diverting the creative energies of peace towards the malign purposes required by a country on a war-footing. He recognised that the young men whom he taught were now men of diverted promise, 'in whom the creative energy existed that would have realised in the world some part at least of the imagined beauty by which they lived'. They had been swept up by the circumstances of the war and of the few whom Russell expected would survive, 'it is to be feared that many will have lost the life of the spirit, that hope will have died, that energy will be spent, and that the years to come will be only a weary journey towards the grave'. When pointing the finger of blame at the elderly teachers in whom, according to him, not only had there been a 'failure to live generously out of the warmth of the heart', but also a failure to recognise this fault, Russell, beset by feelings of guilt and frustration, was not averse to including himself in this group. 'Let us come out of this death', he wrote, 'for it is we (the old) who are dead, not the young men who had died through our fear of life. Their very ghosts have more life than we ... out of their ghosts must come life.'[23]

To Russell, any action to promote 'the greater good' of common humanity as well as enlightened happiness and social progress was justified, even war itself in some cases. As one of his biographers has pointed out, Russell was a consequentialist when it came to the justification of war.[24] Although he opposed war, and specifically *this* war, he was not a 'total' pacifist, as he admitted in an interview with Royden Harrison (undertaken shortly before Russell's death in 1970) during which he commented that his approach had always been utilitarian and a case of balance between the effects of conflict or surrender. He had earlier written that, during the first few weeks of the war, 'I was myself tortured by patriotism. The successes of the Germans before the battle of the Marne were horrible to them. I desired the defeat of Germany as ardently as any retired Colonel.' Nevertheless, he set aside his love of England ('a very difficult renunciation') as his personal feelings were 'swallowed up by the magnitude of the tragedy', and he realised that there were higher priorities at stake.

In the case of the Great War, Russell,

> ... never had a moment's doubt as to what I must do ... when War came I felt as if I heard the voice of God. I knew it was my business to protest, however futile protest

might be. My whole nature was involved. As a lover of truth the national propaganda of all the belligerent nations sickened me. As a lover of civilisation, the return
to barbarism appalled me. As a man of thwarted parental feeling, the massacre of
the young wrung my heart. I hardly supposed that much good would come of opposing the War, but I felt that for the honour of human nature those who were not
swept off their feet should show that they stood firm.[25]

Alternatively, in some other situations of conflict, Russell believed that if the
results of a war were promoting some greater good, such as the hypothetical
spread of European 'civilisation' as a consequence of colonial wars of expansion or the repelling of an aggressive invading army, then it could sometimes be
justified.[26] However, Russell realised that the majority of war's consequences
were mostly harmful in their effect upon mankind and thus made conflict very
hard to justify in the majority of circumstances, if at all. Any justification of
violence had to be balanced against war's impact on society, an impact that in
the majority of cases was likely to be detrimental.

As the State reorganised ready for war, some of those opposed to the coming
of war also organised themselves – most notably in Russell's sphere, the Union
of Democratic Control. This group, born of meetings at the Morrell's in London's
Bedford Square in September 1914, was not a pacifist organisation, though the
jingoistic Northcliffe press soon labelled them 'pro-German'; rather, it was
aligned more towards principles shared with Russell, whose mind, according to
the later recollections of the writer Mary Agnes Hamilton, dominated the group's
thinking at that time. Talk centred around a distrust of politicians and 'secret
diplomacy', support for an international peace body and opposition to the growth
of 'Prussianism' and decline of personal liberty in wartime Britain. Any similar-
ity of aims between Russell and the UDC was only of a general nature however.
Russell was somewhat sceptical of most of the initial UDC leaders involved –
he famously described them to Lady Ottoline as 'eight fleas talking of building
a pyramid' and later remembered, 'I was interested to observe that the pacifist
politicians were more concerned with the question of which of them should
lead the anti-war movement than with the actual work against the war.'[27]

Russell was always distrustful of politics, especially during war. 'I don't want
to be in Parliament; it seems to me one is freer outside, and can achieve more',
he wrote to Lady Ottoline in November 1914, concluding, 'I should want ... to
be unfettered in saying what I believed.' A significant proportion of the initial
founders of the UDC were from an Independent Labour Party background and
Russell also commented that he would only 'swallow socialism for the sake of
peace' in order to better plan for a secure post-war world and fight the current
tyranny of the war.[28] In July of the following year he declined to join the Independent Labour Party when it launched a large campaign to recruit new members for the UDC, and by the summer of 1916 he was protesting to his mistress
Constance Malleson that socialism did not adequately embody the spirit of
freedom in which he placed so much value.[29]

For all his distrust of the leadership of the UDC Russell recognised their similar goals,[30] and he attended the first meeting of the General Council of the UDC on 17 November 1914 as well as the first public meeting of the Cambridge branch (which had initially met in Goldsworthy Lowes Dickinson's rooms at King's College) on 4 March 1915 – Russell was later to become President of this branch. By October of that year he found himself a member of the General Council of the UDC.

By 1915, Russell had been totally subsumed by the war, both mentally and physically, and he wrote in May that:

> I have been without any personal feelings at all – all private affections seemed swallowed up in horror. And my own inward struggle to keep hold of reason and love used up my force … England, Europe, Civilisation, are more real and vivid to me than oneself or anybody at such times – all my passion goes to them.[31]

This culmination of mental upheaval and final recognition of the war's effect upon his personal priorities was to mark the start of Russell's more independent line of thought and action. The change in his position can be marked at roughly the same time as he was publicly able to sum up his private musings on the first year of the war in his paper, 'The Philosophy of Pacifism', delivered at Caxton Hall in London 8–9 July 1915 as one of a series of lectures gathered under the overall title, 'The Pacifist Philosophy of Life'.[32]

Once he realised that there was little chance of bringing an early end to the war, Russell commenced his work on the psychology behind not only the war in progress, but also war in general. Some of the results of this early work appeared as articles in the various newspapers and more radical journals willing to publish them, as Russell's protesting voice was seldom heard in the popular press. His study (which eventually crystallised as the lectures constituting *Principles of Social Reconstruction*, given between 18 January and 7 March 1916) acted as Russell's personal opposition to the war, drawing on his academic background and intrinsic pacifistic and forward-looking feelings. This formulation of his personal stance was largely isolated from his more practical day-to-day work with the UDC, despite sharing similar objectives. Russell publicly analysed the reasons behind the war-mood which had swept over the nation and so horrified him in his article 'Why Nations Love War', written for Norman Angell's journal *War and Peace*, pointing out factors such as the herd mentality of populations stimulated by patriotism, a general suspicion of those whose customs were foreign resulting in collective hostility to strangers (which Russell saw as the root of the love of war) and, most powerful of all, a desire to let loose activities which were instinctive but normally kept in check by the restraints of a civilised life, such as the avowed Bloomsbury goals of pursuit of goodness and the contemplation of beauty in life as well as art.

According to Russell, modern patriotism was the stimulus upon which primitive instincts towards conflict, such as hostility to strangers, depended and, as such, had become an ideal (however false) which must always generate strife at some point. For Russell, the 'ideal' of patriotism was only partial and inadequate and hence not valid. This ideal, being imperfect and fragile, could then be more easily removed in its role as a stimulus to aggression. Thus any further risk of war could be similarly removed.

Russell also placed his faith in the individual. He commented that, 'a stable peace can only be attained by a process of popular education and by a gradual change in the standards of value accepted by men who are considered to be civilised'. As a starting point, Russell had faith that belief in most of the old, barbarous standards of value, such as the championing of the rightness of physical force, 'has largely died out as between individuals in a civilised country'.[33]

As early as March 1915, Russell pointed out to an American readership in *Atlantic Monthly* the evils of secret international relations, national pride and mistaken fear as well as the virtues of diverting public opinion away from aggressive instincts and the establishment of machinery for settling international disputes. He pointed out that the rapid development of industry and commerce stretching back to the previous century had resulted in a 'savage community' in which the natural instincts of man had been left behind by the rapidly changing nature of the prevailing materialism. This lack of balance between instincts and real needs had created a system of false beliefs underpinned by unrecognised amoral passions, and it was these which the pacifist found himself in opposition to. The task of the pacifist, according to Russell, was to highlight the falseness of the prevailing beliefs in order to expose the amorality of those emotions lying beneath. This target of false belief was to be found embedded in the essential conflict of interests between nations and could be easily recognised 'by any candid mind'.[34] Russell placed his faith in the common individual, ideally unaffected by war-fever and false patriotism. The war corrupted statesmen, whatever their nationality; 'What is true here in England is equally true in Germany. There, too, those who decide the nation's policy, being men accustomed to power, have a far greater lust for dominion than is to be found in the ordinary citizen'.[35]

Russell continually appealed to the common humanity and collective wisdom of the individuals who constituted 'the patient populations', while bypassing the rulers and statesmen in whom he felt pride had destroyed individual humanity. This type of appeal is evident in Russell's article 'Can England and Germany be Reconciled After the War?' which he wrote for the *Cambridge Review* in early 1915 and in which he postulated the idea of a post-war international navy to guard against potential future arms rivalry.[36] This was Russell writing on a local, academic level in territory he thought he knew well but in which he felt increasingly isolated and under attack from fellow academics – such as Professor Sorley, who had publicly rejected Russell's call for reconciliation with Germany in the *Cambridge Review* since, according to Sorley, that country had been responsible, if the media were to be believed, for the bayoneting of children and other atrocities. Russell was forced to defend himself in a letter to the *Review* which was published under the heading of 'Mr. Russell's Reply to his Critics'. He upheld his naval ideas whilst pointing to the 'Christmas Truce' of 1914 and the difficulty of keeping the soldiers of both sides from fraternising as an example of instinctive common humanity overcoming the jingoistic prejudice of the media. 'If Professor Sorley believes this', Russell wrote of the bayoneting rumour, 'it seems surprising he should not hate them [the Germans]; but it is not surprising that they should hate us, if we believe such things'.[37]

Instead of concentrating on the actions of the politicians and statesmen at the centre of attempts to make international relations more accountable to ordinary people, Russell focused on the ordinary people themselves and the war's effect upon them. 'In conflicts between civilised nations', he wrote, 'whatever difference there may be in the political aims of the government, there is probably little difference in the intrinsic value of individual men.' It was some of these 'individual men' on whom the war's effect would be most devastating, he declared. The more sensitive and humane type of soldier was prone to nervous collapse, in some cases so complete as to require months of medical treatment, and in others producing a terrible listlessness and lack of creative effort. He warned that 'It is to be feared that those in whom the war does not produce a callous brutality will be broken in will and incapable of playing their part in the national life.' This was what mattered to Russell above all else after watching his undergraduates march off to a war they had no part in starting, only to return unable perhaps to complete their studies and fulfil their potential or to fit back into 'normal life' at all. Some, Russell lamented, had never returned at all and had been robbed of all chances for future creative development.

To Russell, the whole climate of war was wrong, including the inversion of former values that he experienced all around him. 'The moral effects of war are almost wholly bad', he lectured, 'Hatred, cruelty, injustice, untruthfulness, love of violence, are all recognised as vices in time of peace; but as soon as war breaks out, they are universally praised and stimulated, while lukewarmness in any one of them is denounced as a form of treachery.'[38] This theoretical side to opposing the war was to Russell as important as practical opposition – the two went hand in hand. He wrote to Lady Ottoline in July 1915 at the time of his 'Philosophy of Pacifism' lecture at Caxton Hall that, 'What is wrong with mere opposition to war is that it is negative. One must try to find other outlets for people's wildness',[39] and although he described the pacifists around him as 'an awful crew', he was referring here mainly to the UDC with whom he was becoming disillusioned, especially over their concentration on the problems of post-war international diplomacy and seeming inability to match theory with action. He had commented to Lady Ottoline before his lecture that, 'I think I will make friends with the No-Conscription people. The U.D.C. is too mild and troubled with irrelevancies.'

Russell complained that the attitude of people around him was 'so Sunday-Schooly' and that they lacked the necessary 'intensity of will' to be effective in his eyes. Indeed, he felt as if their attitude was perhaps adversely affecting his own, as if 'some great force for good were imprisoned within me by scepticism and cynicism ... How passionately I long that one could break through the prison walls of one's own nature.'[40] Above all, despite his UDC activities, 'it all makes one feel very lonely', he admitted, acknowledging his feelings of frustration and the more isolated position towards which his individual position on the war was drawing him.

Russell was attracted to the No Conscription Fellowship mainly due to its firm stance over the issue of compulsion, an issue which he was firmly against and which the UDC had decided not to oppose. In January 1916, the month that the Military Service Act and hence conscription became law, Russell wrote to Lady Ottoline that he felt the situation was hopeless, as the nation was clearly still in the mood for a victory at all costs, and he personally felt helpless until the general mood of the country changed – a change he hoped the eventual unpopularity of conscription would achieve. For the time being, he wrote, 'The whole conscription outlook seems utterly black. The conscriptionalists have all had the cleverness and all the driving force'. He concluded (and affirmed a personal creed), 'Politics is no good just now – one must work through individuals.'[41]

Russell came to develop a great respect for the leading individuals of the N.C.F. such as Fenner Brockway and Clifford Allen for, although he would not in peacetime have been in total political alignment with them (they both came from staunch, journalistic/Labour backgrounds), a shared opposition to war united them, and he was drawn to their strength of independence and moral fortitude set against an overwhelming tide of adverse opinion. Russell had observed the work accomplished by the organisation since its early beginnings in November 1914 and began to work officially for the N.C.F. as soon as men above military age were permitted to join in spring 1916.

By the first half of 1916 Russell had moved on again from his position a year earlier. From defining his own stance on the war, he now took full charge of his own destiny within the anti-war movement and put his concept of theory and action going hand-in-hand into full effect: he switched to the N.C.F., he worked on *Principles of Social Reconstruction* and he continued to author letters and articles such as 'The Danger to Civilisation', which appeared in America.[42] In this article, Russell again pointed out that the war was leading civilisation towards self-destruction (this was an extension of his private early fears, expressed to Lady Ottoline, that the war had to be halted, 'before the tradition of civilisation has died out'),[43] but the writing was now backed up by an obvious weight of experience and associated continuity of thought. He delved below the crossfire of blame and political diplomacy, warning that, 'There is some risk of forgetting the good of individuals under the stress of danger to the state: yet, in the long run, the good of the state cannot be secured if the individuals have lost their vigour',[44] while declaring that the State existed only in the separate lives of its citizens which now were directly threatened both at home and abroad.

Russell also looked to the near future and warned that the longer the war continued, the more conflict would be viewed as a natural state of affairs, with a corresponding increase in general callousness, cynicism and despair as well as the sinister growth of an unquestioning passive obedience towards those who continued to head the war effort. Above all, in Russell's eyes, the conflict meant, 'humane feeling decays'. Hence he was strident in his warning that, 'War is perpetuating this moral murder in the souls of vast millions of combatants; every day many are passing over to the dominion of the brute by acts that will kill what is best within them.' He concluded by actualising the collective effect of the individual 'moral murder' that the war was responsible for: 'If the war does not come to an end soon, it is to be feared that we are at the end of a great epoch, and that the future of Europe will not be on a level with its past.'[45]

With continuing articles such as 'The Danger to Civilisation' combined with his activities for both the UDC and N.C.F. and increased celebrity resulting from this work (not to mention his forthcoming very public prosecution), by the early summer of 1916, with *Principles of Social Conscience* completed, Russell had thus moulded a public anti-war face which gave shape to his internal fusing of intellect and passion. Once the lectures constituting *Principles of Social Reconstruction* had been delivered (on Tuesday evenings at Caxton Hall in London between January and March 1916), Russell lost no time in moving again from the theoretical to the practical side of protesting. While on a short post-lecture holiday, Russell was sent an appeal for help from Catherine Marshall, who had come to the N.C.F. from the Women's International League and who now found herself overwhelmed with work organising the N.C.F. office at 6 St John Street. Russell typically pledged his free time from as soon as he returned to London on 1 April. Marshall chose well, as Russell, who could not be called up due to his age, was able to stand by in readiness to take over positions on the national committee should any members be sent to prison. He also became an associate member and thus able to work immediately on the Associates Political Committee, the initial meeting of which had already taken place while Russell was on holiday. Russell also helped with the liaison between the organisation and Parliament as well as with the 'converting' of significant individuals to the cause, such as the Bishop of Oxford (with help from Lady Ottoline).

As well as this work, there were now also the individual cases of men trapped by their consciences under the Military Service Act. The Act made use of the same system of tribunals as the previous Derby scheme, but it was not until the summer of 1916 that proper guidelines for the hearings of conscientious objectors were issued by the War Office. By then, the 2,086 tribunals had already had to deal with almost six thousand objectors, many of whom were now in military hands. To Russell, the whole issue of compulsory military service 'was the epitome of illiberalism' and as such, became the main focus of his anti-war work from the spring of 1916. He described the tribunal system to Lady Ottoline as 'monstrous', let alone the hasty legal framework which supported it, which he regarded as 'bad enough'. 'It is simply a madness of persecution', he wrote, the only hopeful aspect being the courage and convictions of the men on trial, the spirit of whom Russell likened to 'the beginning of a new religion'.[46] He also declared his frustration at not being able to fully experience this new 'religion' by not being liable for call-up.

However, his chance to be in the dock soon arrived with his summons, under the Defence of the Realm Act, for admitting authorship, via a letter to *The Times*, of his article (published anonymously by the N.C.F. on 19 April) defending Ernest Everett, a teacher and member of the Liverpool branch of the N.C.F. sentenced to two year's hard labour. Russell used the very public opportunity of his hearing before the Lord Mayor on 5 June to declare that, along with respect for the individual conscience, the tradition of liberty was the 'supreme good' that Great Britain had produced, the inference being that both were under direct threat from the authorities who, Russell declared, under 'the stress of fear' had forgotten these traditional principles, the result of which would be a tyranny of 'disastrous' proportions unless the whole system of persecution were resisted. He was then interrupted by a bellicose Lord Mayor who declared he was not prepared to listen to a political speech.

The remainder of Russell's argument was later published in the *Tribunal* on 6 July and contained the clearest statement yet of Russell's personal course of action from then on:

> The noblest thing in a man is the spiritual force which enables him to stand firm against the whole world in obedience to his sense of right; and I will never acquiesce in silence while men in whom spiritual force is strong are treated as a danger to the community rather than as its most precious heritage.

Although Russell was pleased with his truncated defence, it was ironic that his public espousal of liberty led directly to a personal loss of freedom and increased persecution in his more private academic world. The authorities moved swiftly and only two days after Russell's hearing (at which he was convicted and fined £100 with £10 costs) the Foreign Office instructed the British Ambassador in Washington to inform the President of Harvard that Russell would not be issued with a passport and hence would not be able to accept the University's earlier invitation to lecture there during early 1917. The authorities had not waited for the result of Russell's appeal, due to take place later in the month and he could only retaliate by writing defiantly to Professor James Woods of the Harvard Philosophy Department that he would not be silenced and that the war was, above all, 'a war for liberty'. However, this letter was intercepted by the authorities and never reached America.

The curtailing of Russell's academic life was further advanced by the abrupt decision of the Council of Trinity College on 11th July to remove Russell from his lectureship, despite the fact that only seventeen months previously the College had offered Russell a Fellowship. The action was taken whilst Russell was conveniently away in Wales on a lecture tour, under the auspices of the N.C.F. and the National Council Against Conscription, where his provocative speeches, such as that given at the Cardiff Friends House on 7 July, cannot have advanced his case with the mostly aged and reactionary dons. Despite this, twenty-two Fellows of Trinity led by mathematician G.H. Hardy signed a memorial to the Council protesting at the action taken. Russell now had no regular occupation and hence made plans for another series of lectures to be financially sponsored by regional Quaker groups. He was freed from his work for the N.C.F. for two days a week in order to prepare.

It was typical of Russell to increase the wider, practical side of his anti-war work in response to the curtailing of his academic activities centred on Cambridge. However, although he had told Lady Ottoline in the years before the war that the University town had become like a home to him and he felt of real use to the young men he so admired, by the middle of the war his attitude had changed. After only a month of war he had complained to Lady Ottoline how remote he now felt from his academic colleagues, how he now found himself, 'in a different world altogether … there is an orgy of hate, running through all their humanity'. He had then predicted, with chilling accuracy, 'I fear sooner or later they will attack me … I want to escape.' He had already experienced tension with his college over his rejection of their offer in February 1915 of a research Fellowship in favour of special leave of two terms duration in order to pursue his anti-war work. He had firmly thrown back the offer made by the College and University to him to nestle further into the academic nest by diving into the mêleé of public anti-war activity.

Russell's decision to pursue his own path was underlined by his growing sadness and disillusionment with a Cambridge robbed by the war of its formerly cherished characteristics. In the spring of 1916, Russell described the city to Lady Ottoline as 'dead' and full of melancholy, apart from 'bloodthirsty old men hobbling along victorious in the absence of youth'. The pervading influence of the war had managed to penetrate beyond the present, in Russell's case, and affect the past also:

> All that one has cared for is dead … I look round my shelves at the books of mathematics and philosophy that used to seem full of hope and interest, and now leave me utterly cold – the work I have done seems so little – so irrelevant to this world in which we find we are living.[49]

Russell had known that sooner or later his activities would be challenged in a more forceful manner by the academic establishment than by letters to the *Cambridge Magazine*, and he was well aware that he was unpopular; 'I am intensely disliked by the older dons and still more by their wives, who think I should not mind if they were raped',[50] he wrote, a month before the dons finally took action.

Russell was under no illusion what his activities could cost him – as he wrote to Lady Ottoline the day before the Council of Trinity met, he realised that he would have to get used to being poor, 'having lost America [the Harvard offer] and probably Trinity'. Despite the war cutting off his academic background, Russell wrote almost joyfully that, 'I have somehow found myself ... I have no inward discords any more'.[51] The action taken against him had further strengthened his purpose and allowed him to emulate, to some extent, the conscientious objectors whom he so admired. He admitted to Lady Ottoline that he thought persecution useful in that it made people see that no good could come out of war.

The fact that the controversy over Russell's dismissal occurred after almost two years of conflict, during the carnage of the first battle of the Somme, and the respect accorded to him as one of the world's leading philosophers and mathematicians meant that the twenty-two Fellows who put their names to the memorial condemning the Council's decision were not the only source of public support which Russell received.

The *Cambridge Magazine* followed the case closely and reported in its first issue of the autumn term how Russell had been 'unceremoniously hoofed out' after the sale of his Cambridge belongings. An article in the same issue protested, 'that Trinity of all places should have wantonly proved false to the traditions of tolerance and freedom for which Cambridge had hitherto stood in the eyes of the world, is beyond all things disheartening'.[52] Comments from contributors and those who had written letters on the issue were printed, such as that of Hilton Young who called Trinity's decision 'more discouraging than a German victory' and that of D.S. Robertson who described the action as 'an inexpressible disaster to tolerance and liberty'. Both Young and Robertson were of Trinity and, interestingly, both on active service. In addition, Gilbert Murray (the Regius Professor of Greek at Oxford) was quoted from his letter to the *Nation* of 23 September in which he commented wryly that, 'the times are indeed out of jolt when Oxford can give Cambridge a dig in the ribs as the home of intolerance and irrationalism',[53] while Jean Nicod was quoted from the French paper *Le Journal du Peuple* in an article describing how the war had stirred 'this famous thinker' [Nicod] to the depths of his soul, uncovering a firm 'moral foundation' which supported Russell in his cause.

By November, the *Cambridge Magazine* was being used as a posting house for signatories to a further memorial for Russell, intended for those outside of Trinity, who also wished to signal their disapproval. They could do so by informing the editor by letter or postcard which would then be sent on to those organising the protest. The idea behind this new memorial was to strengthen the hand of Russell's supporters inside the college.

In addition to attaining a new level of notoriety, Russell had by now moved further in terms of confidence in his practical and public persona due to the success of his Welsh anti-war speaking tour during the summer. Although an academic approach lay behind all his ideas and actions, he firmly rejected the chance to return to the world of mathematics when it was offered to him; he had discovered a firmer voice and the time of accepting lecturing work at Harvard or anywhere else was over.

Russell's possible return to mathematics was suggested by General Cockerill, the Director of Special Intelligence at the War Office, who offered that the ban on Russell's movements, which he had incurred as a direct result of a supposedly 'vehemently anti-British' speech in Cardiff, would be lifted if Russell returned to his former life. Russell, although cordial towards Cockerill, rejected the offer and, remembering the cheers that had greeted him in Wales, set out on a second tour in October 1916 which he entitled 'The World as It Can Be Made'. He had been barred from most of the British coast and all large 'sensitive' cities following his Cardiff speech of 6 July, in which he had warned that if the war ended in bitterness, post-war artistic, social and scientific progress would all be impossible. He had written in the *Cambridge Magazine* that, 'under the stress of war, everything that had been learnt has been forgotten, and conscience must once more fight the old fight to free the human spirit from the tyranny of fear'.[54]

This theme of the war's effects and the consequences for future civilisation was carried over to the second lecture tour, and Russell's lectures were read for him in areas where he was prohibited from travelling to, such as Glasgow. The text of that particular speech, read by the President of the Miner's Federation, Robert Smillie, was later published as an N.C.F. pamphlet, making a nonsense of the Government ban, which Lord Hugh Cecil described to Home Secretary Herbert Samuel as 'both oppressive and timid – as though we were rather afraid of what might be said against us'[55] – evidence of Russell's concept of a 'tyranny of fear', induced by the war's effects. By the end of the year, Russell had reached a new level of confidence in his public actions which he was never to lose and which he could finally match to his formidable academic background and intellectual gifts. As he wrote to his new mistress, actress Constance Malleson, known as Colette, 'Quite lately I have had a sense of freedom I never had before'.[56]

However, Russell's personal wartime apogee did not last for long; quite apart from the continuance of the war itself, he could not be totally satisfied with the disparate activities and motives amongst the organised anti-war movements. 'Odd things give me a sense of failure', he wrote to Lady Ottoline, 'for instance, the way in which the C.O.'s all take alternative service, except a handful'.[57] He was also disappointed by the relative failure of his open letter to President Wilson, smuggled to America and published in the *New York Times* on 23 December 1916, in which he appealed to America to bring a swift peace to an ailing Europe, only to be confounded, four months later, with America's entry into the war, which Russell complained would help prolong the war by delaying the exhaustion of Europe. Although on the domestic front there was still plenty of work to do by the first few months of 1917 with over one thousand 'absolutist' conscientious objectors serving prison terms, Russell felt as if he lived in 'two layers' by this point in the war:

... one superficial, in which I have plenty of life and good spirits, and another under-neath, where I feel lost and worn out and isolated and rather hopeless – that is the deeper feeling but I keep on fighting it off with an effort of will. Nothing can be done for it while the war lasts.[58]

The winter of early 1917 was a particularly bleak period for Russell, as it was for so many others. As he later admitted to Colette, during that period he lost all his active love for mankind, which was replaced by despair and hope-lessness. He now found the human race to be 'hateful' and all former well-springs of affection to be dried up after over two years of war. Not just feelings of affection seemed to have disappeared; he complained to Lady Ottoline in the spring that, 'I have no vivid feelings at all except constantly increasing horror of the war',[59] and, two months later, 'just now all fundamental feelings are rather dead in me',[60] adding that only superficial feelings remained and that the last time he had felt alive was when lifted by the hope of his letter to Wilson. He ended by reiterating that he now had no love for humanity; instead, 'vehement hatred of all that has happened since the war began has made one think worse and worse of mankind'.

Russell also admitted to Lady Ottoline in his earlier letter that he was losing interest in the NCF – the earlier 'spirit of freedom' that it had provided him with via his anti-war work had ebbed by this point. As Russell pointed out, all the best people such as Clifford Allen were in prison, and the rest, as earlier with the UDC, now incurred Russell's frustration with their 'petty quarrels and sordidness'. His friendship with Lady Ottoline was cooling by this time due partly to his continuing relations with not only Colette, but other women such as Vivienne Eliot (the wife of T.S. Eliot). His emotional life and search for love became further complicated as he lost patience and faith with the sincerity and emotional truth of a wider world at war with itself.

The late spring and summer of 1917 saw the zenith of his affair with Colette and an associated re-awakening of his academic interests. He expressed to her a desire to study the psychology of opinion and especially the 'unmasking' of the ferocity hidden at the base of opinion, hidden behind a veil of morality. The war and its effect on individuals had emphasised to Russell the duplicitous nature of the human character; the aggressive strength of man's nature, which Russell had warned must be channelled in the right direction to avoid conflict, was not always immediately recognisable, and Russell was motivated by what he saw as an opportunity to highlight it. 'I am creeping back into life', he wrote to Colette, 'but not N.C.F. life – scientific rather'.[61]

As Russell later admitted to Lady Ottoline, 'I realised that I had been much too optimistic about human nature.' By this stage in the war he felt that his only motivation was despair while human life had come to seem valueless and pos-sessing of no possibilities for the future – gone now was the earlier optimism of *Principles of Social Reconstruction*. He described himself, not for the first time, as an alien amongst people he could not communicate with anymore. 'I simply don't know how to express the utter devastation inside me', he explained, 'I feel I am rotting away inwardly.' He even confessed that he felt he had no real hold on life and that sometimes he longed for death, 'with the same kind of intensity with which I long for the end of the war'.[62]

Despite the excitement and hopefulness associated with the Russian Revolution and the meetings of support in Great Britain (at which violence often broke out before his appalled eyes), Russell found he had to re-evaluate his own position completely. At the end of the summer he declared:

> I used to live with a sense of some kind of co-operation with the community – even the most abstract work always appealed to me instinctively as part of the life of the world. Since the war, I have lost that feeling. That is the root of the despair that comes over me.[63]

By the autumn, he was resigned to at least another two years of war, especially since he was forced to recognise that the 'Russian outlook' was getting steadily worse.

Although he still thought that the pacifist movement would bear fruit in the end, Russell no longer felt he could predict what those results would be and on a personal level, he no longer believed in the effectiveness of what he could achieve for peace 'beyond writing books'. All pacifist work, he told Lady Ottoline, except by those who had not been pacifists from the start of the war, seemed to him now to be 'quite useless', and he announced that a return to his books would be a return to sanity, although a sanity of a 'sober and drab' nature. At the end of the year he resigned from the executive of the NCF, and one of his few solaces at this time was a visit to Westminster Cathedral where the chanting of the choir drew his mind away from the exasperation and hopelessness of yet another year of war and towards the 'permanent' beauty and splendour of the church and timeless music.

Notwithstanding his resignation from the NCF executive, the start of 1918 found Russell still contributing articles to the *Tribunal*, one of which, entitled 'The German Peace Offer', gave the authorities the excuse they had been waiting for to prosecute Russell again, this time more harshly than before. The article was submitted on 3 January and suggested that an American garrison in England (and capable of intimidating strikers) would be the result of any further prolongation of the war. It was this supposedly dangerous comment that resulted in Russell's appearance before magistrate Sir John Dickinson at Bow Street Magistrates' Court in early February. Sir John interrupted Russell's impassioned defence and pronounced a sentence of six months in prison under the harsh second division, though this was later commuted (due to the influence of powerful sympathisers) to the first division to allow Russell to continue with his philosophical studies. This he did, working on *The Analysis of Mind* and his *Introduction to Mathematical Philosophy*, whilst also managing to read over forty books and articles during his time in prison – one of which was Strachey's *Eminent Victorians*, which he greatly enjoyed.

Though he was now more at peace than previously, Russell read of the war's daily development in *The Times* and still worried about the conflict's effects on the world outside. 'I feel mankind is these days like a pitiful dumb animal with an open wound out of which the blood drops and life is oozing away', he wrote to Colette, 'and one's own life must go with it, or else one must grow callous for the time'. He began to resent being separated from the people and events of his former world: 'One's life is not life unless it is linked on to that of the world.'[64] Luckily for Russell, he was released on 14 September, before the end of his sentence. He soon moved in with Clifford Allen (whose own imprisonment had aged him dramatically) and continued to devote his time to academic work, while resuming his affair with Colette.

Russell's war was effectively over; his personal conflict and the wider one had sapped his spirits, and he wanted merely to continue with the academic work he had long planned and begun while in prison, using the energy that remained to him. 'I am gradually crawling back into the atmosphere of philosophy', he wrote to Allen with relief.[65] He confided to Colette of his acute loneliness and the fact that the world he encountered on leaving his confinement seemed 'small and sordid' and most of the weary people 'loathsome'. He kept apart from the celebrating populace of London on a rainy Armistice Day, merely observing the damp crowds and feeling like a pale ghost from a different sphere; the war to him had resulted in a drabness that the flagged colours of victory could not assuage. Nothing seemed vivid or worth the pain of existence, and he complained to Lady Ottoline of a 'weariness of spirit' and a lack of energy for 'new beginnings', for there would have to be some kind of new start, he realised; a picking up and rearranging of the pieces left by the shattering impact of the arrival of war four years earlier. 'What is wanted', he had written to Lady Ottoline from prison, 'is to carry over into the new time something of the gaiety and civilised outlook and genial expansive love that was growing when the war came.'[66]

He had summed up his outlook and position with regard to his own observances of the war to Colette shortly before he had been released:

> It is so difficult to forget the horror of the world. There is knowledge that has to come to one, during the war, that one can never forget. Old men at tribunals, every bit as cruel as a cat with a mouse. Envy and fear, the two great motive forces. I find it so difficult not to hate; and when I do not hate I feel we few are so lonely in the world.

The only alternative to hate for Russell was a 'pitying comprehension, which removes me to such a terrible distance that I shiver from the cold of isolation'. He felt as if the war had somehow disconnected the vital link that had previously linked his life to that of the world. 'Something seems destroyed, some connection severed', he wrote, and this had left him isolated from previously familiar and trustworthy precepts; 'although politics may be better or worse, I can never again make them a vehicle for ideas', he realised. All that was left was the future and this was in peril from those, scarred by the experience of combat, who might simply return from battle 'into mutual admiration and a set of soft lies in which vitality is smothered'.[67]

The war was a critical juncture in Russell's long life; propelling him from the dry world of academia to an embattled public arena which he effectively was never to leave. The year 1915 (particularly his speech at the Caxton Hall in July on the 'Philosophy of Pacifism' and the concurrent build-up of ideas which would later constitute *Principles of Social Reconstruction*) marked a turning point in the way in which he articulated his individual protest against the war, even if this course meant greater personal isolation and eventual imprisonment. The conflict presented to Russell a stimulus that was both intellectual and emotional in origin and tone and was of such strength that its call diverted part of his thinking towards an examination of wider areas of philosophy and sociology, concerning the instincts of human beings towards war and peace and the effect of total conflict upon both the individual and the moral value system of society at war. This interest was born of Russell's passion for learning and his extreme despair at observing his undergraduates and other young men marching to war, their latent creative talent being stifled or simply blown away at the front. Russell's awareness of the war's 'diverted promise' of youthful spirit was to be echoed in the thoughts and actions of others.

The moral weight of the war upon his conscience deprived Russell of his former faith in human nature and brought him near to total despair. Yet the war did not crush Russell to the point of complete nullity, 'emotionally he remained fundamentally a liberal individualist'[68] as he exhibited in another letter from prison, this one addressed 'To All and Sundry':

> Once men get away from … the struggle to take up more room in the world than is their due, there is such a capacity of greatness in them. All the loneliness and the pain and the eternal pathetic hope – the power of love and the appreciation of beauty – the concentration of many ages and spaces in the mirror of a single mind – these are not things one would wish to destroy wantonly, for any of the national ambitions that politicians praise. There is a possibility in human minds of something mysterious as the night-wind, deep as the sea – calm as the stars and strong as Death, a mystic contemplation, the 'intellectual love of God'. Those who have known it cannot believe in wars any longer, or in any kind of hot struggle. If I could give to others what has come to me in this way, I could make them too feel the futility of fighting.

However, he concluded crucially, 'I do not know how to communicate it; when I speak, they stare, applaud, or smile, but do not understand'.[69] The war both interrupted and then transformed Russell's life. From the last days of peace, his response was one of both heart and mind – even as he began his descent into despair, he was organising petitions and writing articles based on his fundamental opposition to the conflict, an opposition which, though it sprang from deep emotion, was then thought out and articulated clearly in his numerous writings as the war progressed.

Russell and others shared the view that theirs was a civilisation gripped by a sudden vertigo in which previously accepted values, as Russell postulated, had been twisted or reversed by intense fear which then produced impulses of hatred and blood-lust. Others also recognised that these intense energies – inflamed by war – could be better harnessed for good in times of peace, while latent impulses of creativity were misdirected, suppressed or nullified entirely during the conflict. To Russell, those that survived the war had 'lost the life of the spirit'. He was not alone. It was a shared awareness of this potential loss that provided others with a platform on which to build their own humanistic opposition to the war.

Notes

1 *Cambridge Daily News*, 1 Aug. 1914, cited in Ronald W. Clark, *The Life of Bertrand Russell* (London, 1975), p. 245.

2 A.C. Benson, 'Military Training at Cambridge', *Cambridge Magazine*, vol. 3, no. 20, 2 May 1914.

3 'The O.T.C. and the Element of Compulsion', *Cambridge Magazine*, vol. 4, no. 1, 10 Oct. 1914.

4 'On Coming Up', *Cambridge Magazine*, vol. 4, no. 1, 10 Oct. 1914.

5 'C.U.O.C.T.C. Progress – Parade Ground Prattle', *Cambridge Magazine*, vol. 4, no. 3, 24 Oct. 1914.

6 'An Illegal Proposal', *The Sportsman*, cited in *Cambridge Magazine*, vol. 4, no. 4, 31 Oct. 1914.

7 Frances Partridge, letter to J.P. Atkin, 28 March 1996.

8 J.K. Stevens, 'From Mons to the Marne on a Motor-Bike', *Cambridge Magazine*, vol. 4, no. 1, 10 Oct. 1914.

9 This fund was established specifically to aid students from the medieval Louvain University, burnt by the attacking Germans.

10 *Cambridge Magazine*, vol. 4, no. 2, 17 Oct. 1914, p. 38.

11 Bertrand Russell, 'Fear as the Ultimate Cause of War', *Cambridge Magazine*, vol. 4, no. 3, 24 Oct. 1914.

12 *Cambridge Magazine*, vol. 4, no. 4, 31 Oct. 1914, p. 80.

13 Caroline Moorehead, *Bertrand Russell* (London, 1992), p. 204.

14 With the Archduke Franz Ferdinand dead and declarations of war fanning out over Europe, Russell privately determined not to be dominated by base instincts and feelings of hate, as he remembered he had been during the Boer War. He placed his faith in Reason ('the force that in the long run makes for peace') even though the situation appeared bleak. 'The war is awful', he wrote to Lady Ottoline Morrell: 'I can't think of anything else. It all looks hopeless now. It seems nearly certain that England will be involved. I don't think we ought to be, but I can see a point of view which makes it seem an honourable obligation. It is a ghastly irresistible fate driving everyone on … war is madness – now there will be a new legacy of hatreds and humiliations and brutal triumphs … Nothing seems of any importance beside the prospect of war'. McM,BRP, B. Russell to Ottoline Morrell, 31 July 1914, no. 1016.

15 Jo Vellacott, *Bertrand Russell and the Pacifists in the First World War* (Brighton, 1980), p. 5.

16 *Ibid.*, p. 4.

17 Bertrand Russell, *Autobiography*, (2 vols London, 1970), vol. 2, p. 18. The breakdown of peace threatened Russell's fundamental beliefs and this, together with the effect of recent developments in his personal life, galvanised him into action. As he wrote in his

Autobiography, 'I underwent a process of rejuvenation, inaugurated by Lady Ottoline and continued by the war'. The conflict also served to cast off the dust-sheets of his old life; it 'shook me out of my prejudices and made me think afresh on a number of fundamental questions'. *Ibid.*, vol. 2, p. 15.

18 Moorehead, *Bertrand Russell*, cited p. 206.

19 McM,BRP, B. Russell to O. Morrell, 14 Aug. 1914, no. 1089.

20 *Ibid.*, no. 1073.

21 B. Russell, 'The Rights of War, the *Nation*, 15 Aug. 1914. Russell expected men in positions of trust and power to act responsibly and with caution. To him, men of intelligence were presumed to intend the consequences of their actions and hence he saw the war in part as a consequence of human pride and self-assertion. He regarded the younger generation as being uncorrupted and full of 'admirable spirit' - in contrast to the older people, most of whom he felt were consumed with the false hatred of prejudice. The old teachers at Cambridge he perceived as being dominated by a ruthless logic instead of reason and hence able to allow the young men to be sacrificed for 'some coldly abstract end'.

22 McM,BRP, B. Russell to O. Morrell, undated [Sept. 1914], no. 1136.

23 *Ibid.*, undated [Aug. 1914], no. 1092.

24 See Alan Ryan, *Bertrand Russell: A Political Life* (London, 1988).

25 B. Russell, quoted in *The Early Memoirs of Lady Ottoline Morrell*, ed. R. Gathorne-Hardy (London, 1963), pp. 267–8.

26 See B. Russell, 'The Ethics of War', *International Journal of Ethics*, XXV, Jan. 1915, pp. 127–42. Russell could be impractical when applying carefully thought-out ideas to practical wartime situations; for example, he tended to overestimate the willingness of people (such as Belgian and French refugees and citizens living under armed occupation) to be passively non-cooperative. In Russell's opinion, passive non-cooperation was the best method of lim-iting the damage that the war inflicted on individual character which, to him, was now one of the main threats that the conflict posed to the fabric of European civilisation. In taking this line, he was echoing the views of his godfather, John Stuart Mill, who had placed great value on the freedom of individual judgement and the placing of this principle on a moral level high enough to avoid interference by the State. The necessity of this principle was, for Russell, thrown into sharp relief by the restrictions implicit in a state continuously mobilising for war.

27 B. Russell, quoted in *Early Memoirs of Ottoline Morrell*, ed. Gathorne-Hardy, p. 266.

28 McM,BRP, B. Russell to O. Morrell, 11 Nov. 1914, no. 1147.

29 The lectures which Russell gave as *Principles of Social Reconstruction* marked a theoretical shift towards a more personal concept of socialism that was decentralised and liberal in character. This was echoed by a gradual move in Russell's anti-war activities away from established groups and accompanying doctrine towards an increasingly individualistic ap-proach. By the middle of the war, Russell had begun to feel isolated. As he wrote in March 1916, 'People with whom I have intellectual sympathy hardly have any spiritual life ... and the others seem to find the intellectual side of me unbearable.' McM,BRP, B. Russell to O. Morrell, 4 March 1916, no. 1123.

30 Russell, looking ahead, commented to Lady Ottoline that Britain was 'likely to be far more successful than would be best for the welfare of Europe' and, in fact, 'no decisive victory of one side is in the interests of either Great Britain or of Europe'. *Ibid.*, 6 Aug. 1914, no. 1095.

31 Ibid., 19 May 1915, no. 1218.

32 Up to this point, Russell had been formulating his response to the war by authoring a series of articles and letters. In penning these articles, he was also acting as an eloquent mouthpiece for the UDC and fulfilling what he saw as his moral duty to publicly protest. George Bernard Shaw wrote to Russell (after Russell had agreed to chair a Fabian meeting on the war) that, 'Our job is to make people serious about the war', while lamenting to his fellow thinker that, 'It is the monstrous triviality of the damned thing and the vulgar frivolity of what we imagine

to be patriotism that gets at my temper'. B. Russell, *Autobiography*, vol. 2, p. 49.

Russell agreed, and to that end he expressed his position on the war whenever he got the chance, such as his reply to H.G. Wells's 'The War That Will End War' in September 1914 in which, while declaring that, 'War will only end when people realize its horrors ... the only road to a secure peace lies through a reform in the thoughts and feelings of common men', he also used the first of many opportunities to appeal to common humanity when he warned that, 'The brutal humiliation of a great and civilized nation is not the road to universal peace.' This would only be sowing the seeds of bitterness 'whose fruit is war' and, if this outcome was to be avoided, the conflict – through the efforts of individuals – 'must produce a different spirit, and above all it must make us forget, in the claims of humanity, our fiery conviction of the enemy's wickedness'. B. Russell, 'Will this War End War?', *Labour Leader*, 10 Sept. 1914. This article was rejected by H.W. Massingham at the *Nation* as too controversial.

33 BR, 'Why Nations Love War', *War and Peace*, Nov. 1914, pp. 20–1.

34 B. Russell, 'Is a Permanent Peace Possible?', *Atlantic Monthly*, March 1915, pp. 367–76.

35 B. Russell, 'How America Can Bring Peace', *The Collected Papers of Bertrand Russell, Volume 13, Prophecy and Dissent, 1914–1916*, ed. R.A. Rempel (London, 1988), p. 130.

36 B. Russell, 'Can England and Germany be Reconciled After the War?', *Cambridge Review*, 10 Feb. 1915.

37 B. Russell, 'Mr. Russell's Reply to his Critics', *Cambridge Review*, 24 Feb. 1915. During the summer of 1915 Russell fought back, specifically targeting the academic arena in an article for the *International Review* titled 'On Justice in War-Time. An Appeal to the Intellectuals of Europe'. He appealed to the international academic fraternity by pointing out that men of learning, of whatever nationality, were the guardians of certain ideals essential to human development, ideals such as just thought and the disinterested pursuit of truth, which were under threat during the moral muddle of the conflict; 'The war is trivial, for all its vastness. No great principle is at stake, no great human purpose is involved on either side. The supposed ideal ends for which it is being fought are merely part of the myth'. B. Russell, 'On Justice in War-time. An Appeal to the Intellectuals of Europe', *International Review 1*, 10 Aug. 1915, pp. 145–51; 1 Sept. 1915, pp. 223–30.

38 B. Russell, 'The Philosophy of Pacifism', *Collected Papers, Volume 13* ed. Rempel, pp. 147–8.

39 Moorehead, *Bertrand Russell*, cited p. 214.

40 McM,BRP, B. Russell to O. Morrell, 11 June 1915, no. 1286.

41 *Ibid.*, 1 Jan. 1916, no. 1344.

42 In *The Open Court, no. 30* (Chicago periodical), March 1916, pp. 170–80.

43 McM,BRP, B. Russell to O. Morrell, 23 May 1915, no. 1214/4.

44 B. Russell, 'The Danger to Civilization', *Collected Papers, Volume 13* ed. Rempel, p. 330.

45 *Ibid.*

46 McM,BRP, B. Russell to O. Morrell, 24 Feb. 1916, no. 1354.

47 Cited in Vellacott, *Bertrand Russell and the Pacifists*, p. 82.

48 McM,BRP, B. Russell to O. Morrell, 10 Sept. 1914, no. 1105.

49 *Ibid.*, 19 March 1916, no. 1361.

50 *Ibid.*, 12 May 1916, no. 1383.

51 *Ibid.*, 10 July 1916, no. 1388/1.

52 *Cambridge Magazine*, vol. 6, no. 1, 14 Oct. 1916, p. 17.

53 *Ibid.* Despite his long-standing public support for Russell (he had been one of the signatories of Russell's statement supporting British neutrality in July 1914) Murray also wrote propagandia for Britain's war progaganda bureau at Wellington House in London. See Peter Buitenhuis, *The Great War of Words* (Vancouver, 1987), pp. 46–8.

54 B. Russell, 'Liberty of Conscience', *Cambridge Magazine*, vol. 5, no. 22, 27 May 1916.

55 Public Records Office, Home Office Papers, HO 45/11012/314670 X. 1. 3173.

56 McM,BRP, B. Russell to Colette, 28 Sept. 1916, no. 711200009.

57 McM,BRP, B. Russell to O. Morrell, undated [Sept. 1916], no. 1423.
58 *Ibid.*, 18 Dec. 1916, no. 1448.
59 *Ibid.*, 2 March 1917, no. 1449/1.
60 *Ibid.*, 5 May 1917, no. 1453/1.
61 McM,BRP, B. Russell to Colette, undated [6 May 1917] no. 711200139.
62 McM,BRP, B. Russell to OM, 27 July 1917, no. 1467.
63 *Ibid.*, undated [Aug. 1917], no. 1492/1.
64 McM,BRP, B. Russell to Colette (via Miss Rinder), 17 June 1918, no. 711200299A.
65 McM,BRP, B. Russell to Clifford Allen, 5 Nov. 1918, Rec. Acqu. 16.
66 McM,BRP, B. Russell to O. Morrell, 27 Aug. 1918, no. 229–30/1 (also numbered 1489L RA by McMaster).
67 McM,BRP, B. Russell to Colette, 1 Sept. 1918, 711200344.
68 Ray Monk, *Bertrand Russell – The Spirit of Solitude* (London, 1996), p. 577.
69 McM,BRP, B. Russell to 'All and Sundry', 30 July 1918, no. 66 of Prison File.

4

Writers at war

Bertrand Russell was just one man largely thinking and acting alone – and therein rests his reputation. But to what extent – whether in private or public – did similar anti-war concerns to those of Russell and the Bloomsbury circle express themselves among the intelligentsia? The bulk of the evidence derives from the letters that sped back and forth between contemporary writers, artists and thinkers, during a time of unexpected conflict – a conflict that provoked much doubt and debate.

In common with Bertrand Russell, E.M. Forster believed the war to be partly due to misdirected destructive energies; forces that could be channelled during times of peace into creative efforts. In a letter to Siegfried Sassoon written as the conflict neared its end, Forster confirmed that 'all vigour these days is misdirected' and that the human race needed time and the opportunity to re-align itself.[1] What of further evidence of similarities of response amongst the wider literary intelligentsia who, though they did not take part in the actual fighting (see Chapter 5), could, as with Bloomsbury and Russell, regard the conflict from a particular aesthetic or humanistic standpoint?

In his letter to Sassoon, E.M. Forster also explained that his other hope for the future, though 'very faint', was for a League of Nations. This was a hope Forster shared both with his frequent correspondent Goldsworthy Lowes Dickinson and with other intellectuals such as the writer and ruralist Edward Carpenter, who wrote publicly on the war throughout its duration. Carpenter's standpoint was derived from his background of mysticism rather than the statistical analysis of Leonard Woolf, for example, who worked slowly on academic reports for the Fabians during 1915 and 1916.[2] Carpenter rushed out books, articles, letters and pamphlets on the war and also found time to produce an autobiography. His 1916 pamphlet *Never Again* (subtitled 'A Protest and a Warning Addressed to the Peoples of Europe') echoed Clive Bell's *Peace at Once* of the previous year in arguing that war was 'abhorrent to our common humanity': the longer the war continued, the greater would become the impulses of hate and revenge. Carpenter's focus on destructive impulses mirrored that of Russell; Carpenter cited Russell's *Principles of Social Reconstruction* in his own *Towards Industrial Freedom* (1917) and highlighted the creative impulses of men set against those impulses which were of a 'Possessive' (i.e. destructive) nature.

In his *The Healing of Nations* (1915), as well as the material loss of war and the mental and physical suffering, Carpenter also recognised that war released 'passions' – resulting in cruelty and vindictiveness – the energy of which, during peacetime, could have been put to good use. Carpenter's idea of a world at peace was one without the economic rivalries of nations bound by the dictates of commerce and, more importantly, without the dehumanisation brought about by scientific advances – advances which were now being used for the malign purposes of war, to take life with such a destructive force that the human spirit could 'hardly hold up against'. Carpenter placed his faith in the simple peasant or agriculturalist, 'the one honest man in the community', a figure close to the land, a creator of food and therefore life who perceived, without illusion, the true 'foolery of war'.

Carpenter's appreciation of the life-force represented by the countryside as a contrast to the slaughter and destruction in France and Gallipoli was matched in a quiet way by Leonard Woolf, who later recalled in his autobiography walking to the Sussex coast from Asheham House with his wife on the day war broke out and wrote, 'I see that part of the civilisation which the war destroyed was the environment, the country and the country life, through which Virginia and I walked that day.' Woolf spent most of the war in the country, writing and caring for his mentally-ill wife. 'If one went for a walk on the downs above Asheham', he recalled, 'one could hear the incessant pounding of the guns on the Flanders front. And even when one did not hear them it was as though the war itself was perpetually pounding dully on one's brain'.[3] Both Woolf and Carpenter looked to the future for consolation. Woolf was glad that the weight of the 'fog and fetters' of the Victorian age had been lifted but was concerned that something constructive, creative and free should take its place – hence his work in drafting plans for a League of Nations in order to provide a calm setting wherein this transformation could be given an opportunity to conclude itself satisfactorily.

Edward Carpenter was impassioned about the possibilities of what he identified as the 'life within', a life of the spirit which even death could not conquer. In common with E.M. Forster, Duncan Grant, David Garnett and others. Carpenter believed that experience of war (even from a distance) was important in the formation of reaction to it, especially that of the 'life within'; 'All these shattering experiences, whether in a nation's career or in the career of an individual, cause one – they force one – to look into the bones of life and to get nearer its realities.'[4] At a time when supposedly civilised nations were acting 'so contrary to the natural laws and instincts of humanity', Carpenter championed the individual. 'Let us recognise', he wrote in *Never Again*, 'the right and the duty of each man to ponder these world problems for himself: to play his part and to make his own voice heard in the solution of them.'[5] He raged against the injustice of conscription; this 'gross folly' would prove to be the war's moral low point, he warned. For, 'to compel a man to fight, whether he will or not – in violation, perhaps, of his conscience, of his instinct, of his temperament – is an inexcusable outrage on his rights as a human being'.[6]

The emotional response of Edward Carpenter and Goldsworthy Lowes Dickinson to the war was matched by that of Henry James, who had also experienced an assault upon rational sensibility as soon as hostilities had commenced, writing on 5 August 1914 that:

> The taper went out last night, and I am afraid I now kindle it again to a very feeble ray – for it's vain to try to talk as if one weren't living in a nightmare of the deepest dye. How can what is going on not be to one as a huge horror of blackness?[7]

James was at Rye on the Sussex coast when war was declared but soon went to London, leaving his studio as a refuge for some of the first refugees from Belgium, displaced by the advancing German army. He threw himself into Belgian relief work in the capital, the atmosphere of which he described as 'monotonously magnificent', while highlighting the inconceivability of the general populace towards the horrors occurring just over the 'blue channel'. He pointed out to his fellow writer Hugh Walpole that every former social convention and habit had broken down and that life in the city made his former life at Rye seem to fade into 'grey mists of insignificance', while London itself had become grey – in 'moral tone' due to the war's blunting of life's usual compass points.

This warping of the values of the outside world severely affected James's inner creative life. 'I myself find concentration an extreme difficulty', he wrote to Edmund Gosse after only two months of war, 'the proportions of things have so changed and one's poor old values received such a shock'.[8] He set himself the goal of clinging onto and upholding his values 'in the very interest of civilisation' but admitted in the current climate of 'measureless rush' that this would be no easy task. James found the 'unprecedented combination of size and suddenness' very hard to accommodate in his personal, everyday world. Where others rushed to enlist or cheered the men to France, to James the conflict was the 'Great Interruption' and the experience of it he likened to living under a permanent dark cloud (the 'funeral pall of our murdered civilisation') which obscured the future and threw back 'so livid a light' on the past – a period which had seemed full of effort and promise and now gone to waste.

The war to James could only be an 'unspeakable giveaway of the whole fool's paradise of our past'.[9] He was not above being stirred by sights of human endeavour, however. Ever since, as a young man, he had visited his brothers on active service in the American Civil War (James had then been unfit for service), the exploits of soldiery had held a fascination for him and, though appalled by the war itself and feeling himself to be 'infirm and helpless at home with the women', he was impressed by the bustle of preparation, writing that, 'I find the general community, the whole scene of energy, immensely sustaining and inspiring – so great a thing … to be present at, that it almost salves over the haunting sense of all the horrors.'[10] While visiting the wounded at St Bartholomew's hospital in London, James found himself amazed by the courage and steadfastness, moral as well as physical, of the returned soldiers. In his essay 'The Long Wards', which was included in *The Book of the Homeless* (edited by the hugely popular American novelist Edith Wharton to raise money for refugees), James marvelled that 'the murderous impulse at the highest pitch', experienced by the wounded solders, had left 'so *little* distortion of the moral nature [my italics]'.[11] James naturally expected that the nearer one came to the horrors of war, the more one's moral sensibilities would suffer damage of some kind.

To some extent, James reconciled the differing experiences of himself and others to a question of age and having lived through years of hope and achievement. As he wrote to his friend Rhoda Broughton at the start of the war:

> Black and hideous to me is the tragedy that gathers, and I'm sick beyond cure to have lived on to see it. You and I, the ornaments of our generation, should have been spared this wreck of our belief that through the long years we had seen civilisation grow and the worst become impossible ... It seems to me to undo everything, everything that was ours ...[12]

He took a similar line with his old Rhode Island friend, Margaret La Farge, bewailing to her that, 'These are monstrous miseries for us, of our generation and age, to live into; but we wouldn't not have lived – and yet this is what we get by it. I try to think it will be interesting – but have only got so far as to feel it sickening.'[13]

Although, in contrast with Henry James, the dry, precise tone of George Bernard Shaw provided perhaps the most prominent intellectual commentary of his time on the war's ebb and flow, Shaw had his emotional side, too. His overriding sympathy for the suffering of the troops of all nations was his Achilles heel in terms of his many critics. As Shaw's biographer puts it, 'His reasoning was impeccable; his offence emotional.'[14] Shaw referred at one point to Germany and Great Britain as 'quarrelsome dogs' and advised the soldiers of both sides to shoot their officers and return home. It was for statements such as this that Shaw found himself blacklisted by many public organs of news and comment, such as the *Manchester Guardian*, whose editor, C.P. Scott, regarded Shaw's stance as one that could only 'exercise and divide' a readership at a time when the duty of public comment was to 'encourage and unite'.

Naturally, the outspoken Shaw, never one for reticence, saw things differently; his 'job' and that of other commentators and intellectuals was, as he wrote to Bertrand Russell, to 'make people serious about the war', and to expose the 'monstrous triviality' of jingoistic patriotism. Michael Holroyd has pointed out that Shaw believed that, 'it was the duty of representatives of art and literature in all countries to keep moral considerations above the nationalistic level of the war'.[15] As Shaw wrote to Russell, it was important that thinkers and commentators (people who could 'keep their heads') conferred with one another from time to time, if only to reassure themselves that it was they who were sane and the outer world given over to madness. Hence Shaw's advice to Clive Bell concerning Bell's tribunal adjudicating over his declared conscientious objection (recognising that Bell would suffer from Shaw's public support due to the built-up prejudice against him and that the tribunal would not accept Bell's art criticism as work of national importance) and his anger when H.G. Wells, J.M. Barrie, G.K. Chesterton, playwright Harley Granville Barker, Oxford professor Gilbert Murray and forty-eight others (all those who supposedly possessed 'the power of seeing what is really going on') signed the War Propaganda Bureau's jingoistic Wellington House declaration of September 1914 condemning Prussia's 'iron' military bureaucracy and contrasting it with the lawful ideals of the Allies.[16] Also, though Russell identified the emotions of primitive destructiveness inherent in war, Shaw, with his 'sophisticated reason' and lack of Russell's occasional despairing pessimism, could not always bring himself to comprehend the 'primitive and irrational' character of the war, despite an emotional element to his reasoning.

One of George Bernard Shaw's stated reasons for making an end to war was the abandonment of the morality of right or wrong in favour of kill or be killed. This ethical reasoning was intermeshed with an emotional response to the loss of life. In common with Carpenter and especially Lowes Dickinson, Shaw deplored a situation whereby the youth of all nations was deprived of its potential creativity representing as it did, 'the loss of so many young men any of whom may be a Newton or an Einstein, a Beethoven, a Michelangelo, a Shakespeare or even a Shaw. Or he may be what is of much more immediate importance: a good baker or a good weaver or builder.' Shaw found himself unable to take sides between nations – his 'quarrelsome dogs'; 'I was as sorry for the young Germans who lay slain or mutilated in no-man's land as for the British lads who lay beside them', he wrote, 'so I got no emotional satisfaction out of the war. It was to me a sheer waste of life.'[17]

In *What I Really Wrote About the War*, Shaw lamented the death from trench fever of Cecil Chesterton, the editor of the *New Witness* who had enlisted as a private, though palpably unfit. Chesterton had asked Shaw to review his *The Perils of Peace* even though he suspected – correctly – that Shaw would not agree with the content and would review the book accordingly. Though Shaw found Chesterton too bellicose on a professional basis, his death was to be personally mourned as a waste of creative talent. 'It was hard enough to see any young man thrown into the common heap of cannon fodder', Shaw recalled, 'but when the young man, possessing a rare and highly valuable talent, was not replaceable, one's hatred of the war bit fiercely in.'[18]

For Shaw, the enemy was not Germany but blind jingoism and militarism wherever they existed and in all nations and although he often criticised the British Government for not taking the right steps towards peace, he commented to his translator, the Viennese Siegfried Trebitsch, that if he had been born a

German he would have attacked the German Government with 'equal fierce-ness' and indeed, Shaw's *The German Case Against Germany* appeared in April 1916 in the *New York Times*.

In early January 1917, Shaw was invited by General Sir Douglas Haig to visit the Western Front and, although he was sceptical about the selection of places he would be allowed to see, he eventually agreed with his wife's insis-tence that he had to observe at first hand the events he was commenting on. Once in France, Shaw asked to visit the ruined Ypres and was taken to survey the shattered Medieval Cloth Hall and later (with the accredited journalist Philip Gibbs) he viewed Vimy Ridge from St. Eloi, south of Ypres. Shaw noted the contrast between the projected image of the warrior and the 'soulless labour' that occupied most of the soldiers' time. 'He [the soldier] has no sight or knowl-edge of what he is doing', commented Shaw, 'he only hands on a shell or pulls a string. And a Beethoven or a baby dies six miles off.'[19] Unsurprisingly, this was not printed until long after the war's end. On his return to England Shaw censored his own articles for the *Daily Chronicle* (for which he was paid £200) and was so effective in this that only two objections were raised by the authori-ties.

Though he did not mention the casualty lists, Shaw was critical of the war's cost and its evident waste: it was all 'a hopeless moral muddle', and he at-tempted to understand the motivations of those who, though opposed to the war in principle, still felt they had to become involved in the fighting. He con-cluded that some found that they could not vindicate 'outraged morality' by surrendering once the sword had been drawn and, in common with Bertrand Russell, he recognised general impulses in human nature towards conflict which 'must finally be satisfied in nobler ways or sternly repressed or discarded'. The soldier's experience was unique and for some involved a separate morality: 'The soldier says that war is hell; but he does not say that it is a crime.' Shaw reasoned that when a man became a soldier and experienced the front, he ceased to blame Germany exclusively for the war and turned away from conventional notions of pacifist morality. The moral aspect to the waste, destruction, terror and suffering of the front as separate elements, although 'codifying and human' to observers and commentators, did not represent the 'true nature' of military experience.[20]

His articles for the *Daily Chronicle* marked a valuable turning point in the perception of Shaw and his stance on the war by the public at large. Hitherto, he had generally been judged as the author of 'Common Sense About the War' which had appeared as an eighty page supplement to the *New Statesman* in November 1914 (which Shaw had spent the preceding three months working on). He had refused to make the journey to London for the War Propaganda Bureau's meeting of literati at Wellington House (despite his comment to Russell that intellectuals should not miss opportunities to pass the time of day, occa-sionally, during the war). His 'Common Sense' had found Shaw echoing publicly what he had been expressing privately to friends such as Mrs Patrick Campbell and Siegfried Trebitsh: namely that the war was a 'perpetual Waterloo' and that a civilisation which was 'tearing itself apart' had failed utterly. Shaw's criticisms and solutions (including a 'League of Peace') contained within his personal manifesto had seen him roundly condemned and he had been forced to step down from the two committees of the Society of Authors and resign both his membership of the Dramatists' Club and his directorship of the *New Statesman* in 1916. Although he was also struck off a list of proposed names for a post-war Reconstruction Committee by Lloyd George, Shaw continued his chairmanship of the Fabian Research Department throughout the war.

In January 1915, Leonard Woolf had been engaged as secretary of a subcommittee of this research department to formulate Fabian policy on peace and the future prevention of war. His report, published as 'International Government' with the *New Statesman* in July 1915, had been studied two months earlier by Shaw, Goldsworthy Lowes Dickinson and others at a meeting in the imposing yet calm setting of the Lake District. This led to the formation of a 'definite scheme' for a League of Nations which was announced within the annual report of the Fabian Research Department for the year ending March 1917. In addition to his work for the department, Shaw had also continued to give lectures throughout the conflict, most notably his participation in the series of autumn Fabian lectures, beginning in 1914 around the time of the appearance of 'Common Sense About the War'. The lecture series of 1915 had been entitled 'The World after the War' and although three hundred people were turned away from the first lecture on 26 October, 'The Illusions of War', press reports of the lectures had been suppressed, with the exception of the *Manchester Guardian*. Shaw had also given the fifth lecture of the series in which he declared that the first action of a war should be the formation of a Peace Council to identify the motivations of the conflict in order to more swiftly bring it to a close. The 1916 lecture series was given the title 'The World in Chains', with Shaw giving the initial and concluding lectures on 'Life' and 'Religion' respectively.

By the time of the 1917 series of Fabian lectures, collectively titled 'The Britannic Alliance and World Politics', and following the publication of his reports from the Western Front, Shaw's public position was more respected, due partly to a growing acceptance of his forthright opinions. By this point, Shaw had also spent a year campaigning publicly against the treatment of conscientious objectors such as Clifford Allen of the N.C.F. (later Lord Allen of Hurtwood), Rutland Boughton (the Director of the Glastonbury Music Festival) and Eric Chappelow, whom Shaw was persuaded by Bertrand Russell and W.B. Yeats to support in the pages of the *Nation*.

Russell had been in the chair to introduce Shaw's initial lecture of the 1915 Fabian autumn series, and Shaw later advised Russell to plead his own case after Russell's arrest in 1918 as well as offering a draft defence via Dorothy Mackenzie to whom he wrote:

> If Russell … is to be savagely punished for writing about the war as a Pacifist and as a philosopher, the intimidation of the Press will be carried thereby to a point in England which it has not yet attained in Germany or Austria and if it really be an advantage to be a free country, that advantage will go to Germany.[21]

This was symptomatic of Shaw's reasoning that it was better for intellectuals and writers to work together against the strictures of war. In July 1917 Shaw dined at J.M. Barrie's in the company of Arnold Bennett, H.G. Wells and Thomas Hardy; three months earlier, he had joined with Wells, Bennett and John Galsworthy in protesting at the ban on the export and foreign sales of the *Nation*, imposed due to a perceived editorial policy of preaching peace by negotiation.

In 1915, Shaw had begun work on 'More Common Sense About the War' and though this was never published, parts of it appeared in other articles and writings. One section was later used to form Shaw's appeal for a 'Coalition of the Intelligentsia' which appeared largely in response to the introduction of conscription in January 1916 and which Shaw, like Edward Carpenter, later viewed as the 'profoundest change' brought about by wartime conditions – the 'lesson' of the war. In his appeal, Shaw attempted to rally the forces of the mind and of creation against the 'stale' and 'soul-destroying' work of the Government. 'Perhaps the grimmest feature of this war, as all wars, is the helplessness of the intelligentsia', he wrote, adding that:

> We loathe war as an abomination forced upon us by crude and corrupt people long after we have morally outgrown it. Being unable to suppress it, we would like to obtain control of it sufficiently to dictate its aims and define its limits. But, though we write the most intelligent and interesting and suggestive articles, we might as well discharge popguns. If it were not for the attacks we make on one another, our utterances would pass without notice. They remain in any case without effect. Intelligence is not organised: everything else is, more or less. The War Office has not so much brains as the brim of Mr. [G.K.] Chesterton's hat; the Cabinet has not as much knowledge of political science or even of the everyday facts of four-fifths of English society as Mr. Arnold Bennett's umbrella: Maxim Gorky and Romain Rolland and H.G. Wells know more of the real needs of civilisation than all the Governments of Europe. Yet these clever people count for nothing in war.[22]

By 1918, Shaw and his opinions were becoming respectable, and he was the featured speaker at the annual meeting of the Society of Authors at Central Hall, Westminster, in May of that year. He used the occasion to point out that those that ran the war were blind to the importance of the threatened cultural life that struggled to exist under the weight of the conflict. The following month he favourably reviewed a performance of Wagner's *Die Walküre* for the *Nation*, commenting specifically on the enthusiastic reaction of the audience and challenging the authorities, in this new climate, to, 'bring along your Dora [the Defense of the Realm Act] and hale me to the Tower'.[23] Shaw spent the final months of the war working on his play *Back to Methuselah*.

When Shaw had called for a 'Coalition of the Intelligentsia', Arnold Bennett had remarked to a friend that the idea was 'idiotic'. Bennett, the popular author of *The Old Wives' Tale* (1908), had also remarked to his literary agent on the appearance of Shaw's earlier 'Common Sense About the War' that some of the detail was 'absurd'. However, he had admitted that about two-thirds of it was 'strictly first class' and overall it was 'quite unequalled'. Although Bennett did not agree with his fellow writer on the causes of war, the fallacy of the Foreign Secretary Sir Edward Grey and the position of Belgium, he stated in the *New York Times* on 18 November 1914 that the greatest quality of 'Common Sense' was its courage in saying things 'that no one else has been able to say', in terms of 'magnificent, brilliant and convincing commonsense'. This was praise indeed from Bennett as he and Shaw rarely saw eye to eye on anything.

Bennett attended the Propaganda Bureau's Wellington House meeting in September 1914. However, during the same month, he described war as 'grotesque, a monstrous absurdity' in his article 'Let us Realise' for *Harper's Weekly*.[24] A month earlier, he had confided to his journal that he regarded the war as a 'mistake on our part'. However, he had concluded sadly, it had also been inevitable and hence resistance was useless. Bennett then developed what he described publicly as a 'stolid attitude' towards the conflict, regarding it as a last battle between the old concept of a noble war for territorial power and modern ideals of democratic and social change. Bennett's biographer has remarked that he, 'saw the true issue of war not as the struggle for territory but as the struggle for ideals – the ideas of democracy, social justice and peace'.[25] He had no love for the German military caste or European diplomats in general (except Sir Edward Grey), and he declared them all to be infantile, ignoble and 'altogether rascally' in articles for the *Daily News* and *Saturday Evening Post* during the second month of the war.

Placing his trust in himself, early in the war Bennett became a representative on the Thorpe Division Emergency Committee for his local area, Essex, established in order to assist the evacuation of civilians in the event of a German invasion. This was only the beginning of his practical involvement in the running of the war. He became the permanent chairman of the Wounded Allies Relief Committee and in March 1915 was asked to tour the Western Front only a few weeks after the first newspaper correspondents. The practical result of this visit was seven propagandist articles, six in *Over There*, published in 1915 and one for the *Daily News* in September of that year.

In *Over There* his disgust at the destruction he witnessed in France and Belgium was clear; he prophesied that the shattered Ypres would become a tourist attraction full of visitors 'like staring sheep' and hotels, touts and tours. 'Nevertheless', he concluded, 'the thing must come to pass, and it is well that it should come to pass. The greater the number of people who see Ypres for themselves, the greater the hope of progress for mankind.' The destruction of Rheims moved him to write that:

It is monstrous that one population should overrun another with murder and destruction from political covetousness as that two populations should go to war concerning a religious creed. Indeed, it is more monstrous. It is an obscene survival, a phenomenon that has strayed, through some negligence of fate, into the wrong century.[26]

For Bennett, this was all symbolic of his belief, shared by other writers and intellectuals such as Lowes Dickinson, that the progress of civilisation had been stalled. He had expressed his view early on in his article 'The Ant Hill' for the *Daily News* of 24th October 1914 when he stated that the war had come about because civilisation had failed in its duty to ignore the tenets of anarchy and competition born of jealousy.[27]

In his controversial novel of 1918, *The Pretty Lady*, Bennett has his main character realise that 'the sense of its [the war's] measureless scope was growing' and that the conflict (which 'transcended judgements' and 'defied conclusions') had sprung not from specific crimes, but 'out of secret, invisible roots of humanity'. The novel concerned the love of a deported French courtesan for a middle-aged English bachelor, and was set in a London under attack. The supreme lesson of the war was 'its revelation of what human nature actually was'.[28] In this recognition that the war had evolved from the latent darker side of humanity, Bennett was here echoing Bertrand Russell's similar conception of a human race that had to be constantly on its guard against malign impulses and hence diverted into creative pursuits.

Bennett's novel was attacked repeatedly in print: H.M. Richardson's review in the *Sunday Chronicle* of 14 April 1918 appeared under the title 'An Ignoble New Novel'. Bennett's book would, according to Richardson, 'destroy the moral [sic] of the people'. The novel's supposedly immoral and irreligious character also incited the ire of the Catholic Federation and the Catholic Truth Society. Some reviews were more positive: W.L. Courtney in the *Daily Telegraph* of 5 April described the novel as 'tremendously up-to-date'. Perhaps the most interesting comment came from James Douglas in the *Star* of 5 April, in which he wrote that had the novel appeared *before* the war it could have been appreciated as a study of decadent London life:

But the war forces the critic to set up a severe standard of aim and intention for art as well as for other forms of national energy. No artist had any right to fall below that standard of aim and intention. If he does so deliberately, he is not a good citizen. It is his duty to enoble his readers and to inspire them with ideals which will make them better fit to do their part in the national struggle.

Bennett had done the country an 'ill turn' by writing this book during the war when 'every English pen ought to be a clean, shining weapon' in order to fight for citizens who, as Douglas was forced to admit, 'are in sore need of mental and moral sustenance'. This was no time to 'regale our hurt minds with glimpses of the nether world'.[29]

Bennett spent the latter half of the war in increasing detachment, severing his links with the Thorpe committee and turning his attention to the issue of social stress generated by the war and criticism of the handling of the introduction and after-effects of conscription. He sided with the forces of liberalism on all issues of legislation affecting social issues and attacked the tribunals and medical boards for their ignorance and incompetence. However, despite describing the Northcliffe press as 'the stunt press' in the *New Statesman*, in May 1918 he accepted Lord Beaverbrook's offer to become director of British propaganda in France; by September 1918 Bennett controlled all international British propaganda except that in enemy countries.

Arnold Bennett's final immersion in the practicalities of the war was mirrored in opposite terms by Thomas Hardy, who had also attended C.F.G. Masterman's 1914 call to literary arms – the meeting at Wellington House. By the end of the war, Hardy was working steadily on his autobiography and his next collection of new (and old) poems. His previous and largest collection, *Moments of Vision*, which had appeared in November 1917, had exhibited a 'new human tone', compared to his earlier *Poems of War and Patriotism*. The poems of the 1917 collection were, according to Hardy's biographer, 'wholly on a human scale ... their concern for human failing celebrates true humanity'.[30]

Hardy had been deeply affected by the deaths in 1915 of both his beloved sister and Frank George, the 'heir' to his home, Max Gate, in Dorset. George, a 2nd Lieutenant in the 5th Dorsets had been killed at Gallipoli. It was from this year that Hardy became more thoughtful and reclusive while still receiving a constant stream of visitors including Virginia Woolf and Siegfried Sassoon. Although he felt that Great Britain was impelled to fight, had strongly disagreed with the Christmas Truce of 1914 and allowed producer and playwright Harley Granville-Barker to mount a popular patriotic adaptation of scenes from his epic poem set one hundred years earlier, *The Dynasts*, in the month preceding the 'truce',[31] in truth, Hardy had always been cautious about the war and its effects as well as his own public attitude to it. He responded to an invitation to comment on the war from the *Daily News* in August 1914 with, 'I do not feel impelled to say anything at present.' This he sensibly ascribed to the insufficiency of available data; later in the war he would publicly support the *Cambridge Magazine*'s inclusion within its pages of translated extracts from the foreign press.

In reality, he and his wife were horrified with the uncertainty of the first weeks of the war, and Hardy felt his creativity to be adversely affected, writing to Sydney Cockerell (the Curator of the Fitzwilliam Museum in Cambridge):

> The recognition that we are living in a more brutal age than that, say, of Elizabeth ... does not inspire one to write hopeful poetry, or even conjectural prose, but simply make one sit still in apathy, and watch the clock spinning backwards, with a mild wonder if, when it gets back to the Dark Ages, and the sack of Rome, it will ever move forward again to a new Renaissance and a new literature.[32]

He recognised that the regularity of his correspondence was becoming 'fitful' and blamed the mental pressure of 'this hideous European tragedy', while being guarded in his reaction to reports of German atrocities in Belgium, commenting that, 'the whole thing is a mystery to thoughtful Englishmen'.

'Nothing effectual will be done in the cause of peace', Hardy wrote, 'till the sentiment of Patriotism be freed from the narrow meaning attaching to it in the past (and still upheld by Junkers and Jingoists) – and be extended to the whole globe.'[33] This comment was made to Percy Ames, the Secretary of the Royal Society of Literature, to whom Hardy wrote supporting the idea of an Entente Committee to promote an 'intellectual entente' among friendly countries and also a Memorandum (from the report of the Society's Educational Subcommittee) proposing principles of international education to uphold ethical ideals of peace. This, though on a wider scale, was not far removed from Shaw's concept of intellectuals coming together to promote peace. Hardy apologised to Ames that he could not attend the Entente Committee which was to be composed of distinguished Fellows of the Society. By this stage in the war Hardy and his wife had retreated to Max Gate: 'living uneventful lives … feeling no enterprise for going about and seeing people while the issue of the great conflict is in the balance'. The only physical reminder of the existence of the war was some young German prisoners of war who had been set to work in the Hardy's garden. 'They are admirable fellows, and it does fill one with indignation that thousands of such are led to slaughter by the ambitions of Courts and Dynasties.'[34]

Although Hardy spent most of the war at Max Gate, the steady stream of visitors, letters and newspapers and journals such as the *Cambridge Magazine* kept him informed of the progress of both the war itself and those affected by it, especially when it interfered with the creativity of his fellow writers. 'I am sorry to hear that [John] Masefield has been aged by his war experiences', he wrote to Sydney Cockerell in January 1917, 'Yet a man of deep feeling like him could not avoid it after coming in contact with the tragic scenes in France. It is grievous to think too that his writing of verse will probably be hindered for a time.'[35]

The poet (and later Poet Laureate) John Masefield was thirty-six in 1914. He had volunteered at the outbreak of hostilities but had been rejected on medical grounds. However, by February 1915 he had gone out to France as a Red Cross orderly. After being shocked by the 'horror, terror and anxiety mixed' of the wounded he planned to create a mobile field hospital which would operate nearer to the front and spent the summer of 1915 inspecting French military hospitals, which only served to increase his horror of the situation. Although the start of the war had found him in a mood of 'simple patriotism', and many of his letters express strong anti-German sentiment, his experience of conditions in France led him to admit that, 'Probably nine tenths of each country involved would be glad to end it now. I would, God knows, if there were any chance of its not springing up again.' The military hospitals he had encountered were 'fearful places' and possessed, according to him, a 'disregard … for life which shocks continually; not that we can blame them now, in this upheaval. I could weep all day for pity of these brave fellows here.'[36]

By August 1915, Masefield was at Gallipoli with a nautical ambulance service using funds raised by himself. It was this experience, he wrote, that 'made me very old'. Despite his emotional reaction, Masefield felt a need for constant war-related activity, perhaps to divert him from his inner disquiet concerning the conflict. He returned to France in August 1916, following an exhausting lecture tour of America, to gather information concerning voluntary aid from America to the Allies in the form of medical units and supplies. The year 1916 saw the publication of his *Gallipoli* (based on his observance of military operations in the Near East), and the writing of *The Old Front Line* (covering the Somme offensive) which appeared the following year. He remained in France until June 1917 and saw as much of life at the front as he was permitted. On a sunny day in March he visited the ruined town of Peronne and wrote to his regular correspondent Margaret Bridges that, 'the sight of all this order and niceness and beauty, all lit up in its defilement, made the heart ache'.[37]

Like Hardy, Masefield was wary of the English press, at one point referring to it collectively as the 'last enemy'. He condemned as 'ghastly' the state of affairs whereby foreign sales of the *Nation* were suppressed while the 'howling and foaming' of the 'patriotic' press continued without abeyance. The final year of Masefield's war was spent on a further lecture tour of America, followed by talks to army camps and work on his book describing the Somme offensive which would appear after the war's end. Although his books on the war meant that he was hardly idle in a literary sense, Hardy's concern had been for Masefield's 'writing of verse' and the future Laureate concentrated mainly on rural subjects for his poetry of the war years, such as *The Cold Cotswolds* and *Lollingdon Downs* (both 1917). The realities of the conflict prevented Masefield from expressing his true thoughts on the war in verse form like, for example, Siegfried Sassoon (discussed in Chapter 5).

Masefield's public opinions on the war and its conduct were limited to his American lectures, at which he was heckled over his presentation of the Near-Eastern campaign, and also to his books; the chivalric, semi-mystical tone of *Gallipoli* was an attempt to refute the criticism of what Masefield would later and privately refer to as the whole Gallipoli campagin as 'that insane move'. His private thoughts on the war are his most revealing. After visiting a wallpapered and electrically-supplied German dugout at Beaumont Hamel in 1917, he was moved to comment, 'To the devil with all this talk of Boche efficiency. War is a degradation of life and these dugouts are fit only for the degraded beings who like war. Paupers would refuse them in times of peace.'[38]

Another literary figure who had met at Wellington House in September 1914 with Masefield, Hardy and Bennett was the novelist and playwright John Galsworthy, the author of moralistic dramas such as *Strife* and *Justice*. In common with Masefield and Hardy, Galsworthy distrusted what he called 'our press', referring to reporters and editors, with a few exceptions, as 'a mischievous lot of irresponsibles', though he differed from Masefield's overt distrust of

German militarism in that he ultimately viewed each side as equally to blame and was not above being critical of his own side; as he wrote to a friend in 1915, 'I don't very much admire the British character … we have no philosophy. The man who has no philosophy, who does not know what he wants, but only that he means to have it, does not know when to stop.' This could be seen as siding with Bertrand Russell's view of the destructive element in the human character being given free reign due to a lack of conception or understanding of the philosophical and creative side to life. Galsworthy continued:

> We are told that we are fighting for Belgium, fighting for France, fighting against Autocracy, fighting for our existence. Some of us may be fighting for all or any of these reasons but my instinct tells me that, once it began, we have been and shall go on fighting because the other fellows said they were better men than we; and we shall simply be unable to stop till we have proved to them that they are not.[39]

Galsworthy also differed from Masefield in that his public utterances tended to mirror his private thoughts from the start. On the outbreak of war, Galsworthy's reaction was similar to that of Henry James. He was appalled at the suddenness of the conflict and entered 'Blacker and blacker!' in his diary for 1 August. The following day he recorded how he had gone riding 'to distract the thought' and complained of an inability to work properly; 'I try not to think of all the poor creatures who are suffering and will suffer so terribly', he wrote, 'but how not to? Wrote some words of Peace, but shan't send them anywhere. What's the use of whispering in a hurricane?' On 4 August 1914, with Great Britain now fully involved, he described his feelings thus:

> We are in … The horror of the thing keeps coming over one in waves; and all the happiness has gone out of life. I can't keep still, and I can't work … If this war is not the death of Christianity, it will be odd. We need a creed that really applies to life instead of taking it.[40]

With his lack of faith in whispering, Galsworthy wasted no time in attempting to shout above the noise of 'the hurricane'. He penned 'First Thoughts on the War' that autumn for the American *Scribner's Magazine*, referring to the conflict as, 'the grand defeat of all Utopians, dreamers, poets, philosophers, idealists, humanitarians, lovers of peace and the arts; bag and baggage they are thrown out of a world that has for a time no use for them'.[41] As in his diary, he referred to the war as representing the failure of hypocritical religion. Like Masefield, he would try, via articles in various American monthly periodicals, to explain to the American citizens England's position on the war. In doing this, Galsworthy could calmly distance himself from the emotional turbulence of his personal thoughts and those of the British press. Also like Masefield, he made use of money for humanitarian ends, dedicating his American earnings to the various relief funds that he wrote appeals for in the national press and, in common with Henry James, he concerned himself with the plight of Belgian refugees, arranging for a number of them to be given placements in Devon.

Galsworthy was of a naturally sensitive nature; his niece later commented that the war had 'damaged him terribly because he felt it so' and that it 'ate into his capital as a writer – he gave too much'.[42] Although he believed that the causes of democracy, justice and 'all that is sacred to true civilisation' was the responsibility of the Allies, unlike many others he could not see how the state of the world was going to be improved by the war. 'The reaction from so prolonged a bout of self-sacrifice and heroism is likely to be tremendous', he wrote and warned that, 'we may look for less brotherhood even than existed before, and that was little enough', before adding crucially, 'The whole edge of sensibility is likely to be blunted for a long while'.[43]

For Galsworthy, there existed two types of modern man: those who possessed an 'extra sensitiveness' and those who did not. In other words, those who appreciated beauty and those who could not. 'Would there still be war in a world the most of whose dwellers had the sense of beauty?' he asked in 'Second Thoughts on the War', again mirroring Russell's championship of creative values as an antidote to conflict. As in his 'First Thoughts', he bemoaned the fact that those individuals who appreciated beauty, 'are tragically compelled to live and bear their part in this hell, created by a world of which they are not', and warned that:

> the war .. will not bring them one jot nearer one to the other ... there is certainly no chance that the sense of beauty can increase within measurable time, so as to give its possessors a majority. No chance that wars will cease for that reason. The little world of beauty lovers will for many ages yet, perhaps always, be pitifully in tow, half drowned by the following surge of the big insensitive world when it loses for a time what little feeling for harmony it has, and goes full speed ahead.

Galsworthy saw his writer's role as a clear one; given an underlying feeling among all men that 'we have grown out of ... savagery', the only 'true realities' lay in a future of peace: 'the great epic of our time is the expression of man's slow emergence from the blood-loving animal he was. To that great epic the modern pen has long been consecrate, and is not likely to betray its trust.'[44] 'Second Thoughts on the War', although like its predecessor first written for *Scribner's Magazine*, was included with 'First Thoughts' in *A Sheaf* which was published in Great Britain in 1916. The volume concluded with a repeated warning that the war was 'a terrible calamity' and as such, 'it will not leave an improved world'.

As in the cases of some of his fellow writers, Galsworthy lent his public support to the campaign against the treatment of conscientious objectors. In the case of one particular individual, his brother-in-law George Sauter, who was imprisoned as an enemy alien in Wakefield Prison, Galsworthy attempted to alert Asquith (Prime Minister until 1916), Winston Churchill and Herbert Samuel (the Home Secretary) to his plight and was Sauter's only visitor in the thirteen months of his confinement. Galsworthy also offered to testify in support of the defendant's character at the tribunal of David Garnett and wrote a letter to *The Times* in defence of H.W. Massingham and the *Nation* when the journal's overseas circulation was prohibited. In spring 1918, Galsworthy assumed the editorship of *Reveille*, a magazine which featured contributions from distinguished authors and artists as well as articles of a more practical nature on rehabilitation for the benefit of the disabled soldier. The August issue sold more than 30,000 copies, and Galsworthy spent the remainder of the war working on his anti-patriotic xenophobic novel *The Burning Spear* which would appear under the pseudonym of 'A.R.P. – M.' in April 1919. The same year saw the publication of *Another Sheaf* which was composed of articles written in the latter half of the conflict, one of which, `The Sacred Work', was written at the end of the war in support of the disabled and wounded.

To Galsworthy, the 'folding back' of the darkness of war in the immediate post-war period revealed 'an earth of cripples' with the 'field of the world ... strewn with half-living men'. He observed that, 'loveliness which is the creation of the human spirit; that flowering of directed energy which we know as civilisation, that manifold and mutual service which we call progress – all stand mutilated and faltering'.[45] As he had warned Massingham of the *Nation* during the dark days of 1917, 'We cannot, as reasonable human beings, let our warped and stunted stocks deteriorate further, and the little remains of our dignity and sense of beauty ooze away utterly underneath pressure of machinery and of the herd of life.'[46]

H.G. Wells had joined John Galsworthy around C.F.G. Masterman's table on 2 September 1914 and both Wells and Galsworthy believed that the cause of the Allies was just, representing, in Galsworthy's phrase, 'true civilisation' pitted against the autocracy of the German system. Wells wrote in his pamphlet *The War and Socialism*, that the war was, 'a conflict of cultures, and nothing else in the world'. To Wells, Germany represented a 'nest of evil ideas' and the war was a material consequence of German 'false philosophy and foolish thinking'. The purpose of the war was to 'clear the heads' of the Germans and their allies and to 'keep the heads of our own people clear'.[47]

However, Wells possessed a more robust moral nature than Galsworthy and was initially less willing to distinguish the potential negative effects of the conflict upon the civilisation being fought over. While Galsworthy swiftly perceived that potentially *less* brotherhood would exist after the war and that sensibilities were under threat, Wells famously convinced himself that the war was worth fighting 'to end all wars' and spent the first months of the war penning numerous articles, many of which were of a propagandist nature. Wells's targets included conscientious objectors and the pacifist movement, as in his *War and the Future* – an attack he later regretted. For Wells, the personal solution of the pacifists was too simple – a 'merely negative attitude' was not facing the reality of a world wherein, as he stated in his autobiography, 'life is conflict' and peace must sometimes be kept by force.

As the war progressed, however, Wells – in common with some of the other Wellington House writers – began to harbour doubts over the continuation of a conflict that revealed only the worst in human nature and looked set to wreck civilisation. While not losing his belief that the Germans were responsible for the outbreak of the conflict, Wells communicated his doubts in his novel *Mr Britling Sees It Through*, which first appeared in October 1916 and which became a bestseller in America. Wells later wrote that although Mr Britling was not a self-portrait (unlike Mr Britling, Wells had no son killed in action, for example), the fictional character was deliberately representative of a man of Wells's 'type and class' and the novel was intended to convey the 'sense of tragic disillusionment in a civilised mind as the cruel facts of war rose steadily to dominate everything else in life',[48] a process which had obviously affected Wells himself, who had admitted in *The War That Will End War* that life under the war was at times a 'waking nightmare'. Mr Britling represented the 'intelligent brain', shared by Wells and other individuals, that Wells later described in his autobiography as being unable to be anything other than 'profoundly changed' by the experience of the Great War; 'our vision of life was revised in outline and detail alike'.[49]

The conflict brought Mr Britling – and, by implication, Wells – to a realisation of what modern war represented. The 'essence of modern war' was:

> the killing off of the young. It is the destruction of the human inheritance, it is the spending of all the life and material of the future upon present-day hate and greed … until the whole fabric of our civilisation, that has been so slowly and laboriously built up, is altogether destroyed.[50]

Britling/Wells here echoed the fears of Bloomsbury and also, in the realisation of the 'spending' of the material of the future on present-day hatred, the concerns of Bertrand Russell contained within his *Principles of Social Reconstruction*.

The war swept the old order away and Wells had at first, like Edmund Gosse, welcomed this scouring away of Edwardian indolence and had looked forward to a new world order. However, he found that the conflict, in a wave of destruction that was both physical and mental, overtook his thoughts and rushed ahead. 'We couldn't get out of it for a time and think it out', he remembered, 'and the young men in particular were given no time to think. They thought it out in the trenches – and in No Man's Land.'[51]

An overview of celebrated writers and their reactions to the Great War would not be complete without an examination of D.H. Lawrence, one of the most extreme examples of individuality in his response to the conflict. Lawrence operated within neither the group of Wellington House propagandists nor the circle of Bloomsbury artists and yet, though an outsider like him, did not affect Shaw's dry aloofness. Lawrence *felt* the war to a greater depth than most other writers and was at the same time able to articulate this feeling with passion and clarity – this alone makes him worthy of attention, in addition to the fact that the themes of his response were mirrored by other well-known writers, and echoed later by less-celebrated individuals.

D.H. Lawrence felt no desire to enlist; soldiers seen drilling at Worthing were to him 'teeming insects' while the job of soldiering to him was 'the annulling of all one stands for ... the nipping of the very germ of one's being'.[52] He felt keenly the humiliation of undergoing the call-up procedure following the introduction of conscription in 1916, describing the experience as, 'a degradation, a losing of individual form and distinction'. In addition, there existed the threat that the war posed to Lawrence's creative powers – a threat recognised by his friend Lady Ottoline Morrell, who had read and appreciated Lawrence's *The Prussian Officer* and had first invited the Lawrences to dine in January 1915 (they were her first guests at Garsington Manor and shared a mutual friend in the critic Gilbert Cannan who accompanied them to the Morrell's new house on a later visit the same year).

Lady Ottoline described the war hitting her 'ultra-sensitive' friend Lawrence like an avalanche and dislodging all his hopes for mankind. The outer turmoil of the war was balanced by a mental upheaval within Lawrence which, 'drew him away from his natural course of creativeness'.[53] Cynthia Asquith – the Prime Minister's daughter-in-law and possibly Lawrence's closest confidante – observed and later recalled his quest for a new set of values and 'moral equivalent' of an alternative life from that which existed under the war. To her it was clear that Lawrence saw the seeming fulfilment found in conflict as the confession of failure of mankind, though her husband Herbert saw that Lawrence was alternately full of hatred and fascination when confronted by the full colours of war, though he concluded that Lawrence's 'passionate individualism had no place in an embattled world, whose urgent commands were in obvious conflict with his whole theory of living'.[54] Lawrence's friend John Middleton Murry (the husband of Katherine Mansfield) went further and stated in his autobiography, *Between Two Worlds*, that Lawrence repudiated the war because of a feeling of 'kinship' with it – an inherent 'blood-lust'. This was ironic, in that Lawrence famously accused Bertrand Russell of being 'the super-war-spirit' when they quarrelled over plans for a joint lecture series and Russell's desire to remain a 'free agent'.

One of Lawrence's reactions to the growing unease with Russell (and the rest of Bloomsbury) was to found *The Signature* with Middleton Murry and Katherine Mansfield and including within it contributions from the likes of Gilbert Cannan and, it was hoped, Russell himself. The magazine was to be financed from Lawrence's advance for *The Rainbow*, which had been rejected by the publisher Methuen in the first week of the war. Lawrence wrote to Russell commenting on the venture and stating that he himself intended to be 'the preacher', Mansfield the originator of satirical sketches and Murry 'the revealer of the individual soul' in terms of its 'real freedom'. Cannan was left, in Lawrence's barbed comment, to 'flounder prehistorically'. The article that Russell sent to Lawrence in response, 'The Danger to Civilization', revealed Russell's fear of the war's effect upon, 'that common heritage of thought and art and ...

humane way of life into which we were born', and upon Europe's 'mental advancement',[55] that Lawrence conversely thought had led civilisation astray from the more vital aspects of life.

Russell's article was the start of the rapidly widening breach between the two thinkers and their worlds. The first issue of *The Signature* appeared on 4 October 1915 but soon afterwards Murry's brother was killed on active service by a grenade and he and Mansfield withdrew from the publication, leaving only Lawrence and his growing hostility towards Russell and his friends. In August, in a letter to Cynthia Asquith, Lawrence had accused Russell and those who supported 'all international peace-for-ever and democratic control talks' of striving merely towards 'an outward system of nullity' which would allow them, within their own souls to be 'independent little gods, referred nowhere and to nothing', or 'little mortal Absolutes, secure from question'.[56]

This bitter and independent stance represented the summation of Lawrence's experience of the war so far. As we have seen, both Murry and Herbert Asquith recognised in Lawrence a fascination with the energies of war; Lawrence confessed to Lady Ottoline that, 'if there was a restoring, creating influence equivalent to the destructive, one would not be so bled'. Paul Delany has written that Lawrence, 'longed to take part in some collective enterprise that might be equally engrossing, equally purgative of selfish concerns, yet constructive rather than destructive'. This desire – on an individual level – reflected Russell's concepts of social reconstruction and yet, with regard to the attitude of Bloomsbury and the anti-war lobby:

> Lawrence's indignant temperament did not permit him to dissociate himself from the war, nor to judge it by the old standards of civility as the pacifists did … If men were to give themselves over completely to hate, he saw no reason why he should not hate the haters – though at the same time refusing all literal participation in the massacres.[57]

On the outbreak of war, Lawrence had described his situation to Edward Marsh ('patron' of the Georgian poets) as suddenly existing in 'a sort of coma', a dream-world – 'like one of those nightmares when you can't move'. This was in stark contrast to the way in which he remembered the world before the war; 'there was *something* in those still days', he recalled to Mary Cannan, 'before the war had gone into us, which was beautiful and generous – a sense of flowers rich in the garden … now the whole world of it is lost'.[58]

Despite this loss, Lawrence soon came to believe (by November 1914) that it was the very business of the artist to try and define the war, 'to follow it home to the heart of the individual fighters – not to talk in armies and nations and numbers – but to track it home – home – their war'.[59] In common with other individuals with an anti-war disposition, Lawrence felt himself drawn to the activity at the front and admitted as much to Lady Ottoline in spring 1915, though in his case 'not to shoot' but rather as a bus conductor or some other non-combatant occupation that might afford him the chance to observe 'their war'. However, Lawrence was always wary of what he later described in *Aaron's Rod* (when commenting on the link between former soldiers) as the 'hot seared burn of unbearable experience', especially to one who intensely disliked the military machine; as he commented to the American poet Amy Lowell after his compulsory medical at Bodmin barracks:

> There is something in military life that would kill me off, as if I were in an asphyxiating chamber ... the pure spirit of militarism is sheer death to a nature that is all constructive or social-creative ... is essentially destructive, destroying the individual ... it is bad.[60]

Lawrence found an alternative method by which to 'track' the war home; a process which, he realised, existed within himself and his own reactions to the conflict. By the middle of the war, he commented to Lady Ottoline that he felt as if he had been fighting in spirit 'every minute' and, while describing himself as 'too raw' for the experience of combat to his friend Catherine Carswell, he justified himself by saying, 'one fights too hard already, for the real integrity of one's soul'.[61] This attitude remained with him for the remainder of the war; when his friend Richard Aldington (see Chapter 5) returned to France in April 1918, Lawrence commented that he felt it was harder to bear 'the pressure of the vacuum' of the domestic front that 'the stress of congestion' of its military equivalent. He was becoming more concerned with the condition of his inner being and, in the process, attempting to cut himself off from the attitudes of others, as evidenced by his split with Bertrand Russell. It was as if he needed to experience the war on his own terms alone, whatever state this might bring him to. As early as January 1915 Lawrence was describing himself as made 'feeble and half alive' by the war with a heart 'as cold as a lump of dead earth'. He made many allusions to being brought metaphorically to a state of near death – the coma/nightmare state of the first weeks of war had become deeper and Lawrence now felt 'corpse-cold'.

By the end of 1915, following his argument and subsequent split with Russell and the failure of *The Signature*, Lawrence began to talk of leaving Great Britain; if his soul was to be rendered 'sightless' by the war, then, he wrote, 'let it ... be blind, rather than commit the vast wickedness of acquiescence'. Despite his criticism of Russell of championing the values of civilisation, Lawrence could not help but reflect to Cynthia Asquith that the golden autumn of 1915 had made him deeply sad, as he saw it representing the passing of the old civilisation and the fading of beauty, although his ultimate sadness was that there were 'no new things coming' to replace the old order. He had previously written to her that while war might be a 'great and necessary disintegrating autumnal process', love represented the creative thrust and unifying solidity of mankind, mirrored by the season of spring within nature. Lawrence's fear, as he expressed it, was that the disintegrating processes of war had become overpowering and:

> if it goes on any further, we shall so thoroughly have destroyed the unifying force
> from among us that we shall become each one of us so completely a separate entity,
> that the whole will be an amorphous heap, like sand, sterile, hopeless, useless, like a
> dead tree ... it is so great a danger that one almost goes mad facing it.[62]

His frustration and fear sprung from his belief that it was his duty to 'speak for
life and growth' amid a 'mass of destruction and disintegration' that was increasing in emotional density as the months passed.

After a final visit to Lady Ottoline's Garsington Manor in November 1915,
Lawrence and his wife left intellectual society for the 'crow's nest' sanctuary of
Cornwall. His hopes of travelling abroad were fading and men of military age
could not emigrate. In addition, the degrading experience of attesting at Battersea
Town Hall in December 1915 (to be repeated at Bodmin the following year and
again in June 1917 and September 1918) had left Lawrence extremely unwilling to face the necessary officialdom of the emigration process. As he became
more immersed in his writing once more and worked on *Women in Love*, his
attitude built on the separations of the year before and became increasingly
individualistic; though he still regarded the war as 'stupid, monstrous and con-
temptible', in the natural solitude of Cornwall, his fellow humans came to mean
less to him and he could admit that, 'I am only myself. At last I submit that I
have no right to speak for anybody else, but only for my single self. War is for
the rest of men ...'[63]

For Lawrence to accomplish 'anything real' he felt he had to eschew all
connections with other collective attitudes, and he singled out Fabianism,
Socialism and 'Cambridgeian' as specific examples. As he had decided not to
'go down with the ship' (as he himself described that option), he was left to
'leave the ship and like a castaway live a life apart'. He also described it necessary for himself to become an outlaw, 'not a teacher or a preacher' as he had
hoped at the time of *The Signature*; 'One must retire out of the herd', he concluded. In July 1916 he told the editor T.D. Dunlop that he esteemed individual
liberty 'above everything' and this admission had been preceded by another to
Lady Ottoline that it was only in 'my individual self ... that I live at all'. Hence
his separation from the world at war and the ignominy of his experience with
the military at Bodmin in June of that year ('I won't be pawed and bullied by
them', Lawrence resolved after being eventually classed as Grade 3 in September 1918). The Lawrences only returned to London after their house at Higher
Tregerthen was searched by the authorities in October 1917, and they were
ordered to leave Cornwall.

To Lawrence, the inhabitants of London, obsessed with air-raids, had become 'factors' and not people while, as he and Frieda moved from place to
place for the remainder of the war, Lawrence felt himself to be 'slowly suffo-
cated in mud', an appropriate metaphor for one who believed he was fighting
his own personal battle. Lawrence also described himself, 'at best only a torn
fragment'; the war had forced him to abandon notions of place, identity and

alter his vision of a new beginning, and postpone plans of an escape to Utopia. As others observed and he admitted, the conflict had become one he had felt within himself and his war was of an intensely personal nature. To Cynthia Asquith, Lawrence wrote, 'In war, in my being, I am a detached entity, and every one of my actions is an act of further detaching my own single entity from all the rest.' He continued and explained how the war had led to his position of isolation:

> You say that war does not prevent personal life from going on, that the individual can still love and be complete. It isn't true. The one quality of love is that it universalises the individual. If I love then I am extended over all people, but particularly over my own nation. It is extending in concentric waves over all people. This is the process of love ... and how can this be, in war, when the spirit is against love?[64]

When Ottoline Morrell spoke of the war diverting Lawrence and his 'passionate individualism' away from his 'natural course of creativeness', she was echoing the fears of other writers; Thomas Hardy supported the concept of an 'intellectual entente' between nations, and Bernard Shaw had called for a 'Coalition of the Intelligentsia'. Just as Bloomsbury believed it to be a dutiful good for an individual to appreciate and uphold the values of art and life, so Shaw believed that it was the duty of representatives of art and literature to uphold moral constants in a world changed rapidly by war. Both the Bloomsbury circle and Shaw attempted to 'keep their heads' and persuade others to keep theirs. The appreciation of the importance of keeping heads clear was shared by H.G. Wells who, in common with Russell and others, and using the fictional device of Mr Britling, pointed out that all 'material for the future' was being squandered on 'present-day hate'. Mr Britling represents the disillusionment of a civilised individual in response to the now tattered fabric of a previously familiar world and value system.

John Galsworthy recognised that civilisation was the 'flowing of directed energy' and that this flow was faltering, as Lawrence had also noted, though Lawrence felt that civilisation had become perhaps *too* refined and removed from its more 'vital' aspects: some kind of purgative was called for – though not armed conflict, which could only result in a literal and metaphorical deadening or snuffing-out of sensation. The war caused creative energies (Galsworthy's 'flowing of directed energy') to be misdirected – E.M. Forster had observed that 'vigour' had been misplaced and mankind needed to re-align itself if civilisation was to be saved. Galsworthy also declared the war to be the defeat of Utopians, dreamers and humanitarians and this view was reflected in others. But Galsworthy and some of his contemporaries wrote from a somewhat distant (though no less valid) perspective. What of writers and artists who found themselves in the arena of battle itself? What were the thoughts of those forced to grapple with death – that great nullifier of creation – on a daily basis?

Notes

1 E.M. Forster to Siegfried Sassoon, 3 Aug. 1918, *Selected Letters of E.M. Forster*, vol. 1, ed. Mary Lago and P.N. Furbank (London, 1983), no. 190, p. 293.

2 Leonard Woolf's two reports – the first published as a supplement to the *New Statesman* in 1915 and the second a draft treaty – were published together as *International Government* in 1916.

3 Leonard Woolf, *Beginning Again* (London, 1964), pp. 147–8, 197.

4 Edward Carpenter, *The Healing of the Nations* (London, 1915), p. 18.

5 Edward Carpenter, *Never Again* (London, 1916), p. 24.

6 Carpenter, *Healing*, p. 154.

7 Henry James to Howard Sturgis, 5 Aug. 1914, *The Letters of Henry James*, vol. 2, ed. Percy Lubbock (2 vols, London, 1920), vol. 2, p. 398.

8 H. James to Edmund Gosse, 15 Oct. 1914, *The Letters of Henry James, Volume Four, 1895–1916*, ed. Leon Edel (Cambridge, MA, 1984), p. 720.

9 H. James, 8 Aug. 1914, *Letters of H. James*, vol. 2, ed. Lubbock, p. 402.

10 *Ibid.*, H. James to T.S. Perry, 25 Oct. 1914, p. 434.

11 Cited in Leon Edel, *Henry James – The Master 1901–1916* (Philadelphia and New York, 1972), p. 517.

12 H. James to Rhoda Broughton, 10 Aug. 1914, *Letters of H. James*, vol. 2, ed. Lubbock, p. 403.

13 Cited in Edel, *James – The Master*, pp. 511–12.

14 Michael Holroyd, *Bernard Shaw, Volume Two – The Pursuit of Power* (London, 1991), p. 356.

15 *Ibid.*, p. 368.

16 The former literary editor of the *Daily Chronicle* and MP, C.F.G. Masterman was appointed head of the War Propaganda Bureau in August 1914 and his confidential work was based in his existing office at Wellington House in London (until the department later became the Ministry of Information). On 2nd September 1914, many of Britain's leading literary figures responded to Masterman's call for help with the government's war propaganda and met in the conference room at Wellington House. See M.L. Sanders and Philip M. Taylor, *British Propaganda during the First World War, 1914–1918* (London, 1982) and Buitenhuis, *The Great War of Words*.

17 George Bernard Shaw, 'As I See It', *The Listener*, 10 Nov. 1937, reprinted 18 Jan. 1979, p. 79.

18 George Bernard Shaw, *What I Really Wrote About the War* (London, 1931), p. 183.

19 Cited in Stanley Weintraub, *Journey to Heartbreak* (London, 1973), p. 218.

20 See Shaw's articles for the *Daily Chronicle*, 5, 7 and 8 March 1917, as cited pp. 227–8 in Weintraub, *Journey to Heartbreak*.

21 G.B. Shaw to Dorothy Mackenzie, 18 March 1918, cited in Weintraub, *Heartbreak*, p. 288.

22 G.B. Shaw, 'Wanted: A Coalition of the Intelligentsia', *New Statesman*, no. 149, 12 Feb. 1916, pp. 445–6.

23 Cited in Weintraub, *Journey to Heartbreak*, p. 310.

24 Cited in Kinley E. Roby, *A Writer at War* (Baton Rouge, Louisiana, 1972), p. 33.

25 *Ibid.*, p. 50.

26 Arnold Bennett, *Over There* (London, 1915), pp. 66, 190.

27 Cited in Roby, *A Writer at War*, p. 50.

28 Cited in *Arnold Bennett: The Critical Heritage*, ed. James Hepburn (London, 1981), p. 383.

29 *Ibid.*, pp. 375–6.

30 Robert Gittings, *The Older Hardy* (London, 1980), pp. 234–5.

31 *The Dynasts* was Hardy's epic verse-drama set a century earlier at the time of the Napoleonic Wars. It was widely admired, particularly by other writers, such as Siegfried Sassoon, who

read it while at the front.

32 Thomas Hardy to Sydney Cockerell, 28 Aug. 1914, *Collected Letters of Thomas Hardy,* vol. 5, ed. R.I. Purdy and M. Millgate (Oxford, 1985), p. 45.

33 *Ibid.,* T. Hardy to Percy Ames, 8 Feb. 1917, p. 202.

34 Ibid. T. Hardy to Florence Henniker, 4 March 1917, p. 204.

35 Ibid. T. Hardy to Sydney Cockerell, 15 Jan. 1917, p. 199.

36 John Masefield to 'Con.', 21 March 1915, *John Masefield's Letters from the Front,* ed. P. Vansittart (London, 1984), p. 71.

37 *John Masefield – Letters to Margaret Bridges,* ed. Donald Stanford (Manchester, 1984), p. 31.

38 *Masefield's Letters from the Front,* ed. Vansittart, 31 March 1917, p. 234.

39 John Galsworthy to André Chevrillon, 14 Oct. 1915, cited in H.V. Marrot, *Life and Letters of John Galsworthy* (London, 1935), p. 738.

40 J. Galsworthy, Diary, 3 and 4 Aug. 1914, cited in James Gindin, *John Galsworthy's Life and Art – An Alien's Fortress* (London, 1987), p. 342.

41 J. Galsworthy, 'First Thoughts on the War', in *A Sheaf* (London, 1916), pp. 186–7. According to his biographer, though Galsworthy's unofficial role as English spokesperson on the war in serious monthly American magazines was not one he sought, requests for comment from the United States fitted Galsworthy's self-imposed need to support relief funds and permitted him to retain a kind of calm distance from the emotions and horrors he felt. Encouraged by editors and correspondents, Galsworthy himself suggested to *Scribner's* his latest volume of collected war articles (*A Sheaf*), writing that, 'this is more or less the moment, seeing that the past is so past, and the future so blind'. Cited in Gindin, *Alien's Fortress,* p. 354. Galsworthy described his articles and essays as 'humanist writings' and his desire to publish them in order to secure funds for hospitals etc. was evidence of Galsworthy's 'wide, deep and sincere humanism'. Cited in Marrot, *Life and Letters of Galsworthy,* p. 460.

42 Dorothy Easton Ivens, letter, May 1974, cited in Gindin, *John Galsworthy,* p. 348.

43 J. Galsworthy to André Chevrillon, 14 Dec. 1914, in Marrot, *Life and Letters of Galsworthy,* p. 730.

44 J. Galsworthy, 'Second Thoughts on the War', in *A Sheaf,* pp. 227–8, 231–2.

45 J. Galsworthy, 'The Sacred Work', in *Another Sheaf* (London, 1919), p. 3.

46 J. Galsworthy to H.W. Massingham, 16 Sept. 1917, cited in Marrot, *Life and Letters of Galsworthy,* p. 771.

47 H.G. Wells, *The War and Socialism* (London, 1915), pp. 1, 3.

48 H.G. Wells, *Experiment in Autobiography* (2 vols, London, 1934), vol. 2, p. 671.

49 *Ibid.,* p. 666. Though the author of many propagandist bodies and articles (such as *When Blood is Their Argument: An Analysis of Prussian Culture*; London, 1915), Wells's Wellington House contemporary Ford Maddox Hueffer also expressed his (eventual) disillusionment with the war in his fiction – though in Hueffer's case, not until after the war. See his *Parade's End* tetralogy, the first volume of which *Some Do Not ...,* appeared in 1924.

50 H.G. Wells, *Mr Britling Sees It Through* (London, 1985), p. 422.

51 Wells, *Experiment,* vol. 2, p. 670.

52 D.H. Lawrence to Catherine Carswell, 9 July 1916, *The Collected Letters of D.H. Lawrence,* vol. 1, ed. Harry T. Moore (London, 1962), p. 459.

53 Ottoline Morrell, *Nation and Athenaeum,* vol. XLVI, no. 25, 22 March 1930, pp. 859–60.

54 *D.H. Lawrence: A Composite Biography – Volume One,* ed. Edward Nehls (Madison, Wisconsin, 1957), p. 315.

55 See *D.H. Lawrence – Letters to Bertrand Russell,* ed. Harry T. Moore (New York, 1948), p. 57. Russell's 'The Danger to Civilization' later appeared in his *Justice in War Time* (London, 1915).

56 D.H. Lawrence to Cynthia Asquith, 16 Aug. 1915, *Collected Letters of Lawrence,* vol. 1, p. 360.

57 Paul Delany, *D.H. Lawrence's Nightmare* (Hassocks, Sussex, 1979), pp. 123–4, 211.

58 D.H. Lawrence to Mary Cannan, 14 June 1918, *Collected Letters of Lawrence*, vol. 1, p. 558.

59 *Ibid.*, D.H. Lawrence to Harriet Monroe, 17 Nov. 1914, p. 295.

60 D.H. Lawrence to Amy Lowell, cited in Delany, *Lawrence's Nightmare*, p. 237.

61 D.H. Lawrence to Catherine Carswell, 9 July 1916, *Collected Letters of Lawrence*, vol. 1, p. 460.

62 *Ibid.*, D.H. Lawrence to Cynthia Asquith, 2 Nov. 1915, p. 375.

63 D.H. Lawrence to Cynthia Asquith, *The Letters of Lawrence*, ed. Aldous Huxley (London, 1932), p. 378.

64 D.H. Lawrence to Cynthia Asquith, 2 Nov. 1915, *Collected Letters of Lawrence*, vol. 1, p. 374.

5

Writers in uniform

In our search for reflections of aesthetic response to the Great War across barriers of experience, the soldier, poet and author Richard Aldington is a good
example of John Galsworthy's identification of the human spirit under the pressure of a seemingly mechanised military existence (the 'herd of life'). Aldington
also represents a further category of experience of the war; that of the recognised
writer, artist or poet on active service and Aldington here introduces a series of
creative men who actually donned uniform at some stage (not always willingly)
and fought at the front.

   Chapters 2–4 have examined the importance to some individuals, both male
and female, of experiencing the war at closer quarters in order to enable them
to grasp more accurately intimate knowledge of the conflict, unavailable from
second-hand sources (especially the jingoist elements of the British press); a
knowledge which could back-up their individual humanistic and aesthetic anti-
war emotions and, in some cases, be used to inform their art. The American
poet Harriet Monroe, reviewing Richard Aldington's poetry collection *Reverie*
in 1918 wrote that:

> The poet accepts war, as he might accept a cyclone, in anguish and bitterness of spirit
> but without revolt. He feels no élan, no conviction of war's necessity or righteous-
> ness, but he takes his place in the ranks and does his part with a grim and resolute
> stoicism. And out of his despair, out of his hunger for beauty, comes a lyric note
> clearer and richer than anything we have heard from him since those earliest poems,
> and an exaltation of spirit as noble and impassioned, and perhaps more humane.[1]

John Galsworthy wrote of the artist's attempts to whisper above the noise
and power of a hurricane, and Richard Aldington used a similar analogy in his
celebrated novel of the Great War, *Death of a Hero,* in which the character
George (a soldier) describes the war as, 'a sort of impersonal, natural calamity,
like a plague or an earthquake'.[2] Although *Death of a Hero* did not appear
until 1929, Aldington had entered the war with a literary background. By the
summer of 1914, he was a published poet and listed as an assistant editor of
The Egoist. His first volume of poetry, *Images*, was published in 1915 as he and
his wife, the poet Hilda Doolittle (H.D.), perhaps seeking to distance themselves from the effects of the war, moved from Kensington to the more rural

Hampstead. This move was followed by another in early 1916 to Devon following the stillbirth of their only child the previous year.

From the earliest months of the war, Aldington had felt almost personally threatened by the existence of the conflict. 'This war is killing us all', he wrote to fellow poet Amy Lowell in December 1914:

> the daily waiting, the anxiety, the constant strain is making us all old ... I cannot concentrate my mind for long enough on beautiful things to be able to write good poetry ... For this is the great war, the war of democracy against autocracy, of the individual against the state.[3]

Like Galsworthy and others, Aldington feared for his creative powers and felt, like Thomas Hardy, that for some, the war brought with it an ageing process of startling rapidity: 'We have become middle-aged before our time', Aldington would write to his wife during the final autumn of the war. He had resisted enlisting until May 1916, describing conscription as 'the Sword of Damocles' to his great friend Frank Flint, to whom he also addressed an unpublished poem which ended:

> Admire, ye faithless, with what speed
> These Christians carry out their creed,
> With what dexterity they shed
> The blood of the unrepented.
> Their love is such they needs must show it
> And make a conscript of a poet.[4]

Aldington and his friend Carl Fallas became infantry Privates in the Devonshire Regiment and underwent training at Wareham in Dorset. It was then that the contrast between Aldington's former literary life and his new military one struck home. In particular, the months immediately before his enlistment had been filled with literary promise combined with great personal freedom while writing and walking in the Devon countryside. The conflict made him feel isolated in his literary aspirations and appreciation of beauty from 'the great herd of men' as he described the war-mad world to H.D. (echoing Galsworthy's perception). The isolation of the training camp, situated on a coast that he described with a poet's eye as a 'grey, sickly peevish line' reinforced Aldington's own singularity, and he wasted no time in likening the 'wild desolate spot' to its earlier role as a prison camp while expressing sympathy with its former labouring convicts who had been forced to construct what were now the barracks out of large blocks of grey Portland stone.

In December 1916 Aldington was promoted to Lance Corporal and shipped overseas. He spent the first half of 1917 serving on the Lens–La Bassée front digging and repairing trenches whilst trying to adjust to army life. He admitted to his friend John Cournos that he was 'living spiritually on letters' and to Flint that 'I yearn for the dear musty smell of old vellum', while Flint's poems, included with his letters were like 'sprays of fresh lilac'. It was also to Flint that

Aldington expressed his view of soldiering, acquired through personal experience and explained to Flint as a warning. Aldington described how he 'exploded into hate' for certain individuals:

> ... those imbeciles who pretend that there is anything fine or ennobling or romantic in soldiering. It is simply dreary routine, dreary endurance, dreary 'heroism' of dying at the word of command! ... Somehow some of us will endure to the end, but what will it all be worth? Don't feel too many scruples at being out of it – you have a certain task ... to keep alive something of the gradually enfeebled tradition of beauty in life which we have received from other times.[5]

This view of the artist as torchbearer of the tradition of beauty was one that Aldington found was different now he was constrained by the actual harshness of military experience. He commented to Flint that he had written only twelve poems since entering the army – hence his bequeathing of the role to the (as yet) unfettered Flint. This awareness of a sense of ebbing beauty in time of war was echoed a few months later in a poem by the young writer Alec Waugh of the Inns of Court OTC and subsequently the Machine Gun Corps. Waugh was also undergoing training and his poem was entitled 'Harrowby Camp':

> It is not the dirt or the ugliness
> Nor the monotony of life,
> But its remembered beauty
> That tears the soul with a turning knife.[6]

Though Aldington came to value the comradeship of the fighting unit and appreciate the bravery of his fellow soldiers, he was constantly troubled by this sense of 'remembered beauty' and his inability to make full use of this beauty in his art and life, despite attempts such as his clinging to the job of assistant editor of *The Egoist* until June 1917. To Flint, Aldington tried to justify his place in the war effort:

> So many better men have perished in this foolish contest that I have no ... right to claim a hope for exemption for myself. I am not a suicide. I am a soldier ... It is not easy to die but one makes it easier by renouncing those things which have made life dear.[7]

Aldington seemed to recognise that it was only through trying to forget Waugh's 'remembered beauty' that one could exist from a position within the war with a clear conscience. Once that position was achieved, one could begin to focus on what one truly felt and wanted to express about the war.

By July 1918, Aldington felt he had found his voice and was writing to Flint on the subject of his new poetry that:

> I *have* spoken of the war more frankly than about any other Englishman – the result is that I could not get my poems published and am in the forefront of the battle. Do you think for an instant that if I had chosen to adopt the official point of view I could not have got a 'cushy job' ... like so many others; Say what you will, I have kept my integrity here and when you read 'Images of War' I think you will admit that I have by implication written a denunciation of the war.[8]

Aldington believed that anyone who read his volume of poems with careful attention would be able to discern 'the indignation, the pity, the anguish underneath' and he placed great faith in the total sincerity of his verse.

By this time Flint himself was in training for military service, having been called up in December 1917, a matter of days after Aldington received his commission. When Aldington learned that Flint was to enter the army he commented that, as a sensitive and quickly-wounded poet, Flint might in some way benefit from the depravities and melancholic aspects of the war in terms of artistic material, 'as they have benefitted me'. He warned that although it would seem as if Flint's friends from his former life had forgotten him, there existed a 'spiritual gain' to the suffering of army life within the 'hard relief' of the experience of war. Courage would be forthcoming, and Aldington counselled his friend to seize the opportunity 'in the gaps of liberty allowed you' and to 'grasp at life with a zest you never before had'.[9] This advice contained the truth of Aldington's own reaction to the army, but, in reality, one side of Aldington hoped Flint would avoid the entire experience and a few months later, in his letter just cited concerning his latest poems (*Images of War*), Aldington stated, 'I do hope you escape the army ... how on earth will you endure the stern, insulting discipline'.

The truth of Aldington's words lay in the 'hard relief' of experience of the war and the possible spiritual gain to the individual which lay therein. By retaining his 'integrity' in the army and an ability to 'grasp at life' in moments of relief, Aldington had found he was better able to communicate a message of truth from the 'cockpit of suffering', a phrase used by the writer John Cowper Powys to describe a war that he thought wicked and absurd. Yet, although Powys described his attitude to the war as 'natural' or as 'feminine ... and therefore singularly close to nature', he also believed that it was more noble to take part than to stand on the sidelines. Although the war was a 'fiery furnace', he made several attempts to join up (though he was almost forty and was rejected on medical grounds) because, as he later explained, 'Persons of spirit hurried to get as close to the flames as they could'.[10]

This attitude towards experience of the war was held by another medically unfit writer, John Middleton Murry who was called up in 1916, classed as unfit for active service (B2) and found himself working for the War Office. To him, the war was 'a pure nightmare, an interruption of some strange and inhuman order of existence'. During Aldington's 'gaps of liberty', when, as Murry later described, 'I was in some sense myself', Murry tried to ignore the war because, 'anything that I could call myself and the war could not co-exist in my consciousness'.[11] Like Aldington, Murry struggled to keep his integrity and was eventually able to turn 'the face of my consciousness towards the war' and achieve a 'true ecstasy'. He found then that, 'Insensibly, inevitably, every faculty of mine was now strained upon the war ... the thing engulfed me'. Also like Aldington, and to some extent Powys, he found a logic in the conviction that, 'one must face the war completely, in imagination and consciousness, to the end; that one must behold it until something happened to the sight, until one was blinded, or one saw'.[12]

Aldington himself – attempting to see – found (and admitted to his wife) that, 'my mind is fired with all this turmoil', though he feared, as he wrote in the same letter, that he would be creatively blinded; 'a kind of mental apathy has seized me and my brain refuses to work'.[13] Amid the 'general futility of things' Aldington's creativity was a dwindling commodity, and he was unsure as to which direction he should apply his remaining 'superfluous energies' – in the invention of stories and tales for his comrades or in poetry. Despite his advice to Flint, in the army he had found a lack of his precious 'gaps of liberty'. 'One must have time to live', he complained to H.D., 'All writing is distasteful if one is without leisure'.

As he entered the final year of the war, Aldington's hope was that though he had found himself emotionally and creatively handicapped by this 'abrupt withdrawal from the rapid current of my life into something alien and painful', he hoped that the experience would be a salutary one. The war and his military life represented a 'pause in my intellectual life', and he was unsure whether this would be the 'final pause' or simply a hiatus preceding 'intense creation'. After receiving his commission in late 1917 and further periods of training at Newhaven and Tunbridge Wells, Aldington returned to France in April 1918 and soon complained in letters to H.D. that he could find no purpose to life at the front, or indeed, life in general and was haunted by an intense loneliness tinged with horror and regret. His attempts to be witty and contemptuous of 'ordinary' people failed because he found himself 'choked and stifled' by thoughts of the dead and the misery of the living.

Though Aldington admitted that there still existed a few of his 'gaps of liberty', there was also 'constant wear' to the mind and body compounded by, similar to Waugh's 'remembered beauty', a recognition of 'having lost somehow the pearl and essence of life'. He described to his wife how he now had:

> a precise sensation that what [Robert] Browning would call the 'poetry of life' is over ... the flash has gone from the gun, the perfume from the flower, the ecstasy from music – I shall never live again in the old intense way, never be thrilled by beauty as before ... never live again.[14]

Aldington, in mourning for his old life, also recognised (and again made use of Browning as a reference) that he had been altered by the war:

> I have changed, through misery, through routine, through the strain of things. Perhaps I may get back my equilibrium, some sort of life, even write again but 'never glad confident morning again'. One acquiesces in the death of a flower but it is hard to admit that the flower of one's unique life dies as surely and nearly as quickly as the summer lilac.[15]

Aldington felt reduced to the level of 'little fruitless gesticulations of exist-ence' and only the letters of friends and the consolations of nature enabled him to appreciate what remained of aesthetic life. At rest and away from the line, he described how the sky ceased to be 'a sinister sneering sort of thing' and instead was transformed into part of the 'great plan' of the natural world, the alterna-tions of seedtime and harvest which embodied the 'spirit of the earth'. He wrote with delight to Flint of how, when lazing in some grass, he had communed with a fieldmouse and to his wife of how her letter allowed him to be part once more of 'that world of ideas which is my world'. He also confided to her, with a combination of relief and fear, that, 'I have found a little of my soul that was lost. Very likely I shall lose it again up in that damnable landscape of war, that wrecked earth which is a blasphemy, an insult to the gods.'[16]

Aldington's wife, being a poet herself, was able to empathise with her husband's artistic predicament. During the final months of the war H.D. de-scribed her husband as, 'a queer, tortured soul. He has a soul, that is why he suffered.'[17] Aldington was above all concerned with the preservation of his 'soul', his creative facility which was under threat from the hostile emotional and physical landscapes of the war and would be necessary if he were ever to write with clarity on the horror and sadness of his experiences. 'To live according to one's character', he wrote, 'to live against the world's way – isn't that to save one's soul?'[18]

Gerald Brenan was another fledgling writer in uniform who, like Aldington, felt his soul threatened by the strictures of war. Though his father had obtained a commission for him in the 5th Gloucesters, Brenan found the long evenings in the officers' mess to be destructive of his 'inner life' and hence rented a private sitting-room in which to read undisturbed. By his twenty-first birthday in April 1915 he was at the front, and he spent most of the remainder of that year as part of the Cyclist's Company digging trenches, usually at night, after which Brenan would often be found writing poetry or reading Flaubert until dawn. Although he repeatedly volunteered for one-man reconnaissance missions be-hind enemy lines and also for the Flying Corps, he was rejected each time and spent most of the rest of the war in observation posts, from which he was able to observe the clumsy terror of the Battle of the Somme and the mocking, fea-tureless plain near his next post on the left-hand side of the Ypres salient. To relieve the tedium he went for long walks and read voraciously: Tolstoy, Gib-bon, the Brontës and the Bible. Like Aldington's 'gaps of liberty', these were characterised as creative periods, when 'the fire' was 'alive'. At other times he worried over the fact that, 'I have ceased to be able to read poetry'.[19]

In March 1917 Brenan was moved to an observation post within two miles of Ypres itself in preparation for the summer offensive, and he found himself acting as a guide to senior staff officers due to his expert knowledge of the trench systems. However, he did not see action until June 1918, due to a shrap-nel injury sustained almost a year earlier which necessitated a lengthy period of convalescence. During his first action, Brenan was again wounded and then shipped back to Scotland to recover from Spanish flu after being awarded the MC and Croix de Guerre.

It is clear that, despite his misgivings about the war and military life, in common with Aldington and others, Brenan sought the experience: 'I could only burn up the impurities in my nature and become a real and authentic person if I sought them', he later wrote, 'Now in the middle of the war, a life in the infantry offered me much the same opportunities'.[20] He considered declaring his anti-war views and submitting to a court martial but opted like Aldington for the military experience and, like Aldington, suffered greatly from the isolation and boredom that those of an aesthetic outlook generally underwent. In common with Galsworthy, Aldington's character George (from *Death of a Hero*) and others, Brenan viewed the war metaphorically at times as a kind of upheaval or interruption of nature; a volcanic eruption in Brenan's case. At other times, when he saw the war as brought about and sustained solely by human intentions, it truly horrified him. Despite this, when he learnt that he was to be sent back to France after recovering from his shrapnel injury, he found himself pleased. This was due in part to his dislike of the 'hatred and hysteria' generated by the popular press and 'old men' at home but also because like many others he found himself drawn to the flames described by John Cowper Powys or, as Brenan called it, 'the Demon' – the spirit of the front line which seemed to offer the only *real* life to be had during that period. As he wrote in a letter of August 1918:

> The Infantry means almost everything that I most dislike and it represents, to my emotions at least, death. But at any rate one is in the full flood; all that there is of life in this generation is there – at the war or else in prison … this war is no interlude, it is a large part of one's life.[21]

Unlike Gerald Brenan, though they felt alike on war's negative aspects, the poet Max Plowman *did* (as we have seen in the Introduction) declare his anti-war position and suffer a court martial. Although Plowman enlisted with a view to becoming a member of the London Mounted Brigade of the Royal Field Ambulance (he ended up in the 4th Field Ambulance), he explained to his brother that he thought the war:

> a bloody mess and how anybody can *want* to be mixed up in it beats me. No man properly alive ever kills another whether by machinery or bayonet so that war demands the grossest and foulest insensitiveness on the part of all who have to do with it – it's an infernal soul-searching job and you're damnably well out of it.[22]

Once training had begun, Plowman found that everything was reduced to 'a matter of obedience and routine', and he came to perceive through his own experience how when an individual became part of the war effort, 'he forfeits his self-consciousness and becomes a tiny piece of machinery', and later, in his 1918 pamphlet, *The Right to Live*, Plowman would describe the war as the 'diabolical slavery of man by a vast inhuman machine'.[23]

This loss of self-consciousness led to Plowman becoming, as he put it, 'dulled to the value of life', both to life in general and his own personal interaction with normal existence – this to such an extent that he found he could suddenly, 'put my head into the cannon's mouth or make mincemeat out of a man in a different coloured uniform'.[24] Plowman struggled with the tension that existed between his dislike of the war and taking part in it and his recognition that it could be right to fight, 'until force is proved an idiocy'. To his friend, the author Hugh de Selincourt, he attempted to rationalise his position:

> Who am I that I should say to another man – You do my killing? I do not yield my principles one iota because I live in a world that does not acknowledge them and am compelled by circumstances to action I would not voluntarily undertake ... I know we have to make our individual consciences into National ones but everyday we suffer something which may remind us of the disparity between individual and communal conscience and we do it without much murmuring ... we don't make our individual conscience law by refusing to recognise our responsibility for and towards national conscience.[25]

Plowman felt that if he had 'preached peace and internationalism' in the period before the conflict this might have given him the moral authority to have declared himself a conscientious objector upon the outbreak of war. Now, however, he felt that he could not reject national responsibility in favour of that of a personal nature when he had taken previous advantage of the rewards of pre-war collective national responsibility ('when the system of things one has prospered under has led inevitably to war'). Experience of war was to enable him to make a choice between public and personal demands. Plowman felt that if it was not for his experience of the military side of the inferno, he would have no right to profess his anti-war views and would have little sympathy with the 'absolutist' conscientious objectors. 'And so I'm here', he wrote to de Selincourt in October 1916:

> in mud and blood and all the damned insanity of war and I wouldn't be out of it, things being as they are, for I can seen no alternative, things being as they were – I know that gradually the individual ideal must permeate the national, but till then how can I, after benefiting by all the nation's virtues, disclaim all personal responsibility for its sins? And what moment shall I choose to protest my individuality?[26]

Almost a year later, Plowman informed de Selincourt that he had begun experiencing what he called 'the pressure of life'. Although he felt that in the army (and thus in the war) the human spirit was confined to a position where it only 'conglomerates and coagulates', Plowman had become aware of and attracted to a latent internal creative force representing 'infinite beauty' which he felt was ever present and waiting only for recognition, 'to become fruitful in us of all we most desire'. The 'pressure of life' resulting from the war was now preventing Plowman and, he recognised, others of a similar nature from utilising this potential energy for creative or peaceful effect. He was in effect being drawn to a similar concept to that of Bertrand Russell and the ideas contained in

Russell's *Principles of Social Reconstruction* concerning the latent creativity within most human beings which could act as a deflection from the destructive impulses that led to war. It was time for Plowman to protest his individuality.

In January 1918 he wrote to the Adjutant of the 52nd Durham Light Infantry that, 'organised warfare of any kind is always organised murder',[27] and proffered his resignation from the army. He was at first arrested for refusing to obey an order and placed in near solitary confinement but his mind was made up; 'What I believe is most urgent now', he wrote to his sympathetic correspondent Janet Upcott, 'is that we should explore the recesses of individual consciousness to discover the ultimate basis of individual freedom' – this in order to find a 'new alchemy' for freedom on a national level. As he saw it, an individual's choice was now clear – to fight in the front line trenches or to fight against organisation for war. In order to fight against the war, one could obtain a 'harmless' war job and then, 'expend all your best energy in practical peace politics', or as Russell had suggested, 'the best work in the world – that artistic work which weans men's and women's minds and hearts and bodies from the perversion of war'.[28] This 'creative praise of life' was, in any case, for Plowman the only natural way of living. When it came to his own choice, Plowman felt that, as he had supported the war machine by fighting, his only option was just as obviously to fight against it by 'getting into prison for peace'.

Despite a trial and appeal, Plowman was sent a call-up notice at the start of July 1918 and became tangled in a web of bureaucracy between the two government departments of Registration and Appeals. He was in danger of being sent to prison as a deserter and not as a conscientious objector, which moved Plowman to comment on the grim irony of a situation which he felt was a, 'complete inversion of all natural order', and the organisation of which he felt to be 'literally anti-life'. Despite his ignominious position, Plowman clung to his belief that, 'participation in war is an individual matter, and the fact that a man is given an individual mind and an individual body and not a national mind and body is proof to my mind that he will be held responsible for the use or misuse he puts that mind or body to'.[29] In *War and the Creative Impulse*, the book he wrote on finally leaving the army, Plowman described the choice that the war had imposed; between the 'appeal of individual consciousness' and 'national consciousness which made the denial of individual consciousness the first duty'. The war was a 'vandal', deliberately slashing at the 'great canvas whereon the spirit of life has found expression', and, specifically citing Bertrand Russell's conceptual example, Plowman called for the reconstruction of society upon a creative basis in order to be able to call forth the 'final passions war now filches for destructive purposes'.[30]

For Plowman and others, the experience of being within the war machine acted both as a compass toward and a justification of his later anti-war stance. Two further examples of this process concerned possibly the most celebrated poets of the war – Siegfried Sassoon and Wilfred Owen. Sassoon has much in common with Plowman: both were rated good officers, both possessed an acute sympathy towards their men and both resigned their commissions as a protest against the war.

In December 1915 the country-loving Sassoon, newly arrived in France as an officer with the 1st Royal Welch Fusiliers,[31] wrote that his immediate experience was that of a 'waking dream' and that, 'my inner life is far more real than the hideous realism of this land of the war zone … I want a genuine taste of the horrors, and then – peace'. Like Plowman, he felt a sense of obligation on a wider level than that of individual motivation to take some part in the war; his military training had 'unsealed' his eyes and although he had been forced to make sacrifices, he felt that he had lived rather too well since his enlistment; 'now I ask that the price be required of me. I must pay my debt.'[32] Sassoon had initially enlisted as early as 3 August 1914 and some of his war poems from *The Old Huntsman* (1917) date from the period during his officer-training before he went to France in late 1915. In one of his earliest 'war poems', 'Absolution' – placed first in his *War Poems* – Sassoon touched upon a fundamental paradox of war;

> War is our scourge; yet war has made us wise,
> And, fighting for our freedom, we are free.[33]

Wilfred Owen on the other hand was more wary of the experience of war and it was not until 21 October 1915 (just as Sassoon was preparing for embarkation), that he visited the headquarters of the Artists' Rifles off London's Euston Road and allowed himself to be examined and passed fit for military service. As Sassoon was enlisting in August 1914, Owen had been staying at Bagnères-de-Bigorre in the Pyrenees and had actually returned to London as late as May 1915 and then gone back to France the following month, still unsure of his future. At one point he was taken up with the idea of joining the Italian cavalry, though this possible course of action was prevented by the fears of his mother. A further option, that of a sightseeing trip to the Near East, was prevented by the prolongation of the Dardanelles campaign. 'I don't want the bore of training', he wrote to his mother after his return to France in June 1915, 'I don't want to wear khaki; nor yet save my honour before inquisitive grand-children fifty years hence. But I do most intensely want to fight.'[34]

Although Owen felt almost a 'mania' to see the fighting, as he believed that the conflict would be 'the last War of the World', he was concurrently 'furious with chagrin to think that the Minds which were to have excelled the Civilisation of ten thousand years are being annihilated'. After observing the many wounded French and German soldiers who began to arrive in Bagnères, he began to conceive the notion that his individual poetic fight was worth protecting; 'my life is worth more than my death to Englishmen', he wrote, commenting that his motivation towards survival on a battlefield would be, 'the sense that I was perpetuating the language in which Keats … wrote'.[35] In this Owen was unconsciously echoing Richard Aldington's view of the soldier-artist having a duty to keep alive something of 'the gradually enfeebled tradition of beauty in life'. Touching upon the familiar theme of the need for greater experience of the conflict, Owen felt that he could not compare the life of the trenches to his own of creativity, 'unless I felt in a manner to have suffered my share of life',[36] and it was during this period, February and March 1915, that Owen was wavering over whether the experience of the war would inform or harm his creative existence. To him the 'fullest life liveable' was that of a poet; it was, 'the *one* title I prize, one clear call audible, one Sphere where I may influence for Truth, one workshop whence I may sound forth Beauty, one mode of living entirely congenial to me'.[37]

Sassoon also placed high value on his role as an artist (being a soldier-poet had 'complex advantages', he recalled in his memoir *Siegfried's Journey*); after less than a month in France in December 1915, he wrote in his diary, 'Wish the Kaiser would let me go back to my work at writing poems'. Although the military life was 'mechanical', Sassoon was able to draw inspiration and hope from his inner life; 'The Angel is still there, Poetry, with bright wings prepared for flights into the dawn'. He also drew strength from nature and the countryside, both remembered (from England) and actual (behind the lines in France). However, the desolation of the natural world at the front had the opposite effect. In Flanders, the sky, instead of being a reminder of the freedom contained within nature, was merely a 'death-haunted appendage' to a land altered by the conflict of human beings. Above the reflected battlefields the sky had lost its former, 'bird-held supremacy of whiteness and clarity'.

Sassoon's first taste of the front line was from March to April 1916, and he was determined to utilise the experience of a life he found 'audacious and invincible' (at least until it was, 'whirled away in enigmatic helplessness and ruin').[38] His aim was to collect 'as many sensations as possible'[39] in order to replace the lost 'music and graciousness of life' and fill up an existence of 'naked outlines and bare expanses, so empty of colour and fragrance'.[40] Nevertheless, he was greatly relieved to leave this period of 'mechanical and strained effort' at the end of April and to find the countryside behind the lines acknowledging the arrival of spring. After training at Flixécourt, Sassoon saw action at the front line in May and for his 'conscious gallantry during a raid on the enemy's trenches' he was awarded the MC the following month.

Despite periods of inner calm and a certain relish for the heightened emotions of battle, he still felt that there was 'no music; the quest for beauty [was] doomed', and he admitted to his diary in July that unless one attempted to place one's viewpoint from a position outside events, 'this life begets a life of mental stagnation ... I try to see everything with different eyes to my companions, but their unreasoning mechanical outlook is difficult to avoid'.[41] He was temporarily removed from his troubling surroundings, however, by an attack of trench fever which saw him awarded sick leave until December 1916.

Sassoon's period of leave marked a further shift in attitude towards the war and the necessities thereof. Whereas previously death in battle had possessed the possibility of attaining nobility, now, however, following the possibly delayed emotional impact of the deaths of Sassoon's brother Hamo on 1 November 1915 (of wounds incurred in the Dardenelles) and his beloved soldier friend David Thomas on 18 March 1916, as well as the start of his involvement with Lady Ottoline Morrell and the pacifists, the very thought of death was 'horrible' and his MC was merely an 'absurd decoration'. In his diary he quoted H.G. Wells's troubled Mr Britling – 'It is a war without a point, a war that has lost its soul' – and resolved to 'get a grip on the idea of life and describing it', while hoping (unlike during the previous year) that he would *not* meet his end in 1917 as 'there's such a lot to say'.

Sassoon was now almost ruthless in his desire to record the true bleakness of the war; 'there is little tenderness left in me', he wrote in February 1917, 'only bitter resentment and a morbid desire to measure the whole ignominy which men are brought to'. He recorded how the soldiers he observed made him feel that, 'there is no hope for the race of men'. Like Bertrand Russell, he saw the potential for good within individuals being smothered by the conflict; 'all that is wise and tender in them is hidden by the obsession of war'. The soldier, to Sassoon, was, 'no longer a noble figure; he is merely a writhing insect among this ghastly folly of destruction', and he feared that, 'the agony of armies will be on every breeze; their blood will stain the flowers', while, worst of all, 'the foulness of battle will cut off all kindliness from the hearts of men'. Sassoon noted how, as soon as men were relieved of responsibility via the army machine, they became 'bovine' and mere 'beasts of burden'.[42] Although he recognised that the soldiers he observed were, 'not their own masters in any way', he found himself 'drawn back into the Machine' as if the responsibility for his own life had been taken from him.

Enveloped by a mood of 'unreasoning acquiescence', Sassoon took part in the spring offensive of April 1917 (the Battle of Arras) and was wounded in the shoulder. He was invalided back to England, and his book of poems *The Old Huntsman* was published in May and reviewed appreciatively by Thomas Hardy, Arnold Bennett, Virginia Woolf and by H.W. Massingham in the *Nation*. The collection was also praised by Sassoon's friend and fellow 'C' Company officer Julian Dadd, who was recovering after having been shot in the throat. Dadd (to whom one of the poems in *The Old Huntsman* was dedicated and who had previously described his friend as 'an artist who really tries to see and write the truth') wrote to Sassoon declaring that the published poems were 'absolutely first rate' and adding that, 'I only hope the majority of people will similarly appreciate the greater truth of your point of view'.[43] It was during May 1917 that Sassoon decided to make his celebrated 'A Soldier's Declaration'. A diary entry from that month reveals that he now perceived his only option, other than a return to the 2nd Battalion and the front was, 'some protest against the war', and with the help of Bertrand Russell, the Declaration was drafted in June, sent to his Commanding Officer on 6th July, read out in the House of Commons on 30 July and published in *The Times* the following day.

During the drafting of the statement (as well as during the months previously), Sassoon had read Russell's *On Justice in War-Time* and entered into correspondence with its author. Sassoon wrote to the academic on 23 June, providing an insight into his view of the war and the motivations which had led to his decision to protest publicly:

> People say to me 'Nothing can stop the war till some glimmering of the truth dawns on the Prussian junkers' – They never ask themselves how long it would take 'the truth' to dawn on *them* if someone was going for them with a loaded stick. I suppose 'the truth' is the infallibility of the British point of view. Sometimes I feel that any appeal to the human element is hopeless – War seems to reduce all that to futility. Fifteen-inch shells are the only things that carry any conviction with them. And the soldiers are gulled into concealing their loathing of the war by the civilians who only half-disguise their own liking for it.[44]

In common with Max Plowman, Sassoon felt an obligation towards a wider sphere than his personal motivations. However, whereas in Sassoon's case it was his need to *proclaim* his case that led to his earlier and more public protest, with Plowman, it was the wider responsibility that held his personal feelings in check for so long until he could restrain them no longer. Commenting on the proposed Declaration, Middleton Murry had written to Ottoline Morrell in June counselling caution, stating that an act of insubordination or deliberate martyrdom made on the spur of the moment and without consultation, 'could make no substantial impression against the gigantic evil of the war'.[45] Though Lady Ottoline found the eventual Declaration to be 'extraordinarily good', others more eminent in the literary world were not so enthusiastic: Edward Marsh thought Sassoon to be 'intellectually wrong', Robbie Ross was 'appalled' (though this sprang from a concern for Sassoon's personal safety) and Arnold Bennett thought the intentions behind the Declaration 'misguided'. According to him, Sassoon should have come out against all wars or 'declared for anarchy', and Bennett accused him of 'spiritual pride' coupled with an indulgence in a right 'to which you are not entitled'.[46]

From others the response was more positive; in his post-war critique *Reputations*, Douglas Goldring pointed out that Sassoon's verses had, he thought, found especial favour with his fellow soldiers as well as with 'the more human and imaginative sections of the English public'.[47] Sassoon's friend and Quartermaster of the 1st Battalion, Joe Cottrell, wrote to him warmly, stating, 'I hope trouble doesn't strike you for sailing too near the wind – telling the truth' and followed this up with a further letter in which he declared that, 'I admire you for your standing out and for having the courage of your convictions … War is hideous and no one knows it more than you and I … One dare not *think* of this war – if so – we should go mad.'[48] Cottrill was unsure of the timing of Sassoon's

Declaration and feared that Sassoon would be court martialled. He had showed Sassoon's letter (presumably containing details of his protest) to two of his fellow soldiers and reported to Sassoon that, while not so sure of the 'opportuneness' of the action, 'they, like me, admire your motives'. In 1929, Sassoon received a letter from his friend Julian Dadd who recalled that summer of 1917 and how, 'We were badly worried at the idea that you were getting yourself into serious trouble with the army authorities in your anxiety to stop a needless war'. Dadd remembered that, 'It was a horrible time, but I do not think you have any cause to regret that. You had a bit of a Bertrand Russell in you as well as a V.C.'[49]

Sassoon had already been sent to Craiglockhart War Hospital by a medical board by the time his Declaration was read out to the Commons on 30 July.[50] A postcard from H.G. Wells in September counselled patience:

> Don't get locked up and out of the way. Then don't do anything exceptive. Do ostentatiously sober things. Take your discharge for 'shock'. Then let any action show that it was a mere excuse, that you are a grave and balanced man set upon the peace of the world. Don't develop into a 'case'. Treat all that happens to you as incidental to the effort of sane men to get this crazy world into a state of order again. Don't seem to become in any way a man with a grievance. If sensitive fine minds allow themselves to be tormented into mere shrieks of protest then the blockheads and blood dunkers will prevail for ever.

Wells concluded that Sassoon and himself were 'in the same line'.[51]

Sassoon decided that he wanted to be passed fit for general service in order to 'share the ills' of the individuals on whose behalf he had made his protest, and he felt that to remain under medical supervision or to be discharged as medically unfit for service would cripple the validity of both his anti-war stance and his resulting war poetry. Similarly, he rejected Ottoline Morrell's plan to 'make a commotion' after leaving Craiglockhart and being passed fit for service. The authorities, he felt, would merely label it a relapse in his condition and shut him away again, perhaps this time for the duration of the war.

Consequently, Sassoon rejoined the Royal Welch Fusiliers at Litherland in December 1917 and spent March and April in the Middle East with the 25th Battalion. Army life was now a mixture of 'crude circumstance' and an inner 'flame-like' spiritual experience. He had now, he thought, acquired a degree of self-realisation and found himself free to study other people and events shaped by the war with an intense scrutiny; 'equipped to interpret this strangest of all my adventures – ready to create brilliant pictures of sunlight and shadow'.[52] He now felt he was 'getting outside it all' (in contrast to his previous intense personal involvement whilst on active duty) and while he felt he was approaching the 'secret places of the heart' he also recognised its 'piteous limitations', concluding that, 'I recognise the futility of war more than ever, and, dimly I see the human weakness that makes it possible.'[53]

Sassoon also recognised the incompatibility between the life of the spirit and that of a life curtailed by martial rules. He had taken an enormous amount of literature with him to Palestine, including Keats, Wordsworth, Hardy, Browning, Trollope, Bunyan, Scott and Plato, and had taken up his reading once more, after a period of training, on his return to France; 'The result is that I immediately lose my grip on soldiering and begin to find everything intolerable except my interest in the humanity of the men. One cannot be a good soldier and a good poet at the same time.'[54] Sassoon's friend Julian Dadd had earlier commented on Sassoon's character – that he supposed it, 'not reasonable to expect anyone to combine the characteristics of a poet and champion bomber with the constitution and nervous system of a horse'.[55]

However, the soldier-poet chose to return to the 'soul-deadening' theatre of war – a war in which there was, 'no time for emotion, no place for beauty. Only grimness and cruelty and remorse.'[56] On his subsequent return to France with the 25th Royal Welch Fusiliers, Sassoon felt a desire 'to share its terrors' in order to 'learn yet more the meaning of it – and the effect'. At the same time, he felt it was 'inconceivable' that he was returning to assist in the destruction of human life. Sassoon reached the front line as 'acting' Captain of 'A' Company in July and almost immediately was again wounded (mistaken for a German and shot in the head by one of his own men) and shipped back to England where he would remain for the remainder of the war.

In the month before he was wounded for the final time, Sassoon's second volume of poetry, *Counter-Attack*, was published. It contained many of Sassoon's now celebrated poems describing in stark detail the war's harsh reality and was widely praised. Max Plowman in the *Labour Leader* declared that Sassoon had 'told the truth' about the war and even the normally jingoistic *Morning Post* described Sassoon as 'a poet of power and precision' who, having 'served gallantly' at the front had thus earned the right 'to enter a minority report'.[57]

On reading *Counter-Attack*, Sassoon's fellow soldier and hunting enthusiast, Geoffrey Harbord, of the Royal Field Artillery, wrote to him exclaiming, 'You poor devil. I never realised 'till I read them how much more some people feel the horrors and bloodiness of it all than I do.' For Harbord, some of the poems struck a raw nerve; '*Counter-Attack* is damn good', he admitted, but he added that, 'it conjures up the smell of dead and mud and that horrible pit of the stomach feeling too vividly'. However, this vividness was necessary for an audience that had not experienced the realities of trench warfare. 'I only hope', wrote Harbord, whose brother Gordon (a regular soldier in the Artillery since 1912 and Sassoon's long-term friend) had been killed the previous month, 'that the people at home get the same feelings out of the book that I do. It must bring it home to them more than anything else they have ever or will ever read.'[58]

It was Sassoon who had encouraged Wilfred Owen to increasingly include and describe the vivid realities of trench warfare in his poetry as part of a more complete and truthful emotional response to the war, a response that Sassoon felt and Owen recognised had perhaps been hitherto lacking. The two famously met at Craiglockhart in the summer of 1917, with Owen having arrived there about a month before Sassoon. The meeting would be a turning point in Owen's war, just as his first experience of the front had been in January of the same year (after fourteen months of training). That he described as 'seventh hell', having spent several hours in a water-filled dug-out. To Owen's poetic eye, No Man's Land had resembled a body 'pock-marked' with disease and even under snow it was like the face of the moon, 'chaotic, crater-ridden, uninhabitable ... the abode of madness'. Owen admitted that, although he could to some extent endure the cold, fatigue and 'face-to-face death', an extra node of suffering for him was 'the universal pervasion of ugliness ... everything unnatural, broken, blasted'.[59] Life at the front was, 'the eternal place of gnashing of teeth'.

Owen was given time to reflect of his first taste of the 'real' war as he spent two months out of the line in February and March 1917, due to his attendance of a course for transport officers and then due to injury, having fallen into a ruined cellar. During this period of reflection Owen, like Gerald Brenan, attempted to contain the suffering of the present within hopes for the future. While Brenan expressed a desire to live in a cottage in Spain,[60] Owen's cottage was to be in rural Kent or Sussex with an orchard with pigs to tend. Owen also commented to his sister that when he had looked into the future on his twenty-first birthday, he had not seen the war coming. 'But if I had', he added, 'I should certainly have borrowed sixpence and bundled over into Spain.' Owen confessed this in May 1917 after almost being buried alive during action with the 2nd Manchesters in the vicinity of Savy Wood during the previous month, an incident which, together with his other front-line experiences since January, caused Owen to suffer a return of psychological problems that had plagued him during 1912/13. He was observed behaving strangely, examined by a psychologist and sent to Craiglockhart.

It was during and after his treatment at Craiglockhart and the commencement of his friendship with Sassoon that Owen began to produce his most celebrated poetry of war. We read that Owen's meeting with Sassoon was regarded by Owen as quietly momentous ('At last ... an event worth a letter') and that simply reading Sassoon's poems sent Owen to a 'high pitch of emotion'. After getting to know Sassoon, Owen's assessment of his friend as 'simply honest about the war' bore out his original assessment of Sassoon's work, made during the period before they met, that, 'nothing like his trench-life sketches has even been written'.[61] Though Sassoon was the more experienced in terms of both military action and poetical expression, there were similarities in both that each responded to; Owen recognised that, 'we have followed parallel trenches all our lives'. Though Adrian Caesar in his *Taking it Like a Man* has written that, 'there were aspects of the war that both found exciting, stimulating and emotionally fulfilling ... this gave rise to massive guilt feelings', Caesar also comments that both were drawn to suffering and death in war in an attempt to assuage their additional guilt over their suppressed homoerotic feelings. However, to say that their protests against the conflict were also an attempt to assuage the overall guilt of attraction to war and made on behalf of 'inarticulate' comrades (and perhaps isolated fellow homosexuals) is to overstate the case. One could surely appreciate the comradeship and loyalties of war while being appalled by its effects.

Owen's time at Craiglockhart helped him to refine his anti-war stance in response to his initial but severe military experience and his desire to develop his poetical output in line with Sassoon's advice and his own growing awareness of what the war meant to him both as an individual and in terms of the future possibilities of mankind. Although he compared himself to a satellite spinning in orbit around the blazing nova of Sassoon himself, it was now time for Owen to 'swing out' and become his own 'dark star'. As he wrote to his mother, 'The tugs have left me; I feel the great swelling of the open sea taking my galleon.'[63] Both poets decided to return to the war.

After leaving Craiglockhart in October 1917, Owen was granted leave and then posted to Scarborough followed by Ripon, in March 1918. He was eventually passed fit for general service in June and returned to France in August. It was during the final period of his life, after his meeting with Sassoon at Craiglockhart and eventual return to service with a renewed confidence in his role as a communicator of the true nature of war and its effects on the men it touched, that Owen wrote the poems for which he is most celebrated, such as 'Dulce Et Decorum Est', 'Insensibility' and 'Strange Meeting'. He famously wrote to his mother on the last day of 1917 that he left that year as a poet, 'as which I did not enter it', and he described the particular 'incomprehensible look' of the men in France 'which as man will never see in England … it was more terrible than terror, for it was a blindfold look, and without expression, like a dead rabbit's. It will never be painted, and no actor will ever seize it', he continued, concluding that, 'And to describe it, I think I must go back and be with them.'[64] It was necessary to return to the heart of the war in order to convey its stark truths with dignity as well as revulsion, even if this meant being a part of the army machine once more, or as Owen described the transformation, becoming a 'cattle-driver', a 'Herdsman' and, worst of all, a 'Shepherd of sheep that do not know my voice'. For his part in the military action during the weeks before his death on 4th November, Owen, like Sassoon before him, was awarded the Military Cross. The fighting had been so intense that the experience of it had passed beyond Owen's sensibilities; as he reported to Sassoon, 'it passed the limits of my Abhorrence. I lost all my earthly faculties and fought like an angel.'[65]

Owen's reaction would have been recognised and appreciated by another famous poet of the Great War, Robert Graves (of the Royal Welch Fusiliers). Graves was adept at smothering over his oscillating private reactions to the war with the routine of military duty and expectation. While agreeing with the humanistic motivations behind Sassoon's Declaration – Sassoon was 'quite right in his views but absolutely wrong in his action', as he wrote to Edward Marsh[66] – Graves believed at the same time that it showed gross 'bad form' and disloyalty to fellow men in uniform, especially those in the Regiment. Graves (who in the same letter to Marsh described himself as a 'pacifist in thought' even though he viewed himself as a 'sound militarist' in deed) was swift to reassure Sassoon at Craiglockhart that, 'of course you're sane. The only trouble is you're too sane which is as great a crime as being dotty and much more difficult to deal with. That's the meaning of an anti-war complex. You see what other folk don't see about the rights and wrongs of the show', concluding that, 'Personally I think you see too much.'

Graves's concern was with the outward effect of an anti-war protest on the very individuals ('the Bobbies and Tommies and so on') that Sassoon was supposedly trying to influence. According to Graves and his belief in military form, these were the people who would be most affronted by any action similar to Sassoon's, which would be regarded as 'bad form'. This in Graves's eyes was 'the worst accusation' possible between friends and comrades-in-arms. The only way to command respect was to share the miseries of the war and, he told Sassoon, to 'finish your contract whatever it costs you' while denouncing the principles behind the conflict, though presumably in a more private way than a statement in the Commons and publication in *The Times*. Thus Sassoon would then be able to do more good both now (though in a subtler form) and after the war and although Graves acknowledged that his friend had 'done your bit', he added (with more than a hint of accusation) that he himself believed in 'giving everything'.[67]

Though both Sassoon and Graves (and Wilfred Owen) were in agreement by this stage on the need to return to the war, their motivations were different; Graves thought a return to the front was necessary because he believed in 'keeping to agreements' and 'biding my time' until such time as a 'sporting chance' occurred to alter the state of affairs. Sassoon, on the other hand, believed a return to the war necessary to validate the sentiments expressed in his Declaration and, in common with Owen, those appearing in his poetry of the war. It is notable that amongst the poems concerning the war within Graves's own *Fairies and Fusiliers*, which was published in December 1917, there is little protest against the conflict, only sentiments of regret and sadness at the loss of comrades coupled with a respect for the regiment and its traditions.

Ironically in view of his advice, Graves by this time (the late autumn of 1917) had become permanently unfit for service at the front having completed four consecutive tours of duty, during one of which he had been famously left for dead. He had become an instructor in an officer cadet Battalion based firstly at Wadham College, Oxford and then, after treatment for his nerves, at Rhyl with the 3rd Battalion. While Graves was getting married and preparing for a more domestic existence, Sassoon was training on a gas course in Ireland in anticipation of further active service in Palestine. Now Graves wrote to Sassoon that the contrast between them made him feel 'ashamed', though he admitted he was glad his friend was being sent to Palestine because there was less likelihood of Sassoon being fatally injured. Graves had decided that to finish one's 'contract' whatever the cost was no longer as desirable as previously; 'I'm most awfully keen on your living', he admitted to Sassoon, in order that his fellow poet, with rested nerves, would be able to produce 'miraculous poetry'.[68] Graves's concept of a poet, as he outlined it to his fellow poet in uniform Robert Nichols, was one who appreciated both the refinements of life (through the splendours of Nature and close friendships) together with its harshness and hence the process of being a poet was comparable to a woman suffering the hardships of a man and thus 'hardening her weak softnesses'.[69]

In his loyalty to his regiment, desire for the experience of combat, horror of 'bad form' and general restless enthusiasm, Graves could be seen to be attempting to harden his 'weak softnesses', and in a letter to his literary mentor Edward Marsh of February 1916, Graves had acknowledged a 'hardening and coarsening and loss of music' within his verse which he readily attributed to 'la guerre'. In reality, Graves, though always by his own admission a 'sound militarist in action', possessed underlying pacifist notions ('a pacifist in thought') coupled to a realistic view of the hatreds that fanned the flames of the conflict. He agreed with Sassoon's Declaration in that he also thought 'our people' should state definite peace terms to bring a swifter end to the misery and, on a more personal level, he was not above praising some of Sassoon's most anti-war poems, such as 'To Any Dead Officer', for which he suggested amendments in June 1917 (the summer of the Declaration), some of which Sassoon had adopted by the time of its appearance in *Counter-Attack* the following year. 'In theory the War ought to stop tomorrow if not sooner', Graves declared to Edward Marsh, 'Actually we'll have to go on while a rat or a dog remains to be enlisted.'[70] Graves was trapped by his own character within the army machine. He had earlier written to Marsh and admitted that, 'I have to live up to my part here as I have learned to worship my Regiment: in sheer self-defence I had to find something to idealise.'[71]

Graves's external need to idealise was born of his inner desperation. His worship of his regiment began to wane after experience of the Somme. The focus of idealisation then perhaps shifted to the military bravery of his (internally anti-war) fellow soldier-poets, who in their military experience exemplified Graves's external regard for honouring 'the contract' while publicly or privately they might express the anti-war views that Graves carried within him and with which he felt a need to empathise. Sassoon, with his bravery both on the battlefield and the moral front, became an object of private idealisation (as he did with Owen), despite Graves's public disapproval of the Declaration.

I send you here my two latest poems, which I have managed to write, though in utmost distress of mind, or perhaps because of it. Believe me, the army is the most detestable invention on this earth and nobody but a private in the army knows what it is to be a slave.[72]

So wrote Isaac Rosenberg in March 1916 while training with the 11th King's Own Royal Lancasters at Aldershot. He came from a background far removed from that of most of the other 'War Poets' – that of the Jewish East End of London – and despite enlisting voluntarily, declared to Edward Marsh that, 'I never joined the army from patriotic reasons', concluding, 'Nothing can justify war'. However, in common with Owen, Sassoon and others discussed in this chapter, Rosenberg recognised the need for direct experience of the war to be able to produce the poetry that could convey its truth to others not involved in the fighting, and inspire the sympathy of recognition in those that did participate at the front line. Hence his acknowledgement that his latest poems were perhaps due to the 'distress of mind' produced by his circumstances.

In common with Wilfred Owen, Rosenberg had been abroad during the first few months of the conflict and, like Owen, had taken his time in deciding to join up. Both Owen and Rosenberg valued their roles as artists extremely highly and were unsure at first of the effect of war experience on their artistic ability. Rosenberg, who painted as well as wrote, observed from Cape Town how Europe had stepped into its 'bath of blood' and imagined himself waiting until the war was over, 'with beautiful drying towels of painted canvas and precious ointments to smear and heal the soul; and lovely music and poems'.[73] He also felt that the world had been 'terribly damaged' in that poets and artists were being sacrificed in 'this stupid business' and felt keenly, as he had told Marsh, 'the immorality of joining up with no patriotic convictions'. However, in October 1915 and under financial pressure ('There is certainly a temptation to join when you are making no money', he had told Ezra Pound), Rosenberg enlisted at Whitehall, 'though it is against all my principles of justice', as he described to Sydney Schiff, his artistic patron.[74] He therefore requested service with the Medical Corps but was rejected due to his height and accepted instead into a 'Bantam' battalion, part of the new 40th Division in which the regulation height had been reduced. To Rosenberg, enlisting was 'the most criminal thing a man can do',[75] and he soon suffered under the harsh reality of life at the Bury St Edmunds Depot. When offered a promotion to Lance Corporal[76] he declined and by June 1916 he found himself in France.

Gerald Brenan wrote that while his poetry and reading ability were adversely affected by the war, he also felt a 'desire to suffer', recognising that the experience could be ultimately beneficial in understanding the conflict and his part in it.[77] Similarly, Rosenberg explained to fellow poet Lawrence Binyon that despite his being (like Brenan), 'cramped intellectually' by the war, he was determined that it:

... with all its powers of devastation, shall not master my poeting; that is, if I am lucky enough to come through all right. I will not leave a corner of my consciousness covered up, but saturate myself with the strange and extraordinary new conditions of this life, and it will all refine itself into poetry later on.[78]

However, Rosenberg's death on 1 April 1918 in the German attack on the British 3rd and 5th Armies near the centre of the Western Front put paid to any chance of future artistic refinement, and the final few months of Rosenberg's life had witnessed his artistic hopes declining: 'there is no chance whatever for exclusion or any hope of writing poetry now', he wrote in February 1918. 'Sometimes I give way and am appalled at the devastation this life seems to have made in my nature', he admitted, 'It seems to have blunted me'. He added in a later letter that, 'we will become like mummies – look warm and life-like, but a touch and we crumble to pieces', an apposite metaphor for the perceived sapping of creative capacity.[79] This was a remarkably similar reaction to that of another soldier-poet, Edmund Blunden, who in June 1917 at Ypres described the war as, 'a sort of slow poison ... that keeps on drugging and deadening my mind', adding that he loathed war and the army life. He had found that, 'literature languishes as a whole in the battalion ... some of us are mummies, only we still carry on the motion of breathing, swathed round with red-tape and monotony'.[80]

From the first, Blunden had been 'not anxious to go', as he recalled at the very start of his memoir *Undertones of War* which, like his poetry, is filled with pastoral images warped by the malign pressure of the war upon the landscape. Like Sassoon, Blunden had been brought up in the rural tranquillity of Kent and shared his passion for the countryside and the natural world. The devastation of France, therefore, made a great impression on him which reflected itself in his later poetry and recollections, in particular Blunden's realisation of the reality of what the war meant and its overshadowing of all else. Rosenberg felt he had been 'blunted' by the war; Blunden, a young countryman experiencing modern war, found his 'sensibility blurred' by the 'general grossness' of the front and the landscape so deadened that to even speak would be 'an act of creation'.[81]

Despite his revulsion of war, Blunden's attitude could be said to resemble that of Graves more than most other major poets of the conflict. Blunden enlisted in 1914 (though did not enter the army until the summer of 1915 due to his Oxford scholarship) and though, unlike Graves, he was more prolific in his poetic output with three volumes published by 1916 (the year he went to France), he kept the realities of soldiering and the writing of poetry as separate as possible. His biographer described him as 'a pastoral poet in a war setting',[82] while Blunden referred to himself in *Undertones of War* as a 'harmless young shepherd in a soldier's coat'. In the midst of intense and bloody activity on the Somme and at Thiepval Wood in 1916, which would result in Blunden being awarded the Military Cross for his reconnaissance missions, he was congratulated

by his colonel on a positive review given to a volume of Blunden's poems reviewed in the *Times Literary Supplement* – a volume which, significantly, was
entitled *Pastorals*. Blunden eventually spent two years in the firing line, more
than Rosenberg, Sassoon (whose poems he discovered in the *Cambridge Magazine*) and even Graves.

Although Blunden, as he wrote privately in 1917, 'loathed' the war and the
military machine, he fought his way through it and, like Graves, only really
found himself able to publicly express his deeper feelings in the years following
the conflict. Hence he was only later able to equate the 'ghostly gallows-trees'
of Thiepval Wood with the 'ruins of the world ... black and unalterable' in
Undertones of War, which was first published in 1928. It is also significant that
he entitled a selection of his *Poems 1914–30* (which appeared in 1930) as,
'War: Impacts and Delayed Action'. The passage of time enabled Blunden to
question publicly the meaning of the war and, in the light of his own long
experience of the front line, he was able to ask:

> Is it nearer the soul of war to adjust armies in coloured inks on vast maps at Montreaul
> or Whitehall, to hear of or to project colossal shocks in a sort of mathematical
> symbol, than to rub knees with some poor jaw-dropped resting sentry, under the
> dripping rubber sheet, balanced on the greasy fire-step, a fragment of some rural
> newspaper of Mr [Horatio] Bottomley's oracle beside him?[83]

It was time for Blunden to point out, as he did in his introduction to a 1930
Anthology of War Poems, that the world in which figures such as Sassoon,
Owen, Graves and himself had come to 'maturity of thought' had been a world
which for that crucial period of time had, 'rolled the individuals into one red
burial'.[84] It was now time for him to question even his own experience, as he
did when he wrote of the aftermath of the fighting in late 1916 around Thiepval
Wood and the Schwaben Redoubt for *The Listener* in 1929:

> After this winter battle we left the Somme – but who were we? Not those who had
> marched South in the time of ripening orchards; a very different body of men. We
> had been passed through the furnace and the quicksand ... There is no escape from
> the answer given on 1st July to the question of the human race.[85]

During September 1914, D.H. Lawrence, critically perceptive as always, had
written to his friend, barrister Gordon Campbell, of his disappointment in watching the majority of mankind make war on itself. They – his fellow human beings – were 'vulgar fools' who could always be expected to make a noise, 'because
they are afraid of the silence'. Lawrence stated that those who deliberately
made war deserved their fate; however, he also admitted himself to be very
concerned for, 'those who, being sensitive, will receive such a blow from the
ghastliness and mechanical, dissolute, hideous stupidity of war that they will be
crippled beings'.[86] Lawrence was here, perhaps unknowingly, describing himself and his own reaction to the war, but there were others, as we have seen, of

the type he feared for. The soldier-poet Ivor Gurney is perhaps a supreme example of a sensitive individual transformed into a 'crippled being' by his experience of the conflict. In particular, Gurney's musical background (at the Royal College of Music, under composers Hubert Parry and Charles Standford) little prepared him for the bleakness of war.

The summer of 1914 had found the naturally solitary Gurney walking the countryside of his native Gloucestershire. However, he initially found the prospect of immersing himself in the war to be of possible artistic value, and he volunteered for active service as soon as conflict was declared, but was rejected due to his defective eyesight. However, a second attempt to enlist in February 1915 was successful, and he was drafted into the 2nd/5th Gloucesters. After training at Park House Camp on Salisbury Plain, he was sent to France in May 1916 from where he wrote to his friend Marion Scott that, 'it would be hard indeed to be deprived of all this artist's material now'.[87] However, in the same letter he quoted Shakespeare's Sonnet 129: 'The expense of spirit is a waste of shame/Is lust in action ...' and described how time out of the company had allowed him to breathe 'the air of freedom almost forgotten'. For one such as himself ('who so much desires freedom') – he recognised that it was painful to dwell too much on the conditions of life at the front and even his initial enthusiasm had been tempered by an inner doubt as to the war's effect on himself. During the period prior to the start of the war Gurney had experienced a stronger need for self-expression and had been made 'cold' with thoughts of the possibility of 'leaving all I have to say unsaid'.[88] His hope now was to somehow utilise any 'artist's material' available to him at the front.

As he tried to overcome the 'thought-vacuum' of military life, Gurney took comfort in the 'store of poetry and accumulation of pictures' within himself and wrote to his friend, the musician Herbert Howells, that, 'You can imagine, too, what the hope of being able to praise England and make things to honour her is in me, as in yourself', though he also confessed, 'You can imagine too what a conflict there is between that idea and warfare.'[89] He also admitted to Howells that the most disturbing thought was all his 'continual striving' and endeavours to become 'a fit and full man' could be ended in an instant by a German bullet. He described himself as 'Hamlet in khaki' – as one who was unfit for army life; 'a being cut off from Civilisation by the fixed gulfs of Militarism'. As the date for his embarkation for France drew nearer, he felt as if he had condemned himself to a kind of 'practical blindness and deafness' which was particularly galling to himself as an artist possibly about to face either death or, 'that which might be so fruitful to him'.

Once in France in June 1916, the full horror of the war displayed itself to Gurney, a man yearning only for the chance for artistic expression. He immediately wrote home that the life was, 'an awful life for an artist',[90] and that he felt that the only chance for him to be a good soldier was if he could forget music and books as, 'a sense of beauty is every hindrance to a soldier'.[91] As the autumn of that year gave way to winter and Gurney's regiment went southwards to Albert in order to join the final days of General Haig's Somme offensive, he was still desperately hoping that his experience would be of some use to him from an artistic point of view, and he attempted to rationalise that it was:

> better to live a grey life in mud and danger, so long as one uses it ... as a means to an end. Someday all this experience may be crystallised and glorified in me; and men shall learn by chance fragments in a string quartet or a symphony, what thoughts haunted the minds of men who watched the darkness grimly in desolate places.[92]

However, the pain of existence in the front line (where Gurney found himself in December 1916) was so great for him that he admitted to Marion Scott that, 'for myself it sometimes comes that death would be preferable to such a life'.[93]

During the harsh winter of early 1917 and a corresponding month's training at Gapennes, Gurney recognised that he had made a conscious decision to be a musician and artist rather than a soldier and hence 'I suffer in proportion to my sensibility'. Despite this, he felt that he could not fully understand the war from a position that was 'right out of it'. His role as a soldier gave him 'a right to talk and walk with braver men than myself and an insight into thousands of characters and a greater Power over Life, and more Love'.[94] As the Germans withdrew to the Hindenburg Line during the spring of 1917, the Gloucesters followed them, and Gurney was wounded on Good Friday and sent to hospital in Rouen. From his hospital bed, Gurney, like Wilfred Owen and Gerald Brenan, expressed a desire for a simpler, peaceful life wherein he could return to being the creative artist he once was; 'Oh for a garden to dig in, and music and books in a house of one's own, set in a little valley from whose ridges one may see Malverns and the Welsh hills, the plain of the Severn and the Severn Sea; to know oneself free there from the drill-sergeant and the pack and to order one's life years ahead'.[95]

In the midst of the war, and, as we have seen, in common with others, Gurney felt his artistic awareness to be waning. He described how he had reached a state where he knew from an objective point of view how good a Shakespeare sonnet was but was unable to 'wrap myself up in it' nor 'dwell on the lines to taste their sweetness'. His soul was now, as he described it, 'sick with disgust', and Marion Scott's letters (as Frank Flint's letters and poems had been 'sprays of fresh lilac' to Richard Aldington), were like 'promises of blue' to Gurney, who longed for peace and beauty of the remembered countryside of home. Life itself, without his music, books and friends, lacked the 'vital impulse and natural joy' of his former existence.

By this time (the summer of 1917), Gurney was fighting in the Third Battle of Ypres and in September was gassed at St Julien and sent back to England. He admitted that his experience of the war had created 'a great gap in my mind' which he should now fill up with 'sunsets, trees, winds, stars and children's faces', all of which he found to be, 'blossoming fairer after so long a drought'. To musician Herbert Howells, he described himself on his return from France as 'frosted up' and after a few days rest he felt 'the beginning of the thaw, the first hint of what joy music might give'.[96] Gurney's first volume of poetry, *Severn and Somme*, was published during this period, in October 1917 (to be followed by *War's Embers* in 1919).

Despite the beginning of a possible 'thaw' within himself, Gurney spent the following few months in and out of hospital, a period which culminated in a breakdown, following further training, in March 1918. He spent the remainder of the war in hospital, coming close to suicide at times. Eventually he was sent home to Gloucester in October 1918 and although he returned to London in an attempt to resurrect his musical compositional training (this time with Vaughan Williams as his tutor), it proved too much for him and by 1922 he was declared insane and committed to the City of London Mental Hospital where he lived until his death in 1937. Ironically, he had in a sense predicted this, when in September 1917 on his return from France he wrote that, 'War brings greater self-control – or breakdown. You must also have mastery of yourself, or perish.'[97]

The ordeal of Ivor Gurney exemplifies the reaction to the war of celebrated writers who donned uniform at some stage during the conflict and thus were presented with direct experience of the war. We have seen in the cases of Sassoon, Owen and Gurney in particular, though opposed in practical or aesthetic terms to the war, the conflict could act as a magnet to some individuals, exerting an initial creative pull on their imaginations. As a poet, Sassoon hoped to collect 'as many sensations as possible' when on active service,[98] while Owen felt that his creative potential would not be fulfilled unless, as he put it, he had, 'suffered my share of life', and Gurney felt a need to utilise all the 'artist's materials' on offer in order to make his voice heard.

Harriet Monroe, reviewing the war poems of Richard Aldington, described the artist's view of the war as that of an individual to a cyclone: with anguish but also stoicism in the face of inevitability. Out of the artist's 'hunger for beauty' and despair, hoped Monroe, a clear 'lyric note' might emerge. The experience of the artist or poet at the front could be crucial if the individual was to find this true voice in regard to the conflict – Sassoon's desire to collect sensations was transformed into 'a morbid desire to measure the whole ignominy which men are brought to', and Owen, though he admitted that the war had made him a poet, was appalled at the prospect of having to return to the front – a place 'of the gnashing of teeth' and only returned after his time at Craiglockhart in order to describe the 'blindfold look' of his fellow men – the level to which humanity had been degraded.

Ultimately, as in the case of Ivor Gurney, the war could impose a gradual stifling of creativity upon artistic individuals – an effect which was more severe if those individuals actually fought and observed the war's effects close up. Gerald Brenan found that not only was he unable to be continually creative at the front, he was less able to absorb the fruits of artistic endeavour – in his case he found himself at times unable to read poetry. This chapter examines how individuals with creative potential resented and felt trapped and then coarsened by the unthinking organisational apparatus of a military existence. Max Plowman recognised that an individual, once part of the war effort, forfeited his selfconscience and became 'a tiny piece of machinery'. Isaac Rosenberg felt he had been 'blunted' by his experience of the war, and Edmund Blunden found his 'sensibility blurred' by his long period of service at the front. We have seen these concerns shared by writers and artists who did not fight – the concern of Bloomsbury for the civilised values of art and culture mirrors Owen and Rosenberg's chagrin over the potential annihilation of the creative minds who were to have carried forward the 'Civilisation of ten thousand years', for example. It is easier, however, to hold these articulate thoughts up to the light of re-examination, as they are so well-expressed and the products of minds that have made their influence felt (whether intentionally or not) through the succeeding generations. But what of the similar thoughts and feelings of those whose shadows across history are perhaps paler and not as lengthy?

Notes

1 Harriet Moore in *Poetry*, vol. 12, no. 1, April 1918, cited in *Richard Aldington and H.D. – The Early Years in Letters*, ed. C. Zilboorg (Bloomington, IN, 1992), p.75.

2 Richard Aldington, *Death of a Hero*, Authorised unexpurgated edition, limited edition of 300 copies (2 vols, Paris, 1930), vol. 2, p. 38.

3 Richard Aldington to Amy Lowell, 7 Dec. 1914, *Aldington, Early Years*, pp. 20–1.

4 University of Victoria, British Columbia, Canada. Doyle Collection (UV,DC hereafter). Photocopies of correspondence between Richard Aldington and F.S. Flint (originals held at Henry Ransom Humanities Research Centre, University of Texas at Austin). Aldington to Flint, 12 June 1916.

5 UV,DC, R. Aldington to Frank Flint, undated (Nov./Dec. 1916).

6 Alec Waugh, *Resentment* (London, 1917), p. 44.

7 UV,DC, R. Aldington to F. Flint, undated (Autumn, 1916).

8 *Ibid.*, 7 July 1918.

9 *Ibid.*, 28 Dec. 1917.

10 John Cowper Powys, *Autobiography* (London 1934), p. 583.

11 John Middleton Murry, *Between Two Worlds* (London 1935), p. 338.

12 *Ibid.*, pp. 432–3.

13 R. Aldington to H.D., 23 July 1918, *Aldington, Early Years*, p. 112.

14 *Ibid.*, 8 Sept. 1918.

15 *Ibid.*, 1 June 1918. The quote is from Robert Browning's 'The Lost Leader' (1845).

16 *Ibid.*, 16 July 1916, p. 108.

17 Cited in Charles Doyle, *Richard Aldington – A Biography* (London, 1989), p. 64.

18 R. Aldington to H.D., 24 July 1918, *Aldington, Early Years*, p. 113.

19 Cited in J. Gathorne Hardy, *The Interior Castle* (London, 1992), p. 117.

20 *Ibid.*, cited p. 127.

21 Gerald Brenan to Hope, 18 Aug. 1918 in Brenan, *A Life of One's Own*, (London, 1975), p. 235.

22 Max Plowman to his brother, 3 Jan. 1915, *Bridge into the Future: The Letters of Max Plowman*, ed. D.L. Plowman (London, 1944) p. 29.

23 Max Plowman, *The Right to Live* (London, 1918), p. 10. Plowman was also the author of a celebrated memoir, *A Subaltern on the Somme*, originally published under the pseudonym

'Mark VII', (London, 1927).

24 *Bridge into the Future*, ed. Plowman, M. Plowman to Janet Upcott, 29 Jan. 1915, p. 32.

25 *Ibid.*, M. Plowman to Hugh de Selincourt, undated, pp. 36–7.

26 *Ibid.*, M. Plowman to Hugh de Selincourt, 18 Oct. 1916, p. 57.

27 *Ibid.*, M. Plowman to Adjunct, 14 Jan. 1918, p. 92.

28 *Ibid.*, Plowman to Janet Upcott, 28 Feb. 1918, pp. 105–6.

29 *Ibid.*, M. Plowman to Adelaide Hunt, 16 April 1918, p. 117.

30 Max Plowman, *War and the Creative Impulse* (London 1919), pp. 18, 32, 120.

31 Sassoon originally volunteered as a trooper for the 1st Sussex Yeomanry on 3 August 1914 but later transferred to the Royal Welch Fusiliers and commenced officer-training.

32 Sassoon, 3 Dec. 1915, *Siegfried Sassoon – Diaries 1915–1918*, ed. Rupert Hart-Davis (London, 1983), p. 22.

33 Siegfried Sassoon, *War Poems* (London, 1983), p. 15.

34 Wilfred Owen to Susan Owen, June 1915, *The Collected Letters of Wilfred Owen*, ed. Harold Owen and John Bell, (Oxford 1967), pp. 340–1.

35 *Ibid.*, W. Owen to S. Owen, 2 Dec. 1914.

36 *Ibid.*, W. Owen to S. Owen, 6 Feb. 1914.

37 *Ibid.*, W. Owen to S. Owen, 5 March 1915, p. 326.

38 *Sassoon Diaries*, ed. Hart-Davis, 30 March 1916, p. 47.

39 *Ibid.*, 31 March 1916, p. 51.

40 *Ibid.*, 14 April 1916, p. 55.

41 *Sassoon Diaries*, ed. Hart-Davis, 13 July 1916, p. 92.

42 *Ibid.*, 22 Feb. 1917 and 15 Feb. 1917, pp. 132, 133.

43 Imperial War Museum (IWM hereafter), Sassoon correspondence, P. 444, (Con. shelf), Julian Dadd to S. Sassoon, 12 May 1917.

44 The same letter contained a re-worded section of the proposed Declaration for Russell's inspection as well as Sassoon's earlier version on the same sheet, with a question mark next to it, which had been corrected by Russell and returned. Both versions contained the proposition that if the purposes of entering the war had been clearly stated at the outset, it would have been impossible to alter them without the knowledge of the soldiers. The original draft then stated that if this was the case, 'the war would now be at an end', while the new version, following Russell's amendments, read, 'had this been done, the objects which actuated us would now be attainable by negotiation'.McM,BRP, Sassoon to Russell, 710.055469, 23 June 1917 (and containing 710.055479).

   Sassoon's letters during these crucial weeks also reveal that there existed at one stage a plan to publish the Declaration as a leaflet. They also exhibit Sassoon's opinion towards the reactions of his superiors, once he had sent the Declaration to his Commanding Officer. 'They [his military superiors] are evidently "keeping me in suspense" in the hope that I may become amenable to a chance of backing out', he informed Russell. However, despite a lack of immediate action and an apparent tolerance and 'amiability' from his superiors, Sassoon revealed to Russell that he had informed them that his protest, 'had gone beyond their control or mine', adding that, 'I don't think they understand in the least what it's all about'. By the start of July, Sassoon had overstayed his period of leave by a week and he sent Russell the telegram from 'the Adjt. 3rd Royal Welch' ordering him to 'Join Litherland immediately', with Sassoon himself commenting to Russell, 'we must get the statement published as soon as possible, and all will be over bar the shouting'. *Ibid.*, Sassoon to Russell, 710.055474 and 710.055475, July 1917.

45 McM,BRP Ottoline Morrell to B. Russell, 710.082632, 11 June 1917. Murry's letter was included with Lady Ottoline's to Russell.

46 See *Sassoon Diaries*, ed. Hart-Davis, pp. 179–81.

47 Douglas Goldring, *Reputations* (London, 1920), p. 108.

48 IWM, Sassoon correspondence, P. 444, (Con. shelf), Joe Cottrill to S. Sassoon, 29 July 1917

and 11 July 1917.

49 *Ibid.*, J. Dadd to S. Sassoon, 1 Dec. 1929.

50 Sassoon's account of his time at Craiglockhart, and his relationship with his largely sympathetic doctor, W.H.R. Rivers, can be found in the initial section of his fictionalised memoir *Sherston's Progress*, which itself forms the concluding part of *The Complete Memoirs of George Sherston* (London, 1937). Craiglockhart becomes Slateford War Hospital. Sassoon's meeting and subsequent friendship with Wilfred Owen is covered in Chapter 6 of the 'factual' *Siegfried's Journey* (London, 1946).

51 McMaster University, Hamilton, Ontario, Canada, William Ready Division of Archives and Research Collection, H.G. Wells Archive, Wells to Sassoon, postcard (Sept. 1917).

52 *Sassoon Diaries*, ed. Hart-Davis, 14 Feb. 1918, pp. 212–13.

53 *Ibid.*, 17 April 1918 and 23 April 1918, pp. 235, 238.

54 *Ibid.*, 15 June 1918, p. 271.

55 IWM, Sassoon correspondence, P. 444, (Con. shelf), J. Dadd to S. Sassoon, 29 March 1917.

56 *Sassoon Diaries*, ed. Hart-Davis, 15 June 1918, p. 271.

57 *The Morning Post*, 2 Aug. 1915, cited in Jean Moorcroft Wilson, *Siegfried Sassoon – The Making of a War Poet: A Biography (1886–1918)* (London, 1998), p. 496. A notably bad review was, surprisingly, that of John Middleton Murry in the *Nation*, though Murry's main criticism was that it was the war and the state of the world thereof that had caused Sassoon to react in the way he had (as an 'instrument of discord … so jangling').

58 IWM, Sassoon correspondence, P. 444, (Con. Shelf), Geoffrey Harbord (14th Division, Mesopotamia Expeditionary Force) to S. Sassoon, 9 Sept. 1918.

59 W. Owen to S. Owen, 4 Feb. 1917, *Collected Letters of Owen*, ed. Owen and Bell, p. 431.

60 *Ibid.*, W. Owen to Mary Owen, 25 May 1917, p. 464.

61 *Ibid.*, W. Owen to S. Owen, 12 Sep. 1917, *Collected Letters of Owen*, ed. Owen and Bell, pp. 493–4.

62 Adrian Caesar, *Taking it Like a Man: Suffering, Sexuality and the War Poets* (Manchester, 1993), p. 151.

63 W. Owen to S. Owen, 31 Dec. 1917, *Collected Letters of Owen*, ed. Owen and Bell, p. 521.

64 *Ibid.*

65 Ibid., W. Owen to S. Sassoon, 1 Sept. 1918, p. 580.

66 Robert Graves to Edward Marsh, 12 July 1917, *In Broken Images – Selected Letters of Robert Graves*, ed. Paul O'Prey (London, 1982), p. 77.

67 *Ibid.*, R. Graves to S. Sassoon, 27 Oct. 1917, p. 85.

68 *Ibid.*, R. Graves to S. Sassoon, 6 Feb. 1918, p. 92.

69 *Ibid.*, R. Graves to Robert Nichols, 2 Feb. 1917, p. 65.

70 *Ibid.*, R. Graves to E. Marsh, 12 July 1917, p. 77.

71 *Ibid.*, R. Graves to E. Marsh, 9 Feb. 1916, p. 39. Graves had a great admiration for the soldier-poet Charles Hamilton Sorley, having been impressed by the deceased Sorley's *Marlborough and Other Poems* ('so entirely after my own heart in his loves and hates'). Both were the same age and had attended Oxford University (Graves at St John's College; Sorley at University College). Sorley had been killed near Loos in October 1915 whilst serving as a temporary Captain in the 7th Suffolks. Although he had enlisted, Sorley had found the military life one of 'routinal coma' and he complained of, 'a large amount of organized disorderliness, killing the spirit. A vagueness and dullness everywhere'. His fear was that he would become 'non-individual and British'. See Jean Moorcroft Wilson, *Charles Hamilton Sorley* (London, 1985), p. 191.

72 Isaac Rosenberg to Lascelles Abercrombie, 11 March 1916, *Isaac Rosenberg – Collected Works and Letters*, ed. Ian Parsons (London, 1984), p. 231.

73 *Ibid.*, I. Rosenberg to E. Marsh, (Oct.Nov. 1914), p. 206.

74 *Ibid.*, I. Rosenberg to Sydney Schiff, 8 June 1915, p. 216.

75 *Ibid.*, I. Rosenberg to Sydney Schiff, 8 June, 1915, p. 216.

76 See Joseph Cohen, *Journey to the Trenches – The Life of Isaac Rosenberg* (London, 1975), p. 130.

77 Gathorne-Hardy, *Interior Castle*, p. 117.

78 I. Rosenberg to L. Binyon, (autumn 1916), *Rosenberg – Collected Works*, ed. Parsons, pp. 248–9.

79 *Ibid.*, I. Rosenberg to Miss Seaton, 14 Feb. 1918 and 8 March 1918, pp. 268, 270.

80 Edmund Blunden, 22 June 1917 cited in Barry Webb, *Edmund Blunden – A Biography* (London, 1990), p. 73.

81 E. Blunden, *Undertones of War*, (Oxford, 1956), pp. 270, 202. Blunden's memoir was first published in 1928.

   In his poem 'Zero', Blunden finds that the beauty of the dawn in the trenches brings no consolation; 'What is the artist's joy to me?' the narrator asks, when, 'Here limps poor Jock with a gash in the poll/His red blood now is the blood I see'. Edmund Blunden, 'Zero', cited in John Silkin, *Out of Battle: The Poetry of the Great War* (London, 1987), p. 109. Originally in Blunden's *Poems 1914–30* (London, 1930) from the section entitled 'War: Impacts and Delayed Actions'.

82 Webb, *Blunden*, p. 50.

83 Blunden, *Undertones*, p. 230. Horatio Bottomley was a notoriously jingoistic writer, journalist and self-publicist.

84 E. Blunden, Introduction to *Anthology of War Poems*, ed. Frederick Brereton (London, 1930), p. 23.

85 E. Blunden, 'The Somme Still Flows', *The Listener*, 10 July 1929 and reprinted 18 Jan. 1979, p. 100.

86 D.H. Lawrence to Gordon Campbell, 21 Sept. 1914, *The Collected Letters of D.H. Lawrence*, vol. 1, ed. Harry T. Moore (London, 1962), pp. 290–1.

87 Ivor Gurney to Marion Scott, 7 June 1916, *The Collected Letters of Ivor Gurney*, ed. R.K.R. Thornton (Manchester, 1991), p. 87.

88 I. Gurney to M. Scott, 16 June 1914, cited in Michael Hurd, *The Ordeal of Ivor Gurney* (Oxford, 1978), p. 54.

89 I. Gurney to Herbert Howells (Oct. 1915), *Collected Letters of Gurney*, vol. 1, ed. Thornton, p. 52.

90 *Ibid.*, I. Gurney to Mrs Voynich (June 1916), p. 90.

91 *Ibid.*, I. Gurney to M. Scott, 21 June 1916, p. 102.

92 *Ibid.*, I. Gurney to M. Scott, 9 Dec. 1916, p. 171.

93 I. Gurney to M. Scott, 7 Dec. 1916, cited in Hurd, *Ordeal of Ivor Gurney*, p. 86.

94 *Ibid.*, I. Gurney to M. Scott, 18 Jan. 1917, p. 191.

95 *Ibid.*, I. Gurney to M. Scott, 11 May 1917, p. 78.

96 *Ibid.*, Gurney to Herbert Howells, 2 Oct. 1917, p. 111.

97 I. Gurney to M. Scott, 26 Sept. 1917, *Collected Letters of Gurney*, vol. 1, ed. Thornton, p. 332.

98 Sassoon hoped this 'for the sake of poetry and poets whom I represent'. Sassoon, 31 March 1916, *Sassoon Diaries*, ed. Hart-Davis, p. 51. The assimilation of sensations could be an aesthetic activity in itself – see Paul Levy, *The Case of Walter Pater* (London, 1978) and David Newsome, *The Victorian World Picture* (London, 1997) which both discuss Victorian cultural aestheticism.

6

Women and the war

The Great War, most people would have agreed at the time, was a *male* creation. Politicians, statesmen and kings bred it and soldiers fought and fed it. Thus far, this study has regarded those women within Bloomsbury whose aesthetic reactions to the conflict provide such a good starting point when examining the war in this context. What of other women, existing independently from that hot-house of creativity, but who felt similarly? Due to their status in society as a whole, women necessarily operated within a different cultural milieu to that of men – even when sharing an enlightened, liberal background with them, as within Bloomsbury and its circle. But women emerged from a range of backgrounds and contexts – including that of political agitation linked to specific political aims – whose motivation towards protest, when confronted by the specifics of war, became more individualistic in character and less a part of an organised 'movement' or liable to be led by the propaganda of the war-state.

Many women in the period leading up to the outbreak of the conflict could lay claim to a history of opposition; during the pre-war period one of the principal focal points of public dissent against the existing political structure had been the women's suffrage movement. This cause, by the nature of its specific political goals, had also been largely political in organisation, character and aspiration, though precepts of greater equality for women outside the political sphere – once they had achieved the vote – were meshed to hopes for the ultimate cultural emancipation of the female sex. It is interesting, then, to observe and comment upon the course taken by this swelling tide of political protest as it crashed violently against the rock of war; namely, that though the strength of dissent was dissipated to some extent, it by no means ran dry. Indeed, a modern commentator has stated that, 'Half the leading women in the British suffrage movement opposed the war'.[1]

Some women were able to formulate their opposition to the conflict on a personal level – over and above the political framework of women's suffrage – through direct experience of nursing or simple observance from the Home Front as the casualties mounted. This 'truth' of the conflict led some women to question their position; not in their decision, in some cases, to nurse, but in stark terms of human suffering. The creation of maimed bodies and minds on an unprecedented scale began to be perceived as wrong – for whatever cause or nationality. Boundaries dissolved – those between nations as well as those that lay between propaganda and truth. The gilt was off war, as a friend of one of the women in this section, Mabel Dearmer, commented to her. Some women were intellectually opposed to the war and expressed their opinions – at no less strength – from a distance in their private conversations and writings. This form of expression of female opposition became the norm, as women found that other accessible outlets for protest were few and far between. Hence in the diaries, letters, memoirs and occasional fictions of some women we are able to observe their turning away from the general call to arms and mobilisation of opinion.

In the evening of 4 August 1914, during the final hours of peace (11 p.m. marked midnight in Berlin and hence a formal commencement of hostilities), a meeting was held at Kingway Hall in London in order to discuss the position of women and the women's movement in regard to the rapidly approaching conflict. This meeting marked a confluence of some of the various leading women's organisations of the day such as the Women's Co-operative Guild, the Women's Freedom League, the Women's Labour League, the National Federation of Women Workers and the sponsor of the meeting, the large National Union of Women's Suffrage Societies, which alone was able to declare one hundred thousand affiliated suffragists, six hundred societies and eight hundred pre-war new members a month. The various groups in attendance were not only British; representatives of the International Women's Suffrage Alliance from nations as far as Finland and Russia were present. The sister of General Sir John French, Charlotte Despard, was also present, although those twentieth-century symbols of suffrage – the Pankhursts and their Women's Social and Political Union were not. This could be seen as paradoxical given the militant nature of the Pankhursts and the relative non-militancy of the National Union of Women's Suffrage Societies. However, other groups such as the Women's Co-operative Guild possessed a history of opposition to war.

A few days after that Kingway Hall meeting, Christabel Pankhurst described the war as a 'horrible calamity' in *The Suffragette* and, more crucially in terms of this study, had already condemned the conflict as a 'mechanical and soulless massacre' in an earlier issue. To her, the war was a by-product of a civilisation that had been dangerously tilted by the weight of men's opinions and actions. In spite of these public declarations, Christabel Pankhurst soon joined her family and the other leaders of the Women's Social and Political Union in their support for the war which, it was decided, could take the form of a 'national militancy', though not all agreed: Emmeline Pankhurst was forced to denounce her daughters Sylvia and Adela for their public pacifism.

The Kingway Hall meeting of 4 August urged immediate mediation from non-belligerents in order to put the brakes on a situation which, it was felt, could soon escalate out of control. The meeting also resolved to call on women's organisations to 'offer their services' to the country at a time of national crisis, though precisely what form this offer of service was to take was unclear. These resolutions were taken immediately to Downing Street. Though there were some calls for strikes and stoppages, most of the women present at the meeting felt a need at this point, either collectively within their organisations or individually, to contribute something to their nation at war and for most this feeling, albeit temporarily, transcended the effort to obtain the vote. This feeling was echoed by women who had been agitating for suffrage in the country at large. Millicent Fawcett, the leader of the National Union of Women's Suffrage Societies, recognised this and later described the day as being one of the most miserable of her life, as she observed at a single stroke the cause of women's suffrage being postponed for an indefinite period. However, despite the electoral position of women remaining weak, in a parallel context, women could be said to have been in a stronger position in that they had had no voting power in the period leading up to the war and hence could not be held responsible for the international build-up of tension that had finally erupted in the summer of 1914. It was recognised by some that the world of hostility and tension had been created by men and this in turn could provide women with a somewhat greater moral freedom as to their personal reaction with regard to the war.

As observed in Chapter 2, freedom from conventional morality was one of the pillars supporting the philosophy of life that bound the individuals constituting the Bloomsbury Group together, both male and female. This freedom from convention served to fuel their responses to the war, as we have seen not only in the cases of the men such as J.M. Keynes and Duncan Grant – it was equally true of the daughters of Sir Leslie Stephen; Virginia Woolf and Vanessa Bell. But what of other women?

It is clear that women experienced a diversion of their political aspirations and energies regarding suffrage into anti-war thoughts and activities. What of women who simply desired to be involved in the war to a greater extent and whose subsequent experience facilitated a (sometimes unexpected) humanistic response to the shattered bodies and loss of life that they observed at close quarters? Although many women responded to their country's call by replacing men in the munitions factories, this response also sprang from a motivation to take advantage of the higher wages on offer in industry of national importance. Grief and strain marked the war experience of countless women; the uncertainty of the survival of a husband, wage-earner, father, brother or son darkened the wartime existence of many and while this may not have resulted in militant anti-war protest, a shared sense of bereavement over many months of unresolved conflict resulted in a simple wish, shared by many at the front, that the war be ended as soon as possible, whether by victory or negotiation. As Sylvia Pankhurst points out in her *The Home Front*, anti-war feeling and emotions were not limited to the arguing intellectuals, but were also to be found 'most firmly rooted' among those attempting to live normal lives in the small villages and towns of rural areas, where most cottages and homes contained photographs, many black-bordered, of soldier husbands and sons.[2] Though not a pacifist himself, the author Wilfrid Ewart commented that for the women of England:

> Death after all became a commonplace thing ... the ethics of sorrow changed, many people following simply instinct rather than the dictates of convention or of principle ... still the dominating note was tragedy. And if the war showed human nature at its least, it brought out, too, astonishing heights of faith, strength and courage in women as it did of 'heroism' in men. The divine humane spark burnt bright in each case.[3]

One in whom the 'humane spark' which, when translated into action, burned particularly bright (and mentioned by Anne Wiltsher in her '*Most Dangerous Women*' and Jo Vellacot in 'Feminist Consciousness and the First World War')[4] was Catherine Marshall who, until 1915, was both the Parliamentary Secretary of the National Union of Women's Suffrage Societies and in control of one of the most active sections of the NUWSS, the Election Fighting Fund. She had spent most of the previous decade mustering support for women's suffrage and, as Jo Vellacot points out, like many other women campaigners, Marshall's ideals of suffrage sprang from a background of liberalism; she had absorbed J.S. Mill's *Liberalism*, for example, and in her case – as in that of others – suffrage (and, later, her pacifism) could be seen as a 'component' of her personal liberal ideals.

After the Women's International Congress of the Hague in April 1915 caused a split to occur in the NUWSS over education for Peace and support for that meeting, Marshall helped to found the British section of the Women's International League for Peace and Freedom, which had emerged from the meeting and which was, according to Vellacot, the most solid achievement of the feminist pacifists to emerge from the war. With the newly emergent freedom of choice of action available to the pre-war suffragists, Marshall then narrowed her work to suit her own goals, as much as Charlotte Despard did by moving from the Presidency of the Women's Freedom League at the start of the war to touring the country in support of a federated Europe by 1918 for the Women's Peace Crusade. Marshall worked for the National Council Against Conscription and also, by March 1916, for the No Conscription Fellowship. Within a matter of days of starting her work for the NCF, she had written on a daily basis (and with eventual success) to a holidaying Bertrand Russell appealing for his help. She also attended the National Convention of the NCF at Devonshire House. Marshall became one of the linchpins of that organisation, especially after many of the leading male activists began to be imprisoned after their individual tribunals.

Another in whom the 'humane spark' manifested itself in practical action (and who worked with Catherine Marshall for the NCF in London during the summer of 1916) was Helen Bowen Wedgwood, who later, as Mrs H. Pease, was to donate to the Imperial War Museum a substantial archive of letters to her from the many imprisoned conscientious objectors she assisted.[5] She was the eldest of seven children and, like Frances Partridge, attended Newnham College, Cambridge. While there, she had been secretary of the Cambridge Fabian Society but had found the Fabians 'too slow' and had subsequently helped to form the University Socialist Society, though, as she later admitted, 'at no time was I a socialist in the accepted sense of the word'.[6] She found moral sustenance for her pacifism in her contacts with the Quakers (though never a Quaker herself) since she found their direct and clear-cut philosophy an immense relief amid the 'endless discussions' of the political pacifists. Wedgwood found it hard to always be seen as part of a minority and constantly questioned on the justification of one's position regarding the war at every meeting and dinner party.

Also in common with Frances Partridge, Wedgwood had been brought up in a family that believed strongly in the strength of the position of an individual and in his or her chosen course of action, without interference from others. Hence her preference for action over argument and her lack of encouragement of others *not* to volunteer while the voluntary system lasted. While at Newnham, she was impressed by the positions of academics such as Goldsworthy Lowes Dickinson on the war and their courage in facing the animosity of colleagues such as the 'last ditch dons' – academics who joined up only at the last minute and then for home defence only. When talk of conscription began to circulate, Wedgwood attended the first meeting of the Cambridge branch of the NCF and became its shadow secretary when the acting secretary was arrested. This activity was set against a background of personal tragedy when her cousin Cecil was killed on the Somme in 1915. She had little patience with those of supposed stature in the peace movement, such as politicians Snowden and Lansbury, both of whom she thought 'woolly-headed' (though genuine and kind). In her opinion, Bertrand Russell offered no help to the rank and file, and this coloured her view of other 'pacifist dons', some of whom she suspected of concealing jobs in the War Office. Suspicion was rife in a university town which, although devoid of the vast majority of its male students, was as much gripped by 'war fever' as anywhere else. For example, Wedgwood recalled a period when Catherine Marshall organised a watch on a railway station in order to make sure no conscientious objectors were taken abroad by the authorities surreptitiously. In addition, rumours abounded of a 'retired colonel' who supposedly invited to tea undergraduates suspected of being anti-war. An opportunity was thus engineered, it was said, for their rooms to be searched for incriminating material.

At the outbreak of war, Wedgwood's father, Josiah, had been Liberal MP for Newcastle under Lyme and had persuaded Winston Churchill to place him in the Armoured Cars, Royal Naval Division while his eldest son Charles, though only sixteen, was allowed to enlist in the 5th North Staffords (and later in the Armoured Cars, again through the influence of his father). After he was wounded in 1915, Wedgwood's father was forced to confine himself to parliamentary activities and a job at the War Office, courtesy of Churchill. While he supported conscription, he also supported the individual's right to choose the path of the conscientious objector. He soon became disillusioned with the War Office, however, describing the bureaucrats as 'vultures' waiting to see what they could get out of the country in terms of statistics and quantities. He then became a Lieutenant-Colonel in the Army and went to East Africa in early 1916.

It had been while her father was serving in Gallipoli that Wedgwood had met Clifford Allen for the first time, at a Fabian conference at Keswick and, by the time her father left the country for the second time, Wedgwood was much more involved with the NCF (she attended a conference in London in spring 1916). She had reached, through her own efforts and observations, a new stage in the development of her personal pacifism; she now described herself as a 'Tolstoyan pacifist', and by this time the strength of her anti-war stance and activities was largely recognised by her own family. This was demonstrated when one of her uncles, despite being a Major in the North Staffords, prevented his mother (Wedgwood's grandmother, who disapproved of her help for conscientious objectors) from stopping her allowance. The money, or lack of it, was not to be used to attempt to coerce Wedgwood away from the dictates of her individual conscience regarding the war and her place in relation to it.

It was at this point, in 1916, that Wedgwood's anti-war feeling took flight. She attended many tribunals and noted the names of individuals mentioned, to use as possible future contacts. The energy and enthusiasm involved in her anti-war activities resulted in her leaving Cambridge with a second class degree. This, however, had little effect on her practical work, and she moved back home to the Potteries to join the Stoke branch of the NCF with her sister, Rosamund. She spent much of her time keeping track of the latest arrests and courts martial and visiting those held in local guardrooms with letters from wives and mothers concealed in various guises – perhaps a devotional work of some kind (usually a prayer book) or in a letter purporting to come from a pious aunt. Wedgwood found that, on the whole, the soldiers she encountered at the guardrooms tended to be friendly and sometimes displayed a tacit appreciation of the plight of the conscientious objectors. She commented on the soldiers that, 'they had a sort of vague feeling that ... they all felt caught up in the machine ... which they were all helpless to escape'. She also noted a general respect amongst the objectors for those in the trenches and an awareness that however bad the treatment meted out in the prisons and guardrooms, it was as nothing compared to the hell of the front. The death of some of her friends and relatives in action, especially that of her cousin, convinced her more firmly of the rightness of her humanistic awareness of the tragic waste of the situation and of her practical response to her feelings; to her, the only logical course of action for those of an anti-war disposition was either to refuse to fight or to help those who made the refusal.

In the autumn of 1916, Wedgwood started to work on behalf of the Women's Trade Unions in factories in the East End of London, though this proved too much for her (she felt unsuited to Trade Union work in particular) and returned to the Potteries. The following year saw her return to the capital, where she helped to found the 17 Club in Gerrard Street in the wake of the tide of hope for peace and a new world order that followed the Russian Revolution. However, with its unruly mixture of revolutionaries, anarchists and pacifists, she felt the club to be badly organised, and she returned to the Midlands in order to help her recently widowed Aunt Kat (whose husband had been killed at the front on Hill 60) and her three children. She re-established links with the Birmingham Quakers and tried her hand at market gardening, forestry and digging potatoes while passing on reports for the NCF, although most of the COs were now in prison or had accepted 'alternative' work (most of the North Staffordshire branch took this course).[8]

When her brother Charles, who had joined the Royal Flying Corps, was shot down over Germany and reported as missing and believed killed in the early autumn of 1918, Wedgwood's health broke down completely, and she went to housekeep for the daughter of her cousin who had been killed on the Somme. Despite her precarious health, she still managed to speak at open-air meetings on the situation in Russia and attend meetings of the local Women's Co-operative Guild. The end of the war was marked for her by the sound of the church clock striking again and by the news that her brother was alive and a prisoner in Germany. Typically, peace brought no rest; after continuing to agitate for the release of the remaining imprisoned COs (including George Horwell and his brother) and for an assurance from the authorities of no permanent conscription, she set to work once more, campaigning for better housing for the poor.

The women peace campaigners of the Great War who possessed a previous history of personal activism through the struggle for suffrage, were naturally at their most vocal and public (whether vilified or, in rare cases, supported by the press) from the very outbreak of hostilities onwards, as they reacted to the latest harsh treatment of individual conscientious objectors and internationally mounting casualty figures. This was in general contrast to the anti-war sentiments expressed by a proportion of women who expressed their opinions on the war, often formulated by first-hand observation as writers, diarists or reporters, or who volunteered to nurse the wounded and dying troops in the various theatres of war or at home. The thoughts and feelings of those women who chose to express them were most often recorded in book form and published in the second half of the war or in the months and years following the Armistice. The majority of women who had trained as nurses had done so in innocence, out of a sense of duty to their country and a desire to be of use – to grasp a long-denied chance for action and experience in the world of men, a world, as it turned out, now unfamiliar even to the men who engineered and dominated it. It was not then surprising that some women were horrified at what they found to exist hidden beneath the rhetoric of newspapers and politicians and were forced to confront their sometimes ill-founded initial motivations for becoming involved in the war at the closest quarters. Some women, however, seemingly needed no public re-examination or questioning of their initial patriotic or idealist motivations, despite perhaps observing hospitals filled with casualties shattered in mind and body.

One such – at least on the surface – was Sarah Macnaughton, who travelled to Antwerp in September 1914 to work in a hospital and who used her subsequent experiences to answer some of the 'women's questions' raised by the war in the final chapter of her book, *A Woman's Diary of the War*, entitled 'From a Kitchen Window'. Was the transformation of a child into mere 'labelled humanity', to then be passed around on a succession of bloodstained stretchers, 'worth the victory'?, Macnaughton asked. Since women had no voice in the making of the war, a woman sitting by a sick-bed 'when the candles are burning low' would be bound to seek some explanation for the 'horrible idiocy' of the situation and, while recognising that the war had to be fought, wonder why it was that men and nations of reason could not settle their differences in a sober manner. In common with other female commentators and observers, Macnaughton stated that since women produced life from their very bodies, 'the whole idea of the value of life is inherent in them'. Hence the war and its careless destruction of life would be viewed frequently by women as illogical; since women had been told repeatedly that the war was one of steel, powerful engines, oil and petrol (all of them previously associated with men and male occupations) then why was it not possible to remove the human element altogether from the equation of conflict?

Macnaughton then proceeded to reply to her own (and all women's) questions by declaring that the 'pious horror' towards war exhibited by women was 'inadmissible' because the concept of honour was a thing of more intrinsic value than life itself, while the reality of war did not lay solely in the resultant suffering. For example, war could mean greater freedom and opportunity for women within society alongside being a struggle for the same concept on an international scale. Besides, the war had shown an emotionally frustrated Great Britain ('we had far too much energy and not enough to do') what was worthwhile and what was not. Belgium had undergone a 'tremendous re-birth' through its experience of suffering while France had learned a 'noble seriousness'. The British dead and the women who mourned them could be assured of the rightness of the cause and the certainty of a joyful reunion: 'We think that when the last roll is called we shall find them still cheery, still unwavering ... and still – who knows! on active service'.[9]

This was the publicly expressed opinion of Macnaughton (and what she knew her domestic audience expected to read) in a text replete with the initial high emotion of the first few months of the war and thoughts of consolation as the war settled into its unexpectedly lengthy course. However, the private

Macnaughton expressed markedly different thoughts which were later revealed in her diaries, published in 1919. Such was the difference in tone that Macnaughton's niece (and editor of the diaries) warned that regular readers of her aunt's books would find her latest volume a 'slight surprise' due to an unfamiliar tone that ran throughout the new volume: 'a note of depression and sadness, and perhaps even of criticism'.[10]

From the time that she arrived in Antwerp to do hospital work in September 1914, Macnaughton had found herself surrounded by pain and suffering on an unprecedented scale and unable to console herself with thoughts of 'the Flag' or religion, in an atmosphere 'of bandages and blood'. As time elapsed and she saw more of the war's effects via her work with Dr Hector Martin's Flying Ambulance Corps near Dunkirk and St Malo, she found that her previously firm views on soldiering and warfare were now wavering. 'All my previous ideas of men marching to war have had a touch of heroism, crudely expressed by quick-step and smart uniform', she wrote after a visit to the shattered town of Furnes, 'Today I see tired dusty men, very hungry looking and unshaved, slogging along, silent and tired ... God, what is heroism: It baffles me.'[11] Macnaughton was particularly affected by Furnes, thinking it a tragic place filled with ghosts which seemed to stifle her thoughts to such an extent that she found writing in her notebook an impossibility and was forced to return to the hospital, 'where at least I was with human beings and not ghosts'.

At La Panne in February 1915 she remarked on the 'peculiar brutality' that existed and animated everything within sound of the constant guns. 'Nothing seems to correspond', she wrote in her diary:

> Are men really talking and dying in agonies quite close to us ... It is one of the singular things about the war, because one always hears it said that it is deepening people's characters, purifying them, and so on. As far as my experience goes, it has shown me the reverse.[12]

In April 1915 at Boulogne she observed the British and Canadian wounded being brought back from Ypres and placed in the casino, the vast plastered rooms of which echoed constantly with sounds of pain. Macnaughton, confronted with these sights and sounds, caved in to her true feelings:

> It *isn't right*. This damage to human life is horrible ... at last, in a rage, one feels inclined to cry out against the sheer imbecility of it ... Why bring lives into the world and shell them out of it with jagged pieces of iron? ... I am *sick* with seeing suffering.[13]

She was asking herself the same questions that would appear in 'From a Kitchen Window' later that year, but, unlike the confident author whose readers required that they be given reassurances, the private woman was unable to find a similar level of consolation. She still felt that creativity was stifled by the coarseness of army life; even the songs of the soldiers were 'forced and foolish'. She lamented the lost opportunity for reading and the fact that nobody seemed to look at pictures with the same intensity as before. 'The poetry of life seems to be over', she concluded whilst continuing grimly with her work, which in 1915–16 included the production of four books, a series of thirty-four lectures to munitions workers throughout the British Isles and visits to Stockholm, Petrograd and Tehran, all accomplished 'in the shadow of the death of youth'. Macnaughton, who died exhausted in July 1916, was driven by an ultimate need to champion life, whether in the form of creative energy, the cause of the survival of youth or ministering to those wounded physically or emotionally by war (she did not find this hard: observing an ambulance of wounded civilian children and orphaned babies, Macnaughton commented, 'I think King Herod himself might have been sorry for them'). This was accomplished with a full knowledge and appreciation of a woman's perspective on life and, it followed, the untimely extinguishing of it by the war. 'I suppose women will always try to protect life', she confided to her diary:

> because they know what it costs to produce it ... At present women are only repair-ers, darning socks, cleaning, washing up after men, bringing up reinforcements in the way of fresh life, and patching up wounded men, but some day they must and will have to say [to men], 'The life I produce has as much right to protection as the property you produce and I claim my right to protect it.'[14]

Macnaughton was not the only female observer of the war to proclaim a populist view while harbouring inner reservations over the validity of a woman's place in relation to a conflict created by men for men to die in. 'These men fell for their country, in the cause of Democracy, against a cruel and relentless form of militarism', wrote Mrs Alec-Tweedie in her account of her visits to various battlefronts; 'Better, more glorious to do so, than to skulk in corners as paci-fists, strikers, Bolsheviks, all of whom are trying to tumble over the very foun-dations of home and family, national life and real liberty. If a country is worth anything, it is worth fighting for.'[15] Kathleen Burke, who visited the French front as an observer, proudly explained to General Petain how a pre-war politi-cal society, the Scottish branch of the National Union of Women's Suffrage Societies, had, 'with that splendid spirit of patriotism which had from the first day of the war animated every man, woman and child of Great Britain', organised itself into the Scottish Women's Hospital movement.[16]

However, even seemingly clear cases of simple, patriotic motivation could be muddied by conscience. The restless journeys for Mrs Alec-Tweedie were prompted by a visit to the grave of her son who had fallen near Loos fighting in the Royal Field Artillery. Although she stated that women and men must play their parts in war (a war which, she admitted, in its modern and mechanised form, could be 'a battlefield of life' and a 'cesspool of false report'), the same was true, she thought, of the search for peace, and she expressed her view, similar to that of Christabel Pankhurst, that the war was a male concept and that women were naturally opposed to war: 'Can any woman ever look upon a battlefield and not feel her very soul revolting against war, fiercely insisting that wars must cease, that she will not bear sons to grow to men and be butchered.'[17]

In addition, Kathleen Burke had also pointed out to Petain that the formation of the Women's Hospitals out of the Suffrage movement, 'was no longer a question of politics, but simply a case of serving humanity … a time for organised effort on the part of all women for the benefit of the human race and the alleviation of suffering'.[18]

The alleviation of suffering, then, was recognised by women themselves as a prime factor in the decision to take up nursing. In many cases, patriotism, as Nurse Edith Cavell had declared, was not enough. Working at a distance from all the inflated rhetoric of the Home Front popular press could provide a different perspective on one's home country, as in the case of Dorothy Cator, who nursed in a French military hospital at the start of the war and commented that, 'We are still wonderfully frog-like in our point of view of anything that is not English. When we get to the top of the hill, though the whole world is lying at our feet, we keep our eyes thrown back on our own land.' Cator hoped that a positive result of 'this awful and costly offering of strong, beautiful life' would be a lessening of Britain's insularity and innate prejudices. ' It seems strange', she lamented:

> that we should be found so lacking in sympathy, but in our ignorance it is so. We have forgotten what we stand for … England has been living on its reputation and has been much to blame, but may it now be wise enough to see its own faults, generous enough to own them, and strong enough to correct them.[19]

A wider perspective on the war and its causes was also experienced by another woman at the front, Olive Dent, who, on volunteering, was accepted for foreign service in the summer of 1915 and was immediately sent to France. When war had been declared, Dent had found the very notion of armed conflict to be an 'unreality' and something that was usually confined to disputes between far-flung nation states. Once in France and able to observe the lines of gravestones at Wimereux, she found herself made fully aware of the youth and beauty that had been consumed by the conflict and the lines of smoothed stones came to represent 'man turned to destruction', while each individual stone called to mind 'a gap in some home across those dark waters'.[20] She found herself so affected by the reality that confronted her that she felt the need to record and communicate her experiences to a wider public – hence her memoir, *A VAD in France*, which was published in 1917.

Many of the memoirs and stories constructed by women from their experiences and feelings relating to the Great War did not appear for some years after 1918, despite the intensity of feeling involved. This was probably due to the slow pace of the alteration of the circumstances of women in the post-war period in terms of financial, creative and emotional independence from men, despite their newly-acquired political freedom (i.e. through the vote given to householders over thirty). The publication of the experiences of nurses and observers of the battlefields during the war had been made possible by the hunger of a reading public eager for descriptions of the circumstances in which their loved ones were living and dying, and a recognition of this appetite by financially-aware publishers. A further contribution to swift publication during the war was the usual tone of the material, which was to a large extent always ready to extol the glorious cause and worthwhile sacrifices, often in order to justify the reality of the situation in the mind of the author; a reality, which if it had been fully exposed, would probably have prevented the work's appearance before a wide wartime public carefully shielded from many of the facts of the front by the popular press.

However, as in the case of works of reportage and literature by men,[21] some of a critical nature did appear early on, though most, again as in the case of material from a masculine perspective, appeared steadily over the next decade and into the 1930s and beyond. One such was that attributed to an anonymous woman of the WAAC (Women's Army Auxiliary Corps) which appeared in 1930 and, like that of Olive Dent, recalled an acute alteration of perspective on the war due to direct contact with it. 'The war turned one topsy-turvy, altered one's outlook on life. I felt I could never be pre-war again', she wrote. The former WAAC officer declared that she did not care to dwell on the memories of her war experience that the writing of the book had thrown up, even after such a considerable amount of time had elapsed since the original events had occurred. She found herself still appalled by the number of men's lives cut short, physically blighted or mentally 'deprived of their reason', and she wondered how women came through the same conflict 'without ourselves becoming insane'. Her conclusion was that:

> we all tried not to think – we had little time for thinking except when off duty, and then we were so exhausted that most of us fell asleep. Yet there were nights when I, and I expect others, cried ourselves to sleep at the inhumanity and brutality of it all.[22]

Nocturnal doubts also plagued those who had not even come into contact with the full reality of the war zone and reveal that it was not always a straightforward decision for a woman to volunteer to go to the front. May Sinclair, the author of such fictional propaganda as *Tasker Jevons* (1916) and *The Tree of Heaven* (1917), recorded the 'frightful anticipation' of the weeks prior to her departure for the continent in order to work with the Motor Field Ambulance Corps in her book, *Journal of Impressions in Belgium*, an anticipation based on both the excitement of coming adventure and extreme fear of the unknown: 'going to bed night after night, drugged with horror, black horror that creeps like poison through your nerves'. She recorded that the mind would eventually forget the ordeal to come under the calming drug of sleep but when one woke the lucid brain would immediately construct yet more mental images of the war, 'a dozen war pictures a minute like a ghastly cinema show, till horror becomes terror'.[23] Whether the reality of war matched or exceeded the terror of anticipation, it was difficult to communicate impressions of horror in letters to those at home who expected reassurances to assuage their own fears. Hence truer feelings were often relegated to private diaries, and it was these impressions that were often used as the basis of a later account of the war, whether as fact or fiction.

The actress, journalist and writer Evadne Price made use of her diaries recounting the lives of the volunteer ambulance drivers in her semi-autobiographical novel, *Not So Quiet – Stepdaughters of War*, which she published under a pseudonym – Helen Zenna Smith. One bitter passage describes, in an almost stream-of-consciousness manner, the denial of truth involved in writing to family at home about events at the front and the uselessness of even attempting to convey the terrible truth; If one told the truth, namely:

> that all the ideals and beliefs that you ever had have crashed about your gun-deafened ears – that you don't believe in God or them or the infallibility of England or anything but bloody war and foul smells and smutty stories and smoke and bombs and lice and filth and noise, noise, noise – that you live in a world of cold sick fear, a dirty world of darkness and despair – that you want to crawl ignominiously home from these painful writhing things that once were men, these chattered, tortured faces that dumbly demand what it's all about in Christ's name – that you want to find somewhere where life is quiet and beautiful and lovely as it was before the world turned khaki and blood-coloured – that you want to creep into a refuge where there is love instead of hate ... Tell them these things; and they will reply on pale mauve speckle-edged paper calling you a silly hysterical little girl – 'You always were inclined to exaggerate, darling'.[24]

Not So Quiet was not published until 1930 and was awarded the Prix Severigne in France as the novel 'most calculated to promote international peace'. The narrative of the four central characters was continued in four further volumes during which the war-blighted life of the narrator became worse and worse, her fear during the first volume of the permanence of mental images of maimed men with burning eyes confirmed:

> I fear them, these silent men, for I am afraid they will stay with me all my life, shutting out beauty till the day I die. And not only do I fear them, I hate them. I hate these maimed men who will not let me sleep ... Oh the beauty of men who are whole and sane. Shall I ever know a lover who is young and strong and untouched by war, who has not gazed upon what I have gazed upon? Shall I ever know a lover in whose eyes reflect my image without the shadow of war rising between us?[25]

Price articulated the feeling that women, too, could have their lives blighted by the war in a personal sense, if not in a professional one, as they, 'smilingly stumbled' from suburban chintz-covered drawing-rooms into an unforseen hell. Price's character posed the question many women who saw the truth of the war found themselves asking; 'What is to happen to women like me when this war ends?' Price's narrator declares that she is twenty-one and yet knows nothing of life but death – as well as fear, blood and the false sentimentality of patriotism. She also realises, after a period of leave, that she has become accustomed to being a machine, 'Outwardly I am Smithy, assistant cook [she has by this point given up VAD work for a lower domestic position in the WAAC]; inwardly I am nothing. I have no feelings that are not physical.'[26] Though sunk in mental atrophy herself, she fears for the following generation, raised in a 'blood-and-hate atmosphere' and fears that, as a result, they will be callous, predatory and 'cruelly analytical'. Price's narrator has become so mentally numbed following her own experiences that her reaction to the news that her fiancé has possibly been killed in action is very muted. Replete with fatalism, she rationalises that if soldiers such as her fiancé are not killed by the gas, guns, and grenades, they are simply patched up and sent back to eventual death: 'It is only a matter of time.'

Evadne Price saw the ordinary soldiers as innocents, caught up in a wider scheme over which they had no control. A similar view was taken by Mary Borden in her fictionalised account of her work as an American VAD in Flanders, the Somme and Champagne in which she highlighted the irony of having to return to the front over and over again. Like Smith, she saw the situation as a larger plan from which the ordinary individual had no escape. 'Listen', she wrote with matching irony:

> you can hear how well it works. There is the sound of the cannon and the sound of the ambulances bringing the wounded and the sound of the tramp of strong men going along the road to fill the empty places. Do you hear? Do you understand? It is all arranged as it should be.[27]

Borden likened the war to a second Flood of biblical proportions and the wounded as 'wrecked men', survivors from a former world. Like the anonymous WAAC officer and May Sinclair, Borden found herself kept awake at night by the 'familiar, muttering' noises of the war; the 'feeble, mewing, whimpering voice of Life' and the 'loud triumphant guttural shouts of Pain plying her trade in the hut next to me'.[28]

Borden's most arresting image was her impression of a French territorial regiment en route from the trenches to a local town. These survivors were also 'wrecked men' in that the war had warped and altered them; from a distance they looked deformed and hunchbacked as they moved laboriously through the dust and everything about them created an impression of age and weariness. 'They had not quite the colour nor the shape of men. The war had spread over them its own colour ... Fatigue and suffering and dirt had soaked through them and had made them this colour.' All were deformed in the same way by the same war:

> The same machine had twisted and bent them all ... There was no elasticity in them, nor any enthusiasm, nor any passion ... Suffering was a part of their rations. They were acclimatised to misery. Death was a part of the equipment they carried always with them.

Borden likened them to trees which had been uprooted from their earthy settings, leaving gaping holes, and carted away to 'the bleak desert of death' where, instead of growing freely, they were now chained and fastened to the earth, pulled down with their burdens of suffering: 'as dark weight scraping the road', in startling contrast to a plane passing overhead above them.[29]

Borden's fictionalised account was not published until 1929, the same year in which Maude Onions' *A Woman at War* appeared, a factual account of her time as an army signaller in France which displayed a similar insight and compassion regarding the plight of the ordinary soldier, especially in contrast with the bland tone of the official bulletins. 'It was only when the mask was drawn aside for a moment that one realised how the seeming futility and endlessness of the war was eating into the souls of the men'.[30] Onions had been surprised by the level of the men's disillusionment she encountered when she arrived in France in 1917 and, like Borden, was painfully made aware of the endless stream of wounded which arrived at all hours of the day and night with 'ceaseless monotony' and was also concerned, like Evadne Price, about the effect of the war upon the following generation as she observed French children travelling daily to school through scenes of utter desolation and ruin.

Onions spent time talking to those with whom her work brought her into contact, and she recorded the uncertainty of a soldier who found himself afraid of returning to civilian life, explaining that, 'my brains you see have run to seed', as well as the puzzlement of a gunner who found it difficult to connect the lamb's wool used for cleaning gun muzzles – which reminded him of his former job of sheep-rearing – and the purpose of the weapon itself, it being hard for him to comprehend the transition he was forced to undergo from the procurement of life to the taking of it. Onions also recorded her conversation with a man who forced her to admit to him that she thought the war to be wrong and then challenged her as to her part in it, stating that to meet wrong with wrong would only aggravate the larger, inherent evil of the war's progression. He then revealed himself to be a conscientious objector and pointed to the paradox that, while each believing the war to be wrong, both of them were in France involved in war-work of some sort. Onions came to the realisation that the separate identities and personal freedoms of both men and women could be adversely affected by the war's infringement upon the course of ordinary life. As she stated in *A Woman at War*, 'From the moment of enlistment in the "War for Freedom", freedom for the individual ceased to exist. The separate identity of men and women became submerged.'[31]

This recognition of the submergence of personal identity – already identified as part of the male experience – was most often applied to those who had actually experienced battle: from Mary Borden's weary French regiment to the wounded survivors observed by the women who cared for them. One nurse likened her patients to ghosts as they all filed into the mess in coloured dressing-gowns, 'gentleman, tinker, and tailor; each having shuffled home from death; each having known his life rock on its base'. All had become 'creatures of habit'.[32] The nurse in question was Enid Bagnold whose memoir of her time as a VAD nurse was published in 1918 as *Diary Without Dates*.

At the outbreak of war, Bagnold volunteered for nursing work and found herself at the Royal Herbert Hospital, Woolwich, where she found herself greatly affected by the wounded men's attitudes towards life as a result of their involvement in the war. She found they had become, 'careless of life ... of all the whims and personalities and desires that go to make up existence', and to her they seemed 'new-born' from the fire of their experience, their personalities wiped clean, and child-like in their unquestioning acceptance of each other and faith in the nurses. She also became aware, like Mary Borden, to what extent the men had been wrenched from their former existences ('Watchmakers, jewellers, station-masters, dress-designers, actors, travellers in underwear, bank-clerks...') in order to be made into soldiers. 'To what a point their lives are suspended', she mused, while considering their motivations for allowing their lives to be altered to such an extent, particularly when one of her anti-war friends visited the hospital and asked a former dairyman why he fought simply because someone told him to.

Bagnold tried to see the situation from a personal, masculine point of view:

> It isn't so simple as that, is it, dairyman? It isn't even a question of the immense, vague machinery behind the sergeant, but just the sergeant himself: it isn't a question of generals or politicians; of great wrongs or fierce beliefs ... but of the bugle which calls you in the morning and the bugle which puts you to bed at night.[33]

She acknowledged that the male, military experience of the war was something in which she, as a woman, could not share and therefore could not fully comprehend: 'I – a woman and therefore of the old, burnt-out world', as she classified herself. Bagnold found herself almost frustrated in her inability to share in the life-altering experience of the soldier, particularly as, 'It must happen to the men in France that, living so near the edge of death, they are more aware of life than we are.' She retained the faint hope that, 'When they come back, when the post-war days set in, will they keep that vision, letting it play on life ... or must it fade?'[34]

Bagnold later joined the First Aid Nursing Yeomanry and served in France as an occasional driver as well as undertaking further nursing, and these experiences formed the basis for her novel *The Happy Foreigner* (1920). When *Diary Without Dates* was published in 1918, she was immediately sacked by the Matron as she arrived for work, although she derived satisfaction from a sympathetic article in the *Daily Mail* (linked to a debate over alleged unfeeling routine in a Rouen hospital) and critic Desmond MacCarthy's typically descriptive appreciation of her courageous stance as a 'Lionetta'.

Enid Bagnold was to build on the fame thrust upon her by the popularity of *Dairy Without Dates* with her many plays and novels whereas the other most celebrated nurse-turned-author of the Great War, Vera Brittain, achieved her (possibly greater) fame solely through her memoir of her war years, published in 1933 – unlike Bagnold's volume, which appeared in the final months of the war. We are now able to study Brittain's actual diaries and letters of the war period, and they reveal that her pacifism was somewhat slow to reach maturity, as recognised by Yvonne A. Bennett, who specified that Brittain's anti-war feeling, 'from its inception, was rationally and pragmatically inspired'.[35] At first, the war gave a 'spurious simplicity' to emotional life, and Brittain, who (like Bagnold) 'longed to live at an intense level', responded with a conventional upper-middle-class patriotism; her 'great fear' in the first few days of August 1914 was that Great Britain's 'bungling' government would declare its neutrality and refuse to assist France, and hence be guilty of 'the grossest treachery'. She urged her brother Edward to volunteer and began to knit garments for the soldiers ('the only work it seems possible as yet for women to do').

However, by 1915 the 'shallow patriotic tone' vanishes from her diaries and letters as she became more disillusioned with the reasons behind the fighting.[36] Eventually, through a combination of personal loss and observation of the war's effect on individuals during her time as a nurse, she came to resemble Evadne Price's narrator in that her coming of age was marred by a too-full knowledge of death. 'O glorious time of youth indeed!', she lamented in her diary in April 1915:

> This is the part of my life when I ought to be living every moment of the full, tasting the sweetness of every joy, full of love and life and aspiration and hope, exulting in my own existence. Instead, I can only think how weary are the heavy hours, wonder how I can get through their aching suspense, wonder when they will end – and how. Ah! Those who are old and think this was so terrible do not know what it means to us who are young. They at least have had their joy, have it now to think of and look back on; for us the chief part of our lives, the part which makes all the rest worthwhile, has either never dawned, or else we have for a moment seen what is possible only to have it snatched from your eyes.[37]

While she continued with her nursing, her emotions became deadened. As she wrote in the winter of 1916 after the death of her fiancé, 'In the utter blackness of my soul I seem to be touching the very depths of that dull lampless anguish which we call despair ... I am crushed – altogether crushed, by life – I have no power of resistance left, no courage – not even any desire for courage'.[38]

Every hope had been blighted. She had felt great personal satisfaction in passing the Oxford Senior Exam in Latin, French, Arithmetic and Algebra in August 1914, as Oxford to her meant, 'a breaking down of oppressive boundaries and a step towards freedom and liberty of thought, work and endeavour'. Instead, she found her hopes and happiness 'transformed by the same grey despondent mist that alters everything now ... This is no longer a time to see how much enjoyment one can get out of life, but to see how much courage and strength one can give to it.' There were now only two possible options – to act and to endure.[39] She turned to nursing partly so as to involve herself in hard manual labour and so perhaps banish constant thoughts of the danger of her fiancé, Roland Leighton, especially after the casualty lists were published after the battle of Neuve Chapelle in March 1915. She realised with regret that 'my

sort of work' (i.e. academic study) was much less easy or needed in an atmosphere obsessed with military victory and, 'when so much of intellectual life
seems at a standstill and the war cry drowns the purer voices of the upper air'.
However, she vowed not to shirk the intellectual life ('the work for which I was
made') simply because the nations had temporarily forgotten that the intellectual life 'reigns supreme above the strife of nations'.[40]

As a woman, Brittain, like Bagnold, felt herself to be an outsider – unable to
experience, share and perhaps understand the dangers faced by her brother and
Leighton; in March 1915, at the same time that she was deciding to become a
nurse, Brittain described herself, as 'a weak imperfect being, whose only interest in the war was through individuals concerned in it'. Her decision to nurse
was also based on a desire to experience more of the war in order that she
might satisfy her growing doubts concerning the motivations behind it and the
truth of the horrors of the actual fighting, as expressed by Leighton in his letters
to her. By the time Brittain commenced her nursing at the Devonshire Hospital
in June 1915, her compassion had already started to reach out beyond the
abstract and embrace others; news came that a former friend had been killed in
the Dardenelles and 'a dull, agonising ache' began. While listening to an organ
recital at New College Chapel, she mused upon her likely reaction to a British
victory and concluded that she would not be one of those taking a happy part
in the triumph; 'Even if I do not lose directly my heart will be too full of what
others have lost'.

The practical observations of nursing brought home to her, as in the case of
Maude Onions and the conscientious objector, the paradoxical element to the
war. After tending to a badly wounded prisoner of war, she found herself 'disturbed' to realise that, 'Wasn't it somehow odd that I, in Etaples, should be
trying to save the life of a man whom my brother up at Ypres had perhaps done
his best to kill? And didn't that argue the existence of some fundamental absurdity in the whole tragic situation.'[41] Also, Leighton had told her before he even
went to the front that he had no personal animosity for the enemy and wished
he were back at Oxford amongst his books. His reasons for enlisting had sprung
from very individualistic motives: an attempt to live up to his own expectations
of himself coupled to an 'indefinite pursuit of heroism in the abstract'. He later
confirmed in a letter to her that he had found no glory in trench warfare, only
endless waiting and the taking of 'petty advantages' and though people talked
of ideals, 'it is all for nothing – for an empty name'.[42]

Leighton was killed in December 1915, at which point Brittain was nursing
at the 1st London General Hospital, Camberwell. She later nursed both British
and German wounded in France in 1917, and it was then that her pacifism and
inspiration for her anti-war writings of the 1920's and 30's came to full fruition
as she sensed the seeming indifference of the belligerent governments towards
the mounting numbers of dead and injured of both sides that she came into
contact with. She likened the war to a snowball gathering volume as it rolled:

Every day seems to take us further from the end. Every month introduces some new and complicating element which further involves all the elements already there. It is too gigantic for the mind to grasp. And through everything, involving things still more, run everyone's personal interests and loves and despairs, most terrible of all.[43]

'The only way to see war is from a hospital'. Such was the view of Mabel Dearmer who volunteered to nurse in Serbia in March 1915. She, like Brittain and other women observing the male world of military might 'from the wings', recognised the inherent paradox of the situation. 'War is the devil's own', she wrote to her friend Stephen Gwynn, 'When I see these wounded here ... I don't see you and Geoff and Chris [her sons, both serving] hurt, but I see all the men that you and Geoff and Chris are going to hurt as these men are hurt – and that is the unbearable thing.' She also was aware of the roles that both men and women were forced to play in a country at war. 'We do live in odd times', she wrote while ill herself in hospital, 'the men go out to kill each other in order to settle some question, and the women – well, if the women can't be ministering angels and brave dangers, they just become horrid little cats and break rules and squabble'.[44] When Gwynn wrote to her that 'the gilt is off war' after the sinking of the *Lusitania*, she replied with astonishment, 'But was there ever any real gilt on war?' She stated that she could be no more angry with the men of another nation for robbing her of her sons than with an earthquake: 'It is all ignorance and folly' she concluded.

Like Vera Brittain and Dorothy Cator, Dearmer became disenchanted with what she referred to as 'this madness of Nationality, this false patriotism' that she everywhere observed while the Serbians were dying around her ('they are human beings wasted'). She also deplored the limited choice open to the individual in a nation geared to war, noting that 'today it is Christ or Kitchener'. To her, the folly of the situation was easy to identify: 'As long as men grab land and think it noble to die for their own bit there will be wars. As though a nation depended on its land! It depends on its spirit and ideals ... This war will not bring peace.'[45] Dearmer died of typhoid in July 1915, and her younger son was killed at Suvla Bay later that year. In his memoir of her, which was published by Macmillan with her letters to him in the year of her death, Gwynn commented that she had left her career as a book illustrator and author of children's plays for the harsh battlegrounds of Serbia, not because she was an Englishwoman or simply followed her husband, but 'because she was a woman'. He recalled that her motivations, 'were born of her own thought, not impressed from outside', and that the war and the resultant situations in which she found herself had produced in her a 'disturbance' far greater than in others: 'For her, no harmony was possible between natural life and these unnatural times.'[46]

Dearmer had volunteered to go to Serbia after sitting through a farewell service at St Martin's in the Field in London which had been arranged by her husband, Percy Dearmer (chaplain to the British units in Serbia), under the auspices of the Church League for Women's Suffrage. The service was a farewell for a unit about to leave for Serbia and organised by Mabel St Clair Stobart who, when approached by an inspired and eager Dearmer at the end of the service, immediately informed her that Dearmer would have to leave her long earrings and fur coat at home if she were to be accepted for a role in the unit as a hospital orderly. Stobart had been approached after the Kingway Hall meeting of women's organisations on 4 August 1914 to do something practical on behalf of women and she had responded by establishing an office and headquarters for the Women's National Service League in St James Street the following day. She also found time to send a letter to the *Daily News* complaining of the double standards of morality imposed by the war between women and men as well as between individuals and nations.

Stobart was the natural choice to surmount the practical difficulties of organising some form of women's hospital unit that would work abroad. She was already nationally celebrated for her role in the establishment of the Women's Sick and Wounded Convoy Corps, a medical unit staffed entirely by women, including the doctors. During the first Balkan War in 1912, she and the corps had travelled to Bulgaria *against* the advice of the British Red Cross Society and had established a hospital at Kirk-Kilisse, the existence of which marked the first time that female doctors had worked at a front-line hospital during wartime. By 1914, Stobart was fifty years old and was putting the finishing touches to her memoirs of her experience of the Balkan conflict – an experience that had convinced her of the futility of war.

Stobart later described the establishment of the Hospital Units (the Women's Imperial Service Hospital) in the first few weeks of the Great War as, 'a protest, passionate, sane, practical, of the civilised against the barbaric; of the spiritual against the material'.[47] Between the establishment of her office in St James Street in the first few days of war and her meeting with Mabel Dearmer on the eve of her departure for Serbia in April 1915, Stobart led an ambulance unit on behalf of the St John's Ambulance association to Brussels and was nearly shot as a spy as the Germans overran the city. She then went to Antwerp where the hospital was in the German line of fire of an ammunition dump and hence at serious risk of bombardment itself. Stobart and her staff were forced to leave with the wounded and were the last to escape the ruined city by way of a hastily-constructed boat bridge before that too was destroyed. She then accepted an invitation from the French Red Cross to set up a hospital at Cherbourg and hence was chosen by the authorities to lead the British hospital unit to Serbia in the spring of 1915.

Stobart's motivations behind her immense practical achievements during the war were clearly defined and set out in her description of her time in Serbia, *A Flaming Sword in Serbia and Elsewhere*, which was published in 1916. In the Preface, she described the stark choice facing humankind: evolution or retrogression. To her, militarism was a retrograde step which would bring the progress of civilisation to a halt.[48] 'The sign-post to devolution is militarism', she declared, adding, 'and I believe that militarism can only be destroyed with the help of a woman'.[49] To women, Stobart declared, life was not a game of chance but an 'individual charge' (and hence their dislike of militarism was 'an instinct') and, since primitive woman had always defended 'individual concrete life' both before and after birth, modern woman was charged on a larger scale with defending 'the abstract life of humankind'. To Stobart, a male disapproval of militarism was based on sentiment or expedience and not on instinct and was, therefore, not forceful enough to have the required effect. Again in common with other female observers of the war, Stobart felt the paradox of the conflict keenly: 'Society holds that no motive justifies murder when it is retail, and concerns individuals; but when that murder is wholesale, and concerns nations, no motive justifies abstention from the murder-fields'. She also, like many other women, worried for the sensibilities of the coming generation in that:

> Civilisation, as we were taught, meant the progress of the human race in ideals, spiritual and moral. Civilisation, as our children are being taught, means progress in the invention of machines for destroying life – the one thing on earth that can't be made by machines.

Modern warfare was 'a business for butchers' and represented a 'negation of civilisation', especially for women: 'Of what use the care and labour spent in science, art, culture, education, it, at the command of militarism, these and their votaries are to be periodically blotted out.'[50] Stobart saw how the war reached out to affect those who would or should have no part in it:

> War is not merely an encounter between rival armies of man. War is, in these days, an encounter between equipped armies and unequipped women and children, with results that are bestial and humiliating; between equipped armies and unequipped civilisation with results that are destructive of civilisation.[51]

As Claire Tylee has pointed out in her *The Great War and Women's Consciousness*, Stobart felt that society needed the more forceful promotion of 'womanly' values in order to, 'channel the courage required by militarism away from the battlefield and into moral, social and spiritual purposes'.[52] In this, Stobart reflected the concepts expressed by Bertrand Russell (*Principles of Social Reconstruction* and *Flaming Sword* both appeared in 1916) surrounding the channelling of the creative and destructive energies of society. Stobart believed that society needed to allow a fuller recognition of the nurturing instincts of women. This proposition was not simply offered from an exclusively feminist perspective, but would benefit both genders (and thus all of society, international as well as national) by promoting peaceful pursuits and thus lessening the chances of future war.

By the beginning of May 1915, Stobart, propelled by her need to minister to the wounds of militarism, reached Kragujevac in Serbia. The 3rd Serbian Relief Fund Unit comprised of fifty staff, including seven women doctors (this number later increased to fourteen). Upon her arrival, Stobart requested and was granted forty more doctors and nurses from England in order to establish a system of roadside dispensaries to combat outbreaks of typhoid amongst the local populations. Each dispensary was soon dealing with a hundred people each day, including home visits using an ox-wagon as a makeshift ambulance. During the first few months in Serbia, approximately twenty-two thousand people received help from these dispensaries. In October 1915, Bulgaria attacked Serbia, and Stobart was asked to form a 'flying field hospital' at the front for the Serbian army which would include persons from the original unit and Serbian soldiers as ambulancemen. Stobart, with her earlier Bulgarian experience behind her, here came into her own as the Serbian–English Field Hospital became caught up in the Serbian retreat and was forced to abandon the motor ambulance and hospital equipment at the foot of the Montenegrin mountains. Stobart, who had – uniquely – been appointed a commander with the rank of Major in the Serbian army, led her column on foot through the often trackless mountains in mid-winter, during which an estimated ten thousand Serbian soldiers and civilians perished (with over four hundred thousand taking part in the actual retreat).

Stobart refused to abandon her Field Hospital and re-join the original Relief Fund Unit; in the end, only five of the original staff remained with her as she became the only commander to reach Scutari in Albania (after three months and eight hundred miles) without a single loss of life. Once back in Britain by way of Brindisi and Rome, she was reprimanded by the Serbian Relief Fund Committee for exceeding her instructions. Undeterred, she then undertook a lecture tour of America, initially backed by the Ministry of Information, which she angered by then insisting on financing herself. She then also donated all profits to the Serbian Red Cross. On her return to Britain, her request for another appointment was ignored, and she never heard from the authorities again. Stobart was left to write her memoirs – and to mourn her son, who died in the influenza epidemic of 1918.

In *Women of the War*, which appeared in 1917 and included an introduction by former Prime Minister H.H. Asquith, Barbara McLaren described Stobart thus:

> No woman has seen the war at closer quarters and in more varied fields of action than Mrs. St. Clair Stobart and no one has worked harder to help the sick and wounded … Everywhere she has sought and found her opportunity to bear her part in the actual campaign – a part such as no woman has ever taken before.[53]

This description was apt because it reflected Stobart's intentions and beliefs as to the role of women during the war. 'The co-operation of women in warfare is essential for the future abolition of war; essential, that is, for the retrieval of civilisation', Stobart wrote, voicing the frustrations of Enid Bagnold and Vera Brittain amongst others. In order to promote the cause of humanity, the cause of war had to be suppressed and this could not be done by men alone, since the society which had failed to prevent the present war had been dominated by men. The spiritual power of women had to be combined with the physical force of men if humankind were ever to reach the 'Tree of Life'. In order to facilitate this co-operation of women in warfare, it followed that it was 'good that Woman shall put aside her qualms, and go forth and see for herself the dangers that threaten life ... that Woman shall record, as Woman, and not as neuter, the things which she has felt and seen, during the experience of Militarism at first hand'.[54] Participation in the war from a nursing or reporting capacity would give women a voice to raise against conflict. 'Until woman had obtained some experience of war, she could only express sentiments concerning war; but now she is at liberty to give opinions as to the meaning of war.'[55]

In her analysis of Britain under the war, *Britain Holds On 1917–1918*, the cultural analyst Caroline Playne examined the effect on daily life on the Home Front, where the war, 'filled up all the already full places of life', and the effect of the 'crushing blows' dealt by the conflict upon the spheres of art and literature. 'In every sense', she concluded, 'the war took the gilt off life, even off literature.'[56] She thought the war too vast an event from which to harness themes for works of literature other than war stories. The complexities of character and adventure (as well as life itself) had 'lost their savour'. Compared to the experience of serving in the war, everything else seemed subsequently small and insignificant while for most others, 'dullness has deadened life'. But was this view perhaps not placing enough faith in the abilities of the artist to catch at least one of the 'myriad faces' of the war? This was the opinion of another female commentator on the conflict, the novelist Storm Jameson, who wrote in her autobiography:

> Do we ... think of the war as an event, an experience too singular or too vast to be tampered with by the conscious artist? Or is it that we half misprize the novelist as a person too cheaply bought off by easy emotions, too facile, not fit to be trusted to handle an experience of this magnitude?

Although she herself thought that no war novel had matched the three or four best personal records of the war, Jameson took to task critics who viewed a war novel as naturally inferior to a 'truthful' memoir: 'We anxiously assure one another that the George Sherston of one book is Mr. Siegfried Sassoon'[57] (alluding to Sassoon's fictional counterpart). The waters of analysis were muddied further by certain memoirs/novels in which an almost deliberately thin line was placed between fact and fiction, as in the accounts of Helen Zenna Smith/ Evadne Price, Mary Borden and others. In addition, it was rare indeed to find a woman's account, fictional or otherwise, of events surrounding individual humanistic anti-war attitudes that was far removed from the 'traditional' scenes of horror and pity of trench and hospital. One such, however, *was* penned by a woman, Rose Allatini, under the pseudonym A.T. Fitzroy.

Allatini's novel, *Despised and Rejected*, traced the development of the anti-war views and actions of the main character, Dennis, a homosexual composer, and those of his like-minded associates, as set against certain events, such as the outbreak of war and the introduction of conscription, as well as the hostile views of both his family and the outside world. During the first few months of the conflict, other characters, such as Lance-Corporal Griggs, are prepared to be tolerant of Dennis' lack of enthusiasm to volunteer which they put down to artistic temperament. Gradually Dennis faces increased criticism as he steadfastly refuses to attest under the Derby Scheme. When the patriotic Mrs Ryan takes him to task over his civilian clothes complaining, 'I should like to know where the war would be if everyone thought like that!', Dennis counters, 'Presumably there would be no war at all.'[58] During a discussion about the merits of music (Dennis' friend Crispin has forsaken military life in order to oppose those in authority who would ban German composers from British concert halls), the character of Henriette declares, 'Who thinks – who has the heart to think of music now? For me, if I were a man, there would be but one music thrilling my soul: the roar of cannons',[59] while Lily Hallard, in her VAD uniform, tells Dennis that the 'proper spirit' should be contained in the desire to get to the front as soon as possible – like Tom Sanderson, who effects a transfer from a cavalry regiment due to lack of action. When Dennis argues that the individual intellect and soul demand satisfaction that the course taken by an individual is for the greater good, Lily declares, 'A fat lot most of our boys think of "intellect and soul"! They just go and do their bit, and don't talk about it.'[60] One of Dennis' severest critics is his father who tends to the view that, 'A little blood-letting won't do the nation any harm', while he regards man as a 'fighting animal' and thinks it 'unnatural' for a man, especially his own son, to have 'no fight in him'.[61] Dennis and his friends represent the 'unnatural' anti-war stances that Allatini wished to plead a case for and that she herself felt and observed in others.

Allatini's leading character is at odds with all the swirl and bustle of wartime life around him: 'The thought of war inspired in him none of those feelings with which convention decreed that every true Briton should be inspired at times like these.'[62] Dennis recognises and deplores what he regards as the general pretence that the war is a game, 'which every Englishman should be proud to be playing', and resolves not to 'give himself up to the machinery of nations trying to prove which could stand the most blood-letting; machinery that organised the murder of individuals by individuals who had no personal quarrel with each other'.[63] Dennis sets the picture of the nations of Europe locked in their 'death-grapple of hatred' against one of the continent in which the rivers flow calmly onwards, 'oblivious of all artificial frontiers, oblivious if it was French or German or British or American blood that reddened them'.[64] He resolves to translate the voices of the nations into his music: 'He would make himself the medium through which their individuality, their thoughts, their dreams, their yearnings should be expressed.'[65] Individuality drowned by the war would re-surface within his music. His symphony would transcend man-made frontiers and claim kinship with all fellow human beings; it would be, 'as international as art itself'.

Dennis struggles to be true to his nature and instincts in attempting to understand the conflict and its effects from an overall perspective. He describes himself as a 'humanitarian' before his Military Tribunal and when his father challenges his views as unnatural, he pleads his case, replying:

> You'll allow a man to conquer nature with his ships and his railways – you'll allow him to widen as much as possible the gulf that separates him from the beast; but when it comes to rooting out the war-instinct – No! He can't overcome that. Why should he? It's always been there, always will be. In fact, you're rather proud of it: it's part of a gentleman's equipment. You want progress and the conquest of natural difficulties in every possible direction and yet you won't admit that a man can conquer himself. You're shouted down as 'unnatural' if you as much as speak of overcoming an instinct that is nothing but a hindrance to civilisation and progress.[66]

Despite his appeal to the tribunal, Dennis is sentenced to non-combatant service and, as he waits to be called up, finds his creative impulses now focused on a symphonic poem which he at first perceives as full of dissonance and counter-rhythms battling to be heard. However, he then recognises that this is a truer picture of the war and that each conflicting noise must be left to make up the whole. 'Each must have its place in the scheme, for each stood for one of the innumerable beliefs and reasons, ideas and madnesses that had led the people into war.'[67] Thus his art can reflect the truth of the reality around him and could act as a conduit for his pacifist and humanistic emotions as he blends all the clamouring voices into one, 'showing their fundamental unity, converting strife and turmoil and the sorrows of all nations into the transcendent harmony of peace'.[68]

In this desire, he is supported by his friend Neil Barnaby, a fellow artist, who laments the wastage of art and intellect that the war has facilitated, stating that:

> There are thousands of men being forced to fight, who are physically and mentally unfit to be of the least use in battle, but whose brains might have given us scientific inventions that would have benefited humanity, works of art, books, music ... No, they won't let them stop at home and do what they can do, but must send them out to do incompetently things against which their whole nature rises in revolt. From the general utility standpoint: in which capacity is the artist of more value to the nation? As a creator of a work that may live, or as a mass of shattered nerves, totally incapable either of fulfilling the requirements of the army or of carrying out his own ideas?[69]

He deplores the treatment meted out to conscientious objectors as 'wilful murder of brains that were fine, sensitive instruments which might have brought some lasting beauty, some lasting wonder into the world', and later concludes, 'From every possible point of view, whether from religion art, socialism or humanity, war is a disgrace to any civilised nation.'[70] Barnaby supports Dennis' need to translate his feeling on the war and his hopes for peace into his music, despite all hostile opinion. Artists have a duty to their art, despite contrary circumstances; as Barnaby urges, 'Let's at least preserve art from the general wreckage.'[71]

The character of Alan, Dennis' lover, represents the 'absolutist' point of view of the conscientious objector in that he declares himself to be against 'passive pacifism' to the same extent as he is against militarism, and he condemns those individuals who take an anti-war stance and yet accept work in munitions factories or at the front line without bearing arms. To Alan, those of a pacifist point of view should be ready to suffer 'the utmost penalty' in the demonstration of their belief ('capitulating means admitting that we believe that black is white, just because the majority says so').[72] Like Bertrand Russell, he expresses the idea that the energy of populations could be channelled towards creativity rather than destruction:

> Think of the heroism and self-sacrifice of those who really 'die gladly' for a mistaken idea; and the tremendous flame of patriotism that's burning in the hearts of all the peoples alike: if all these tangible and intangible splendours could have been used in the furtherance, instead of in the destruction of civilisation![73]

Despised and Rejected was published by C.W. Daniel in May 1918. Daniel, a pacifist who had already been prosecuted for his publication of an anti-war pamphlet, was again prosecuted, not for obscenity (the novel featured – shockingly for the period – openly lesbian and gay characters), but as, 'likely to prejudice the recruiting of persons to serve in His Majesty's Forces, and their training and discipline'.[74] Daniel was fined £460 and was forced to relinquish any unsold copies to the authorities while he declared, in a volte-face, that he would rather the book be burned than, by implication, lend support to pacifist homosexuals. Paradoxically, Stanley Unwin, who had earlier rejected the book for publication when the manuscript was offered to his firm, was one of the main contributors to the appeal launched by the *Herald* to help pay the fine imposed on his rival publisher. The *Times Literary Supplement* had described the book as well written and the author's plea for toleration open enough to, 'rob the book of any unpleasant suggestion',[75] while Allatini herself hardly featured in the widely reported court case and publicity surrounding it. Sadly, her book was not published again until 1988, ten years after her death. In her *The Great War and Women's Consciousness*, Claire Tylee cites three principal 'pacifist' novels by women to emerge from the experience of the war: Rose Macaulay's *Non-Combatants and Others*, Mary Agnes Hamilton's *Dead Yesterday* and *Despised and Rejected*. Of the three, Tylee proclaims only Allatini's novel to be truly radical in its approach. The book had proved too uncomfortable in its truths for a wartime audience. Allatini obviously drew upon the real sensibilities of herself and those of people she knew to lend credence to the vivid anti-war emotions displayed in her novel.

Storm Jameson later commented that the value of fictional accounts of personal reaction to the war lay in the fact that the experience involved the whole self – both physical and emotional – and at a time when the author was perhaps 'most sharply alive'. No other experience cut so deep into individual personality and achieved a greater level of glaring reality, and this was true in spite of varying critical opinion on the level at which individual experience became articulate fiction. Jameson believed that the war fiction of the generation of the Great War was the category of literature that would bequeath the most ultimate value to succeeding generations, in particular its power to convey the reality of the horrors of war rather than its glories. Her generation, she felt, had been without this 'prior knowledge' and thus, 'For us, and all those who like us were without the ballast of experience, the war came as a sudden wave, lifting us high before it threw us under.'[76] She also acknowledged that the 'gulf' of experience between women and the men who actually fought the war was 'impassable', commenting that, though, in geographical terms, the distance between her wartime home on the south coast and the Western Front was short, 'measured in human experience it is infinite'. However, she counted both herself and her brother who fought and did not survive as part of the same blighted generation, a continued blight which showed itself in a draining away of the human spirit: 'the drying up of vitality, the lack ... of resilience and warmth', concluding, 'In a year of war, the spirit lives out a lifetime of experience.'[77]

Like Bertrand Russell, Jameson recognised that the tendency towards war involved a diversion of the peaceful human spirit via the distorted impulses of natural passions operating at a destructive level. Commercial interests, greed, false patriotism were parts of a general corruption that took hold with the arrival of the war:

> War, like any powerful passion, like the passion of jealousy, begins by destroying the very source of reason. It becomes a state – of being – from which people argue, as the old astronomers argued their conception of the universe from the existence of god. Then to say, 'But this war is madness' becomes heresy and treason.[78]

The concepts of Russell concerning the potential of the creative and destructive impulses of society were also mirrored by the actress, journalist and author Cicely Hamilton who believed that the science of war was the enemy of progress and gradually evolving civilisation, especially when its enormous power was placed in the hands of a 'fallible and emotional humanity, liable to outbursts of passion'.[79] Hamilton worked in a war hospital on the edge of the forest of Chantilly for almost three years, and it was when she witnessed a hit on an ammunition dump in the Somme valley that, 'the world was suddenly changed for me', with the strange, angular silhouette of the aeroplane flying overhead representing the capabilities of a new and terrifying science of destruction. The fiery spectacle around her, she later wrote, 'made havoc of my old beliefs in progress and the onward march of humanity', and she found herself 'stunned and purposeless' for a time.

This abrupt change in her emotional and creative life echoed the earlier effect of the start of the conflict upon Hamilton's writing, the flow of which had halted in the latter half of 1914. This stifling of creative ability did not simply affect her, as we have already seen. A literary agent later informed her how difficult it had been to procure any writing from his authors in the first few months of the war. When she inquired of the dramatist Harold Chapin, whom she encountered on a bus, how the writing of his plays was progressing, he told her there was only one thing that mattered now and gestured through the window towards the passing drill-ground of the Duke of York's barracks. Hamilton clearly identified the dangerous effect of the war upon creative impulses: 'Our morals, inevitably, are affected by the company we keep, and the machine, our constant companion, being merciless, has trained us in its own indifference.'[80] She only managed to find new inspiration herself in her work for the 'Concerts at the Front' organisation (linked to the YMCA and run by Lena Ashwell).

The reaction to the war of Cicely Hamilton was similar to that of another educated and observant female writer, Mary Agnes Hamilton: 'We were unprepared, morally and mentally. War in 1914 was a revelation of evil outside our categories', Hamilton wrote in her own memoir of the war. She recalled that there had been no talk of the concept of peace in the years before 1914 because there had been little talk of war to inspire it: war had seemed very remote and unreal and hence the outbreak of the conflict in 1914 had carried with it:

> the force of a bomb which blasted us, suddenly, violently and with acute pain, out of our habitual thinking, broke up our patterns and violated our standards. It was a charge of dynamite applied not only to the forms of our lives but to the ideas by which we have lived.[81]

Mary Agnes Hamilton – feminist, suffragist and early member of the UDC was the author of *Dead Yesterday* (1916), another of Claire Tylee's three principal pacifist novels by women to emerge from the war.[82] In common with Frances Partridge and Helen Wedgwood, Hamilton had attended Newnham College, where she had read and appreciated G.E. Moore's *Principia Ethica* and remembered that arguments over the nature of the concept of good were very much 'in vogue' at the time at Cambridge and that J.E. McTaggart had also been regarded as 'a major prophet'. She had also read and been impressed by Bertrand Russell's 1903 essay 'The Free Man's Worship' at a time when her and her friends were extremely critical of their own attitudes and those of the world around them and were, in Hamilton's words, 'chockfull of conscience, social and individual'. When war came she was on the staff of the *Economist* under the editorship of F.W. Hirst (one of Foreign Secretary Sir Edward Grey's harshest critics). Although she had previously joined the Independent Labour Party which now condemned secret diplomacy as the root cause of the war but placed Germany in the moral wrong for its violation of Belgium, Hamilton admitted that her resistance to the war was 'primarily emotion'. For her, a 'just war' was a contradiction in terms and to declare the war inevitable, 'was to abandon reason and proclaim despair'. She saw the war, with its 'high sensationalism', as an artificial creation with all the 'jarring suddenness of a theatrical transformation scene' and was appalled by the way in which the 'elevated chatter of publicists and parsons' masked what she saw as a universal pretence in denying the sufferings of those at the front.

In common with other female commentators, Mary Agnes Hamilton recognised the gap between those experiencing the conflict at first hand and those whose exposure to it was controlled by censored letters and deadlines. She described this gap as being like a smokescreen, 'dense, hot and excited', which divided those at home from the soldiers who, unable to impart the true horror, 'locked their fearful experiences in their breast'. Hamilton felt unable and unwilling to take part in what she described as a 'mass conversion' to the acceptance of war; the very phrase 'belief in war' now had a 'remote, unnatural ring' to it, especially those, like Hamilton, who refused to swim with the tide of war. 'We refused to un-say and un-think what we had thought before about war itself: insisted that, having happened, it was still horrific ... we alone *felt* the war, realised its horror, minded it; were kept awake by it.'[83]

In 1916, Hamilton left the *Economist* with Hirst and both moved to *Common Sense*, based at 44 Essex Street and which was, as Hamilton described it, 'a sort of pacifist G.H.Q.'. It was at this point that she began to write *Dead Yesterday* ('inspired by an intense feeling against the war') as well as numerous anti-war speeches and articles until the 'dark waters' that she felt had closed over her head in 1914, submerging and stifling her, finally receded in 1918 ('we were in the air'), although she commented that the gaiety which followed the end of the war was 'all unthinking'.

It was all so different from the state of the world at the war's beginning. Although united on the question of female suffrage, many women were naturally divided in their response to the war. Some of the female opponents of the war, such as Catherine Marshall and Helen Wedgwood, emerged from the suffrage movement and their reaction, in common with much other female opposition to the conflict, was based on a humanistic appreciation of the value of life. Women were perhaps more likely, given their 'passive' position in society and natural role as the facilitators of life, to be individuals in whom, in Wilfrid Ewart's phrase, the 'humane spark' burned brightly.

Men were regarded by some women as aggressive warmongers, both in the form of the politician – the originator of the war – and, to a lesser extent, the soldier – the executor of military policy. By contrast, the female was seen as the life-giver, the mother of sons forced to experience violent conflict and perhaps be killed or wounded for an increasingly spurious cause. In this context, the soldier could be seen as merely a dumb instrument, reduced to the level of a child – hence perhaps the protective role adopted and the terminology employed ('my boys' etc.) by women in their roles as nurses. In their specifically humanistic approach to the apparent wrongness of the war, we have seen how certain women of differing circumstances articulated not only a similar reaction to the conflict but also similar themes of reaction to some of the (male) individuals covered in the previous chapters. In common with some of the male writers and commentators (in particular Owen and Sassoon), direct experience of the war was also regarded by some women as having a serious role to play in their conveying of its essential truths. It was important that a woman both could and should, in the words of Mabel St Clair Stobart, 'go forth and see for herself the dangers that threaten life', in order that she could then convey these dangers to others and also be in a better position to promote feminine/nurturing instincts through helping to channel destructive energies away from the battlefield towards more moral and social purposes – a strategy that was supported and publicly promoted by Bertrand Russell. This premise of 'the value of experience' – along with other familiar themes – were to be echoed yet further.

Notes

1 Anne Wiltsher, '*Most Dangerous Women': Feminist Peace Campaigners of the Great War* (London, 1985), p. 1.

2 Sylvia Pankhurst, *The Home Front* (London, 1932), p. 369.

3 Wilfrid Ewart, *When Armageddon Came* (London, 1933), pp. 360–1. See also Ewart's bestselling novel, *Way of Revelation* (1921) in which similar concerns are explored.

4 Contained in *Women and Peace – Theoretical, Historical and Practical Perspectives*, ed. R.R. Pierson (London, 1987).

5 Imperial War Museum (IWM hereafter), file of Mrs H. Pease, 76/179/1.

6 IWM, Sound Archive, Helen Bowne Pease, transcript 821/20.

7 *Ibid.*, p. 49.

8 She was particularly close to George Horwell, an 'absolutist' and man of extreme principles who often mentioned to her in his letters of his concern that the public should be kept fully aware of the difference between the 'absolutists' and the 'Scheme men' (those that had accepted alternative work under the Home Office Scheme). He had asked her to take over his job as secretary of the Stoke NCF when he was arrested and court martialled in May 1916 after organising two outdoor anti-conscription meetings and calling publicly for an immediate peace. Horwell subsequently spent time in Whittington Barracks at Litchfield, Perth Penitentiary, Wormwood Scrubs, and prisons at Durham, Newcastle and Wakefield, where he was part of a committee which voted not to accept new conditions proposed by the authorities ('They prove to be the Home Office Scheme in another form ... I am not prepared to do compulsorily what I refused to do voluntarily two years ago', he wrote to Wedgwood – IWM, file of Mrs H. Pease, letter from G. Horwell, Sept. 1918). By August 1918, Horwell had served a total of 27 months in prison in between various courts martial and his release due to ill health. Throughout, Wedgwood corresponded with him, sent him items such as a German dictionary and Norman Angell's *The Great Illusion* and provided financial assistance to his mother and brother Harry, who was also imprisoned for some of the war as a conscientious objector.

9 Sarah Macnaughton, *A Woman's Diary of the War* (London, 1915), p. 168.

10 Sarah Macnaughton, *My War Experiences on Two Continents*, ed. Mrs L. Salmon (London, 1919), Preface, p. xi.

11 *Ibid.*, 21 Oct. 1914, p. 34.

12 *Ibid.*, spring 1915, pp. 103, 113.

13 *Ibid.,* April 1915, p. 115.

14 *Ibid.,* 16 Oct. 1914, pp. 30–1.

15 Mrs Alec-Tweedie, *A Woman on Four Battle-Fronts* (London, 1919), p. 35.

16 Kathleen Burke, *The White Road to Verdun* (London, 1916), pp. 49–50.

17 Alec-Tweedie, *Woman on Four Fronts*, p. 18. For more on the perspective of Mrs Alec-Tweedie, see Sharon Ouditt, 'Tommy's Sisters: the Representation of Working Women's Experience', in *Facing Armageddon – The First World War Experienced*, ed. H. Cecil and P. Liddle (London, 1996).

18 Burke, *White Road*, p. 50.

19 Dorothy Cator, *In a French Military Hospital* (London, 1915), pp. 89, 95–8.

20 Olive Dent, *A VAD in France* (London, 1917), pp. 25–6.

21 For example, see C.E. Jacob, *Torment* (London, 1919), a personal reminiscence which combined jingoism with criticism of army bureaucracy and Gilbert Frankau, *Peter Jackson, Cigar Merchant: a Romance of Married Life* (London, 1920), a patriotic war novel which reflected the stance of its author.

22 WAAC, *The Woman's Story of the War* (London, 1930), p. 35.

23 May Sinclair, *Journal of Impressions in Belgium* (London, 1915), p. 16.

24 Helen Zenna Smith (pseud. of Evadne Price), *Not So Quiet: Stepdaughters of War* (New York, 1989, first published 1930), pp. 30–1.

25 *Ibid.,* pp. 163–4.

26 *Ibid.,* pp. 216–17.

27 Mary Borden, *The Forbidden Zone*, (London, 1929), pp. 121–2. *The Forbidden Zone* was a collection of poems and narrative sketches from the 1914–18 period as well as stories written during the post-war period.

28 *Ibid.,* p. 54.

29 *Ibid.,* pp. 24–9.

30 Maude Onions, *A Woman at War* (published privately in 1928; then by C.W. Dent, London, 1929), pp. 17–18.

31 *Ibid.,* p. 22.

32 Enid Bagnold, *Diary Without Dates* (London, 1978, first published 1918), p. 6.

33 *Ibid.,* p. 104.

34 *Ibid.,* p. 24.

35 Yvonne A. Bennett, 'Vera Brittain and the Peace Pledge Union' in R.R. Pierson (ed.), *Women and Peace – Theoretical, Historical and Practical Perspectives* (London, 1987), p. 193.

36 See Deborah Graham, 'Vera Brittain, Flora Macdonald Denison and the Great War: The Failure of Non-Violence' in Pierson, *Women and Peace*, pp. 142–3.

37 *Vera Brittain, Chronicle of Youth – War Diary 1913–17*, ed. Alan Bridges (London, 1981), 19 April 1915, pp. 179–80.

38 *Ibid.,* 30 Jan. 1916, p. 313.

39 *Ibid.,* pp. 99–103.

40 *Ibid.,* p. 163.

41 Vera Brittain, 'From War to Pacifism' quoted by Bennett in Pierson, *Women and Peace*, p. 193.

42 Cited in *Brittain, Chronicle of Youth,* ed. Bridges, 25 April 1915, p. 184.

43 *Ibid.,* 7 Oct. 1915, p. 286.

44 Mabel Dearmer, *Letters From a Field Hospital* (London, 1916), pp. 157–8.

45 *Ibid.,* pp. 158–9.

46 Stephen Gwynn, 'Memoir' in Dearmer, *Letters*, pp. 2–4.

47 Mabel St Clair Stobart, *Miracles and Adventures* (London, 1935), p. 147.

48 Although writing from a different context, the Fabian Beatrice Webb also recognised a 'return to barbarism' heralded by the war. Though she had little sympathy with the plight of the conscientious objectors (even though the noted CO Stephen Hobhouse was her nephew), Webb exhibited a horror of the escalating casualty lists which resulted in a mounting pessimism.

She also recognised – in common with Bertrand Russell – malign impulses at work: 'I see the fine energy and cheerful self-sacrifice, the eager self-effacement of our recruits', she wrote to Lady Betty Balfour in December 1914, 'but it is a tragedy these splendid qualities should be insolubly connected with all the vulgar impulses of national domination, delight in the loss and suffering of other races, and in many cases with the horrors of lust to kill and injure individually. It is after all a return to barbarism – to animal pugnacity; and the heroism of the trenches has its likeness in the heroism of the wild animal.' B. Webb to Lady Betty Balfour, 8 Dec. 1914, cited in Carole Seymour-Jones, *Beatrice Webb – Woman of Conflict* (London, 1992), p. 289.

Webb also wrote in her diary of an 'indescribable torrent of misery and bestiality' which she perceived as affecting those individuals caught up in the fighting. 'This was seems a universal bankruptcy of human intelligence and human goodwill', she concluded. See *The Diary of Beatrice Webb – Volume Three: 1905–1924, The Power to Alter Things*, ed. Norman and Jean MacKenzie (London, 1984), p. 289. The missing body of another of Webb's nephews, Noel Williams, was found three weeks before the Armistice.

49 Mabel St Clair Stobart, *A Flaming Sword in Serbia and Elsewhere* (London, 1916), p. vii.
50 *Ibid.,* pp. 311–12.
51 *Ibid.,* p. 314.
52 Claire Tylee, *The Great War and Women's Consciousness* (London, 1990), p. 37.
53 Barbara McLaren, *Women of the War* (London, 1917), p. 32.
54 Stobart, *Flaming Sword*, pp. viii, 4.
55 *Ibid.,* p. 311.
56 Caroline Playne, *Britain Holds On 1917–1918* (London, 1933), p. 430.
57 Storm Jameson, *No Time Like the Present* (London, 1953), p. 148.
58 A.T. Fitzroy (pseud. of Rose Allatini), *Despised and Rejected* (London, 1988, first published 1918), p. 151.
59 *Ibid.,* p. 169.
60 *Ibid.,* p. 188.
61 *Ibid.,* p. 194.
62 *Ibid.,* p. 150.
63 *Ibid.,* p. 150.
64 *Ibid.,* p. 199.
65 *Ibid.,* p. 200.
66 *Ibid.,* pp. 194–5.
67 *Ibid.,* pp. 317–18.
68 *Ibid.,* pp. 317–18.
69 *Ibid.,* pp. 241–2.
70 *Ibid.,* p. 244.
71 *Ibid.,* p. 157.
72 *Ibid.,* p. 288.
73 *Ibid.,* p. 240.
74 *Ibid.,* cited by Jonathan Cutbill in his Introduction to the 1988 edition.
75 *Ibid.,* cited by Cutbill.
76 Jameson, *No Time*, p. 189.
77 *Ibid.,* p. 100.
78 *Ibid.,* p. 207.
79 Cicely Hamilton, *Life Errant* (London, 1935), p. 150. Hamilton was the author of the war novel *William – An Englishman* (London, 1919).
80 *Ibid.,* p. 152.
81 Hamilton, *Remembering My Good Friends*, p. 63.
82 Tylee, *Great War*, p. 119.
83 Hamilton, *Remembering My Good Friends*, p. 68.

7

Obscurer individuals and their themes of response

The destruction of nature as reality and metaphor

This chapter casts the net wider. Following the responses of the small but influential Bloomsbury circle, the earlier chapters have encompassed the experiences of other celebrated thinkers and writers (especially Bertrand Russell), some of whom donned uniform, and also certain women, well-known and otherwise, some of whom travelled to the war-zone as nurses or observers. It has became clear that similar aesthetic–humanistic responses occurred *outside* the confines of Bloomsbury and aesthetic viewpoints manifested themselves within particular themes of response, such as the blunting of individual personality and stifling of creative efforts. The further we get from the creative nexus of Bloomsbury, will the same hold true? In other words, will the anti-war reactions of further obscurer individuals still be linked by the familiar and recurring themes experienced among the more celebrated?

A particular expression of personal disquiet with the war 'in its operation' and involving a contrasted appreciation of nature and landscape was exhibited by one of the first individuals included in critic Laurence Housman's edited collection of war letters, which appeared in 1930 and contained a significant amount of anti-war material.[1] Captain Arthur Innes Adams of the Cambridgeshire Regiment, writing to his sister in July 1916, contrasted the freedom of his Sunday walk behind the lines near Boulogne with the usual 'ridiculous military precision' and the 'appalling … deadening nature of the instruction' inherent in army life. Adams resented the intrusion of the hand of the military Englishman with its usual 'vulgar effect' into this peaceful landscape of corn and poppies and wished for the end of the war when, 'the true business of life will begin – to teach men the beauty of the hill-sides'. For the present, however, his love of nature and the contrast it forced upon him, 'gives me a fierce feeling of hatred of the present bondage that is hardly to be borne – and there are times on parade when it seems impossible to do what one is told'.[2]

Reporter W. Beach Thomas echoed Adams's horror of the ugliness of the war in a diary entry, written after five months of fighting on the Somme in 1916. 'The power of ugliness could no further go', Beach Thomas observed,

'Everything visible or audible or tangible to the sense – to touch, smell and perception – is ugly beyond imagination. The hanks of wretched and rotted wire suggest that the very soil has turned into a sort of matter hostile to all kindly productiveness.'[3]

The travel-writer Stephen Graham, in his *The Challenge of the Dead*, contrasted not only the pre-war Somme with the post-war 'incomparable Somme silence', but also the devastation of Nature brought about by the war with the destruction of man wrought by the same conflict. 'Now the desolation of Nature alone suggests what a desolation there was of man', he wrote in 1920, 'The terrible woods are impressionist pictures of the ruined vitals of great regiments, and you can hold a forest in your mind as you would a skull in your hands and say, "This was a forest. This was an army".'[4] This view of the destruction of the natural world being intrinsically linked to the deaths of countless soldiers was duplicated by Lieutenant R.H. Pickering of the Royal Field Artillery in a letter to his brother in September 1915. Pickering found thoughts of 'happy days' before the war impossible when contemplating the thousands of his fellow soldiers who had been killed during the previous four months in his battle-sector – 'this wretched hole' – which covered only a square mile. 'These woods were lovely once', he wrote, 'now the trees are all bare and strafed and blackened, they lie broken against one another, they lie on dead men squashing them.' He had formerly observed the pre-war names and initials of lovers carved into the bark of the trees, 'How little did those happy sweethearts imagine the desolation and death that now reigns here – the neighbourhood is a stinking cemetery.'[5] For Pickering, the image of the 'death' of the trees and the close proximity of the human dead served to heighten the contrast that the war had brought about with the former days of life and growth.

The conflict's effect on the limited world of an individual at the front could be total, with the blighting of nature via the war's man-made effects seemingly to then reach further and affecting the continuum of time itself. In his last letter before being killed, Sergeant James Duncan, formerly a coal merchant, wrote:

> It is now getting late. The sun is sinking over the ridge to the right of Cambrai. Its setting glory is hidden from me by the murky pall of smoke, or the fog of war that stretches across our horizon beyond Douvai and Lens. The coming of the night does not bring us rest and peace. We go on in an endless cycle, whirling in the ether of man's inhumanity to man.[6]

Even if a soldier contemplated a peaceful summer landscape behind the lines, a sense of the war's insidious effect could still be apparent, as in an observation of Corporal H.L. Currall, ASC in July 1918. 'The fields were a blaze of colour', he wrote to his future wife, 'I have never seen so many wild poppies and cornflowers – brilliant red poppies and blue cornflowers – every now and then the former were so thick the fields gave the impression of being splashed with huge patches of blood.'[7] Currall deplored the acute devastation that the war brought to former centres of humanity such as Lens, which he observed was reduced to mounds of bricks while he noted that, on a larger scale, from Arras eastwards for approximately fifteen miles there was nothing but scenes of total desolation. He also commented that, as Ypres had been 'the bloodiest battleground in the history of the whole world', it should be left in its devastation as a monument to the dead who had fallen around it.

Currall found the sense of finality he saw everywhere hard to convey to his sweetheart, someone who was living in a different frame of existence and could not therefore fully appreciate the war's immediate effects on the mind:

> This war defies description – it is indescribable – no words or photographs can picture the awful scenes of carnage and destruction, and unless one has been actually face to face with the horrible sights, one cannot possibly conceive the magnitude of the slaughter, desolation and waste – no matter how vivid one's imagination may be.[8]

A parallel observation is to be found in the diary of 2nd Lieutenant J.B. Herbert, MC of the 5th Battalion, the Royal West Surrey Regiment. Herbert interrupted his battle narrative to reflect on the destruction of the countryside around Mount Kemmel that he observed when, ostensibly on duty but in reality wanting to see the state of the surrounding area, he went on a morning walk in the final months of the war. He recorded that, 'It was the country we had advanced over and had been the first to explore. In those first days we had been the only men on the landscape.' After four years of war, the 'chief feature' of this landscape was now one of movement, with men making roads, collecting salvage, filling up shell holes or simply moving about on foot or with transport, usually ambulances. Not only was the countryside now dominated by man and his war in the flesh, but also by the debris of that war. Herbert also observed a landscape full of shells, trench mortar, bombs, rifles, ammunition, timber, elephant iron for dugouts and machine gun mountings, all in various states of decay and disrepair. Some of this material was German in origin, as the area had for some time been under German control, but, as Herbert noted, the British had been there initially, and the ground was littered with hundreds of broken huts – the remnants of an early British rest camp. The cumulative effect on the countryside was the same, Herbert noticed, no matter that most of the small dugouts and shelters captured from the Germans had been constructed originally by the British. Now German and British dead lay side by side in a jumble of stray limbs, smashed skeletons, steel helmets full of bullet holes and old field dressings dyed ochre with old blood.

Herbert wrote that he had heard of how the countryside around the hill used to be before, and during, the war and how the hill itself:

> was once the pleasure resort and beauty spot of the land, covered in forest and wonderful with lover's walks and fairy ringed glades. Why even in 1916 and 1917, people were living there, running estaminets on the hill itself and that very smashed fragment on the summit I sat on for a few minutes on August 30th was a prosperous farmhouse a year ago. Not a tree lives on that hill now, though the stumps show the

stately things that once were, not a bird stirs, not even a rabbit can live in the gas that poisons the ground, not one square yard, but is torn and mangled by the fury of bygone shells.[9]

Herbert, who was later to become a respected judge, could not help but feel the wrongness of the situation. Nature and the landscape had been transformed by the unnatural frenzy of war. He noted the irony of the formerly obscure main road of the area, down which prosperous farmers once easily drove or strolled from village to village, now achieving a notorious fame in its ruination. 'I had to plough through a foot of mud', he recorded:

> skirt a hundred shell holes, broken carts, heaps of shells, masses of brick from a church whose site was fifty yards away, pick my way where the road narrowed to a yard, where it once was eight, trip across tangled iron which once was a railway. And so, back home to my company H.Q.[10]

The dereliction of the natural world was so total and shocking in many areas that to those who were great appreciators of nature and its link to an assumed sensitivity inherent in man, the havoc wrought by the war was seen as the ultimate betrayal of former values embedded in man's relationship with a landscape initially unaffected by industry and mechanisation. The ugliness of a landscape blighted by the conflict could bring home in a particular way the ugliness of war itself – especially to an individual possessed of acute sensibilities. Even a seemingly unaffected landscape could conceal stark reminders of the human cost of war upon close inspection. Lieutenant Bernard Pitt of the Border Regiment and formerly a tutor at a working-men's college described in a letter to his friend, Lionel Jacob, the still hilly and wooded region of the Bois de Souchez as being:

> poisoned with human relics, limbs and bundles of clothes filled with rotten flesh and even those poor remains of men which pious hands have buried are daily disinterred by plunging shells. S—— itself is merely a heap of bricks and stones, and it reeks to heaven of mortality. Do you wonder that, reading Wordsworth this afternoon in a clearing of the unpolluted woodlands and marking the lovely faded colours on the wings of hibernated butterflies, and their soft motions, I felt a disgust, even a sickness, of the appalling wickedness of war.[11]

In a similar manner, the sight of the Somme valley brought forth bitter feelings from anonymous soldier 'Bombardier X' in his *So This Is War*, published in 1930. 'How ghastly is this great desert they call the Somme!', he wrote during the war to his mother:

> Only a carcass of a district, festered and rotten. War, like a mighty steamroller has crushed it. Derelict trenches everywhere cut across the land. They are hacked out of the dead clay, and built with the blood and sweat of men ... Hand-in-hand, war and death have danced a grisly ballet over the land that was tilled and developed by a patient people. They have left ruin and devastation behind. Still the dance of death goes on, but they set the stage farther alone and call it 'a great British victory', when

we capture three thousand square yards of graveyard. War is the devil's own spawn. How he must laugh when he sees us puny men hurtling death and destruction at one another.[12]

To a lover of the natural world, the rare sight of nature flourishing amid the devastation of war could provide a glimmer of hope and inspiration when all else seemed black. W.B. Kitching, a signaller with the Royal Garrison Artillery, found himself inspired by a beautiful spring morning and the unfamiliar sound of birdsong to record in his diary that, 'this free open air life makes one feel the beauty of nature and her charms ... who knows, perhaps soon the day of peace will be with us again and then we can re-start a new life, let us hope, changed for the good ... to a higher mode of thinking'. However, he found himself constantly aware of the conflict happening all around; 'this awful calamity which broods over the earth'.[13]

Kitching was able to come nearer to his personal God through his communion with Nature. He contrasted the 'jarring monotony' of the official Army observances with the freedom of the landscape behind the lines where, 'the woods and surrounding countryside are the true temple'. He also found the destruction of once thriving towns painful to witness. In particular, the sight of shattered Ypres with its 'gaunt walls and gaping rents' (the only remnants of the old Cloth Hall, Hotel de Ville and Library) he described as, 'a veritable city of the dead: a standing witness of the curse of war'.[14] In this he echoes the earlier view of Corporal H.L. Currall of the ruined city of Ypres as a monument to the evil of war.

The devastation of Ypres was viewed in a similar fashion by Norman Cliff of the Grenadier Guards, who later recalled how, 'closing my eyes and picturing Ypres as the dream city it must have been, and then observing the sad wreckage around me, I felt a helpless, irrepressible rage'. Cliff likened the battered Cathedral to an injured animal, 'raising its wounded head with awe-inspiring dignity, as if in mute protest against wicked mutilation by men gone mad'. Despite this sense of 'proud dignity', Cliff felt that this merely served to emphasise, 'That only man is vile'. 'There was', he wrote, 'no escaping the overhanging permeating fog of war', particularly when he observed the shells of former houses ('with the life gone out of them') and surveyed the Ypres Salient after heavy shelling had destroyed rebuilding work:

> So this was the malodorous, festering garbage heap we had to keep out of the grasping hands across the way, and for which so much rich blood must still be spilled. This vast muck-heap valued so much more than lives. If those who held this view were sane, I must be mad.[15]

It seemed as if the vast upheaval in the natural world brought about by the war was now mirrored by a reversal of 'sane' values in the world of man.

It was perhaps easier to draw contrasts between life and death when one was an ardent lover of Nature, a point exhibited by Charles Douie in his memoir, *The Weary Road* (1929). He had been at rest behind the lines near the villages of Millencourt and Mentigny and recalled that:

> I watched the coming of Spring in the woods and the young corn in the fields and the men, the flower of every shire in Britain, on the march towards the chalk uplands of the battlefield. I wondered often how many of those whose eyes were delighted by the glory of these fields would see the harvest, and I thought of the other harvest which death would reap.[16]

Douie also pointed out that much of the 'material havoc' wrought by the war in the form of the trenches scarring the landscape had been made good in the decade following the war's end. It was his hope that the 'moral havoc' also wrought by the war, this time in the minds of men, had also been repaired to the same extent. Again, a contrast was specifically drawn between the disintegration of the physical world compared to that of the mental landscape.

The direct experience of mechanised battle and the resulting destruction thereof could sometimes chisel away at the ability of an observer to appreciate the beauty of the natural world; instead of surviving flora and fauna acting as a reminder of tranquillity and the normal order of things, senses were dulled to such an extent by the war's grey routine and surroundings or worn away by the constant artificial highs and lows of battle and rest that it could become hard to attain former levels of communion with nature.

The wartime author (largely of propaganda for the Allies) and serving soldier, Patrick MacGill, wrote after the battle of Loos of how he had gone out to help a fellow soldier caught on the wire only to find that the huddled heap of clothing was by that time a rotting corpse. He observed that in the half-light of the pre-dawn, the body was not repulsive but, rather, 'almost beautiful'. The head of the dead soldier was sunk low on the wire and the face could not be observed, so that the man seemed to be merely weary and at rest. To MacGill, this figure represented the 'Futility of War', not in harsh terms but in a context of infinite pity and forgiveness towards all soldiers of whatever nationality. Then the sun came up and as the light became stronger MacGill's perception was altered. 'I saw now that He was repulsive, abject, pitiful lying there'. MacGill tried to turn the head of the corpse upward so as to observe the face but discovered that it was fastened to the wire by rusted barbs through the eye sockets. For MacGill:

> The glory of the dawn had vanished, my soul no longer swooned in the ecstasy of it ... that which endured the full light of day was the naked and torturing contraption of war. Was not the dawn buoyant like the dawn of patriotism? Were not the dew-decked wires of war seen from far off? ... But a ray of light more, and what is He and all with Him but the monstrous futility of war.[17]

The sun, which formerly had represented a life-force and nature at its most powerful now served only to highlight and reinforce the destruction and death wrought by man, a contradiction which MacGill was painfully aware of.

Despite his role as a propagandist, for MacGill personally the war represented a negative force: 'What is to be the end of this destruction and decay? That is what it means, this war. Destruction, decay and degradation.' Even time, in the form of linear human progress, seemed set in reverse by the totality of modern conflict. 'We who are here know its degradation', he wrote, 'We, the villa dwellers who have become cave dwellers and make battle with club and knobkerry'. MacGill warned that, although the world had become acquainted with the destruction and decay of war, 'Man will recognize its futility before he recognizes its immorality.'[18]

It was only well away from the scene of battle, on home leave, that a person could perhaps begin to recover their equilibrium and adjust to what sometimes seemed a different or former life. This could be a cruel irony in itself, if and when the individual had to return to the front. Lieutenant Wyn Griffith, return-ing from leave in May 1916, later wrote in his memoir *Up to Mametz* how he realised that he now had more to lose, 'for the deadening power of months of trench habit had been lifted from my mind leaving my fibre bare to the weakest blast of war'. For, as he described, back in the trenches the world was altered once again from the familiar patterns of home, not merely in the routines of life but the very framework of existence became warped.

> Sound, sight and smell were all challenged at once, and they must in concert submit to the degrading slavery of war, chained to a ridiculous chariot heading for utter destruction. Sense and soul were of no account ... in this mad runaway we had cast sanity to the winds. If ever war was meaningless, it was on this sunny afternoon in May, as I walked on my winding way towards the line.[19]

In Griffith's case, it was only because his judgement was sharp after his leave and not dulled by life at the front that he could appreciate the 'irredeemable idiocy' of war. For Griffith, there was no equality or stability at the front; it was a false world, 'governed by a force operating ruthlessly in one direction', in which war became 'the very negation of all value'. He felt himself pushed by the mechanics of the operation down a path on either side of which was a steep wall. All that was possible was a quickening of slower movement in one direc-tion, 'lacking knowledge of our destination'. If resistance to this operation was futile, individual non-acceptance became the only method of internal protest. The mechanical nature of life at the front Griffith likened to the mood of a man constantly sullen in temper (while battle was the same character when enraged), and he described how this mood could extend from the trench and permeate the surrounding landscape: in his particular case, that of Givenchy. He could not believe that this extension of mood was due in totality to war's mechanical aspect and would vanish when the war ended or moved away: that peace would reign once again over Givenchy when the noise of the guns abated. 'No such metamorphosis was credible, so strong was the feeling of the presence of malig-nant fate hovering above this hillock in a plain.'[20]

The quiet of pre-war days could not return; all hope for a return to 'normal-ity' had faded. When Griffith wrote that 'the eye could catch no promise in the landscape' he was referring to the hope of spring and of a renewal of life. To him, spring stood for sanity in a mind dominated by the greyness of the all-

pervading mud and ruins. 'There was ugliness everywhere one looked, the ugliness of smashed new brick and new plaster, a terrible ugliness, inconceivable to
one who has seen no ruins but those of aged walls, mellowed by sun, wind and
rain.'[21] Spring also represented the usual progression of the seasons and hence
of time, the natural processes of which the war had mechanically interfered
with.

Even the process of decay itself was not immune from the war's overpowering effects. To Griffith, the ragged profiles of the smashed houses physically
represented a mood of 'unyielding futility' and resembled the faces of 'gibber-
ing idiots, mad and meaningless'. Again, as in the case of MacGill, the sun
animated the scene but only served to mock the hopelessness of the situation:
'When the sun shone full on those red masks they seemed to be laughing emp-
tily, like a maniac, who has no fear of evil.' The ruins of former dwellings
seemed only to 'screech their defiance of man's mastery over their poor and
tenuous bodies'.[22]

The very earth seemed to protest against man's warrior activities on its surface. 'Everywhere the work of God is spoiled by man', observed 2nd Lieutenant
William Ratcliffe, aged nineteen, of the South Staffordshire Regiment a month
before his death in action. 'One looks at a sunset', he wrote, 'and for a moment
thinks that that at least is unsophisticated, but an aeroplane flies across, and
puff! puff! and the whole scene is spoilt by clouds of shrapnel smoke!' To
Ratcliffe, this despoliation of the natural order served only to make men more
bestial in character. Formerly, he had believed that the experience of war could
have a beneficial effect upon the minds of men. Now, however, he wrote to his
parents bleakly:

> What is there here to raise a man's mind out of the rut? Everywhere one sees prepa-
> rations for murder; nearly every person one sees is a filthy, dirty man with some
> implement of destruction about his person. The countryside and the beauties of
> nature, which, as you know, always have a beneficial effect on a man, are all spoilt
> by the dust and mud of motor lorries and by huge camps.

Ratcliffe became convinced that, 'war has an almost degrading effect on the
minds of soldiers'.[23]

The particular theme thus highlighted by Ratcliffe and those preceding him
in this narrative is the destruction of the former landscape by the war's mechanical processes and the comparisons drawn between this process and
that of the breakdown of the 'civilised' human condition by both the Army
'machine' and the generally soulless aspect of modern warfare. If, as Ratcliffe
noted, the beauties of the natural world could have an improving effect upon
the human character, then the destruction of these aesthetic aids to betterment
and their replacement with scenes of wearying ugliness could only produce the
opposite effect. Ratcliffe's identification of the 'degrading effect' produced by
the war on the minds of individuals will be echoed later in this chapter by
others similarly affected.

Morality and individuality under threat

In the Introduction to his 'miscellany of the Great War', the writer, Guy Chapman, perhaps in response to the growing threat of a second global war (his compilation appeared in 1937), wrote that, 'stripped of that grandiose word "tragedy", war affects individuals – And that is all this book tries to show … that there was a moral disintegration, both of troops and civilians …'[24] Chapman placed this disintegration of moral values higher than the sacrifice of a generation in his personal scale of the effects of the war and their relative gravitas. In this, he echoed the view of the author R.H. Mottram who, when he examined the post-war state of things in *Three Personal Records of the War*, counted the 'moral exhaustion of civilised peoples' as 'most serious of all' of the resulting problems that he could identify.[25] Chapman pointed out that war altered the routine of life because, according to him, the 'intoxication' of war brought with it a corresponding replacement of reason with emotion (a process which, as discussed in Chapter 2, Bertrand Russell had also identified), while schemes for individual futures – the 'longer vision' – became obscured in a fog of wartime opportunism. Chapman warned that, 'Men, dressed in a brief authority, have the power to ignore the civilisation they are defending.'[26]

Chapman was not alone in his perception of a general moral disintegration caused by the war; we find this view echoed by others, such as Captain J.E. Crombie of the Gordon Highlanders, who commented to a friend a month before his death, aged twenty, in spring 1917, that he found the morals of the war to be 'horrible'; in fighting the Germans, he felt the English could only 'become all that we hate', with an Allied victory becoming a victory for Prussianism. Instead of meeting force with pacifism (as Bertrand Russell had suggested), the Germans had merely been given back their own example and 'top-dog' attitudes would prevail – whoever won. Crombie thought the whole situation had a music-hall unreality to it – it was, in his words, 'Gilbertian', while the basic point remained, as he wrote, 'that by fighting we have hopelessly degenerated our own morals'.[27]

Crombie's opinion was similar to that of Arthur Osburn, a Medical Officer initially with the 4th Irish Dragoon Guards, who commented that soldiers on leave, in moral terms, seemed to have 'sunk below men', and he realised that it had become impossible for them to experience months of exposure to war, 'without beginning to feel an even greater contempt for Life than they acquire for Death.'[28]

In some cases, individual events associated with their experience of the war were enough to demonstrate all too clearly the distance that had grown between former and wartime values. For Lieutenant Colonel A.A. Hanbury-Sparrow, it was his experience of Passchendaele: 'It shattered our moral force', he later wrote in judgement in his memoir, *The Land-locked Lake*. The awfulness of the experience had cast aside any remaining moral prerogatives to 'fight the good fight'.

War had been stripped to its animal-like essentials: former civilising moral codes had given way to merely bestial impulses. He recognised that the mental trauma together with the extreme physical conditions had broken him to the extent that he only lasted for three more months after his experience before a nervous breakdown brought to an end his military involvement in the war.

Not only was 'moral force' broken by the experience of battle: on the Home Front, the strictures of the Military Service Act were seen by some as an infringement of the moral right to personal liberty. Former accountant Eric Southall claimed exemption from military service not only on the usual religious grounds; as he declared to his court martial in October 1916, 'My real offence is that I have maintained that all war and the Military Service Act are morally wrong.' To assist in the conflict would be to ignore individual conscience and make an 'unworthy bargain' with those prosecuting the war. Most crucial to Southall, however, was the fact that while the British army claimed to fight for freedom on the continent, on the Home Front, 'it is being used to reduce the law of the land to a scrap of paper and to crush moral liberty'.[29]

An individual 'moral sense' of some kind was useful to possess, especially when at the front, as a means of justifying one's participation in the slaughter – fighting perhaps to prevent the following generations from undergoing a similar experience or as a means of placing the Central Powers squarely in the wrong when it came to handing out explanations of cause and blame. Alternately, a moral value system could provide a personal justification for anti-war attitudes that were not based specifically on religious or political precepts. However, it was often difficult to maintain a set of previously held values, whether for or against war in general, when faced with the upheaval of this war's specific effects on virtually every aspect of life.

A Padre at the front, C.G. Raven, was forced to comment, 'We out here … get so sick of the strain and ghastliness that our conviction of the moral values for which we are fighting gets overbalanced.' This was partly the result of regarding the Germans as individuals and not as 'the enemy', after observing with pity shell-dazed prisoners of war and the stoicism of the captured wounded enemy.

Raven, who was Padre with the 1st Royal Berkshires, observed that life at the front was like a 'separate incarnation' from the other 'sweeter and saner' life at home and that only those placed outside that artificial world at the front could possibly retain their jingoistic perception and desire the deaths of fellow human beings. Raven realised that, in principle, the war had to go on until its 'full and victorious' conclusion; after all, whole ideals of the human race were at stake ('we have the permanent thing, man, to think for') but he could not help admitting that, at the front, the killing was so terrible, sometimes, to behold, that, 'no sacrifice of abstractions is too heavy a price to pay for the stopping of it'.[30] Personal morality surrounding the ethics of killing here outweighed a national morality of blind patriotism and popular press.

Stephen Bowen, a former cleric and now in uniform, found himself clinging to what he identified as a 'moral courage myth' as he enlisted in 1915, in order to overcome a subconscious dread of discomfort, wounds and death, as well as a full realisation that fighting and shell-fire, 'even if they spared the body must wound the mind'. Once in France, after initial training at Aldershot, Bowen suffered ill health and dreams haunted by a bullet-shattered face. He began to sleep-walk, and this led to an accusation of desertion and the ordeal of the notorious Field Punishment No. 1. Bowen then succumbed to an 'inner blight' that affected others at the front to varying degrees; 'a constant disintegrating menace, eating at the mind – or is it soul? One day dormant, yet always dully present; the next, springing to crush essence out of reason'.[31] Years later, when he wrote up his memoirs, Bowen had not fully recovered from his ordeal, and he warned that the essence of war, once instilled in a man via experience, was permanent and that, 'war haunts through the years, making Death a companion of the living', and hence 'dead' men were still living on, though years were drained, for them, of life, 'years dragged aforetime out of their future, rendered down in an extract of vitality – in a trench-sump of hope – and blasted out of life forever ... the guns eat on'.[32]

C.G. Raven, on the other hand, did not succumb to the 'inner blight', the fear of being afraid which swallowed Bowen. Raven's difficulties were of a more focused and specific nature; he found the almost entire lack of intellectual or like-minded spiritual comradeship in the army hard to bear, and he longed constantly for letters from home, the bonds with the 'sweeter and saner' life he remembered. Meanwhile, his growing hatred of the war was based upon physical hardship and mental exhaustion, but there also existed a friction, as he himself recognised, in spiritual terms. Raven began to see the conflict as a test of his faith and described himself as 'crying in the wilderness' with nobody wanting or able to respond. He felt guilt for, as he admitted, placing the concerns of family, friends and comrades before those of God and hence felt that his ordeal was a form of punishment: 'Shall I come out of it with self or Christ triumphant', he wondered, 'or shall I just stay in this hell until it winnows my nerves and breaks my brain?'

In January 1918, Raven was sent to work in No. 10 Stationary Hospital, BEF, formerly a large Jesuit College situated near a Chaplain's School where he began to lecture. He was sorry to leave his 'lads' but filled with relief to be out of it, especially when on leave in April, back in England amid aspects of his former life and those individuals who, in his own phrase, 'have been saved from passing through the cloud'.[33] In Raven we see a specific recognition of the war's possible effect upon personality: the conflict threatened both the nerves and mind – the physical and the mental. Since Raven in the end narrowly escaped 'passing through the cloud', his view of the war as a danger to personality as well as, in his case, moral/religious codes is all the more interesting for being slightly more objective.

The first chapter of Guy Chapman's celebrated memoir of his wartime experiences, *A Passionate Prodigality*, begins:

> For a long time I used to think of myself as part of a battalion, and not as an individual. During all that time the war, the forms and colours of that experience, possessed a part of my senses. My life was involved with the lives of other men, a few living, some dead. It is only now [i.e. the 1930s] that I can separate myself from them.[34]

Chapman acknowledged the large degree of comradeship and loyalty to one's battalion that formed a considerable part of his and of so many other's experience of war, but he also recognised the cost of this, combined with the 'sensual' effect of the conflict, to his strength of personality, in particular his sense of oneness as an individual as he found his personality subsumed to such an extent that it was years later before he could once again think of himself as an individual.

This adverse feeling of a submersion of personality under the waves of war was felt in many other instances – for example in a cache of letters from a British soldier to his American sweetheart which was found left in a dugout and later published in the final year of the war as *Love of an Unknown Soldier, Found in a Dug-out*. Although the unknown soldier admitted that the war had generally brought forth men's souls and clad them in 'the armour of duty', he himself, with his future mapped out, had never dreamt of fighting, and killing had been inconceivable. To him, then, war meant terror and a change of self to combat this:

> One had to sink personality and ambition; throw aside everything for which one had been trained; take up a way of life that was abhorrent to one's nature; place oneself in a position where one must be inefficient; and stand the strong chance of dying shortly, in a manner which seemed incommensurately obscure and out of proportion ghastly.[35]

Not only was personality forced to sink from the pressure above, but what was left was forced to operate in an inefficient manner and never up to full strength. In any case, aware of the mounting casualty lists and surrounded on most sides by wholesale slaughter it became increasingly easy to become, as one Lieutenant (who was awarded the MC) grimly pointed out, 'careless of the mere individual'.[36]

For some, the experience of war was a struggle to deflect the conflict's effect on individuality by the use of a form of self-distortion of normal existence. For one subaltern, his personal battle to 'solve' the front (ie. to make some sense of it) could only be won, in his own acknowledgement, 'when actuality has been wholly swallowed up by imagination'. Only then would there be some form of unity of perception, 'and I shall no longer be perpetually passing from one extreme state of mind to another'. His struggle with the false dualism which the war had created in his vision of things depended upon him casting to one side 'the first law of Nature, or any other individual consideration'. In other words, a self-denial of personality.[37]

The suppression of the individual was recognised even by those who did not regard its effects as adverse. One such was Captain Charles B. Brooke of the Royal West Surreys, who wrote in a letter to be passed on to his parents in the event of his death (he was killed only a few hours later, on the first day of the Somme), 'It is impossible to fear death out here when one is no longer an individual, but a member of a regiment and of an army.'[38] Brooke, like many, found refuge a lessening of individual responsibility, the fraternity of military service and the knowledge that he had dutifully responded, like many of his contemporaries, to the demands that his country had placed upon him.

There had been a tradition of the individual responding to the call of patriotism in times of crisis or conflict from the Boer War back to the Napoleonic threat and beyond, and this tradition had been widely recognised. However, on further examination, some expressed disquiet at a situation wherein the demands placed upon the individual were perceived as unfair:

> Society indeed does not distinguish between those who have large stakes to defend and those who have none, nor between those who are willing and those who are unwilling, those who understand and those who do not. Society demands equality of sacrifice though it does not bestow equality of rewards. But society is defeated in its demand. The only equality is that recorded by the rude, rough graves of the battle zone. And after those who have given their lives come the wounded, mangled and maimed who crawl from the stricken field – Who stands before these claiming 'equality of sacrifice?[39]

Hence a wide variation existed in the scale of the individual's response to the demands placed upon him by his own society in wartime and it was the individual's responsibility, as C.E. Jacomb (who had been a Lance Corporal in the 23rd Royal Fusiliers) suggested in his *Torment – a Study in Patriotism*, to construct a personal Profit and Loss account in order to discover what had been gained or lost in the sum total of the individual's war experience. To some, this was an easy and obvious calculation to make. 'Intelligent mechanics and clerks', commented R.F. Mottram on the end of the war:

> were under no illusion as to the nature of the 'fighting' in which they had been engaged. They made no revolution, [sic] as did their like across more than half Europe. They just wanted to go home ... It was only too clear to what pass years of dishonest or inept politics, new industrial methods and the obliteration of the individual had brought us.[40]

Many soldiers based their moral standpoint on the assumption that, in H.G. Wells' phrase, the war was one to end all others and hence worth the fight. 'Thank God we are fighting to stop war', wrote the Oxford-educated schoolmaster Theodore Cameron Wilson, 'otherwise very few of us could go on.' Not only was he forced to view the beauty of Nature constantly through a 'veil of obscenity, as a madman may see beauty', but he felt guilt for the fact that war had always been taught as a romantic subject when, in fact, the rhetoric of valour was dangerous because it showed 'nothing of the individual horror, nothing of the fine personalities smashed suddenly into red beastliness, nothing of the sick fear that is tearing at the hearts of brave boys who ought to be laughing at home'.[41]

There seemed to be no official recognition of the 'individual horror' of the experience, especially in the army, which merely 'enforced a uniform upon the soul itself, a prison uniform', as Stephen Graham described the process in *A Private in the Guards*. The army was not constructed to contain a firm base on which to place and proclaim one's individuality, and those that recognised this and resented it could do little to avoid it other than protest at their tribunal hearings and courts martial. One such was George Kaufman, who declared at his court martial in January 1917:

> I do not think it right that a man should hand himself over body and soul, to a military authority which can command him to kill his fellow men – men with whom as an individual he has no quarrel, and who are as innocent as himself. I believe wars can only be made to cease by such a realisation.

Kaufman had been arrested as an absentee under the Military Service Act and, when he had refused a medical at Whitehall, had been attested without signing any statement to that effect and assigned to the 31st Middlesex Regiment. He was sent to Wormwood Scrubs for most of 1917, and the experience affected him deeply, particularly his concept of the individual in war. After his release from prison, he found that he had lost faith in the prospect of a future peace and the steady advance of civilisation. Instead, all he perceived ahead was further strife, confusion and darkness. He wrote to his friend Helen Wedgwood that he used, like a 'good Fabian', to seek fulfilment in life through the possibilities inherent in physical existence and material things. Now, however, rather like Bertrand Russell, he recognised that many impulses to pain and violence existed and sometimes emanated from within himself and other individuals. Therefore, peace could not come from the external, material world; from without, but from within. He concluded, 'I am not meaning that I am now in favour of physical violence. But it seems to me far more an individual matter and not necessarily wrong for everybody.'[42]

If physical violence was not regarded as wrong by some, this did not mean it became automatically right and the only other option available. One who wavered between these extremes was Lieutenant A.V. Ratcliffe of the West Yorkshire Regiment, educated at Cambridge and Heidelberg and a published poet. He was described as a man who possessed 'a very high moral courage' by a Lieutenant Wooler, whose letter was published posthumously in *The Microcosm*, a literary magazine founded by Ratcliffe's sister-in-law and financed by his uncle, a former Mayor of Leeds. Ratcliffe's own thoughts on the ethics of fighting were published in the same magazine before his death (he was killed in action at Fricourt on 1 July 1916) in an article in which he rationalised his decision to fight and wear khaki, 'the dress of the pest slayer'. He wrote that, although he objected to helping the war by taking part in it, 'I cannot help helping', whether in an active or passive role. He was responding to the call of a 'dormant kinship' with other Englishmen fighting to protect their homes and willing to kill Germans not as individuals but as implements of something more powerful.

This deliberate dehumanisation of personality was a device to enable Ratcliffe to conquer his dislike of war as a concept and as a state of affairs. His stance contained an ironic element, given his support for the concept of individuality coupled with a knowledge, born of experience, of how war clashed with that concept: 'War is not concerned with the individual', he wrote, 'but with the whole sum of individuals, the state'. He stated that 'to submit to military tyranny, to give up that which one should value most in life – one's liberty – to measure oneself with other men not by the standard of ideals but by the standard of inches', as well as having to handle weapons and learn how to inflict death by various methods:

> all these things in peace time are morally indigestible to me. My whole being revolts against war and the usages of war, for I love life, and war is the tyranny of death ... If I have conscientious objection to the subjugation of ego and to the vulgarisation of the standards of living and of thought produced by the military mechanism, I have a tenfold stronger objection to war.[43]

Ratcliffe was a clear lover of life, an individual for whom the war meant a loss of personality in the military machine in its role as the facilitator of war, and who possessed a clear moral objection to the concept of war itself. His recognition of a further threat – that of a 'vulgarisation' of standards of life, and, by implication, of individual sensibility, is echoed again in the following section.

'Surrendering to the machine' – the coarsening of sensibility and imagination

In his Introduction to a volume similar to that of Guy Chapman's 'miscellany of the Great War', though published almost a decade earlier, C.B. Purdom stated that his overwhelming reaction to the various personal narratives of the Great War that he had edited was one of the senselessness of the whole thing. As a method of State action, it had no positive qualities, while on an individual basis, although men managed to retain in many cases their courage and spirit of self-sacrifice, these qualities had begun to lose their intrinsic value under the more or less constant sense of oppressive futility.

For Purdom, the war had been evil not only because men had been forced to suffer and die in it, but also because, 'it destroys the meaning of life'. To him, personal life could not be valued under the old standards any more and hence went into reverse while everything that had made it worth living faded away when a man, 'surrenders himself to the machine'.[44] Thus a new kind of state was formed in which the freedom to act according to one's conscience was severely curtailed. This, in turn, could affect the very value of individual personality, especially when one was forced against one's will – in Purdom's phrase, to 'surrender to the machine' and submit to the mechanised processes (both in thought and action) of the war.

The ties of comradeship in the armed forces could be very strong and were genuine in most cases but, as Stephen Graham observed, 'there is a deep hypnotical effect produced by the great army machine. Moving in its splendour and terror before the eyes, it suggests the thought to the heart: You have ceased to be anything or to count for anything in yourself.' Graham suggested that some who found themselves in the army – and perhaps would have made some stronger protest against the demands placed upon them as individuals – had entered a 'false sleep' in the army's presence, but, when the army was absent, 'the painful process of fighting the illusion begins'. He saw the modern way of war as a mechanised process which included the human beings involved. The one needful thing for the private soldier was obedience while imagination and thought, along with fear, love and even hate were regarded as out of place.

Graham found it difficult to consistently maintain his precept that the individual man was better than the army in which he found himself in the face of military brutality of thought, word and deed. He observed how this brutality was supported by some individuals in the army who were not in themselves brutal but cultivated that spirit 'to get the army tone', a tone which he thought especially marked by a deficit of 'life'. Graham, on the other hand, sought to humanise himself by reading poetry by the fireside in the barracks, the sensation of which he likened to the soft, calm touch of a woman. This was in response to the coarseness of life at the barracks – he had sensed himself, 'becoming duller, less sensitive to sights and sounds, more a possession of the army, more ready to kill and destroy than to be and to enjoy.'[45] Not only were bodies in uniform (which, to him, betokened 'hard duty and bondage'), but souls also, and Graham worried that it would take longer eventually to demobilise the souls than the bodies, a process that, in his view, could be aided by an appreciation of poetry, love and Nature.

For Graham, war robbed the individual of important, natural characteristics: reverence, tenderness and, most of all, 'the hush of awe which should silence and restrain'. He highlighted the 'immense gulf' that seemed to divide two categories of being that he identified: firstly, the man who was creative in some way and possessed an awareness that the hardest part in the reaction to army discipline was (as we have seen in the case of A.V. Ratcliffe and others) 'the suppression of individuality, the unconditional surrender of the individual-istic ego to the will of the nation'.[46] Secondly, the man who, in Graham's phrase, 'shoulders the rifle'. Both these states of being could be experienced by a single individual, as in Graham's case; 'When for the first time after many months I took up the pen again and tried to write', he wrote, 'I felt that even my hands had changed.'[47]

There existed a fissure, crucially exacerbated by the war, between the artistic individual and the ordinary soldier/citizen, through which much inspiration and initiative had drained. The war generation was deprived of its creative force and peacetime found men robbed of energy. 'As the floods of war slowly subsided', observed Lieutenant Colonel A.A. Hanbury-Sparrow, 'it revealed them for what they were, a land-locked lake, impotent to join the main stream of life; impotent to convey to it the deeper lessons of the war that they alone had sensed.'[48]

Many of those who left jobs and home life to go and fight, whether voluntarily or under duress, had assumed however, not unreasonably, that if they survived they would return, their labours ended, to a life much as they had left it. 'I gained a comforting security that the possibilities of my old life were being preserved, held in trust against the day when I should be able to resume them', wrote Arthur Graeme West of the Public Schools Battalion on the occasion of his last weekend leave before embarking for France.[49] He, like so many others, possessed a certain confidence that this preservation of life at home would be their reward for taking part in 'The War to End all Wars', an activity that was, to some, an escape from the ordinary routine of life while to others, simply anathema. West's initial army training in March 1915 offended his sensibilities with its 'irredeemable ugliness', but this was perhaps not surprising in one who had a great love for beauty, Nature and books and was, as described in the Introduction to his published diaries, a 'quiet, effaced sort of individual' and, 'a man of marked individuality and keen susceptibilities ... he had a habit of independent thinking. He was an individualist who hated routine and system as devices for suppressing men's differences.'[50]

West had been at Oxford when war had broken out; he had returned there in autumn 1914 to find most of his friends had already enlisted, and he acted on their example, as well as from an innate sense of duty. From then on his life became a succession of training and trenches which instilled in him an 'intense abhorrence' of army life. He never at any stage agreed with the killing (violence of any kind was also 'abhorrent to his nature') and returned to France with a commission in September 1916 with a deep sense of wrong, his pre-war belief in patriotism and the army having been severely shaken, with his former faith in its 'companionship, suffering courageously and ... noble necessity undergone' transformed to 'violent revulsion', while his personal concept of God had been reduced to that of a 'malignant practical joker'. He recognised that he had been under many delusions when at first he had joined up, but that most of these ('especially the religious ones') had faded under the 'beastly and degrading' nature of war.

Prior to returning to France, West had read Bertrand Russell's *On Justice in War-Time* and agreed with him that the war was trivial despite its vastness. He also met some conscientious objectors in whom, along with philosophers like Russell, he found hope for the future ('the living force ... the light that must come sooner or later'). Rather like Bloomsbury, he believed that to bring happiness into the world was the only worthwhile aim of human activity, while action undertaken with any other aim in mind was wasteful, and he deplored the fact that many individuals could only see the war as the most important thing in the world, thus overlooking the ideal trinity of Truth, Beauty and Love.

A month before he returned to the front with his commission West contemplated desertion, 'pained, bored and maddened' by the fact that the army had an automatic right to demand that he give up his chance of obtaining happiness. He likened himself to a creature caught in a net 'by the proprietors of some travelling circus and forced with formal brutality to go through meaningless tricks'.[51] He attempted to place his faith in the promise of a life begun again after the war and in Nature, which he thought would not suffer to see harmed 'a lover so loyal and keen-sighted'. However, he could not restrain himself from asking of what use a life of intellectual training and 'sensitising myself to exquisite impressions' had been if he were merely to be snuffed out at random for a cause so far from his own. He began to realise, under the weight of raw impressions, the 'absolute nonentity' of all he held dear and the lack of permanent value or goodness in the world he now observed. All existence now seemed at times futile and even his former life now appeared vacant and stale, 'when all books seemed to have been written, all pictures painted, all experience and sensation opened up for no good reason at all', and the world was, 'a silly blind drift, purposeless and unintelligible'.[52]

On leave in London, he had a sense that both himself and the external world would not return to their former, pre-war states; he felt that both he and the city itself had been too deeply 'stained' by the war to revert back to normality and that, coupled to his loss of faith, his former softness had drained away, leaving him harder and 'more ferocious in nature', a process which he railed against and felt symbolised the effect of the war upon individuals:

> Duty to country and king and civilisation! Nonsense! For none of these is a man to be forced to leave his humanity on one side and make a passionate destroying beast of himself. I am a man before I am anything else, and all that is human in me revolts.[53]

There seemed a side to the war that denied or suppressed creative thinking and all that had been civilised in thought and expression, a war that, to some, increased in illogicality the further it progressed and the more it was observed with a critical eye. 'I have seen roads and railroads lined with unrecognisable creatures, living, cursing, dead and utterly forsaken, all struggling and trying to turn their blind efforts at what we call patriotism to some kind of individual peace', wrote Captain E.G. Venning of the Royal Sussex Regiment to his sister in the early summer of 1915.

To Venning, the war was stultifying in that it consisted only of 'meaningless orders obeyed by brainless heads', and he was much struck by the 'smallness' of it all in terms of the individual experience contrasted with the whole 'mighty business'. He found that his pre-war view of the individual had not only re-mained but become stronger when set against the conflict: 'the individual counts', he was moved to reiterate, while noting the extreme meanness of the army's practise of 'aggressive herding'. Venning was almost glad that the war had acted on some to harden the individual's fragile carapace of sensibility as this prevented in some cases a full realisation of the futility of the situation. 'Hap-pily', he wrote, 'one has no chance to think. The "why?" and "what is it all about?" trouble only the few'.[54]

If one spent time analysing the situation, one might come to the conclusion that the only good aspects of a war-life were a warm billet and good company: the rest being not only a waste of energy but also a draining of energy, an increased roughness of personality, so that a warm billet was perhaps all that one was capable of enjoying. Any deep thought or analysis only led one to appreciate the 'unsettling influence' of the war and the, 'precarious tenure of our time, and the insignificance of any individual efforts'.[55]

These comments were expressed by Stephen Hewett, a 2nd Lieutenant in the Royal Warwickshire Regiment who had won a scholarship to Balliol College, Oxford in 1910 and who had applied for a commission in December 1914. 'In this military life', he wrote while undergoing training at Windmill Hill Camp:

> or perhaps I should say for everybody in this time of war, one is made to lose that old dependence upon what seemed the greatest element of happiness – the sense of per-manence and stability and a singleness of aims in one's work and movements ... one is the worse for losing that sense. But now one must grow coarser or at all events harder.[56]

Hewett's chief consolation during this process was the camaraderie of his fel-low officers, which he likened to the friendships he had experienced at Oxford, although he realised that too many recollections of his former life and thoughts of personal ambition were 'unnatural' in the setting of the unreal time of the front and better left, 'until one can shut one's study door again, and know that one's time is one's own', although in this mixing of past academic memories and future hopes, he was well aware that the return of those days was anything but certain.

In common with E.G. Venning, Hewett commented on the 'littleness' of the life at the front: 'one develops a kind of myopia ... by which one's vision is confined to very little things'.[57] A man was forced to live from day to day and be satisfied with 'an animal life' amid the desolation of the theatre of war in which the things that decided the fortunes and major events of the war literally passed over the heads of the insignificant infantryman in the form of shells and other high explosives. Any interest that lay in dug-out life and the ruined land-scape was confined to novelty, a novelty which quickly wore off and could only sustain the contents of a single letter, the writing of which had become difficult in itself. 'Another reason for my general slackness in writing letters (to everybody) is the gradual coarsening of one's feelings, due partly to the sameness of one's experiences', Hewett explained. This process was inevitable, he continued, 'for, if one did not quickly lose one's first sensibility, one would have to knuckle under and come home.'[58]

Hewett recognised that the experience of war was worse for those who appreciated life and for whom the pre-war period had meant a chance to do some work of lasting value, work which could not be accomplished by fighting. He commented to his sister Mary that the artist or individual who 'lives for the expression of beauty' stood to lose far more by the loss of their creative life than those of a religious persuasion and who 'enjoy a good which eternity cannot take away'. He felt that the war, at its close, in addition to leaving 'a scar upon the very earth' would also leave a 'stain on the imagination' of those who experienced it, despite the process of coarsening and hardening of attitude towards the crudeness and bleakness of the front. For, as he pointed out, it was not as easy to be hardened towards the pathos of things. One might get used to sights of terrible injury and death in the trenches, 'but the feeling of spring in a quiet orchard and repose behind the line ... have the power to make one *think*'.[59] It was perhaps better to be in the midst of action of some kind. Accordingly, Hewett led out his platoon in an attack on 22 July 1916 on the Somme and never returned.

For some, then, even the power of thought and imagination was sullied or immured by the war's drain on the senses. This was not true for all, of course; some were oblivious while others, such as the poets of the war, found themselves stimulated into creativity by their experiences – stimulated to protest in some cases. Many soldiers had, in any case, gone straight from school to slaughter, and the war was simply just another experience. But for some, it was different: 'I was far more immature than my contemporaries', recalled Monk Gibbon of the ASC (a non-combatant corps) who had left behind an open History exhibition at Keble College, Oxford for an army commission, 'but I had learnt to philosophise. And it was a bad moment to do so.' In the 'reign of unreason' that war had come to be, the individual soldier was lost if he attempted to find structured patterns of behaviour and motivation in the chaos around him. 'It is fatal for him to question his individual conscience', warned Gibbon in the Foreword to his memoir, *Inglorious Soldier*.[60]

Like Stephen Hewett, Gibbon recognised that time spent not engaged in combat was time to think and hence dangerous time to the Army who were in the business of disciplining men's minds as well as their bodies. 'The men out here are not encouraged to think', he wrote to E.D. Morel of the UDC in August 1917, 'but at the same time the Army realises that every man in being allowed a certain amount of time off duty, is in danger of perhaps spending part of that time thinking.' Hence all the concert parties and cinemas existed to fill leisure time collectively and keep the men from escaping the system, the net result being that, 'man ceases to believe in his own individuality'.[61]

Gibbon, the son of a Dublin clergyman and who served fourteen months in France from July 1916, had already stressed this fact – that army discipline meant 'death to individuality' – in a letter to his sister during the previous winter. 'The soldier today', he wrote, 'is a man goaded by his nation into fighting for so-called ideals; never given chance to see things in perspective, never given a chance to think for himself, never given an opportunity to consider the other side except in the most distorted form.'[62] At this point in the war, Gibbon was afraid that if men did not start to think for themselves, the conflict would be prolonged for years rather than months. He had felt his sense of the logical to be affronted by his experience of the war which in turn had brought forth an anger at the injustice and tragedy he observed as well as an acknowledgement that his was a minority view and that most people who had lost a loved one in the conflict would not react kindly to suggestions that the fallen had been sacrificed for a mistaken ideal.

It was during the summer of 1917 ('A summer of the seasons but a winter of the spirit'), after serving a year in France, that Gibbon suffered his most intense inner anguish over his role in the war. He found himself fighting to the north of Arras and on Vimy Ridge amid a landscape of desolation contrasted with 'tragically accidental greenery' when he wrote his second letter to his commanding officer asking to be removed from his position in the army. He had sent the first letter, supported by his friend Sir Francis Vane, at the start of 1917 and had been advised to give his 'theories' a rest and instead busy himself with ordinary duties. His second letter contained his resignation of his commission and stated that he had initially applied for military service under the influence of 'brass bands and the daily press'. The letter also requested that he be given work in connection with the Royal Army Medical Corps.

For Gibbon, a righteous war was now a contradiction in terms, and patriotism was either sentiment or self-interest. He could find no justification for the slaughter and realised that whichever side achieved victory, the world as a whole was bound to be poorer materially as well as in spirit, as was the individual. In a poem written at Souchez, he had expressed his perception of the war's coarsening effect: 'We have hardened our hearts within us … We have forgotten softness'. Sir Francis, who wrote to General Haig on Gibbon's behalf, agreed with him; the war, wrote Sir Francis, was 'a perversion of intelligence' and 'not in the least enabling to the individual, generally speaking – on the contrary, with the exception of a very few choice spirits, it is degrading'.[63]

The War Office awarded Gibbon merely compassionate leave, though he was later admitted to hospital suffering from shell-shock and eventually sent home. However, he decided against taking up once more the open History exhibition at Keble College, Oxford, and so remained in the army, classified 'permanent Home Service'.

Gibbon and the men like him provide evidence for a specific awareness amongst some soldiers of the effect of the military machine upon individual

minds: a coarsening or roughening of previously fine-tuned intellects or aesthetic sensibilities that was as unexpected as it was resented. The dead
otherworldliness of the front and savage reality of armed combat was a
world removed from any previous peacetime University Officer Training
Corps or Military Training Programmes. Now some men were unable to
think, work or appreciate former valued elements of life to the same degree
as in their former lives. This recognition and the awareness of it echoes the
sentiments of Bloomsbury, Bertrand Russell and other individuals observed
in the earlier chapters, whether in the front line or in familiar surroundings.

Representatives of life, civilisation and the imagination

The value of life to a soldier at the front could become grossly exaggerated
amid the constant danger of extinction. However, the opposite could also be
true for some individuals. Some men who fought the war were in danger of
losing their sense of the value of life. 'Religion, philosophy, the arts: what have
they to do with us? Words, words', confided one soldier to his diary, when
allowed time to reflect whilst at rest in Amiens. 'The war has cheapened life till
it is of little or no value', he concluded.[64]

To some observers the danger of conflicts involving the very value of life was
obvious. To Stephen Winsten, a contemporary of Issac Rosenberg at the Slade,
the position to take was clear: 'I could see the significance of pacifism, the
destructive against the creative aspect.'[65] The reactions of Winsten and his wife
to the war are an example of the struggle at work between creative and destructive forces during the war.

Winsten was a teacher in Wapping and worked on a voluntary basis for the
National Council Against Conscription (alongside Lytton Strachey and the writer
and critic Gilbert Cannan) during the first half of the war. He believed that
some form of practical protest was the only response to a situation he found
both to be ignoble and shameful. He refused the exemption which was offered
by his local tribunal in 1916 (as this would mean the pretence of doing land
work whilst in fact resuming his teaching and thus in effect a silencing of his
convictions). This refusal came after he had already endured two months of
solitary confinement in Wormwood Scrubs. He was then sent to Bedford Prison.
His wife left the Central School of Arts and Crafts in protest at a proclamatory
notice prohibiting German students from attending classes. She then joined the
NCF and took a cottage near her husband's prison and found teaching work in
the surrounding area. Winsten read and appreciated Bernard Shaw's *Common
Sense about the War* and found himself thinking that, after the initial glorifica-
tion of war, an attitude of common sense which might put an end to the conflict
could only occur when the mass of individuals involved in it reached what was
to him, 'a kind of moral sense'.

Another overview of the war from one who, like Winsten (though in a different way) stepped back from it was recorded by William Bell, an architect, who, towards the end of the war worked for the Friends War Victims Relief Committee erecting temporary accommodation for civilians displaced by the conflict around them. In the area of the liberated Marne he noted French and German graves lying together by the road to Chatillon and found himself forced to search for some kind of deeper meaning to the war, as a means of justifying the fact that former enemies were now side by side, equalled in death. 'In spite of all the diplomatic twaddle about world conquest', he wrote, '... One cannot look upon such tragic memorials without cogitating on the causes which have produced such pathetic effects.'

Bell found no end to justify the means and instead found it inexplicable that 'some harmless Prussian lad' should have been marched from some small hamlet in eastern Germany in order to fight to the death with an equally harmless young French boy, both now lying together as if brothers. Of course, they had been brothers – in humanity, he concluded, and not enemies. They had been sent by the real enemies, the statesmen, to blindly grapple with each other 'like fighting-cocks in the back-yard of an inn'.[66]

Near Chateau-Thierry, Bell regarded salvage-dumps by the roadside made up of abandoned guns and heaps of scrap-iron. 'What a monument of misplaced energy was represented in this wilderness of waste', he found himself thinking, 'What a pygmy man actually is in the face of such damning evidence of his so-called greatness.' Then, like Patrick MacGill and Charles Douie, he compared the spoliation and waste around him to that of an earlier period of human history to illuminate the negative effect of 'modern' warfare: 'The primitive flint-bludgeons of the cave-dwellers that we see nowadays lying in the museums, are no more an anachronism than are those highly complex weapons of the modern trench-dwellers that lie on the green heights above Chateau-Thierry.'[67]

When Bell surveyed the destruction of Rheims Cathedral he fumed at the 'colossal presumption' of modern man in laying waste, for modern motives, the evidence of the motives and ideals of an earlier age. He had much experience both of the actual military movements (such as the Allied armies' retreat from the Somme) and of the ruin done to people and communities as the conflict passed over them and this affected him deeply:

> To have seen the physical suffering and the mental anguish caused to innocent people – civilians and soldiers alike – by Lord Roberts' quack prescription labelled War – 'the only natural tonic'; and to have witnessed the broken homes and blighted lives of those I have dwelt among during the past winter – is an experience both spiritual and physical, to which it is utterly beyond the compass of my vocabulary adequately to give expression.[68]

Bell wrote his memoir of the war in the months immediately following the Armistice, and his thoughts naturally turned to the future and his hope that 'those who believe in the common brotherhood of Humanity' would 'blaze the trail of spiritual Principle' in order to set a blighted civilisation back on the true road of progress and understanding. He cited specifically several of those individuals whom, though thought of as 'outlaws' during the war by much of modern society, Bell felt represented the future of the 'newer' civilisation: Bertrand Russell, Edward Carpenter, Israel Zangwill, Patrick Geddes, Henri Barbusse and Siegfried Sassoon. This 'newer' civilisation would discard living soldiers as well as toy ones and would enable man to understand his adversary instead of trying to destroy him, while common humanity would be expressed by a shared appreciation of beauty and the processes of creation rather than destruction, as Russell had also hoped. Reason would triumph over material force: principle over policy and love over hate.

It had been largely the practicalities of rehousing the dispossessed that had informed Bell's war experience and gave him a needed stimulus to carry on during a reign of destruction which to Bell, especially considering his profession as an architect and creator, was horrific. In tandem with the practical process of reversing the damage done by the conflict was Bell's hope for a brighter future and a new civilisation to follow the old.

For many, the war had marked a transition between one era and another – most commonly, a transition from a time of achievement, progress and familiarity to one of random change and general uncertainty. The novelist Stephen McKenna, who, having attended Westminster School and then Christ Church College, Oxford (from 1906), had been fully part of the 'Edwardian Generation', saw this change as one affecting all aspects of life: socially, economically, politically, intellectually and ethically.

In common with William Bell, McKenna identified and praised the individuality of those 'spirits dwelling in isolation' who 'struggled to preserve detachment' such as D.H. Lawrence, John Masefield and Gilbert Cannan. Again like Bell and Patrick MacGill he highlighted the state of a modern civilisation convulsed and degenerated by war to resemble a 'society' of the distant past, commenting that during the war and especially during times of particular crisis such as the German offensive of March 1918, 'the restraints of modern civilisation were burst on the resurgence of primitive man'. Those of a sensitive nature (who had 'fared delicately and lived softly') were 'dragged back across the ages' to a state of self-seeking intrigue and intoxication. The tide of civilising influence had gone out leaving only a state in which, 'the bravery of the savage emerged hand in hand with the savage's philosophy, his licence, his superstition and his credulity'.[69] McKenna described the war, especially during its early period, as being 'organised fury' and, in this extremely focused and hence constricting atmosphere, he deplored the fact that, in terms of the experience of many writers, artists and thinkers, 'Meditation was not allowed to become articulate until the armistice', a state of affairs that some felt as an extreme pressure.

'I have never had time to think', wrote R.H. Kiernan, who had joined up, in October 1917 aged seventeen, 'I have had nothing, nothing. I want to get back from all this, back out of it – and sit and think, and look at clean things.' Kiernan had attested rather than wait to be conscripted, following in the footsteps of his two elder brothers. At first, after training at Catterick Camp, he served with a Mercian Regiment but was then transferred to 'the Huntshires'. At Catterick he was often caught reading when off duty and this led to his nickname of 'College' and to some physical abuse, usually at night. He saw six months of active service near Ypres, the Marne and the Somme which was cut short when he was wounded in September 1918 and out of action from then on.

Kiernan's youthful enthusiasm and desire to emulate his brothers did not prepare him for his experiences in Belgium and France where, 'death seems to hang in the very air. We live in it, and it's always heavy round us, even when one is thinking of something else.' The grey sky of the dawn mirrored for him the uncertainty of the coming day, and his own future, while above the landscape constantly seemed to hover an 'awful spirit', and fear pressed him down and enveloped him like a 'shapeless shadow'. His only emotions were a strong desire to get away from all this and a sense of frustration that, as he said, he had no time to think properly. This was prompted by an analysis of Rupert Brooke's poem 'The Soldier', which Kiernan found that he could not empathise with. Kiernan felt that he did not possess Brooke's experiences of life, love and travel nor his opportunities to think and appreciate – hence Kiernan's 'I have had nothing' cry – borne of thwarted ambition and regret. Above all, he recognised that, at the front, 'every man seems to be living in a small life of his own', shrunken and contracted from the norm. This was not unfriendliness but the isolation of constant fear; 'I know that Death is talking to them all.'[70]

The values of loyalty and comradeship still existed and were demonstrated, but sometimes only on the surface. 'It would seem as though most of those who come over here have a dual personality, a dream-life and a real one', wrote G.B. Manwaring, an officer in 'Kitchener's Army', in a letter back home of summer 1917. To some, the actualities of the war represented the real life, and the old life in England seemed imagined, but for others, the reality of home life was a source of strength when confronted with the nightmare of life at the front. Manwaring saw that, 'mine is not a nature that is really shaped for war', and that, in common with Stephen Hewett and Monk Gibbon, 'A vivid imagination is here a handicap, and it is those who have little or none that make the best soldiers.'[71] He admitted his love of beauty in all its forms, the appreciation of which was almost like a religion to him, the 'gospels' of which were beautiful creations and the 'apostles' the great artists of music or literature. Like Kiernan, he used his time off duty at night to read and write in order to counteract the effects, worse in the still of the night, of the constant carnage and desolation all around which, 'must tinge one's mind towards gloom'. Manwaring found that his imagination had become stained: 'One's pictures are set in sombre colours and one's pen reflects mainly their darker hues.'

Like William Bell, Manwaring's hope was that a new society would be born of the chaos and that, 'we who come back will do so with new standards and ideals', which could be used as the first building blocks in the construction of this new order. Only with this hope could the sacrifice demanded be worth the price paid in life, limb and ambition, a precept brought home to him by his job of censoring the letters of other soldiers. These 'dips below the surface of life' with their individual longings to return to families and normal life reinforced his own view of the war as a destroyer of life, beauty and the natural order of things. Mixed with his hope for a new humanity and faith ('whose prophets are the poets, whose Godhead is nature') was a fear that the war's effect would be *too* detrimental to the soul for a resurgence of the human spirit to occur: 'Will the present generation ever know contentment again, or will there come to them in the silence of the sleep time a vague yearning for "Life again?"'[72]

George Baker, a former bank clerk from Kent, also championed the values of a threatened civilisation – to such an extent that he was eventually imprisoned for it after being caught up in the net of the 1916 Military Service Act. In common with Patrick MacGill, William Bell and others, Baker deplored the backwardness of the war's effect on society and especially the youth of that society. The politicians of Europe had, according to Baker, persuaded the young men of Europe to, 'dig two long and narrow ditches across Europe's face' and then had compelled youth to become, 'ditch-men and cave-men, and to translate Stone-Age barbarities into terms of poison-gas, liquid-fire, land-mine and aerial torpedo'. He felt no affinity with organised Socialism and with its tendency, as he saw it, toward uniformity, and he disliked what he saw as the same negative aspect of the NCF. He read and largely supported Shaw's *Common Sense About the War*, despite its 'war-acquiescence', and described anti-war MP Philip Morrell as 'my hero'.

Baker appealed to his local tribunal as a 'free-lance pacifist' with strident objections: 'For myself, I would be neither ditch or cave-man', he decided and instead 'stood for' civilisation against the encroachment of barbarism, peace against patriotism and love against hate. 'I had not a conscientious objection against war so much as an intellectual and emotional objection', he later wrote.[73] On these grounds he claimed total exemption from all military service, both combatant and non-combatant; however, he was only granted non-combatant exemption, and his subsequent appeal was turned down by the Canterbury Appeal Tribunal.

After a failed attempt to go on hunger-strike in April 1916, Baker was sent to Shoreham Camp and passed around from the 16th Royal Fusiliers to the 3rd Eastern Company, Non-Combatant Corps, (while trying to resist various attempts by the Plymouth Brethren to make him 'see the light' of their particular religious outlook). Baker was then forced to load ships with food and drink for the army at Newhaven and spent the winter of 1916-17 in Lewes before he was sent to Larkhill Camp on Salisbury Plain to build and destroy roads and then, finally, to Wormwood Scrubs where he met a few like-minded individuals. One was a painter known as 'Mac'. Baker was relieved to have met a man who, 'though he cared for peace ... cared more for creative beauty', and he compared his own experience and aims to those of men like Sassoon and Graves – 'I, whose prison-life was their trench-life's complement'. They were all individuals in whom 'the heart's desire was not Cause spelt with a large "C", but Beauty with a large "B".' Both he and 'Mac' grew angry when they regarded a spectacular sunset from the prison window, a reminder that the politicians had 'filched beauty' from their experience and were, 'biting from our lives the best days of the best years'.

Reviews of some of 'Mac's' (whose real name was Alan McDougall) translations appeared in the *Athenaeum* and *Saturday Review*, though by that stage 'Mac' was too weak to read them. To Baker, McDougall the former man seemed dead and in his place existed, 'a walking number in mis-fitting broad-arrows and shuffling shoes'.[74] The two lovers of beauty were reunited in Winchester Gaol, after Baker had been taken under guard to Bulford Camp near Stonehenge to face a District Court Martial, at which he was sentenced to eighteen months hard labour. Baker (who was not released until April 1919, aged twenty-four) finally reconciled himself somewhat to prison life as a method of showing his solidarity with the soldiers at the front via a shared lack of both freedom and an ability to appreciate the finer things of life.

This chapter has uncovered a collection of lesser-known individuals united by various themes of aesthetic, humanistic and moral opposition to the war and its effects. Monk Gibbon's lamenting of a 'forgotten softness' was characteristic of those who viewed the conflict as a coarsening of aesthetic sensibilities. For those who took, like George Baker, the trinity of truth, beauty and love as their ideals, the war effected, in the words of Stephen Hewett, a 'stain on the imagination' that proved hard to remove. Hewett also recognised that this effect was mirrored by 'a scar upon the very earth' – the warping of the natural world at the front, though to be deplored in itself, was also a physical expression of the inner mental turmoil that affected many individuals, particularly those of a sensitive or artistic disposition. The army was likened to a ravening beast without a soul which consumed individuals without thought, or it was merely a machine, the operation of which processed personality into uniformity.

Men found themselves sunk to the levels of animals (literally nearer to the earth) and were treated as such. In Chapter 4, we noted John Galsworthy's description of 'the herd of life' that he felt existed at the time, and the 'herding' of men became a common metaphor employed to describe the situation. In addition to the coarsening effect of the war, there existed also a recognition of a corresponding submersion of personality within the army machine and the enveloping physical and mental landscape of the war. This decline in individuality and growth of personal isolation – with a soldier pushed into 'a small life of his own' (R.H. Kiernan) was mirrored in the eyes of some by a moral exhaustion – a degeneration of morality which seemed to set back the clock of progress. Just as nature had seemed to revert to primordial chaos, so the decline of civilised values pointed to a reversal of time and, as Stephen McKenna described, a 'resurgence of primitive man'. What hope from this new 'stone age'?

Notes

1 'A large majority [of contributors], though firmly convinced that what they do is right – or right in the sense that it is inevitable – show their detestation of war in its operation.' Some of the letters contained 'the cry of a violated conscience'. Housman pointed out that the men who fought and died in the conflict were not all 'lovers of war, or believers in war ... many of them learned to hate the war, from having known it, as they could not have hated it before'. Those who 'tasted war' (and 'in their souls turned from it in loathing') had as much right to claim the Cenotaph as their memorial as those that died 'more happily accepting war as a means and believing that good might come out of it'. Introduction, *War Letters of Fallen Englishmen*, ed. Laurence Housman (London, 1930), pp. 5–6, 10.
2 *Ibid.*, Captain A.I. Adams (to his sister), 9 July 1916, pp. 21–2.
3 W. Beach Thomas, *With the British on the Somme* (London, 1917), p. 275. Beach Thomas was an accredited war correspondent.
4 Stephen Graham, *The Challenge of the Dead* (London, 1921), p. 95, Graham was also the author of *A Private in the Guards* (London, 1919).
5 *War Letters*, ed. Housman, Lieutenant R.H. Pickering, 1 Sept. 1915, p. 215.
6 *Ibid.*, Sergeant James Duncan, 5 Sept. 1918, p. 98.
7 University of Leads, Liddle Collection (UL,LC hereafter), file of Corporal H.L. Currall, typescript of letter dated 1 July 1918.
8 *Ibid.*, typescript of letter dated 30 Sept. 1917.
9 *Ibid.*, file of J.B. Herbert, diary entry, Sept. 1918. pp. 22–4.
10 *Ibid.*
11 *War Letters*, ed. Housman, Lieutenant B. Pitt, 31 March 1916, p. 216.
12 'Bombardier X', *So This is War* (London, 1930), Feb. 1918, p. 148.
13 UL,LC, file of W.B. Kitching, diary entry, 18 April 1917.
14 *Ibid.*, diary entry, 5 Dec. 1917.
15 Norman D. Cliff, *To Hell and Back with the Guards*, (Braunton, Devon, 1988), pp. 63–6.
16 Charles Douie, *The Weary Road* (London, 1929), pp. 152–3.
17 Patrick MacGill, *The Great Push* (London, 1916), p. 253.
18 *Ibid.*, p. 251.
19 Wyn Griffith, *Up To Mametz*, (London, 1931), pp. 111–13.
20 *Ibid.*, p. 73.
21 *Ibid.*, pp. 73–4.
22 *Ibid.*, pp. 73–6.
23 *War Letters*, ed. Housman, 2nd Lieutenant W.H. Ratcliffe, June 1916, p. 225.
24 *Vain Glory: A Miscellany of the Great War 1914–18*, ed. Guy Chapman (London, 1937), p. x.
25 R.H. Mottram in R.H. Mottram, John Easten and Eric Partridge, *Three Personal Records of the War* (London, 1929), p. 140.
26 *Vain Glory*, ed. Chapman, p. xi.

27 *War Letters*, ed. Housman, Captain J.E. Crombie, 3 March 1917, p. 83.

28 Arthur Osburn, *Unwilling Passenger* (London, 1932), pp. 221–2.

29 UL,LC, file of Eric Pritchard Southall, defence of E.P. Southall and written for his court martial at Littlemore Camp, Weymouth, 19 Oct. 1916.

30 UL,LC, file of Revd C.G. Raven, letter to Burgess, Fellow and former Dean of Emmanuel College, Cambridge, 27 June 1917.

31 Stephen Bowen, *Forsaken – Confessions of a Priest who Returned* (London, 1931), p. 91.

32 *Ibid.*, pp. 232–3.

33 UL,LC, file of C.G. Raven, letter to Burgess, 16 June 1917.

34 Guy Chapman, *A Passionate Prodigality* (London, 1965), p. 1. Chapman's book was originally published in 1933.

35 *Love of an Unknown Soldier, Found in a Dug-out*, ed. John Lane (London, 1918), pp. 36–7.

36 *War Letters*, ed. Housman, Lieutenant A.C. Stephen MC, RFA, Sept. 1916, p. 261.

37 Charles Edmonds (pseud. of Charles Carrington), *A Subaltern's War* (London, 1929), letter of Oct. 1916, pp. 28–9 and letter of Dec. 1916, pp. 221–2.

38 Charles Berjew Brooke, *Letters from the Boy* (privately published, Imperial War Museum collection), 30 June 1916.

39 Frank Gray, *Confessions of a Private* (Oxford, 1920), p. 202.

40 Mottram, Eastern and Partridge, *Three Records*, p. 139.

41 *Letters from the Front*, ed. John Laffin (London, 1973), Captain Theodore Cameron Wilson, to Mrs Orpen, 3 May 1916, p. 8.

42 Imperial War Museum (IWM hereafter), file of Mrs H. Pease, 76/179/1, transcription of the defence of George Kaufman at his court martial, 19 Jan. 1917 and letter to Helen Bowen Wedgwood, 30 Oct. 1917.

43 UL,LC, file of Alfred Victor Ratcliffe, 'The Conscientious Objector', *The Microcosm*.

44 C.B. Purdom (ed.), *Everyman at War: Sixty Personal Narratives of the War* (London, 1930), p. vii.

45 Graham, *A Private in the Guards*, pp. 84–5.

46 *Ibid.*, p. 347.

47 *Ibid.*, p. 25.

48 Lieutenant Colonel A.A. Hanbury-Sparrow, *The Land-locked Lake* (London, 1932), pp. 299–300.

49 A.G. West, *Diary of a Dead Officer* (London, 1919), diary entry, 7 Nov. 1915, p. 4.

50 *Ibid.*, p. xiii.

51 *Ibid.*, p. 23.

52 *Ibid.*, p. 10.

53 *Ibid.*, p. 58.

54 *War Letters*, ed. Housman, Captain E.G. Venning, to his sister, May and June 1915, pp. 281–3.

55 Stephen H. Hewett, *A Scholar's Letters from the Front* (London, 1918), to F.F. Urquhart, 1 March 1916, p. 23.

56 *Ibid.*, to Mrs Robertson, 18 Oct. 1915, p. 3.

57 *Ibid.*, to Mrs Robertson, 11 April, 1916, pp. 52–3.

58 *Ibid.*, to Charles Robertson, 27 May 1916, p. 84.

59 *Ibid.*, to F.F. Urquhart, Fellow of Balliol, 2 April 1916, p. 51.

60 Monk Gibbon, *Inglorious Soldier* (London, 1968), p. xii.

61 *Ibid.*, letter to E.D. Morel, 20 Aug. 1917, reproduced pp. 332–3.

62 *Ibid.*, p. 194.

63 *Ibid.*, p. 227.

64 Edmonds, *A Subaltern's War*, diary, Dec. 1916, pp. 221–2.

65 IWM, Sound Archive, file of Stephen Samuel Winsten.

66 William Bell, *A Scavenger In France* (London, 1920), pp. 247–8.

67 *Ibid.*, p. 259.
68 *Ibid.*, pp. 92–3.
69 Stephen McKenna, *While I Remember* (London, 1921), pp. 144–5, 221.
70 R.H. Kiernan, *Little Brother Goes Soldiering* (London, 1936), pp. 120–4.
71 G.B. Manwaring, *If We Return* (London, 1918), pp. 17, 137.
72 *Ibid.*, p. 162.
73 George Baker, The *Soul of a Skunk* (London, 1930), p. 115.
74 *Ibid.*, pp. 199–200.

8

Three individuals

A new type of warfare demanded a new type of response. Amid the jagged and broken setting, the metaphorical usage of the overwhelming effect of man's new and mechanised forms of warfare on the natural landscape became common. We have seen in Chapter 7 how this, in turn, could act as a trigger on some individuals to encompass a humanistic appreciation of the wrongness of war itself.

An awareness of the conflict's malign effects seemed to reach beyond the desolation of Nature. There now occurred a perceived alteration of the steady progress of time itself, its linear structure sometimes compressed to give the effect that time had actually halted, as in Lieutenant Wyn Griffith's account of the battle of Mametz Wood.[1] For some, the effects of the war seemed to turn time in upon itself, thereby unwinding the clock of human development to a darker age peopled by trench-dwelling brutes who had lost comprehension of what they were fighting over.

This 'throw-back' concept was highlighted by H.S. Innes of the 23rd Battalion (later 20th), the Middlesex Regiment. At the battle front, H.S. Innes found himself comparing the area around the dug-outs of the front line with that around the 'outer dug-outs' further back and hence less affected by the physical effects of battle. The scene he observed at the front during the bleak winter of early 1917 was, 'the abomination of desolation. From eaves such as primitive man might have occupied we looked out over a shell battered valley.'[2] He noted the few remaining trees on the hillside and the stench from the lower ground, and he likened the 'canyon' over which shells whirred incessantly to one from the bleakness of Arizona. By the end of the year, he wrote that the mud all around had become a normal feature of life and that, 'war without mud would not be war'.

The unnatural and blighted landscape was once again linked directly to the war's effect on a way of life and a setting that became increasingly primordial with time. The story of H.S. Innes represents an awareness of the retardation of civilised values and the idea of man being transformed to an altogether more primitive state – in addition to the concept of individuality under threat and, as Innes put it, 'the importance of each man to himself' radically reduced.

Innes had been one of the earliest men to be called up in February 1916, though he had not been sent to France until early December of that year, after training at Shoreham camp. Like many others, at the beginning of his training he was optimistic in outlook and clear in his motives. 'Remember', he wrote to his mother in March, 'when I am forced to be away from home as I am, that it is all in order that we may all have many happy years in peace afterwards, years which we shall value the more because we shall have paid for them'.[3] His mother had attempted to persuade him to avoid army service and appeal against his calling-up, but Innes had noted that men were being taken from non-combatant bodies and placed in the infantry regiments and that it was impossible at that time to obtain a transfer from one regiment to another. He remarked that he had done what little he could to avoid going to France but to no avail; the Military Service Act had transformed Britain in his view to a 'conscript country', and he rationalised the situation by submitting to the forces of destiny and a desire to have some part in the overthrow of Prussianism. Crucially, he knew that many had already volunteered ('a thing I never did'), and he felt he had to undergo the ordeal of the front in order to meet others afterwards with similar levels of experience. 'When I meet people after the war who have lost sons or brothers or friends', he rationalised, 'it will be easier for me to look in their faces than it would be if I had stayed out of it.'[4]

The rigours of army life did not appeal to him and, when presenting arms to a visiting general, he likened himself to a performing dog and wrote with some degree of rancour to his mother that, 'A soldier is a man only when off duty, on-duty he is regarded as a well trained animal.'[5] Being a pianist himself, his main pleasure during his training were the camp concerts, though he deplored the situation whereby some of the more talented artists were forced to lower their classical standards. Most concert items were popular chorus songs, and Innes noted critically the murmurs of boredom during one of the few classical items presented, a duet from Verdi's opera *Il Trovatore*. After a few weeks of training, he arrived at an explanation of why a *private* soldier was so-called – because, according to his experience, all the thoughts, affairs and interests of an individual were of an entirely solitary nature 'and are not admitted to exist' by the army hierarchy. The more private affairs that concerned an individual, the more they would act as an encumbrance. 'The army is no place for a man of intelligence', Innes wrote, 'or one who is used to active independence, whether in business or in his spare time.'[6]

The burden of his experience pressed Innes to greater depths of criticism of his new, regimented life and the anomalies he found therein, such as the wastes of labour and instruction apparent when he observed qualified farriers or signallers being sent abroad as ordinary privates as well as the decisions of one day being reversed the next for no apparent reason. All this left Innes with little confidence in his future and the daily practicalities of life. He could only place his faith in abstracts and thus attached his uncertain fate to that of 'the nation', in whose future he felt more confident ('The duty of the nation is the duty of the individual'). This reasoning relieved the pressure of conscience to such an extent that he now found himself able to examine the inequality of service that he saw existed around him, such as those individuals who had innocently obtained jobs before the war only to find these posts assuming irrational importance in time of war and hence were able to serve their country with honour without having to actually engage in any form of combat, while others were protected from the firing line by specially selected 'safe' military positions hastened into at the outbreak of hostilities.

Innes also highlighted the general hostility that he found existed in the army towards secure civil occupations with long hours, high pay and security. In addition, he noted that during the confusion of the early days of the war some of a timid nature had been able to 'make havens for themselves' while others, bound up in a mood of reckless patriotism, 'went out early and died long before the country knew what it was they were suffering, or what they were fighting against'. Now, in late 1916 and after conscription, Innes deplored the fact that so many individuals with careers and responsibilities before them had been obliged to set their lives to one side to make way for the demands of the war. He concluded, 'The importance of each man to the country has increased, and consequently the importance of each man to himself has decreased'.[7]

Patriotism had to consist of deeds as well as words: in other words, positive action of some kind. Innes saw this but felt that there should be no glory attached to the individual's choice of action which in any case had been stifled to a certain extent by the constraints of a wartime society and, most especially, in the army where individuals were generally treated like animals, according to Innes' observances. Suitably, in his own case, once Innes reached France (feeling himself 'unfit for battlefield by physique or temperament') he was set to work constructing dug-outs amid clouds of chalk dust. Despite his support for positive action of some kind, Innes found his mind turning in other directions. 'I long to be somewhere where the decent side of life is to be seen', he wrote to his mother 'Perhaps my ambitions will revive after the war – but at present all I want is a quiet life on a moderate income and a bicycle in an English countryside and you to look after (I should have put you first)'.[8]

In March 1917 he realised that it would soon be Easter ('I have sufficiently regained a sense of time') and mused upon the Resurrection which he could not help evaluating in terms of his present existence. He found himself wishing for, 'the resurrection of this life', for, as he had found, 'this existence is death, mental and usually spiritual'.[9] At the end of May, Innes was summoned back to base in order to appear before a medical board, and he hoped to be marked down for permanent base duty. At the base, while awaiting his result and watching troops passing in and out, with some bound for the front, he expressed unease at the vagaries of existence and the lack of certainty in things, with men heading towards different fates: an anonymous death or the VC, depending upon war's caprice. He found himself struck by the 'the element of dreadfulness' in this intersecting of artificial existences.

Although he was assigned to permanent base duty and became a Field Cashier at the headquarters of the XIV Corps of the BEF, he still found himself unhappy and unfulfilled, despite varying his 'programme' by walking in the nearby woods on fine evenings and occasionally playing the organ at Sunday evening services. 'Things worth living for are rare in the army: duty and preparation for duty ... occupy one's entire existence',[10] he wrote in the summer of 1917, during which time he noted how easy it was to become indifferent to the war when one was behind the lines for a length of time. However, he admitted, any element of the old uncertainty (and even the bleakness of trees rustling dismally in a gale) 'brings back its [the war's emotional impact] hard side' immediately.

In September 1917, Innes was granted leave and transferred from the Middlesex Regiment to the 273rd Employment Company of Field Cashiers. Back in London, he found that his 'conscript country' had become worse, to the extent that, as he noted, the practice of saluting when on leave had been forcibly revived:

> so that apparently harassed and war-worn men are in theory obliged to stand to attention in overcrowded Tube carriages (if they are not doing so at the time) whenever an officer enters, or the latter's hand on its way to seek support from the nearest strap must not omit to pause distinctly, if briefly, in the region of his hat-peak.[11]

By the end of the year, he found himself sent to Italy and established in a draper's shop which acted as his billet and office. By mid-1918 he had only received fifteen days off in the previous eleven months, despite working for nine hours every day, seven days a week. He became 'stale' and realised that he could never be content until the war was over 'and everybody has a fair chance again'.

Ironically, Innes would suffer delayed demobilisation and not return to his former life until September 1919, becoming increasingly frustrated with a life that he had never been in tune with, even during the urgency of war. 'With constant thought for the morrow and constant devising of ways and means', he had written during the uncertain period of the last great German advance of spring 1918:

> life ceases to be life and becomes existence. When one's desires and inclinations are cramped and thwarted on all sides, monotony, if not slavery, results ... the whole world is in a fever with this war disease and things cannot go on in the usual way ... we still measure life by the old standards, while the fact is that the better comparison is not with what we have known but with what we shall have to face. War upsets the routine of civilisation; the world goes backwards instead of forwards.[12]

In his explicit recognition of the conflict's upset of civilisation's calming and steady progression and all that implied about the state of mankind and hope for the future, the experience of H.S. Innes reflects in greater detail the concerns and feelings of other similarly-minded individuals, many of whom have already been discussed elsewhere in this book.

Occasionally an individual can be identified in whom many of the various humanistic objections to the war and the minutiae of the conflict (embodied to greater or lesser extents in the individuals previously considered) existed side by side – though not in isolation. Indeed, they seemed to coalesce and create a personality which, to some extent, was a result of the abrasion between a humanistic approach to life and a sense of duty which assumed forced contact with circumstances of death and destruction. Frederic Hillersdon Keeling is not remembered to any great extent as one of the major figures of the war, but after his death on 18 August 1916, he was mourned by those that had known him as a perfect example of the 'gentleman-soldier' and as 'one of the most remarkable men in the army', according to the captain of his regiment – a regiment in which he had become something of an institution by the time of his death.

Keeling mixed in various circles and recognised from personal experience (in common with Bertrand Russell) that there was little common ground between the 'demagogic Socialists' and the 'Hypersensitive aesthetic intellectuals'. He knew Rupert Brooke and, like him, had started to drill with the Artists' Rifles in August 1914 though, unlike Brooke, Keeling refused a commission, deciding instead to enlist in the 6th Battalion, the Duke of York's Light Infantry as a private because he wanted to have a wider knowledge of experience of the war. Joining up, he felt, was, 'not dishonourable in itself and gives one direct experience of another side of life and another way of living altogether'.[13] By this action he also felt that he had more in common with the ordinary soldier. This decision was nothing out of the ordinary for Keeling, a man who, despite his First from Cambridge, had chosen to manage the Leeds Labour Exchange in 1910, when he was only twenty-three.

When war was declared, Keeling felt a sense of duty and a desire to be part of the coming experience though he appreciated that his feelings did not involve any 'war cult' and that the individual did not have to share in the national and racial tension that engulfed the country ('a miserable vicarious emotion'). It was enough to recognise that this feeling existed and to perhaps be wary of it, while deploring the lack of sense exhibited by all nations and English insularity in particular. He had just visited Germany and found himself feeling a kind of 'secondary patriotism' for that nation and found himself more suspicious of Russia than he was of any Teutonic threat. He found himself greatly disturbed by the 'damnably mean' treatment meted out to German shops, governesses and servants by the British press and people. If there had to be war, it must be fought without passion or bitterness but with respect for the 'enemy'; he wanted Great Britain to triumph on the sea and Germany on land and then both to keep the peace thereafter. This was Keeling emoting, as he inferred, on a practical level, as a 'political animal'. On a deeper level he expressed more passion; 'As a man', he wrote on 2 August, 'I detest the conception of one national culture regarding itself as essentially the enemy of another'.[14]

He also thought of the situation in moral terms, wishing that any moral results of the conflict, such as those of comradeship and brotherly love, would outweigh the inevitable material losses, and he found himself frustrated by what he saw as a lack of perception of these potential material losses by the general populace; the holidaying people he observed at Cowes and in the train did not seem to him to see that they were all on the brink of the 'greatest abyss in history'. Amidst the whirl of patriotic headlines, speeches and calls to arms he wrote sadly from the National Liberal Club at midnight on Monday 3 August that, 'There is no room for one's personal feelings now ... It is too awful for words.'[15]

The German destruction of the medieval city of Louvain did not move him as much as he expected it to, due partly to the fact that during the first few weeks of the war, as he commented, 'The everyday life of the present is my main interest', and he found Louvain and its history to be rooted too deeply in the past, although he imagined that if he were to be ordered to destroy a beautiful town he would probably be horrified – however on reflection, he speculated, 'perhaps it wouldn't if one had been engaged in fighting for weeks on end', which indicated his recognition of a coarsening of sensibility that went hand in hand with military action. He was determined to avoid all cant and false emotion: 'I am not going into this job in a simple swelling mood of patriotism', he wrote, 'That is there, but there are a lot of other things, personal and impersonal, which complicate it.'[16] Although he admitted that the destruction of Louvain by his beloved Germans was a 'blunder', he found it impossible to work up any feelings of animosity towards them, and he realised that 'We're all capable of pretty bad things given the least encouragement to barbarities; it is absurd to blame the men.'[17]

Keeling's main concern was that civilisation, as he saw it, was slipping backwards, and there was no guarantee at this early stage in the war that the world would emerge any saner at the end of the conflict. He worried that his own countrymen would be encouraged by politicians and pressed to learn to hate the Germans over time, a mood which would obscure that of international brotherhood that he believed in so keenly. 'I expect I shall be a stronger pacifist after the war than any of the people who are pacifists now', he wrote, adding crucially, 'But I don't feel one will have earned the right to be one unless one has gone in with the rest.'[18] The war was to be a test of the strength of his personal anti-war feeling.

Once in the army and kept busy training, Keeling found himself as he had feared, suffering a blunting of his sensibilities and was shocked to find out how easy it was, now that the army staked a claim to his soul as well as his body, to become immune to the beauty of a sunset or early morning mists. Only occasionally did he find that these sights brought back a 'grubbing in one's wretched soul'. Most of the time he felt isolated and devoid of feelings; now, his 'most real life' was with his own inner thoughts, and this encouraged him to the resolution (as it had Siegfried Sassoon) that, 'one must keep an inner life going', if one wished to preserve anything of an individual's former independence of thought if not of action. His feeling of comradeship was one of the few positive features he identified from the circumstances of army life and the wider conflict ('What a brotherhood there will be between all those who shared the experience!'). He could not believe that the ordinary soldier harboured feelings of intense hatred towards the Germans and was sure that these feelings were the product of 'ranters and intriguers'; journalists, pro-war intellectuals, politicians and the highest ranks of the army.

There was also the excitement of the unknown, the thrill of 'the greatest game' (as he referred to his progress towards the front) which existed whatever the moral or immoral results of the war. Keeling felt that the process of facing up to the imminence of death could lend one a more realistic sense of values in life, especially that of liberty, or the lack of it, and he was quick to praise voices of perception and calm common sense, such as George Bernard Shaw's 'Common Sense About the War' in the *New Statesman* which he described as 'magnificently sane'. Besides the simple attraction of certain excitement, however, there was a deeper need to be part of things in some that Keeling saw as a psychological necessity: 'I don't think an average man can be sure of being sane about this business unless he knows he is going to face death like the rest', he wrote from Witley Camp in April 1915.[19]

It was at this point that Keeling finished his training and embarked for France, possibly suspecting (from the stories of those who had returned) that what he had already undergone was as nothing compared to the horrors ahead. He was now somewhat used to the routine of the army, especially expressed by the calls of the bugle ('They have eaten into my soul') though he was still depressed by the spirit of hatred that abounded and was forced to place his hope in some kind of international outburst against the war which all soldiers who had experienced the front would respond to. Once on the continent he found that, on his time off, he had more opportunity than before to appreciate the beauty of the scenery although this was contrasted with the 'rough standard of physical civilisation' to which he had sunk when forced to endure sleeping rough, lice and the 'obnoxious' inequality of the army's standards between officers and common soldiers.

More seriously, he found that his relationship to all things, both external and internal, was, 'under the shadow of the big gun'. He continued, 'One lives – enjoys life full-bloodedly and even thinks and feels aesthetically now and again – but having come away, one knows that there was a special abnormal tinge over the whole of life.'[20] He saw that the limit of experience of the infantryman in this war was greater than ever before and hoped that, in response, there would be a correspondingly large wave of practical pacifism after the war in which he determined he would play a part by going to Germany and re-establishing ties with German life as well as creating new ones where possible. 'It is the soldiers who will be the good Pacifists – just as every decent Pacifist should be a soldier', he wrote to a friend.[21]

It was his direct experience as a soldier that compelled Keeling to write a powerful article for the *New Statesman* against the issue of compulsion. 'Now that I know what one's experiences in the firing-line at their worst actually are', he wrote, 'I cannot as a responsible citizen of a democratic community be a party to compelling any man willy-nilly to share them'. He stated that he was not concerned with the logical end-result of this point of view in terms of the state's relation to the individual, only that no man should be forced against his will to experience the 'hell' that he had undergone, concluding that, 'I feel a moral objection to compulsory service which I never felt before I had come to France as a soldier.'[22]

Despite his anger, hope and convictions, Keeling was becoming tired of the 'mud, monotony and murderousness' of his circumstances by late 1915. The constant edge of death had transformed the experience from artificial adventure to actuality with no opportunity in the spring of 1916 to enjoy that which he most craved – time to enjoy the beauties of nature in peace, away from the guns. 'Every pleasant landscape now seems to suggest the horrors of war by contrast', he wrote wearily in March. Even the sound of the larks at dawn now only brought him unhappiness through their reminder of peaceful gardens of former days: 'Here one knows that the larks sing at seven and the guns begin at nine or ten.'

Frederic Keeling was killed later that year, in August 1916 – caught by a bullet as he stood on a parapet. His Captain, Barrington-Ward, recalled Keeling's disciplinarianism, his energy and most of all, his kindness (and bad language) towards his men. 'We shall be hard put to re-arrange ourselves without him', he commented. No less a figure than H.G. Wells provided the Introduction to a volume of Keeling's letters which appeared in 1918 and wrote in stark tones that, 'Keeling's life was a full and vivid one, but it was largely wasted ... What a fund of vitality, what a power of work, what a promise of youth, fell back into darkness with this one life!'[23] Wells saluted Keeling's supreme individuality, best expressed by Keeling himself who, having no use for religion ('it seems no good in this hell'), misdirected hatred and the false rhetoric of politics and press, affirmed that, 'speaking as a man face to face with the chances of death, I can honestly say that humanity and England's contribution to the Temple of Humanity are the only ideal conceptions for which I have any use'.[24]

If Frederic Keeling represented a standpoint on the war that was charged with feelings of both duty and repulsion, with pity and concern for humanity emerging as paramount concerns, then that of D.H. Calcutt of the Queen's Westminster Rifles was of a less emotionally complicated nature, based on much more practical objections. Calcutt, a civil servant with the Home Office since 1910, possibly suspecting that conscription was inevitable and close, applied on impulse and was accepted by the armed forces in late 1915 – much to his surprise (and that of his employers), as he had expected to be rejected on medical grounds, as he had been by the Home Office on the occasion of his first (pre-war) job application. In August 1914 Calcutt had been entrusted with the task of informing all 222 Chief Constables of the British Police Force of the outbreak of hostilities between Britain and Germany, and Calcutt's wry, fussy, objective tone is initially evident when he noted that the telegrams he sent read that Germany had declared war on Britain when, in fact, the situation had been the reverse, lending, as he saw it, credence to the adage that the first casualty in war is truth.

Right from the start of his military career, Calcutt harboured feelings of resentment and unease, feeling himself to be something of a coward and disliking being forced to associate with others of poor physical condition, 'from all points of the compass'. Like H.S. Innes, he was frustrated by the elevation to hight rank of those 'with apparently no higher mental delights than are to be found in seeing a lot of men making a single inane movement simultaneously'.[25] More seriously and in common with others such as E.P. Southall and Guy Chapman, Calcutt was worried by the general lowering of moral standards that he felt was produced by the war. An aspect of this was to be found in the conduct of the authorities in coercing the manhood of Great Britain to join the colours. As Calcutt saw it, this involved a gradual breaking down of the resistance of small categories based on marital status, occupation, age, etc., leaving the remainder either full of false hope of being spared the front or placed forcibly and publicly in a morally dubious position. According to Calcutt, the remaining adult male population of late 1915 had been 'prized out of their niches individually' by an unfair sleight only to be shunted around like so many milk churns, once in the army, sometimes left in a siding for hours at a time. He described the common soldier as being like a horse in a horse box gazing backwards rather vacantly with blinkered vision, never able to discern the true direction of the road ahead.

After some training, all the less physically fit soldiers were transferred to the Rifle Brigade Garrison Battalion at Falmouth and in December 1916, after a year in the army, Calcutt was shipped with his regiment to Egypt. He described the crowded conditions on the Mail Packet *Connaught* as a sea of khaki – 'ugly, utilitarian clad bundles of humanity' with their meagre possessions scattered about them. The boat was torpedoed in the Mediterranean and at the church service following the incident Calcutt noted the tendency towards deeper religious feelings when threatened by acute danger. He also observed that the army Padre had 'easy stuff' to work on with a collection of scared men and boys many miles from familiar surroundings. All that had to be mentioned for them to 'ooze religion' were the usual homilies such as 'friends at home', 'old folk' and 'wounded and distressed'. However, Calcutt also observed how soon this pious atmosphere could be shattered by a command to 'fall in' for the march back from church to camp. 'Oh – if only we had the courage of our thoughts and inclination', Calcutt recorded in his diary:

We are not afraid to die, we are afraid to live. The Church merely tries to bridge the gulf between reason and practise by 'His will' and talk and prayer. Send high explosives over and then pray for the recovery of the wounded. Love them that despitefully use you. Oh! What a coward I am.[26]

His self-denunciation was for his lack of courage in his own convictions: for not refusing to take part in the service. As it transpired, the following week church parade was declared voluntary due to lack of interest. Calcutt's bitterness here was also a (perhaps unrecognised) self-taunt for not possessing the ability or will to publicly proclaim his views on the army and the conduct of the war itself.

Calcutt's stance was fed by his general attitude towards religion, which he thought of as a cloak put upon a man at birth and worn forcibly for the remainder of his life. In Calcutt's view, it was unfair to clothe a man externally in a particular point of view with no respect for any independent internal outlook. Religion was an action performed on a man not unlike vaccination and for it to be effective it had to spring naturally from inside, though, 'the man who thinks at all, as often as not, finds it does not suit him'.[27] He contrasted the powerful position of the Church in the Middle Ages and at the start of the twentieth century during wartime and found them to be oddly similar, describing the modern ecclesiastical stance during war as, 'selling buns to conscript serfs at places where buns are not otherwise available'.

By the spring of 1917, Calcutt was stationed at Kantara in Egypt, and it was at this point that he found himself in contact with some of the more direct effects of the war. At the 24th Stationary Hospital some of the worst cases made him feel 'more anti-war than ever', and he worried on behalf of the wounded that the frequent grumbling of the stretcher-bearers would only serve to remind the casualties that they themselves were still in the army. He still retained his eye for the odd or slightly ludicrous; one example was his newly arrived substitute, a small, deferential old man in an ill fitting drill tunic, baggy trousers and rumpled puttees whom Calcutt likened to a bird, especially since the man's broken spectacles hung from one arm on a piece of string and were continually being held up to his left eye and peered through. Calcutt thought him a figure of mirth until the man spoke of his son of twenty-one, killed in France. Calcutt saw this personal loss and the man's subsequent loss of dignity as a whole and representative of the material tragedy of the war, especially when he learnt that the man was fifty-seven and had claimed to be thirty-eight in order to enlist.

Calcutt remained angry with himself for failing to take some kind of personal stand; in a letter from Kantara he wrote that he wished he had declared himself a Conscientious Objector from the beginning. 'I have sold my soul to the Directors of British Interests for £45 a year', he lamented, 'I am in a whirl of circumstances, like the rest of us, but I clearly see the circumstances and instead of proclaiming it ... I allow myself to drift along as fate and the medical boards decree. We are not free, we do not follow our own inclinations for a moment.'[28] He found it easy to be cynical; church parades were a travesty, the addresses of Brigadier and Commanding Officer 'hesitating and unconvincing' and full of 'fulsome rubbish' respectively. Divisional concerts were the army's method of ordering the men to be 'cheerful by numbers' and a soldier's personal discretion was continually interfered with 'right down to a strap and a buckle'. He was well aware that for many his objections were not an issue, but he felt forced to uphold the moral and aesthetic standards of himself and others for, 'honour and susceptibilities, like taste and appreciation of art, are subtle things' and an order could easily transcend the realm of self-respect and degenerate to the level of self-humiliation. He privately berated others for being too thick-skinned to be aware of these regular intrusions.

Calcutt's chief consolations were his extensive reading (his book list for September 1917 included Jane Austen, Byron, Wordsworth, Browning, Matthew Arnold and Marcus Aurelius) and his stretcher-bearing, which he regarded as action directed at saving life rather than destroying it. He appreciated most forms of natural life in the desert and possessed an almost child-like interest in small creatures, especially the lizards (though not a six-inch spider attracted by his evening candle; 'I screamed'). He found depressing the lack of greenery or feature in the barren landscape ('not unlike the downs around Winchester but unrelieved *dust colour*'), and he was especially plagued by the constant flies. By the end of 1917, Calcutt was exhausted after many marches in wind and rain, disturbed sleep under wet blankets and worsening sciatica, though he tried to make light of the physical hardships and recognised that his mental state was more fragile. Physical hardship could be linked to obvious cause (though not reason) whereas on a mental plane he found himself plagued by 'some irritation I could not see the reason for'.

Calcutt found himself constantly frustrated by the random illogicality of military activities. He cited the occasion when his company spent two days marching away from Jerusalem at the end of December in appalling conditions only to be told they would be returning there forthwith. There was also the time in February 1918 when, in pouring rain, they dug trenches and were ordered to scatter the resulting earth around the camp, turning the whole place into a sea of mud. Then they received orders to collect all the dirt again and make a 'trench pile' on one side. Finally, the notorious Captain Flower ('dry as a bone') ordered the trenches to be filled in again as they were crooked. This, combined with episodes of arduous road-making in freezing conditions, brought Calcutt to the edge of despair, especially since he had been largely unable to make friends in the army and now admitted in his journal to a feeling of 'absolute loneliness in a crowd' coupled with the 'maddening' frustration of the pettiness of military life. He described himself at this time as being, 'Mentally, morally and physically SICK and FED UP' amid the 'usual atmosphere of RUSH and MADDENING INSPECTIONS and ETERNAL FAULT FINDINGS.'

Calcutt sensed that he was being drained of any remaining personality by the impersonal nature of the army's treatment of the individual, especially when he was referred to simply as 'the man who dropped his rifle' by the sergeant-major. As he noted, 'The expression of one's *own* personality *is* life, and the cramped, limited, dog's life under military discipline is not worth living at all.'[29] He regretted the filtering away, as he saw it, of natural emotions such as true courage and honour. The courage that he observed after a day's drilling on the parade ground was merely 'the courage of discipline' and, as he later recorded, 'all restraining senses of decency vanish under discipline'.[30]

In June 1918, Calcutt embarked on the *Indarra* for Southern Italy. His physical condition was now so bad that he was admitted to the 79th General Hospital at Taranto with a temperature of 102°F. After his recovery, he was transported by train through Italy and into France.[31] In the autumn of 1918, the Division started to take 'civilian life' courses. Calcutt chose shorthand, journalism and French, hoping grimly that he lived to make use of them. He was also granted leave unexpectedly and returned home to find his mother out, which gave him time to hide his 'horribles' (rifle, gas helmet etc.) in the larder before she returned. Despite his attempt to settle back into the comforting gossip of home life ('Cathie is married and Em'ly jilted … Cecil well in tow'), he could not forget the war and found himself walking restlessly around Kensington Gardens and Hyde Park as his leave dwindled away. A visit to the theatre in Drury Lane was spoilt by an inebriated Major who was sick over a girl's dress in front of Calcutt and his party. This incident seemed representative of the false gaiety and intoxicated emotions which only partially concealed the war-weariness of the conflict's closing months.

It was a weariness that, in Calcutt's case, had tinted his view of events for many months, and the approach of the end of the war brought no lessening. The landscape of France he saw when travelling by rail to the Divisional HQ after his leave was 'the most awful picture of destruction I have ever clapped eyes on. Derelict tanks, rain sodden, shell torn, trench cut country, railway lines and concrete all over the place. Miles and miles of this …'[32] To him it seemed as if the landscape was as worn out and shattered as those experiencing the war. He encountered a German placard, aimed at the Belgians, depicting the English dropping bombs on German hospital trains, and Calcutt saw this as a symbol of the mutual messages of hate and lies which were hurled around between the belligerents, the only result of which was 'misunderstanding beyond reconciliation', and the suffering of innocents. He came across a battered village on the banks of the Scheldt river only a week before the Armistice and mused that a fortnight previously it had been relatively peaceful and now, though it had been 'recovered' or 'freed', this had meant its virtual destruction. All that was left was, 'a painful reminder of human suffering'.

It was the suffering of the man in the field and the innocent civilian that Calcutt could not forget once peace was declared. The date 11 November was marked by squad drill, instruction in the manipulation of the Lewis gun and little else; 'we have not facilities for rejoicing … Henley's brother is dying. Corporal Jacob's brother has just died. Newson's brother killed last week. A few Very lights are fired but very weak as a daylight demonstration …'[33] To Calcutt, there seemed no 'victory' to celebrate, and the highlight of his day was a game of pontoon before turning in. A speech given by a General at the end of the month confirmed Calcutt's identification of the gulf that existed between a Divisional General and 'the poor clod in the line', a gulf across which real understanding of the latter's 'daily humiliation' was impossible. The General's remark that the troops had never looked better and would not be recognised when they returned home provoked an outburst of indignation from Calcutt. 'What of the dead? Poor Sergeant Sheperd rotting on the top of a desolate mountain-top in Palestine looks well doesn't he? And Pat Brady and Calvery and Geeson. Are we to forget them all so soon …' As the General entreated the men to remain in the army in the period following the war, Calcutt likened the insensitive, business-as-usual attitude to Prussian militarism. Reviews, parades and pageants could only result in 'the dead and mutilated at the bottom of a mud-soaked trench'.

He did not return to England until June 1919, when he was granted a month's leave prior to demobilisation. Despite Calcutt's emotional turbulence and physical illness, he had carried on and tried – like so many others – to make the best of it, perhaps realising that he was undergoing a defining experience. He stopped his diary on his return home, and his last entry described a visit to the theatre to see a play about Napoleon at which the audience, still affected by 'war-fever' to some degree, applauded the deriding of the Austrian national anthem by a French chauvinist when, to Calcutt, it was obvious that, at the time of the Napoleonic Wars, France stood for militarism. 'Still', wrote Calcutt characteristically, 'it showed constancy anyway. After that we went home by bus and told each other when we got home that we had enjoyed ourselves. So I suppose we had.'[34]

The war had wrenched Calcutt from an ordered, if slightly insular, life and constantly underlined his sense of being out of place and involved in something against his nature. His facility for critical observation, which privately balanced his public shyness, was forced to the fore by the events he was compelled to undergo or witness, but this was not to the detriment of his real kindness and sympathy for those he regarded as trod upon or exploited. He was painfully aware of the war and its stripping away of all façade and pretence to the essentials of life, however petty. 'What a prosaic, unromantic war this is', he wrote, 'All the little refinements and secret sensitiveness are torn aside and love finds expression in a cake of soap'.[35]

Within the personal stories of H.S. Innes, F.H. Keeling and D.H. Calcutt, there lie buried familiar shards of aesthetic, humanistic and moral opposition to the war. Innes' awareness of the 'abomination of desolation' at the front mirrored the bleakness of the 'conscript country' that he felt Britain had become.

In Innes' opinion, conscription and the war's general demand for men had allowed the importance of each man to himself to decrease. Individual personality was becoming submerged and life itself, as a consequence, was being reduced to the level of 'mere existence'.

Keeling's recognition of the 'abnormal tinge' created by the war enveloped his 'inner life', leaving, as he saw it, no room for personal thoughts and feelings. Added to this was the parallel reaction of his identification with the life of the soldier as a means to 'earning the right' to pacifism through channels of 'direct experience', and his hope that this brotherhood of experience would result in a shared understanding of the horror of war and thus a reduction of future international conflict. This recognition of the importance of experience to a full appreciation of the meaning of the war is a theme already observed in this study, particularly in the cases of Sassoon and of Owen in Chapter 5, who resolved not to be satisfied until he had 'suffered my share of life'.

Just as Keeling expressed a moral objection to the introduction of compulsion, Calcutt deplored the general lowering of former standards of morality by which he had fixed his life and values. At the same time, he came to see what the war ultimately meant to him, a realisation facilitated by the acute observances of his reluctant participation within it. Calcutt was keen to view himself as upholder of moral and aesthetic standards on behalf of not only himself, but also of others. He was aware that standards of personal honour and sensibility could easily be transgressed by both the horror of the front and the artificiality of the structure of military life. Self-respect was continually at risk, and this intrusion into standards of individual morality was what caused the greatest torment to the sensitive Calcutt and others like him. For all three soldiers the war had upset, in Innes' words, 'the routine of civilisation' – not only in the wider sense of their awareness of altered standards of public morality, but also in the conflict's warping of their personal hopes, dreams and aspirations. Thus the war divorced them from their own lives.

Notes

1 'Past and future were equidistant and unattainable.' Wyn Griffith, *Up to Mametz* (London, 1931), p. 212.
2 University of Leeds, Liddle Collection (UL,LC hereafter), file of H.S. Innes, letter to his mother, 5 Jan. 1917.
3 *Ibid.*, H.S. Innes to his mother, 6 March 1916.
4 *Ibid.*, 9 May 1916.
5 *Ibid.*, 26 April 1916.
6 *Ibid.*, 13 July 1916.
7 *Ibid.*, 30 Oct. 1916.
8 *Ibid.*, 9 March 1917 and 23 March 1917.
9 *Ibid.*, 24 March 1917.
10 *Ibid.*, 3 July 1917.
11 *Ibid.*, 20 Sept. 1917.

12 *Ibid.*, 1 May 1918. For details of a similar reaction to that of H.S. Innes, see file of R.M. Gale (also UL,LC), a Royal Marine in the Divisional Engineers of the Royal Naval Division. The former Post Office telegraphist describes the 'soul-destroying slavery' of military life and how he feels that it, 'drives iron into a man's soul'. (See Diary 3, 26 June 1917 and 15 Jan. 1918).

13 *Keeling – Letters and Recollections*, ed. E.T. (London, 1918), p. 185.

14 *Ibid.*, 2 Aug. 1914, pp. 178–9.

15 *Ibid.*, p. 180.

16 *Ibid.*, Aug. 1914, p. 187.

17 *Ibid.*, Aug. 1914, p. 187.

18 *Ibid.*, Aug. 1914, p. 187.

19 *Ibid.*, April 1915, p. 202.

20 *Ibid.*, to J.C. Squire, BEF, 7 Aug. 1915.

21 *Ibid.*, to R.K.C. Ensor, 23 Dec. 1915, p. 259.

22 F.H. Keeling [writing as 'A Sergeant in a Line Regiment in Flanders'], 'A Soldier on Compulsion', *New Statesman*, vol. 5, no. 130, 2 Oct. 1915.

23 H.G. Wells, Introduction to *Keeling – Letters and Recollections*, ed. E.T., p. xiv.

24 *Ibid.*, p. 264.

25 Imperial War Museum, file of D.H. Calcutt, transcribed diaries, Introduction – 'Beneath the Veneer', p. 1.

26 *Ibid.*, vol. 1, 2 Sept. 1917, p. 97.

27 *Ibid.*, vol. 1, Memo (no date), p. 103. Calcutt was particularly unimpressed with the Padre of his own Regiment, a character who conversed continually in 'timid parables'. The nonconformist Parson met with equal lack of enthusiasm, not only from Calcutt, but from most of the other soldiers as well. Calcutt described a church parade over which the parson presided as being a 'chronic wash-out'; the chosen sermon – that of the Good Samaritan – did not reflect the war nor the relationship between the Church and Army, while silence greeted both the hymns and even 'God Save the King'.

28 *Ibid.*, vol. 1, letter to Pat, 31 July 1917, p. 90.

29 *Ibid.*, vol. 2, 27 Feb. 1918, p. 21.

30 *Ibid.*, vol. 2, 15 May 1918, p. 52. The general misery, bewilderment and loss of direction that Calcutt experienced was amply demonstrated by an incident on the Nabour Road in the spring of 1918. Calcutt and his company had been marching north and, in order to reunite with the main battalion, they had left the road to climb over higher ground, in what was presumed to be a short cut. After hours of clambering around in the hot sun without a 'long halt', it was decided to find a road again and look for the Battalion. It was 3 o'clock in the afternoon by this point, and the men had had nothing to eat since sunrise. After scrambling down a hill, a road was found and followed until it was realised that the company was now marching south – and in the opposite direction – on the very road it had left that morning. In order to reunite with the Battalion, Calcutt and the men had to completely retrace their steps, including returning to the far side of the hill they had just scrambled down and partially skirted. Almost inevitably, they found that the Battalion had completed the job in three hours, including three halts.

Calcutt recorded this incident with a tone of self-satisfaction, as if this proved, once and for all, that his pessimism was entirely justified. He still felt isolated and stifled; he was 'reduced' to reading *Mrs Mason Protests* by Anthony Hope and the acquaintances he had built up he labelled 'Friends of Convenience'. Nothing could be real or resemble the friendships of the old life in a situation precarious with uncertainty and fairweather values. 'We do not live', he wrote in May 1918, 'We are in a whirl. Not a minute to yourself. One thing after another. We just exist.' *Ibid.*, vol. 2, 28 May 1918, p. 57.

31 Calcutt found himself passing through numerous towns and cities ('St. This and St. That') seemingly untouched by the war, such as Cannes and Marseilles. His spirits improved slightly

when he observed the beautiful wooded scenery along the banks of the Seine as he travelled northwards. However, the pleasure evaporated when he noticed the lumbering being carried out for war purposes – the extra lines being added to the railway and the construction of more embankments and bridges.

Just as the altering scenery was speeding past his train window, so life at home was passing him by, affording him only glimpses of altered circumstances. He received a letter from his niece Eileen, who had started school. 'I had no idea she was so old', he wrote with astonishment. Once at the Western Front, Calcutt went into a shell-torn house to have a look around and found that he could not help but view it as the home it once had been, particularly since a Singer sewing machine and numerous Virgin Marys were in evidence, as well as family photographs, in cracked frames, still on some of the walls. It was these 'intimate threads of life ... ruthlessly broken off' that he felt brought forth the true tragedy of the war to a greater extent than even the remaining gaunt trees of France, 'stretching their stricken forms upwards, silhouetted every instant by shell flash and Very light'. *Ibid.*, vol. 2, Sept. 1918, pp. 96–8.

32 *Ibid.*, vol. 2, 26 Oct. 1918, p. 121.
33 *Ibid.*, vol. 2, 11 Nov. 1918, p. 128.
34 *Ibid.*, vol. 2, 24 June 1919, p. 65.
35 *Ibid.*, vol. 1, 18 July 1917, p. 85.

9

Public commentary on familiar themes

The 'herd instinct' versus the individual

Throughout this book, contemporary evidence has been the key to unlocking the emotions of the past – both private and public. Although some excerpts have appeared from the numerous books and memoirs generated by the war (and largely written *after* the event), comparatively little evidence has been cited from the wider contemporary sphere, the exception being the case of the *Cambridge Magazine*'s vocal support of Bertrand Russell as part of its balanced and humane view of the wider conflict. Now it is perhaps appropriate that some attention is drawn to contemporary newspapers and periodicals – journalistic reactions fully exposed to public scrutiny and in contrast to the enclosed world of intimate diaries and letters.

In summing up one of the main themes of humanistic and aesthetic opposition to the Great War – the friction that existed between the structure of the war-state with its resultant 'herd instinct' and notions of the sacredness of the individual – there is perhaps no more apposite personal example than that of Gilbert Cannan, an individual who, like Bertrand Russell, specifically projected his concerns into the public sphere. Cannan was a friend of D.H. Lawrence (who, together with his wife, had moved to Buckinghamshire in August 1914 to be near Cannan and his wife Mary), and he saw himself as a defender of that which he described as 'a man's most precious possession' – human dignity.

He had first expounded on this theme in an article for the *Cambridge Magazine* in November 1914 in which he wrote that, 'Every day strips this war of a little more of its dignity, even of the dignity of death, for it is not dignified to die in a trench armed with a rifle and bayonet against a machine miles away out of sight behind a hill'.[1] This commodity of dignity was, he felt, almost the sole guarantee of decency in human affairs, 'the magnetised needle which swings to the points of the moral world', violations of which caused 'untold secret suffering', due to the fact that many men would submit to indignities in the name of the State rather than see their dignity impaired by the taint of accusations of cowardice, moral or otherwise. Cannan commented that thousands had, by submitting to the dictates of the war-state, inflicted the very damage they sought to avoid ('though they have realised it only too late'). He concluded sadly that in the world created by the war, 'the living are more ghostly than the dead'.

Cannan and the views he expressed in print later attracted the ire of Douglas Goldring, who in his survey of the writings of the war, *Reputations* (1920), thought that the war had narrowed Cannan's outlook and indeed 'impaired his mental equilibrium'. Goldring accused Cannan of turning away from everything 'genuine and essential' and instead focusing on 'sub-human types' who were able, in Goldring's view, to forget the war and whom he described as 'wasters and artistic riff-raff'.[2] Presumably Goldring included Cannan himself in this category, as Cannan had faced a tribunal in 1916 and claimed exemption from military service on the grounds of his work as a writer being of national importance: work which, via his American publishers, brought in three times as much money as the alternative agricultural work. The tribunal, although granting him exemption from combatant service, would not accept his writing as an alternative to military service and gave him a month to find other work of national importance in order to avoid being called up.

It was this supposed injustice that revealed to Cannan the precarious nature of individuality within the war-state and led to the writing of his book, *Freedom* (1917). Initially, Cannan had fired off a letter to the *Nation* in September 1916 in which he railed against the regulations resulting from the Military Service Act of earlier that year, regulations which he felt, 'were not framed with any regard for the intellectual life of the country'. The strictures governing the aesthetic and spiritual frames of life within the war-state made every day for Cannan and those with similar concerns one of 'acute suffering'. He continued:

> The convention, the icy gaiety, the hypnotic phrases, the affectation of cynicism, which for most men seem to make the situation tolerable, are useless to me. I believe that only the mind and the will can find an issue from this general degradation and that young men also must contribute thought and imagination if life is to be made sweet again.

Cannan believed that the 'spiritual impulse' that was needed from the young men was under threat: 'It is crushed in those who fight with their bodies by military discipline', he continued, 'It should not be crushed in those who fight ceaselessly with their minds by the misapplication of the Military Service Act.' He concluded that there existed certain 'enduring things' in life that were unaffected by the supremacy of the nation in which they existed, things from which human life took its form and quality and, although politicians rarely recognised them, 'artists must' and therefore must be mentally free to do so. Hence those resisting attempts to make them act against their convictions represented the only force which was capable of winning the moral victories, 'without which victory on the battlefield will be utterly without meaning or potency'.[3]

In November 1916, and by now seen as a voice of dissent due to his writing and experience before a tribunal, Cannan was invited to address the Cambridge University Socialist Society, and he used the opportunity to reiterate his themes of the grave threat posed to the 'spontaneity and spiritual content' within individuals by the 'heresy-hunts' of the war-state, and the State's inability to realise and appreciate the value of the freedom that lay at the heart of each individual that constituted it. With *Freedom*, Cannan was able to expand further on the concerns and concepts he had already expressed, such as that of a war of morals being fought alongside that of territory; the conflict was 'a suspension of the moral law' by agreement between states, the terminal result being a 'moral vacuum' in which 'thought can hardly live'.

Bertrand Russell had written in the *International Journal of Ethics* that the young men and their potential creative impulses were being 'brutalised and morally degraded' by the war[4] and for Cannan in *Freedom*, as for Russell, war was the 'removal of the mask of civilisation' and a subsequent submersion of peaceful creativity in favour of destructive, barbaric impulses. The energies of the people were 'sucked up' in the creation and maintenance of sovereign states; according to Cannan, the world of states could be likened to, 'a great bubble blown out of the energies of humanity'.[5] Here Cannan again mirrored Russell, especially when he (Cannan) went on to state that, though every human being was to some extent mechanical within the routine of habitual actions and thus could be regulated, the impulsive and passionate side of an individual's life could not be so harnessed 'without the most injurious suppression' and hence should be allowed to find liberation and expression via unobstructed creative channels, a process without which the individual would become 'warped and rendered less effective', as was occurring within the war-state.[6]

Cannan recognised that the machinery of the State was composed of individuals with their own susceptibilities, and, hence, the State would be most effective in a situation wherein individuals were left to themselves to adjust the balance between mechanical and creative functions. This was especially true in the case of 'the artist' within whom life and work were fused into a single passion; here the idea of any form of control was 'simply ridiculous'.

The war for Cannan signalled a return to a situation of chaos in which the anarchy of the State was able to override the (potentially creative) 'anarchy of the individual'. Military discipline only served to hold men together under conditions which were a violation of instinct:

> It serves its dreadful purpose, is itself dreadful, and for the purposes of peace worse than useless … it can only be achieved by relieving men of all moral responsibility for what they do under orders. There is then a complete severance of their public and private lives, and from this severance both must suffer.[7]

This was especially the case when it involved an artist or creative individual in whom the public and the private were most closely intertwined. Cannan surmised that the concept of the 'state as machine' had its supporters in that it promised a modicum of existence for all. However, he identified a minority for whom mere existence was not only not enough but which also implied a detestable 'moral death'. To them and Cannan, the State was only concerned with existence, while they were 'eager for life', a life doubly denied to them by the confines of the war's moral and social parameters. Cannan concluded that, 'Only the release of the spirit of liberty can restore the health of humanity.'[8] At the same time he warned that the banner of liberty could also be used to lure men deeper into the 'morass' because, although the war illuminated the lack of freedom of the individual, those individuals were encouraged to win back that liberty at the expense of that of individuals of other nations – a clear 'abuse of patriotism'.

Cannan's article for the *Cambridge Magazine* of November 1914 on the loss of dignity inherent to the war had stirred up fierce debate within its pages with (the possibly pseudonymous) G. Udny Yule of St John's College writing to protest that Cannan's words were 'enough to make a decent dog sick'. The editor, C.K. Odgen, defended the right of all opinions to be expressed in the pages of his magazine and asked Yule to contribute £5 to the fund for Belgian University Refugees if the paper could find a dozen British army officers ready to publicly endorse Cannan's article. By the end of the following month (January 1915), the paper had been inundated with signatures from serving officers willing to support Cannan, as well as messages of support from civilians such as one individual, Leonard Doncaster, who applauded the paper for, 'doing a real service, not only to the University, but to the nation, in encouraging the expression of all shades of opinion'. Ogden summed up the stance of the *Cambridge Magazine* as, 'primarily an institution whereby free discussion may be kept alive in troublous times, whether of peace or war'.[9] As if to back up this claim, Cannan's original article was reprinted together with a further one in which he declared that, 'It is for the soldier of 1914 not only to do and die but also to reason why.' Each soldier, Cannan warned, would have to pass through the 'moral ordeal' of battle and he cautioned that it would be well for the young, 'to set about the detections of unnecessary fictions before their lives and their minds are so encumbered and impaired with them as to be unable to act except through prejudice'.[10]

Gilbert Cannan's description of military service as a test of morality was later echoed by the poet and dramatist Robert Nichols, who wrote that the very essence of war was compulsion by violence or threat of violence and such compulsion entailed 'moral suffering'. The act of enlisting (Nichols served in Flanders) signified an exchange of 'individual liberties for anonymous and collective bonds'.[11] This thought was in turn reflected in a published letter to the *Nation* of October 1915 from the cultural analyst Caroline Playne who cautioned against the coming of compulsion, pointing out that the military standard imposed by compulsion in other nations had already 'deadened countless individual souls and produced one vast human machine perfected in brutality', a result which would, given the opportunity, duplicate itself and thus divert whole populations from the path of progressive civilised enlightenment. 'We might learn to exploit and dominate rather than how to rule and replenish the earth in its fullness', her letter warned, 'What of the loss of individuality, loss of common humanity, and of some of the rational grasps of the higher purpose of human existence and of human destiny.'[12]

In August 1914, the *New Statesman* had publicly reminded its readers that while war meant 'the tragedy of broken human relationships' and admitted that, 'no man can be satisfied with the idea that war will be one of the permanent moral agencies of the world', the rush to arms also possessed a 'nobler aspect': that of comradeship, men marching as brothers and 'the spirit of subordination of the individual to the common life'.[13]

One of Gilbert Cannan's principal themes was this threat, as he perceived it, to the role of the individual within the State posed by that state at war, a war waged against other states and also, in effect, on some of its own citizens. He began a chapter in *Freedom* on 'The Man in the Street' with the maxim, 'You may make all men don uniform, but you cannot thereby secure uniformity. The infinite variety of humanity remains and will not be denied.'[14]

There had been much debate concerning the war's revival of the 'herd instinct' amongst populations and the consequent loss of the strength of individual personality. In July 1915, the *Nation* commented upon an essay by Gilbert Murray (Regius Professor of Greek at Oxford and occasional propagandist) entitled 'The Herd Instinct and the War', in which Murray argued that the progress of civilisation had not only suppressed this latent collective instinct but had also served to educate and emphasise qualities of individual judgement. The war had reversed this process. Feelings of danger and alarm had drawn out the dormant herd mentality, much as Bertrand Russell argued that it brought forth and encouraged the latent destructive impulses within people. The *Nation* concluded its comment by warning that if the war continued, the capacity for individual thought, built up over many years, could become fatally damaged and individual personality totally submerged under that of a tribal nature. For when war brought forth the herd instinct:

> The individual ceases to be a separate source or centre of thought or feeling; his particular nature, what we call his personality, is inhibited. He becomes highly suggestible both to feelings and ideas ... The individual member of the herd not only need not, but must not, feel or think for himself.[15]

In the same month as the analysis of Murray's essay appeared in the *Nation*, the *Quarterly Review* carried an article on 'Patriotism' by W.R. Inge in which he described that concept as a subtle blend of the noble and ignoble and recognised that to many, it marked, 'an arrest of development in the physical expansion of the individual'. While patriotism for ideals was needed for the peaceful progress of humanity, patriotism of a military aspect could only result in 'depreciating the value of individual liberty'.[16] In the November 1914 issue of the *Cambridge Magazine* (which also included Gilbert Cannan's article on the danger to human dignity posed by the war), a letter was published from 2nd Lieutenant N.B. Bagenal of the Cambridgeshire Battalion, the Suffolk Regiment, formerly of King's College, in which he stated that some soldiers, including himself, believed that they were fighting for something more than the concept of patriotism: 'the English soldier of the 20th Century is fighting for Humanity'. Bagenal thought that England should 'sacrifice our pride' and be the first to offer peace terms, and he thought it necessary for those who felt unable to join the army to 'raise their voices' against the spirit of greed and hatred that abounded. He pointed out that the soldier who was fighting for humanity took a unique position in that 'his feet are in the mud, but his head is in the stars; he is battling in the tempest, against the temporary forces of unreason'.[17]

The danger to the forces of reason and the threat of the herd instinct were still being pointed out during the final months of the conflict. An article in the *Nation* of June 1918 entitled 'The Havoc of the Mind' concluded that the war had sapped the supports and 'undermined the rules of reason' and thus left reason prey to not only passions of hate and fear but also to 'the instinct of herding together'. For four years the war had demanded (as a 'safe condition' of its duration) that the minds of individuals be reduced to a state, 'in which the power alike of personal judgement and of the general will has been inhibited'. As the conclusion of the war neared, following the failure of the German spring offensive of 1918, the author of the article was relieved to point out that he, at least, perceived a 'slow struggle back towards the sanity of individual judgement' occurring as well as an effort 'to throw off the passions and superstitions of the herd'.[18] After the Armistice, in early 1919, the *Nation* concluded that the true 'disaster of the war' could be attributed to, 'a consequence of the increase of the herd by the mechanical annihilation of obstacles between individuals'.[19]

The war as gaoler of the imagination

What had also become apparent to many since the summer of 1914 was the war of minds and words that existed within the war-state and which was waged by some with an equal tenacity to that of the rifles and bayonets which framed it. A gulf existed between the politician and the pacifistic artist or intellectual in terms of the freedom of ideas and the limitations placed upon this concept. This was apparent to the author of an article in the *New Statesman* on George Bernard Shaw's supplement 'Common Sense about the War' of November 1914. With evident approval, the article described Shaw's dealing with public affairs to be from an artistic point of view rather than a political one; the approval of Shaw's words was due not only to his ideas but to their origin – his independent stance and freedom of expression. As the article pointed out, 'The politician tells you what you ought to think; the artist shows you what you ought to see and leaves you to think what you like.' The article deplored the fact that, 'just when it is of the utmost importance that public opinion should be kept as healthy and active as possible', there existed a 'conspiracy' to prevent the expression of differences in opinion on issues of the war, 'though in point of fact we all differ violently about them'. Independent thought was being 'gravely depreciated and sternly suppressed'.[20]

The imaginative mind was at risk. In August 1914, the *New Statesman* commented on 'War and the Imagination' and the helplessness of the ordinary mind in comprehending the true nature of war. The 'ordinary citizen' was liable to be plunged into gloom by news of a military defeat or the build up of anxiety. However, if that citizen were 'an imaginative man', he would find constant reason for sadness, 'even in a victory'. Regarding the future of civilisation, the *Statesman* warned that:

> Even if we approved of a war yesterday, or approve of one today, we do not necessarily believe that the bursting bomb is going for ever and ever to be the leading agent of dissemination of righteousness among the nations. We may not be a pacifist for the present, but the more the imagination dwells on the actualities of the battlefield, the more likely we are to shrink from war as the natural appeal of statesmen at variance.[21]

While the *New Statesman* saw imagination as an indicator of war's horrors and thus a tool for peace, the *Nation* looked back over four years of conflict in the weeks following the Armistice under the heading 'The Defeat of Imagination', declaring that in its essence, the war was the struggle between the power of imagination and 'the sluggish soul'. Imagination had been prohibited because it weakened the power of the fighting machine and 'made units men again'. As a result, a wall, knit together by a 'cement of blood and iron', had grown up between men of imagination and the rest of mankind. The *Nation* commented that imagination and a 'sense of the ideal' depended for their existence on 'the effort of the individual mind'[22] and that on one side of this wall there existed, 'an incapacity for imagination hardened into a deliberate refusal to imagine', and on the other (that of men of thought), 'imagination was purified and completed by experience'. The *Nation* concluded that if imagination had been free of artificial restraint and deliberate refusal to comprehend, 'it would have known that victory could not be bought at such a price of pain. Its will to action would have been paralysed by knowledge.' Instead, the gap of imagination amongst many was filled by 'experience of pain', as the war that was already a struggle of the imagination became 'an orgy of necessity'.[23]

Hence there existed public recognition in some quarters of the threat posed by the war to the independence of both the work of the creative individual and the direction of thought. This recognition was apparent not only in the pages of journals but also in books of the period such as E.S.P. Haynes's *The Decline of Liberty in England* which appeared in 1916. Although Haynes's study looked to the Germans and Prussianism for many of the threats to individual initiative, it also singled out more general concerns, one of which was the misery caused by the war in being allowed to bring about the 'death of British freedom'. Contained within this concept existed 'the progressive contempt of the mob for the freedom and privacy of the individual' which in time of war, grew in direct proportion to, 'the speed with which these blessings are abolished by politicians'.[24] In a companion volume, *The Case for Liberty* (1919), Haynes concluded bluntly that war and the fear born of war had always been 'necessarily ... the worst enemies of liberty'.

Also published in the year of Haynes's 1916 work on the danger to liberty was an analysis of the effect of the war upon art and literature by Lawrence Haward, the curator of Manchester City Art Gallery. In this tract, which had originally been given as a lecture at the University of Manchester in February 1916, Haward stated that though the figure of the artist represented a positive and constructive nature, the war was both negative and destructive and, 'in its general methods it remains blindly and hideously impersonal; it is based on the suppression of the individual, on the emphasis of national distinctions, and on the merging of the will of the unit in the collective impulse of the crowd'.[25]

Creative work required the concentration and detachment of the individual, states of mind not easily attained during a period of intense conflict and propaganda, the patriotism of which, Haward stressed, was not only temporary and local but also of a vague and mystical nature, 'rather than human'. He also commented that the theory that the war would draw creative powers out of men via new emotions showed, 'little appreciation of the working of the artist's mind or that of the real character of modern warfare'. The notion that contact with war would engender heroic emotions rather than fear and bitterness was, he felt, based on the popular, romantic view of war, and he concluded that modern conflict was no longer – if it ever had been – a romantic adventure: 'it leaves little room nowadays for make-believe except in so far as it leads to a lowering of standards'.

Writing in 1922, the former chief of Britain's War Propaganda Bureau, C.F.G. Masterman, agreed. In terms of literary output, he declared that although the 'broken ends' of normal life were slowly being re-joined, 'not only has the war given no real inspiration and the great victory passed unsung, but among the young men, bitterness and cynicism and contempt of human life and the foolishness of men is far more noticeable than any ... new inspiration'.[26] Frank Swinnerton, in his survey of *The Georgian Literary Scene*, declared that the imagination of writers had been 'soured' by their experience of the war, while John Rothenstein, also looking back from the 1930s but, in his case, specifically on British artists and the Great War, concluded that although the war had temporarily closed the 'gulf' between art and life (which had been in the process of widening) this had not necessarily been a positive process. Such was the starkness of the war's reality that 'few and insignificant' were the artists who had remained unaffected by it. He described its effect as 'omnipresent, disturbing, terrible ... a reality too powerful and too tangible for artists to be able to neglect', and hence most were 'drawn into the maelstrom'. He concluded that, 'individual opinions regarding it therefore were of little moment'.[27]

These later views of the war's influence upon the creative spheres of art and literature were, as shown in the case of Lawrence Haward, not simply recorded with hindsight. In 1915, Henry James declared in an interview with the *New York Times* that the war had:

> used up words; they have weakened, they have deteriorated like motor car tires; they have, like millions of other things, been more overstrained and knocked about and voided of happy semblance during the last six months than in all the long ages before and we are now confronted with a depreciation of all our terms, or, otherwise speaking, with a loss of expression through increase of limp-ness, that may make us wonder what ghosts will be left to walk.[28]

During the same year as James's public warning, John Galsworthy could be read in the *Times Literary Supplement* ruminating on 'Our Literature and War'. He stated that 'to practically all imaginative writers of any quality war is an excrescence on human life, a monstrous calamity and evil'. Galsworthy was at pains to point out that the fact that creative writers comprehended the 'gruesome inevitability ' of the war in no way lessened their 'temperamental' horror at its waste of life and talent. He employed the word 'temperamental' to indicate that the creative being would naturally be horrified at any such spectacle of carnage; this was the natural reaction of the artist or writer since, 'the nature of the imaginative artist is sensitive, impressionable, impatient of anything superimposed, thinking and feeling for itself, recoiling from conglomerate views and sentiment'. For 'this particular sort of human being', war held no glamour as it perhaps did for other categories of person. Indeed, writers for whom the war *was* glamorous he declared, 'were not those who produce literature'.

Though horrific, the war in Galsworthy's opinion had to be endured in order that artists and writers could attempt to preserve, 'that humane freedom which is the life-blood of any world where the creative imagination ... can flourish'. Galsworthy thought that for some young artists, 'innocent hitherto of creative powers', the experience of the war could possibly be a 'baptism into art', and hence creativity could be born of the conflict in some quarters – as discussed in Chapter 5 in the cases of Siegfried Sassoon and, possibly to a greater extent, Wilfred Owen. However, according to Galsworthy, the 'intense identification' of the artist and creative writer with the struggle of the war was of a 'spasmodic, feverish and almost false' nature, and possessed a kind of 'deep and tragic inconsistency' which was, he stated, 'too foreign to the real self within him'.[29]

Galsworthy admitted that for some the ordeal of war could be a 'baptism into art' and in this he was undoubtedly correct when one takes into account the mass of art, literature and verse that emerged from individual experience of the Great War. In October 1918, the critic Arthur Waugh surveyed the poetic output of the war in the *Quarterly Review* and reached a similar conclusion. He identified that an intellectual aspect of response to the conflict, over and above the 'material realism of lamp-black and lightning', was possible and that this had provided poetry with a new scope. This was despite the fact that war in its chaotic aspect possessed 'the worst antagonists of the poet's art'. If the poet took the war at face value, its aspect was 'too barren, too hard, too hideous to issue in poetry'. However, if the poet brought an intellectual aspect to his experience (which Waugh labelled the 'secret interpretation' though this was concurrently, 'the very antithesis of war itself') then the poet might be able to discover 'the soul beneath the surface' of the war and be able to express it in creative terms. Waugh hailed this process as unique: 'it would seem to be not so much an act that the war has made poetry – as that poetry has, now for the first time, made war – made it in its own image'.

The outstanding characteristic of the significant poetry of the war for Waugh was a passionate determination to picture the war as it revealed itself, 'not to the outsider, but to the enlightened combatant himself'. The key to unlocking a significant response was the personal revelation of direct experience on one who was able to bring an intellectual gaze (which was itself 'enlightened') to bear on events witnessed and emotions felt. Something of the true meaning of the war could be revealed in poetry and art, 'not because war had any virtue in it that would make a poet out of a man, but simply because the poet has himself turned soldier, and concentrated upon the ugly and monotonous business of war the keen searchlight of interpretation'.[30]

Waugh identified differing stages of this vital experience of war, the first being a 'startling retrogression' from the universal to the personal point of view. An individual swept onto the field of battle, Waugh maintained, was suddenly 'disconcertingly conscious of his own individuality'. Following initial experience of the zone of battle this sense of self vanished to be replaced by an awareness of the war as a 'toiling, moiling business, beset with detail, loaded with obligations', in the midst of which the individual was merely a small cog in a vast machine. The final stage of experience involved a growing appreciation of the value of comradeship and of the fact that the war was made up of human beings, each with a significance and history of their own. By this stage, 'the man has passed out of himself into the heart of others'. Waugh warned of the 'insistent claim of personality' exerted by the war and, in common with John Rothenstein, the danger to individual opinion. The war had brought with it a realisation that, 'no man's life can belong to himself, even for a moment, and that, when all is said and done, the individual life is of very little concern to the world at large'.[31]

In 1915, also within the pages of the *Quarterly Review*, Lascelles Abercrombie had divided the poetry of the war into two categories: that of a 'patriotic nature', such as the gush of verse trumpeting the onset of hostilities (Julian Grenfell, Rupert Brooke etc.) and, secondly, that which was content to merely describe the fact of the war in one or many of its facets, usually with brutal detail, as in Owen and Sassoon. The poetry and art of patriotism – that which was 'temporary and local' to Lawrence Haward and which most easily succumbed to the 'insistent claim of personality' in Waugh's view – Abercrombie had found to be 'polarised ... by a pre-determined purpose of morality; in fact, it is a kind of didactic poetry'. The second category of stark expressiveness Abercrombie saluted as 'very valuable', due to the order and form of the *manner* of its realisation, even if in its nature it conveyed the chaos of war and the mental danger thereof – a danger the war presented 'by throwing thought into disorder and incoherence'. 'It is terribly likely', Abercrombie warned, 'that these events and emotions when we are most conscious of them, are least submissive to mental control'. Here Abercrombie publicly acknowledged what others had been thinking in private: the vandalism that direct experience of the conflict could inflict upon the canvas of the mind.

The value of experience

Despite the warning of Lascelles Abercrombie, it was sometimes deemed necessary to experience the war directly in order to inform one's art and hence to be able and 'qualified' to react against it. This chapter has shown Arthur Waugh's view that direct experience could trigger an 'enlightened' searchlight of artistic interpretation and the *Nation* proclaiming that, in some cases, imagination could be 'purified and completed' by experience. An apposite example of the importance of experience in formulating a response to the conflict is that of the War Artist Paul Nash. Although Nash regarded the conflict as 'a war of negatives', he wrote, 'I expect I should hate the slaughter – I know I should, but I'd like to be among it all'.[33] He made this comment while training at the barracks in Roehampton, a situation he described as like being among a 'herd of beasts'.

Nash had enlisted for Home Defence in the Artists' Rifles and had been eventually accepted after initial rejection for being under the original (6 ft) standard height requirement. His thoughts on the war and his part in it are graphically illustrated in his letters to the essayist Gordon Bottomley, who had helped persuade him to register at the Slade in 1910 and had acted as a father-confessor figure from that time (also the year of Nash's mother's death). During the first weeks of the war, Nash had volunteered for farm work to replace enlisting farm-hands. He commented that he was 'not keen' to rush off and be a soldier, describing himself as 'a gentleminded creature' unsuited for the ordeal ahead. However, with Bottomley's advice to strengthen his resolve, he eventually decided to enlist. 'We thinkers love art and poetry better than war', Bottomley wrote, 'but this is one of the times of the world when men must fight if they want to preserve the foundations on which art and poetry can alone be possible.' Bottomley looked forward to a time when his 'pupil' might be able to bring, 'a new world of experience to your art'.[34]

In May 1916, Nash became a map-reading instructor at Romford where he formed a close friendship with the rural poet Edward Thomas. Later that summer he began officer training, and he was gazetted as a 2nd Lieutenant in the

3rd Hampshires and sent to France in February 1917. Before his embarkation, Bottomley had written to him that he was envious of the fact that Nash's vision of life would potentially 'be keener and more various for these next month's experience' and he wished for Nash, 'the mental energy to let it all feed the various purposes of your art'.

Nash's first drawings from the Western Front were exhibited in June 1917 and then in a much larger exhibition in May 1918 at the Leicester Galleries under the title 'The Void of War'. By this time, Nash and the experiences of war recreated on his canvasses were much further in the public eye – in October 1917 he had been seconded to the Department of Information as an official War Artist after a recommendation from John Buchan to C.F.G. Masterman. Following several weeks back in France in November 1917 (after recovering from accidental injury in England for five months), he was granted leave to work up his drawings – this leave was eventually extended to the end of the war.

Nash found himself profoundly affected by what he saw and felt at the front, a place where, 'Sunset and sunrise are blasphemous, they are mockeries to man … It is unspeakable, godless, hopeless.' More crucially, he now felt his status as an artist had changed: 'I am no longer an artist interested and curious. I am a messenger who will bring back word from the men who are fighting to those who want the war to go on for ever.'[35] In July 1918, while working on one of his most celebrated pictures, 'The Menin Gate', Nash commented to Bottomley on how difficult he found it, while painting in the peace of the English country-side, to recall and 'brood on those wastes in Flanders, the torments, the cruelty and terror of this war'. However, Nash and the artist within him felt compelled to do so, 'for it seems the only justification of what I do now – If I can help to rob war of the last shred of glory, the last shine of glamour'.[36]

In addition to a desire to put himself to the test, the artist and poet Herbert Read, a 2nd Lieutenant in the Green Howards by January 1915, also hoped to use the war for artistic purposes. Read hoped the passion of conflict would make him a writer. However, by the time he was wounded and invalided back to England in 1916, it was the passion of anger against the war that fuelled his anti-romantic essays and poems (during the same period he also began a novel which was later abandoned). He claimed not to be afraid of death, only fearful (like Ivor Gurney) that the 'high projects of my ambitious spirit' would remain thus incomplete. By the time he returned to the front in April 1917, Read had decided that his possible death would not be for King and Country but for 'the salvation of my own soul'. At the front, he had found that he had begun to appreciate the values of comradeship and the character of the common soldier; 'the simple soul', symbolised by 'a stout heart' and the fellowship of endeavour. Conversely, he began to distrust the 'bombast and swank' of the military 'machine'.

Although he was awarded the Military Cross and the DSO, the end of the war found Read, 'dazed, indifferent, incapable of any creative action'.[37] The final months of the conflict had seen him much changed as the war exerted its effect over his previous socialism. He found that he now disliked crowds and mobs and instead placed his hope in 'beautiful anarchy' and declared that, in order for mankind to comprehend the wrongness of war and thereby arrive at a realisation of its common humanity, 'I have only one faith ... faith born in the experience of war.'[38]

Even some of those who themselves recoiled from the various theatres of war felt themselves drawn to the intense emotions involved and saw fit to offer advice and comment to others who went when they could or would not. Henry James, despite writing from England (to Hugh Walpole, serving with the Red Cross on the Russian Front), described the war as an 'unspeakably intimate experience', and he advised Edward Marsh to 'entertain the pang and taste the bitterness' of the overall experience in order to comprehend the process of change that was, in James's opinion, bound to affect individuals caught by the conflict. To James, experience was valuable, and it was worth enduring the 'aching anguish' of it in order to, 'press one's poor old ponderous and yet so imperceptible "moral weight" into the scale'.[39]

It was important to make one's point felt, however faintly, amid the clamour of conflict, and one's point of view would be reinforced by direct (or indirect, in James's case) immersion in the altered and altering life during wartime. In an article on war-weariness and the search for peace in 1917, the *Nation* was moved to comment that, as it understood the movement of public opinion, it was not a military decision that was going to bring about the end of militarism but rather a 'general sense, bred of personal experience, that war is folly and waste and suffering'. The author of a 'typical' letter from the front to the *Cambridge Magazine* in 1916 specifically stated that a motivation in enlisting and going to France had been the fact that 'we thought we could be better advocates of peace by seeing with our own eyes the futility and ingloriousness of war'. He described himself as a conscientious objector, though not on an official level, because his conscience was not of a religious nature and hence, he thought, would not be recognised by the Military Service Act. There had also been a price to pay for using experience as a tool of peace; he described the result of eighteen months of experience at the front for himself and his fellow soldiers as being as if they had all, 'sold our souls to unreason, as converts do to the Roman Catholic church'.[41]

In the spring of 1919, the *Nation* observed that many 'soldier minds' were returning to academic courses delayed or cut short by military service. That these soldier-academics were able to find hope renewed was due to their experience, commented the article, entitled 'Back to the Muses'. Having passed through action, they could now approach the 'realms of thought' with greater maturity:

> Only those who have learnt through action the true meaning of beauty and of knowledge can know how abundantly it [their hope] will be justified ... But, above all, we

look to them with urgent hope for a new form of literature – a literature of reality, not made from cobweb fancies and tender suppositions but from profound truths of life as they have been revealed to them along the hardworn ways of action.

The returning soldier-thinkers, it was sincerely hoped (though no one had asked them), were to be the prophets of a new age of reason, one rejecting all the base values they had encountered in confrontation with the war. 'For our country', the article in the *Nation* concluded, 'as for the whole region of mind and beauty, they may lead towards a new birth, a later and finer renaissance. It would be hard indeed to over-estimate the value of action upon the thinker's mind.'[42] As Henry James had noted, immersion in war, however bad for the soul, was valuable in honing one's thoughts down to sharp, accurate truths. The war could be thus insidious to specific individuals; so many who opposed it were concurrently drawn to it, especially in the case of the artist or one conscious of aesthetic values.

The creative results of the artist venturing forth to test his sensibilities in the arena of war – in order to present as true an impression as possible – could be dramatic or muted, immediate or delayed, as in the following, concluding example. As late as 1922, in a review of Edmund Blunden's *The Shepherd and Other Poems*, the critic Cobden Sanderson remarked that Blunden had 'suffered the war and survived it' and that there had been little about the war in his earlier (though post-war) volumes of verse. This was, Sanderson commented, forgivable, as the poems had been written, 'under the more or less immediate impact of its stupendous and irreducible experiences'. Now however, 'Mr Blunden has seen Ypres; the iron has been driven into his soul ... We can understand why his instinct as a poet was to reserve his experience and perfect his craft.'[43] If regretful time could not bring back the dead, it could, it seemed, bring some measure of understanding.

Notes

1 Gilbert Cannan, 'Kept Alive', *Cambridge Magazine*, vol. 4, no. 8, 28 Nov. 1914, p. 154.
2 Douglas Goldring, *Reputations* (London, 1920), pp. 60–1.
3 Gilbert Cannan, letter to the *Nation*, vol. 19, no. 24, 9 Sept. 1916, pp. 729–30.
4 Bertrand Russell, 'The Ethics of War', *International Journal of Ethics*, vol. XXV, Jan. 1915, p. 130.
5 Gilbert Cannan, *Freedom* (London, 1917), p. 12.
6 *Ibid.*, p. 55.
7 *Ibid.*, p. 13.
8 *Ibid.*, p. 61.
9 *Cambridge Magazine*, vol. 4, no. 10, 23 Jan. 1915, pp. 187, 189.
10 *Cambridge Magazine*, vol. 4, no. 10, 23 Jan. 1915, Gilbert Cannan, 'Addenda and a Soft Answer', p. 191.
11 Robert Nichols, Introduction to *Anthology of War Poetry*, ed. Nichols (London, 1943), pp. 39, 47.
12 C.E. Playne, letter to the *Nation*, vol. 18, no. 5, 30 Oct. 1915, p. 183.

13 'War and the Imagination', *New Statesman*, vol. 3, no. 70, 8 Aug. 1914, pp. 555–6.

14 Cannan, *Freedom*, p. 44.

15 'Life and Letters: The Herd Mind', the *Nation*, vol. 17, no. 15, 10 July 1915, p. 479. This was a comment on Gilbert Murray, 'The Herd Instinct and the War' in Humphrey Milford ed., *The International Crisis in its Ethical and Psychological Aspects* (London, 1915). Murray had pointed out that, 'in time of danger the Individual subordinates himself to the herd'. (p. 31).

16 W.R. Inge, 'Patriotism', *Quarterly Review*, vol. 244, no. 444, July 1915, pp. 71, 82.

17 N.B. Bagenal, letter to *Cambridge Magazine*, vol. 4, no. 8, 28 Nov. 1914, p. 157.

18 'The Havoc of the Mind', the *Nation*, vol. 23, no. 10, 8 June 1918, pp. 245–6.

19 'The Nature of Civilization', the *Nation*, vol. 24, no. 14, 4 Jan. 1919, p. 400.

20 'The Moral Outcast Theory', *New Statesman*, vol. 4, no. 84, 14 Nov. 1914, p. 124.

21 'War and the Imagination', *New Statesman*, vol. 3, no. 70, 8 Aug. 1914, pp. 554–5.

22 'The Nature of Civilization', the *Nation*, vol. 24, no. 14, 4 Jan. 1919, p. 400.

23 'The Defeat of Imagination', the *Nation*, vol. 24, no. 13, 28 Dec. 1918, p. 376.

24 E.S.P. Haynes, *The Decline of Liberty in England* (London, 1916), p. 219.

25 Lawrence Haward, *The Effect of War upon Art and Literature* (London and Manchester, 1916), pp. 32, 8–9. Haward met Siegfried Sassoon via a mutual friend, Edward Dent, when Sassoon visited Manchester in December 1917 (in order to see Goldsworthy Lowes Dickinson, who was also in the city).

26 C.F.G. Masterman, *England After War* (London, 1922), p. 192.

27 John Rothenstein, *British Artists and the War* (London, 1931), pp. 20–1.

28 Henry James, interview in *New York Times*, 21 March 1915, cited in Leon Edel, *Henry James – The Master 1901–1916* (Philadelphia and New York, 1972), pp. 527–8.

29 John Galsworthy, 'Our Literature and the War', *Times Literary Supplement*, no. 695, 13 May 1915, p. 157.

30 Arthur Waugh, 'War Poetry 1914–1918', *Quarterly Review*, vol. 230, no. 457, October 1918, p. 383.

31 *Ibid.*, p. 399.

32 Lascelles Abercrombie, 'The War and the Poets', *Quarterly Review*, vol. 224, no. 445, October 1915, p. 397.

33 Paul Nash to Emily Bottomley, cited in *Poet and Painter – Letters between Gordon Bottomley and Paul Nash 1910–46*, ed. C.C. Abbott and A. Bertram (Bristol, 1990), [late Oct.] 1914, no. 96, p. 76.

34 *Ibid.*, Gordon Bottomley to P. Nash, 2 Oct. 1914, no. 95, p. 75.

35 Paul Nash, *Outline* (London, 1949), p. 211.

36 P. Nash to G. Bottomley, 16 July 1918, *Poet and Painter*, p. 99.

37 Herbert Read, *The Contrary Experience* (London, 1973, first published 1963), p. 217.

38 Herbert Read, 'Our Point of View', written in January 1918 for the *New Age* and cited in *The Contrary Experience*, p. 117.

39 Henry James to L.C. Perry, 17 June 1915, *Letters of Henry James, Volume IV: 1895–1916*, ed. Leon Edel (Cambridge, MA, 1984), p. 758.

40 'A Peace of Conciliation', the *Nation*, vol. 21, no. 18, 4 Aug. 1917, p. 444.

41 *Cambridge Magazine*, vol. 5, no. 18, 29 April 1916, p. 408.

42 'Back to the Muses', the *Nation*, vol. 25, no. 4, 26 April 1919, p. 104.

43 Review of Edmund Blunden's *The Shepherd and Other* Poems, Times *Literary Supplement*, no. 1060, 11 May 1922, p. 305.

Conclusion

In addition to a dawning comprehension of what had occurred, the chief legacy of the Great War was change. On 2 September 1914 *The Times* printed for the first time Rudyard Kipling's poem 'For All We Have and Are' in which the nation's poet lamented that, 'Our world has passed away/In wantonness o'erthrown', the only solid things remaining being 'steel and fire and stone'. If the realities of war focused attention on the basic elements of existence and survival, the well-spring of grief and self-examination that characterised the post-war world did not allow this attention to lapse.

Throughout this book we have encountered opposition to the Great War which emanated from individuals who, motivated by aesthetic, humanistic and moral concerns, reacted against this reduction of life to its basic – and, they felt, *baser* – constituents. This cultural abrasion was comprehended by some during the period of reflection following the war. The social analyst Caroline Playne in her *Society at War* (1931) stated that:

> Thoughtful people, people of artistic temperament, felt the war years to be a long-protracted, acute form of nightmare. They felt themselves held up from constructive tasks; and, at the same time, falling apart from civilised standards, divided, estranged from their own ideals. The goodness they might have pursued evaded them, whilst regard for beauty vanished, as it seemed for ever. The faith that might have upheld them, being constantly trampled in the mud, ceased to function. Instead of help when they cried aloud, they must endure the perpetual trumpeting of falsities – the war for freedom and justice, the war to end war.

Playne concluded – and we have observed – that the experience of thinkers and artists who had languished under the conflict was just as real as that of the shattered soldiers:

> Just as the nerves, the minds of the strongest soldiers broke down under their endurance of the continuous noises, vibrations, shocks of intensified bombardments, so whole-hearted followers of mercy and truth broke down under the prolonged moral shock and disappointment.[1]

Bloomsbury, perhaps typically, reacted to the Great War on an individual basis. Other people also based their objection to the conflict on aesthetic or humanistic grounds and did so from a wider cross-section of the cultural land-scape. Although most of these people were from the educated middle-classes, similarly linked anti-war reactions occurred throughout the war and beyond and emanated from differing contexts; from the equally well-known to the obscure, from male to female, from those who fought to those who did not. As early as 1 August 1914, the *Manchester Guardian* carried a letter from one Louis Kletz, who declared that Great Britain should remain neutral in the approaching conflict, 'first and foremost because war at the best of times is not only a calamity, but an outrage on humanity'.[2] Bloomsbury were *not* exclusive in their response to the Great War and, in fact, could be viewed as merely the 'tip of the iceberg' of aesthetic or humanistic opposition.

As we have found, though not the totality of anti-war feeling, occurrences of individualistic aesthetic, humanistic or moral opposition were both varied and widespread. To a certain extent, this was due to cultural legacies from the previous century – a period which had witnessed the solid individualism of entre-preneurial endeavour, entrenched notions of self-help and, in culturally influential circles, a growing appreciation of aesthetics. In an address during his tenure as President of the Royal Academy (1879–93), Lord Leighton had offered a philosophy of the ideal. The source of all art was, 'the consciousness of emotion in the presence of the natural phenomena of life and Nature'.[3] This advocacy of a life lived through the senses was similar in concept to that proffered by Walter Pater in his aesthetic championing of, 'the cult of beauty in everything [and] the pursuit of pleasure'.[4] The Victorian Romantic movement had sought to afford to the individual a higher perception via the imagination, and Pater had not only defended this power of imagination but advocated its extension. His crusade had been embodied, in the words of one of his undergraduates, in a drive to 'cultivate the art of vivid sensation'.

The essential attributes of the Romantic movement had been a 'vibrant individualism striving to emancipate itself from the false conventions of the age', coupled with 'the belief in the higher perception afforded by the imagination' and a certainty that, 'ultimate truths belonged more to the heart than the head'.[5] Humanistic and aesthetic links between the late nineteenth and early twentieth centuries were strong; the Red House of William Morris at Upton near Bexley Heath foreshadowed the Charleston of Vanessa Bell and Duncan Grant. Paul Levy, in his biography of that 'father' of Bloomsbury, the Cambridge philosopher G.E. Moore, has pointed out that:

> Among ... general attitudes that have become to be associated with Moore were several that were common to 'Cambridge Humanism', and which were shared by Apostles such as [Harry] Sedgwick, [J.E.] McTaggart and [Goldsworthy] Lowes Dickinson. A belief in rationality and the power of reason was the chief of these. All these philosophers believed that men's minds could be changed by rational argument, and that belief could affect action, so that it was in the power of mankind to decide rationally to follow a certain course of action.[6]

It was when mankind refused to act rationally in a collective sense (and went to war) that the individuals of Bloomsbury and their circle felt the need to follow independent and, to them, rational courses of action. According to Bloomsbury authority J.K. Johnstone, that circle of individuals desired 'understanding rather than power', and both Johnstone and Levy draw attention to a 'Cambridge Humanism' that was, 'even more important to Bloomsbury than Moore's philosophy'. These 'Victorian' tenets formed the basis not only for Bloomsbury's response to the Great War but that of others also – all of them, 'individuals in a world in which individualism [was] threatened daily'.[7]

The individualism of the Victorian period had had to vie with the new collectivist approach of movements such as Guild socialism, feminism and the more abstract impulses of patriotic imperialism. With the advent of the Great War, conflicts of morality ensued, as some individuals who were used to sublimating themselves in work for the common good found the call of individual conscience hard to ignore. Those who volunteered for military service in the early months of the war *voluntarily* laid down individualistic claims for a variety of reasons, not least due to the pull of pre-war collectivist patriotism and a resulting sense of moral duty – this was, after all, in H.G. Wells's famous phrase, the 'War that Will End War'.

With the coming of war, a new moral order was established. 'The present War is a conflict which admits no truth or reconciliation, between two conceptions and ideals of life', declared the *Quarterly Review*. 'Liberty, democracy, and the moral law are ranged in battle order against physical force, militarism and the claims for universal domination.'[8] Moral battle-lines were drawn, but as we have seen, not everyone rallied to the same standard. The *Manchester Guardian* warned that:

> These will be times to try men's souls. Those who have from pulpit platform and press, have prated so lightly of war as a moral purge, a discipline, a tonic, will have a chance to show how much their faith in war is worth … it will not be only the men who go to the front who will have to drink of that purge and who will find it a bitter draught.[9]

The men and women in this book found the war a 'bitter draught'. To some, accepted standards of morality had been corrupted and independence of character forcibly reduced by the war. 'The fact that men of character and moral strength were forced down to primitive levels fixed such levels for the general mass', Caroline Playne later commented. It was these men, she continued:

> … possessing powers of original thought and intellectual initiative who would in former times have maintained their independence of judgement, exercise of reason – it was these men who were badly broken in the course of being shaped to the military pattern by rude and brutal methods.[10]

We have observed how the conflict was perceived by some as, in Henry James's phrase, 'the great interruption' in human progress. In some quarters, this interruption was seen as the herald of *positive* change, and this was to be celebrated rather than condemned. In September 1914, the *English Review* trumpeted that 'This war will be the great clearing house of civilisation.'[11] Despite the *Manchester Guardian*'s warning to all those who had talked of the coming of war as 'a moral purge' or 'a tonic', Edmund Gosse, in an article entitled 'War and Literature', described the conflict as, 'the sovereign disinfectant . . . the Condy's Fluid that cleans out the stagnant pools and clotted channels of the intellect'. To Gosse and others, the war was a 'refreshment of the spirit' and a chance to sweep away Edwardian lethargy, both physical and mental. However, even Gosse was forced to admit that the conflict was 'the great scavenger of thought'.[12]

It is clear that while not all those viewing the war from an educated aesthetic or humanistic standpoint necessarily regarded its effects as disastrous, a significant proportion did so. Henry James clearly saw the war's adverse effect upon human progress. 'The plunge of civilisation into this abyss of blood and darkness', he wrote to a friend,

> is a thing that so gives away the whole long age during which we have supposed the world to be, with whatever abatement, gradually bettering, that to have to take it all now for what the treacherous years were all the while really making for and meaning is too tragic for words.[13]

The thoughts and feelings of the people described in this book reflect both private and public concerns, and the *Manchester Guardian* publicly voiced James's private lamentation. In an article entitled 'On the Brink', the paper warned that Britain should not make itself 'an accessory to the crime against reason and human happiness that is now beginning'. Entering the war would be to 'throw away in a wild gamble the accumulated progress of half a century, to starve every hope'.[14]

Gilbert Murray, the Regius Professor of Greek at Oxford, mused upon the paradoxical nature of the conflict. He highlighted the necessarily 'hideous' character of the activities of war – 'so hideous, indeed that at times it seems strange that we carry it out at all of this war of civilised men against civilised men, against our intellectual teachers, our brothers in art and science and healing medicine, and so large a part of all that makes life beautiful'.[15] The Great War was not only a paradox; George Bernard Shaw described it as a 'monstrous triviality'. While Shaw was driven largely by his scepticism concerning the motives of government and public morality, Bertrand Russell described the conflict as 'trivial for all its vastness'. We have witnessed both Russell's despair for mankind and his hope that the lesson of the conflict would produce (via individuals) a 'different spirit': a calmer, creative state of mind in contrast to the destructive 'fiery conviction' of the war years. In addition, Russell's concerns were echoed, often independently, by other individuals, whether celebrated or obscure.

The ground was being laid for the organised voice of historian Martin Ceadel's 'humanitarian pacifism' of the 1920s and 1930s.[16] It is clear that aesthetic and humanistic anti-war feeling was not simply an inter-war 'innovation', but existed much earlier during the actual conflict and emanated from differing sources on an individual basis in its expression.

The inter-war years and especially the early 1920s were potentially a time for reflection and reassessment on what had gone before. However, the accredited war correspondent Philip Gibbs noted in 1921 that the period since the Armistice, instead of being one of peace and analysis had been, 'three years of blundering, moral degradation, and reaction to the lowest tradition of national politics'.[17] It seemed as if the fears and warnings of humanity being jolted from the path of progress by the force of the conflict contained some truth. Victory celebrations had been muted and short-lived, and the post-war period was a time of uncertainty and instability.

Gibbs had revisited the notion that the war had effected a 'rapid decline in ordinary morality' and a 'lowering of spiritual ideals' amongst individuals. In his memoirs, he cited reprisals carried out against those who had supposedly been pro-German in occupied Belgium and the all-consuming desire of the French for revenge as examples of the human spirit brought low by the war.[18] He had perceived an attitude amongst intellectual and aesthetic observers during the war; namely that the conflict had 'demoralised and spiritually weakened' human nature, thus enabling 'a coarseness and cruelty of mind' to evolve in the vacuum thus created. This, in turn, Gibbs concluded, produced a 'degrading' action, a 'poisonous reaction' which 'deadens the sensitive nerve cells of the mind'. He reiterated that the overall effect had been 'a subtle coarsening process' which had, 'overtaken the most refined minds and blunted their finer sensibilities', while the least refined minds had 'relapsed into brutishness'.[19]

Within Philip Gibbs's post-war assessment of the conflict's effects, lay some of the resulting major themes of individual aesthetic, humanistic or moral anti-war reaction. Gibbs's recognition of a 'moral degradation' reflects the climate of 'moral fear' which Caroline Playne saw as pervading the war years and after, as well as the public recognition of a new moral order in the pages of journals such as the *Spectator*, the *Quarterly Review* and the *Nation*. Writing from his intellectually crag-like vantage point, George Bernard Shaw declared the war to be a 'hopeless moral muddle', and we have seen how men with experience of the front came to comprehend an altered moral climate, such as Colonel Hanbury-Sparrow's claim that Passchendalele shattered the force of any moral argument for war. Some men, such as E.P. Southall at his court martial, declared an exemption from the war on specifically moral grounds and, as in Southall's case, displayed a recognition that the strictures of the war-state could only 'crush moral liberty'.

The 'coarseness and cruelty of mind' and resultant mental degradation that war correspondent Philip Gibbs identified could be said to be similar to the metaphor of 'iron' entering the soul of poet Edmund Blunden and other writers and artists in uniform like him, a process which Blunden had to not only struggle against, but, but, more crucially, shut off from his creative consciousness if he were to continue to be a poet in the short term. Hence Blunden's apparent inability to produce 'war poetry' immediately after his experience of the front. Gibbs's observations also mirror the experiences of other individuals, such as E.G. Venning and Stephen Hewitt, who both discerned a hardening of sensibility and a growing insignificance of individual efforts within the apparatus of war.

Experience of the conflict resulted in a 'winter of the spirit' for many. This mental climate was publicly pointed out and debated within various periodicals during the war itself. In a spiritually heightened review in the *Nation* of Goldsworthy Lowes Dickinson's *The Chance Before Us* in 1917, the reviewer had warned that war had a detrimental effect upon the spirit as well as the body. According to the review, the conflict had imparted, 'a kind of hardness to human nature. It accepts suffering, cruelty, injustice, all the evils, for their effect is inducing this hardness.' The review made clear that, on the other hand, peace was based on love and, therefore, inclined to the values of liberty and the richness and diversity of human character: 'Thus peace comes not to destroy the individual, but to fulfil him.'[20] A letter published in the following issue carried the analysis further, stating that the 'effective pacifist' was one who expressed a positive spirit which was 'healing and creative'. The pacifist was not a 'retailer of formulas' (which were 'dead things' and belonged, therefore, to the realm of war) but rather, he exhibited an 'intense effective personality' which could thus in wartime become, 'a rallying point for all those unseen creative forces which will slowly but surely overcome the destructive forces of war'.[21] The practical truth of this lies in the struggles of Bertrand Russell.

The journalist H.M. Tomlinson was a war correspondent in France for the *Daily News* from 1914 to 1917. He was eventually withdrawn by the Newspaper Proprietor's Association for being too 'humanitarian' in his outlook; his experience of the conflict 'left him with a bleeding soul' according to Philip Gibbs. Tomlinson's *Waiting for Daylight*, published in 1922, detailed in thirty-three precisely dated sections, one man's reaction to the war and its aftermath. According to Tomlinson, following experience of the conflict, nothing could be viewed or discussed innocently again. The common soldier represented not only 'a desolation of the mind', but also, 'the ghost of what was fair, but was broken, and is lost'.[22] Despite the possibility of this 'desolation of the mind' resulting from experience of the war, we have seen how for some, a major component of aesthetic or humanistic opposition to the conflict was direct experience of it – men like F.H. Keeling and Wilfred Owen sought out the experience in order to validate their individual stance on the conflict. Owen, in particular, felt that he would not be content until he had, 'suffered my share of life'.

Tomlinson noted that the war had produced a 'lethargic' state of mind and that, 'we have learned it is possible to habituate humanity to the long elaboration of any folly . . . folly and cruelty become accepted as normal conditions of human existence'.[23] The ordinary conditions of life were warped by the war to such an extent that the world that emerged from the conflict was not the one that had entered it and that men had rushed to defend. Observing this new world in April 1921, Tomlinson wrote that:

> The Spring is not for us ... We have cleverly made a way of life that exacts so close an attention, if we would save it from disaster, that we are now its prisoners ... The Spring we see now is in a world not ours, a world we have left, which is still close to us but unapproachable.[24]

Later still, Tomlinson wrote that his experience of battle had cautioned him that life would not be the same again.

'The shadow of the battles of the Somme was of a nature that no radiant May morning of a better year could ever lift', he admitted, linking metaphorically and emotionally across time to one of the earliest observers of the war, Geoffrey Winthrop Young, the author of *From the Trenches – Louvain to the Aisne, the First Record of an Eye-Witness*, who described the war of movement that he had newly witnessed as a form of cloud, shifting, 'from village to village, from week to week, only to let us see in its track nature outraged, emotion degraded, humanity defaced',[25] an apposite summary of aesthetic, humanistic and moral concerns.

After the passing of the shadow of the cloud, Tomlinson recalled, both the physical and mental landscapes were altered:

> We faced a world that had an aspect changed and obdurate, that would have a future we could not guess; even our standard roses would never bring Summer in the old way; and life faltered within us. We began to surmise that the world we have known, which was fair, had gone the way of Eden and youth, and that it would not return.[26]

Commenting on the Great War, the Weimar playwright, satirist and war-veteran Carl Zuckmayer stated that: 'What really happened in 1914, and how it took place, can be reconstructed only from the experience of the individual.'[27] The fabric of this book has been constructed with this premise in mind. In his cultural survey *England After War*, C.F.G. Masterman placed his faith in 'the return of men trained in the art of war to the pursuits of peace', as did Bertrand Russell and others, as we have witnessed. However, Masterman was overly optimistic, postulating that 'all experience of incredible suffering, danger and upheaval' brought about by the conflict had 'vanished like a dream' while 'the broken ends of normal life have joined together again, as though the interval had never been'. We have seen this was not so – how could it be, given the variety of individual experience created by the war? For all his optimism, Masterman was forced to admit that, 'Amidst all these millions who suffered, each individual suffered *alone*'.[28] By this he meant that everyone who suffered the war, both in the sense of actual suffering and also of simple experience, did so in an internal manner, known only to themselves. Thus when the waters had subsided, they were each of them left looking at the world from an individual vantage point – islands of personal experience – and thus uniquely alone.

A month after the Armistice, in December 1918, in its review of *Fields and Battlefields* by an anonymous sergeant in the Royal Army Medical Corps ('no. 31540'), the *Nation* commented on the surveys, such as C.F.G. Masterman's, and official histories, military or otherwise, of the war that were bound to appear in the years to come. 'But the real history', the review predicted, 'the one that men and women will want, will be something quite different. It will be the record, broken, perplexed and partial of what individual soldiers were really thinking and feeling; the reflection and refraction of the tragedy in human souls.'[29] This book has attempted to put a mirror to the soul of the war as it triggered responses within men and women possessed of certain aesthetic, moral or humanistic sensibilities and thus capture something of the nature, cause and effect of the personal tragedies reflected therein.

Notes

1 Caroline Playne, *Society at War* (London, 1931), p. 373.

2 Louis Kletz, letter to *Manchester Guardian*, 1 Aug. 1914, p. 10.

3 Cited in Stephen Jones, 'Attic Attitudes – Leighton and Aesthetic Philosophy' in *Victorian Values – Personalities and Perspectives in Nineteenth Century Society*, ed. Gordon Marsden (London, 1990), p. 69.

4 Michael Levy, the *Case of Walter Pater* (London, 1978), p. 21. In his *Studies in the Renaissance* (1873), Pater had exhorted individuals to seek out and experience new sensations – to 'burn' with 'that hard, gem-like flame' that drew its fuel from the pleasure of emotion rather than cold rationality.

5 David Newsome, *The Victorian World Picture* (London, 1997), p. 79.

6 Paul Levy, *G.E. Moore and the Cambridge Apostles* (Oxford, 1981), p. 62. The Apostles were the 'secret' discussion society (founded in 1820) of Cambridge undergraduates, dons and ex-students.

7 J.K. Johnstone, 'The Philosophic Background and Works of Art of the Group known as Bloomsbury', PhD thesis (University of Leeds, 1952), pp. 444, 445.

8 'The German Spirit', *Quarterly Review*, vol. 223, no. 442, Jan. 1915, p. 41.

9 'The Mental Attitude to War', *Manchester Guardian*, 6 Aug. 1914, p. 3.

10 Playne, *Society at War*, p. 74.

11 'The Task of the Allies', *English Review*, Sept. 1914, p. 254.

12 Edmund Gosse, 'War and Literature', *Edinburgh Review*, vol. 220, Oct. 1914, p. 313.

13 Henry James to Howard Sturgis, 5 Aug. 1914, *The Letters of Henry James*, ed. Percy Lubbock (2 vols. London, 1920), vol. 2, p. 398.

14 'On the Brink', *Manchester Guardian*, 3 Aug. 1914, p. 6.

15 Gilbert Murray, *Hibbert Journal*, vol. 13, Oct. 1914, pp. 80–1; later reprinted in Gilbert Murray, *Faith, War and Policy* (London, 1918).

16 See Martin Ceadel's *Pacifism in Great Britain 1914–1945: The Defining of a Faith* (Oxford, 1980).

17 Philip Gibbs, *More That Must be Told* (New York, 1921), p. 1.

18 See Philip Gibbs, *The Pageant of the Years* (London, 1946), p. 235.

19 *Ibid.*, pp. 85, 87.

20 The *Nation*, vol. 22, no. 2, 13 Oct. 1917, p. 72.

21 Edward G. Smith, letter to the *Nation*, vol. 22, no. 3, 20 Oct. 1917, p. 95.

22 H.M. Tomlinson, *Waiting for Daylight* (London, 1922), p. 121.

23 *Ibid.*, p. 105.

24 *Ibid.*, p. 224.

25 Geoffrey Winthrop Young, *From the Trenches – Louvain to the Aisne, the First Record of an Eye-Witness* (London, 1914), p. 301. Young was a volunteer with the Friends Ambulance Unit.

26 H.M. Tomlinson, *All Our Yesterdays* (London, 1930), pp. 411–12.

27 Carl Zuckmayer, *A Part of Myself* (London, 1970), p. 137.

28 C.F.G. Masterman, *England After War* (London, 1922), pp. 5, 8.

29 The *Nation*, vol. 24, no. 10, 7 Dec. 1918, p. 294.

Bibliography

Primary sources

Manuscripts

McMaster University, Hamilton, Ontario, Canada, William Ready Division of Archives and Research Collection
Bertrand Russell Papers
Referred to as McM,BRP in notes following initial citation.
1073–1492
    Letters from Bertrand Russell to Lady Ottoline Morrell.

711200-
    Letters from Bertrand Russell to Lady Constance Malleson ('Colette').
Rec. Acqu. 16.
    Letter from Bertrand Russell to Clifford Allen.

710.082-
    Letters from Lady Ottoline Morrell to Bertrand Russell.
    Bertrand Russell, Prison File, no. 66.

710.055-
    Letters from Siegfried Sassoon to Bertrand Russell.

H.G. Wells Papers
Wells to Siegfried Sassoon, postcard (Sept. 1917).

University of Victoria, British Columbia, Canada, Doyle Collection
Referred to as UV,DC in notes following initial citation.
Photocopies of correspondence between Richard Aldington to F.S. Flint. Originals held at University of Texas at Austin, Henry Ransom Humanities Research Centre.

British Library, Manuscripts Collection
Referred to as BL,MC in notes following initial citation.
Add MSS.59732
    Letters from Lytton Strachey to Duncan Grant.
Add MSS.57933
    Letters from Duncan Grant to Lytton Strachey.
Add MSS.60659
    Letters from Clive and Vanessa Bell to Lytton and James Strachey.
Add MSS.60660
    Letters from Francis Birrell to Lytton Strachey.

Add MSS.60666
  Letters from E.M. Forster to Lytton and James Strachey.
Add MSS.60710 and Add MSS.60711
  Letters between Lytton Strachey and James Strachey.
Add MSS.62888 and Add MSS.62889
  Letters between Lytton Strachey and Dora Carrington.

Tate Gallery Archive, Charleston Trust Papers
Referred to as TGA,CTP in footnotes following initial citation.
8010.2.-
  Letters to Clive Bell from Vanessa Bell and Roger Fry.
8010.5.-
  Letters to Vanessa Bell from Clive Bell, Roger Fry and Duncan Grant.
8010.8.-
  Letters to Roger Fry from Vanessa Bell.

University of Leeds, Liddle Collection
Referred to as UL,LC in notes following initial citation.
File of A.V. Murray, letters from A.V. Murray, Helen Murray and K. Murray.
File of S. White, CO/FAU section [containing: Clifford Allen, 'The Faith of the N.C.F.' in *The No Conscription Fellowship Souvenir – the N.C.F. 1914–1919* (London, 1919)].
File of J. Sadler, CO/FAU section [containing: Society of Friends – Friends Service Committee, *The Absolutists' Objection to Conscription – A statement and an appeal to the Conscience of the Nation* (London, 1917) and the *Manifesto of the N.C.F.* (London, 1915)].
File of Frank Shackleton, containing 'All My Tomorrow'. Manuscript of autobiographical novel.
File of Cpl. H.L. Currall, typescript of letters.
File of J.B. Herbert, diary.
File of W.B. Kitching, diary.
File of R.M. Gale, diaries (3 vols).
File of H.S. Innes, letters.
File of E.P. Southall, containing a defence of E.P. Southall, written for court martial at Littlemore Camp, Weymouth, 19 Oct. 1916.
File of A.V. Ratcliffe, containing 'The Conscientious Objector', *The Microcosm*.
File of Revd C.G. Raven, letters.

The Imperial War Museum
Referred to as IWM in notes following initial citation.
File of Mrs H. Pease (formerly Helen Bowen Wedgwood) 76/179/1. Letters from 'Standon' (to his parents), G. Horwell to Wedgewood and George Kaufman to Wedgewood, including a transcript of his defence at his court martial, 19 Jan. 1917.
File of D.H. Calcutt, transcribed diaries (2 vols, including an Introduction, 'Beneath the Veneer').
Siegfried Sassoon Correspondence, p. 444 (Con. Shelf). Letters to Sassoon from J. Dadd, J. Cottrill and G. Harbord.

Public Records Office
Home Office Papers, HO 45/11012/314670 X.1.3173.

Other primary sources

Imperial War Museum Sound Archive
File of Steven Samuel Winsten.
File of H.C. Marten, 383/6.
File of Helen Bowen Pease (formerly Wedgwood), 821/20.

Frances Partridge
 transcript of interview with J.P. Atkin, 18 Jan. 1995 and letters to J.P. Atkin, 18 Nov. 1994 and
  28 March 1996.

Printed original sources

Books, memoirs, edited contemporary letters and diaries etc.
Abbott, C.C., and Bertram, A., (eds), *Poet and Painter – Letters between Gordon Bottomley and
  Paul Nash 1910–1946* (Bristol, 1990).
Adams, Bernard, *Nothing of Importance* (Stevenage, 1988). First published 1917.
Aldington, Richard, *Death of a Hero*. Authorised unexpurgated edition, limited edition of 300
  copies (2 vols, Paris, 1930).
Alec-Tweedie, Mrs, *A Woman on Four Battle-Fronts* (London, 1919).
Asquith, Cynthia, *Diaries 1915–1918* (London, 1968).
Bagnold, Enid, *Diary Without Dates* (London, 1978). First published 1918.
Bagnold, Enid, *The Happy Foreigner* (London, 1920).
Baker, George, *The Soul of a Skunk* (London, 1930).
Bell, Anne Olivier, (ed.), *The Diary of Virginia Woolf, Volume One, 1915–1919* (London, 1977).
Bell, Clive, *Art* (London, 1914).
Bell, Clive, *Civilization and Old Friends* (Chicago, IL, 1973). *Civilization* originally published
  1928.
Bell, Clive, *Peace at Once* (London, 1915).
Bell, William, *A Scavenger in France* (London, 1920).
Bennett, Arnold, *Over There* (London, 1915).
Blunden, Edmund, *Pastorals* (London, 1916).
Blunden, Edmund, *Poems 1914–30* (London, 1930).
Blunden, Edmund, *Undertones of War* (Oxford, 1956). First published 1928.
'Bombardier X', *So This is War* (London, 1930).
Borden, Mary, *The Forbidden Zone* (London, 1929).
Bowen, Stephen, *Forsaken – Confessions of a Priest who Returned* (London, 1931).
Brendan, Gerald, *A Life of One's Own*, (London, 1975). First published 1962.
Brereton, Frederick (ed.), *Anthology of War Poems* (London, 1930).
Bridges, Alan (ed.), *Vera Brittain, Chronicle of Youth – War Diary 1913–1917* (London, 1981).
Brooke, Charles Berjew, *Letters from the Boy* (privately published, Imperial War Museum collec-
  tion).
Burke, Kathleen, *The White Road to Verdun* (London, 1916).
Buxton, C.R. (ed.), *Towards a Lasting Settlement* (London, 1915).
Cannan, Gilbert, *Freedom* (London, 1917).
Carpenter, Edward, *The Healing of the Nations* (London, 1915).
Carpenter, Edward, *Never Again* (London, 1916).
Carpenter, Edward, *Towards Industrial Freedom* (London, 1917).
Cator, Dorothy, *In a French Military Hospital* (London, 1915).
Chapman, Guy, *A Passionate Prodigality* (London, 1965). First published 1933.
Chapman, Guy (ed.), *Vain Glory: A Miscellany of the Great War 1914–18* (London, 1937).

Clarke, T., *My Northcliffe Diary* (London, 1931).

Cliff, Norman D., *To Hell and Back With the Guards* (Braunton, Devon, 1988).

Cole, Margaret I. (ed.), *The Diary of Beatrice Webb, Volume Three: 1912–1924* (London, 1952).

Cooper, Diana, *Autobiography* (1 vol. edition, London, 1979).

Dearmer, Mable, *Letters From a Field Hospital* (London, 1916).

Dent, Olive, *A VAD in France* (London, 1917).

Dickinson, G.L., *After the War* (London, 1915).

Dickinson, G.L., *The Choice Before Us* (New York, 1919). First published London, 1917.

Dickinson, G.L., *The European Anarchy* (London, 1916).

Dickinson, G.L., *Letters From John Chinaman and Other Essays* (London, 1901).

Dickinson, G.L., *The Meaning of Good* (Glasgow, 1901).

Dickinson, G.L., *Problems of International Settlement* (London, 1918).

Dickinson, G.L., *War: Its Nature, Cause and Cure* (London, 1923).

Dickinson, G.L., *The War and the Way Out* (London, 1914).

Douie, Charles, *The Weary Road* (London, 1929).

Doyle, Arthur Conan, *A Visit to Three Fronts* (London, 1916).

Edel, Leon (ed.), *The Letters of Henry James – Volume Four, 1895–1916* (Cambridge, MA, 1984).

Edmonds, Charles (pseud. of Charles Carrington), *A Subaltern's War* (London, 1929).

'E.T.' (ed.), *Keeling – Letters and Recollections* (London, 1918).

Ewart, Wilfrid, *Way of Revelation* (London, 1921).

Ewart, Wilfrid, *When Armageddon Came* (London, 1933).

Farrer, Reginald, *The Void of War* (London, 1918).

Fitzroy, A.T. (pseud. of Rose Allatini), *Despised and Rejected* (London, 1988). First published 1918.

Forster, E.M., *Goldsworthy Lowes Dickinson* (London, 1934).

Foxcroft, Frank (ed.), *War Verse* (New York, 1918).

Franklin, Gilbert, *Peter Jackson, Cigar Merchant: a Romance of Married Life* (London, 1920).

Fussell, Paul (ed.), *The Ordeal of Alfred M. Hale* (London, 1975).

Galsworthy, John, *A Sheaf* (London, 1916).

Galsworthy, John, *Another Sheaf* (London, 1919).

Garnett, David, *Flowers of the Forest* (London, 1955).

Garnett, David, *Great Friends* (London, 1979).

Gathorne-Hardy, Robert (ed.), *The Early Memoirs of Lady Ottoline Morrell* (London, 1963).

Gathorne-Hardy, Robert (ed.), *Ottoline at Garsington – Memoirs of Lady Ottoline Morrell 1915–1918* (London, 1974).

Gibbon, Monk, *Inglorious Soldier* (London, 1968).

Gibbs, Philip, *More That Must Be Told* (New York, 1921).

Gibbs, Philip, *The Pageant of the Years* (London, 1946).

Gibbs, Philip, *The Soul of the War* (London, 1915).

Goldring, Douglas, *Reputations* (London, 1920).

Graham, John W., *Conscription and Conscience* (London, 1922).

Graham, Stephen, *The Challenge of the Dead* (London, 1921).

Graham, Stephen, *A Private in the Guards* (London, 1919).

Graves, Robert, *Fairies and Fusiliers* (London, 1917).

Gray, Frank, *Confessions of a Private* (Oxford, 1920).

Griffith, Wyn, *Up to Mametz* (London, 1931).

Gurney, Ivor, *Severn and Somme* (London, 1917).

Gurney, Ivor, *War's Embers* (London, 1919).

Hamilton, Cicely, *Life Errant* (London, 1935).

Hamilton, Mary Agnes, *Dead Yesterday* (London, 1916).

Hamilton, Mary Agnes, *Remembering My Good Friends* (London, 1944).

Hanbury-Sparrow, A.A., *The Land-Locked Lake* (London, 1932).

Hart-Davis, Rupert (ed.), *Siegfried Sassoon – Diaries 1915–1918* (London, 1983).

Haward, Lawrence, *The Effect of War upon Art and Literature* (London and Manchester, 1916).

Haynes, E.S.P., *The Decline of Liberty in England* (London, 1916).

H.D. (Hilda Doolittle), *Bid Me to Live* (London, 1984). First published 1960.

Hewett, Stephen H., *A Scholar's Letters from the Front* (London, 1918).

Hinchliffe, A.H.S., *The Bar Sinister* (London, 1935).

Housman, Laurence (ed.), *War Letters of Fallen Englishmen* (London, 1930).

Hueffer, Ford Maddox, *Some Do Not ...* (London, 1924).

Hueffer, Ford Maddox, *When Blood is their Argument: An Analysis of Prussian Culture* (London, 1915).

Huxley, Aldous (ed.), *The Letters of D.H. Lawrence* (London, 1932).

Jacomb, C.E., *Torment* (London, 1920).

Jameson, Storm, *No Time Like the Present* (London, 1953).

Keynes, J.M., *The Economic Consequences of the Peace* (London, 1919).

Keynes, J.M., *Two Memoirs* (London, 1949).

Kiernan, R.H., *Little Brother Goes Soldiering* (London, 1936).

Laffin, John (ed.), *Letters from the Front* (London, 1973).

Lago, Mary and Furbank, P.N. (eds), *Selected Letters of E.M. Forster*, vol. 1 (London, 1983).

Lane, John (ed.), *Love of an Unknown Soldier, Found in a Dug-out* (London, 1918).

Lawford, Stephen, *Youth Uncharted* (London, 1935).

Lubbock, Percy (ed.), *The Letters of Henry James*, vol. 2 (London, 1920).

Macaulay, Rose, *Non-Combatants and Others* (London, 1916).

MacGill, Patrick, *The Great Push* (London, 1916).

MacKenna, Stephen, *While I Remember* (London, 1921).

Macnaughton, Sarah, *A Woman's Diary of the War* (London, 1915).

Manwaring, G.B., *If We Return* (London, 1918).

'Mark VII' (pseud. of Max Plowman), *A Subaltern on the Somme* (London, 1927).

Marrot, H.V., *Life and Letters of John Galsworthy* (London, 1935).

Masefield, John, *Gallipoli* (London, 1916).

Masefield, John, *The Old Front Line* (London, 1917).

Masterman, C.F.G., *The Condition of England* (London, 1909).

Masterman, C.F.G., *England After War* (London, 1922).

McLaren, Barbara, *Women of the War* (London, 1917).

McNellie, Andrew (ed.), *The Essays of Virginia Woolf*, vol. 2 (London, 1986).

Milford, Humphrey (ed.), *The International Crisis in its Ethical and Psychological Aspects*. Lectures delivered in February and March 1915 under the scheme for Imperial Studies in the University of London at Bedford College for Women (London, 1915).

Montague, C.E., *Disenchantment* (London, 1922).

Moore, G.E., *Principia Ethica* (Cambridge, 1922). First published 1903.

Moore, Harry T. (ed.), *The Collected Letters of D.H. Lawrence*, vol. 1 (London, 1962).

Moore, Harry T., *D.H. Lawrence – Letters to Bertrand Russell,* (New York, 1948).

Mottram, R.H., Easten, J. and Partridge, E., *Three Personal Records of the War* (London, 1929).

Murray, (George) Gilbert, *Faith, War and Policy* (London, 1918).

Murry, John Middleton, *Between Two Worlds* (London, 1935).

Nash, Paul, *Outline* (London, 1949).

Nichols, Robert (ed.), *Anthology of War Poetry* (London, 1943).

Nicholson, Nigel (ed.), *'The Question of Things Happening', The Letters of Virginia Woolf – Volume Two, 1912–1922* (London, 1976).

Onions, Maude, *A Woman at War* (published privately in 1928; then by C.W. Dent, London, 1929).

O'Prey, Paul, ed., *In Broken Images – Selected Letters of Robert Graves* (London, 1982).

Osburn, Arthur, *Unwilling Passenger* (London, 1932).

Owen, Harold and Bell, John (eds), *The Collected Letters of Wilfred Owen* (Oxford, 1967).

Pankhurst, Sylvia, *The Home Front* (London, 1932).

Parsons, Ian (ed.), *Isaac Rosenberg – Collected Works and Letters* (London, 1984).

Pitt, B., *Essays, Poems and Letters* (London, 1917).

Playne, Caroline, *Britain Holds On 1917–1918* (London, 1933).

Playne, Caroline, *The Pre-War Mind in Britain* (London, 1928).

Playne, Caroline, *Society at War* (London, 1931).

Plowman, D.L. (ed.), *'Bridge into the Future': Letters of Max Plowman* (London, 1944).

Plowman, Max, *A Subaltern on the Somme* (originally published under pseud. 'Mark VII') (London, 1927).

Plowman, Max, *War and the Creative Impulse* (London, 1919).

Powys, John Cowper, *Autobiography*, (London, 1934).

Purdom, C.B. (ed.), *Everyman at War: Sixty Personal Narratives of the War* (London, 1930).

Purdy, R.L. and Millgate M. (eds), *Collected Letters of Thomas Hardy*, vol. 5 (Oxford, 1985).

Read, Herbert, *The Contrary Experience* (London, 1973). First published 1963.

Rempel, R.A., Brink, A., Moran, M. (eds), *The Collected Papers of Bertrand Russell, Volume Twelve – Contemplation and Action, 1902–1914* (London, 1985).

Rempel, R.A. (ed.), *The Collected Papers of Bertrand Russell, Volume Thirteen – Prophecy and Dissent, 1914–1916* (London, 1988).

Rothenstein, John, *British Artists and the War* (London, 1931).

Russell, Bertrand, *Autobiography* (2 vols., London, 1970).

Salmon, Mrs L. (ed.), *Sarah Macnaughton: My War Experiences on Two Continents* (London, 1919).

Sassoon, Siegfried, *The Complete Memoirs of George Sherston* (London, 1937).

Sassoon, Siegfried, *Counter-Attack* (London, 1915).

Sassoon, Siegfried, *The Old Huntsman* (London, 1917).

Sassoon, Siegfried, *Siegfried's Journey* (London, 1946).

Sassoon, Siegfried, *War Poems* (London, 1983).

Scott Duckers, J., *Handed Over* (London, 1917).

Shaw, George Bernard, *What I Really Wrote About the War* (London, 1931).

Sinclair, May, *Journal of Impressions in Belgium* (London, 1915).

Sinclair, May, *Tasker Jevons* (London, 1916).

Sinclair, May, *The Tree of Heaven* (London, 1917).

Sitwell, Edith (ed.), *Wheels* (London, 1916).

Smith, Helen Zenna (pseud. of Evadne Price), *Not So Quiet: Stepdaughters of War* (New York, 1989). First published 1930.

Sorley, Charles Hamilton, *Marlborough and Other Poems* (London, 1916).

Stanford Donald (ed.), *John Masefield – Letters to Margaret Bridges* (Manchester, 1984).

Stobart, Mabel St Clair, *A Flaming Sword in Serbia and Elsewhere* (London, 1916).

Stobart, Mabel St Clair, *Miracles and Adventures* (London, 1935).

Strachey, Lytton, *Eminent Victorians* (London, 1986). First published 1918.

Swinnerton, Frank, *The Georgian Literary Scene: a panorama* (London, 1935).

Thomas, W. Beach, *With the British on the Somme* (London, 1917).

Thornton, R.K.R. (ed.), *The Collected Letters of Ivor Gurney* (Manchester, 1991).

Tomlinson, H.M., *All Our Yesterdays* (London, 1930).

Tomlinson, H.M., *Waiting For Daylight* (London, 1922).

Vansittart, P. (ed.), *John Masefield's Letters from the Front* (London, 1984).

'W.A.A.C.', *Letters of Thomasina Atkins – Private* (London, 1918).

'W.A.A.C.', *The Woman's History of the War* (London, 1930).

Waugh, Alec, *Resentment* (London, 1917).

Wells, H.G., *Experiment in Autobiography* (2 vols, London, 1934).

Wells, H.G., *Mr. Britling Sees It Through* (London, 1985). First published 1916.

Wells, H.G., *The New Machiavelli* (London, 1911).

Wells, H.G., *The War and Socialism* (London, 1915).

Wells, H.G., *The War that Will End War* (London, 1914).

West, A.G., *Diary of a Dead Officer* (London, 1919).

Williamson, Henry, *The Patriot's Progress* (London, 1930).

Williamson, Henry, *The Wet Flanders Plain* (Norwich, 1987). First published 1929.

Willis, Irene Cooper, *England's Holy War – A Study of English Liberal Idealism During the Great War* (New York, 1928).

Woolf, Leonard, *Beginning Again* (London, 1964).

Woolf, Virginia, *The Common Reader* (2 vols, London, 1925).

Woolf, Virginia, *Roger Fry* (London, 1940).

Woolf, Virginia, *A Room of One's Own* and *Three Guineas* (London, 1993). *Three Guineas* originally published in 1938.

Young, Geoffrey, Winthrop, *From the Trenches – Louvain to the Aisne, the First Record of an Eye-Witness* (London, 1914).

Zilboorg, C. (ed.), *Richard Aldington and H.D. – The Early Years in Letters* (Bloomington, IN, 1992).

Zuckmeyer, Carl, *A Part of Myself* (London, 1970).

Pamphlets and essays

Allen, (Reginald) Clifford, *Conscription and Conscience, Presidential address to the National Convention of the No Conscription Fellowship, November 27th 1915* (London, 1916).

Allen, (Reginald) Clifford, 'The Faith of the N.C.F.' in *The No Conscription Fellowship Souvenir – The N.C.F. 1914–1919* (London, 1919). Reprinted 1940 as part of *Troublesome People*, issued by London III, Miscellaneous Institutions, Socalists and other bodies, Central Board for Conscientious Objectors.

Murray, (George), Gilbert, 'The Herd Instinct and the War' in *The International Crisis in Its Ethical and Psychological Aspects*, ed. Humphrey Milford (London, 1915).

No Conscription Fellowship, *Compulsory Military and Alternative Service and the Conscientious Objector* (London, 1916).

Plowman, Max, *The Right to Live* (London, 1918).

Society of Friends – Friends Service Committee, *The Absolutists' Objection to Conscription – A statement and an appeal to the Conscience of the Nation* (London, 1917).

Articles and letters in journals and newspapers
Atlantic Monthly
Bertrand Russell, 'Is a Permanent Peace Possible?', *Atlantic Monthly*, March 1915.

Cambridge Daily News
Cambridge Daily News, 1 Aug. 1914.

Cambridge Magazine
A.C. Benson, 'Military Training at Cambridge', *Cambridge Magazine*, vol. 3, no. 20, 2 May 1914.

J.K. Stevens, 'From Mons to the Marne on a Motor-Bike', *Cambridge Magazine*, vol. 4, no. 1, 10 Oct. 1914.

'The O.T.C. and the Element of Compulsion', *Cambridge Magazine*, vol. 4, no. 1, 10 Oct. 1914.

'On Coming Up', *Cambridge Magazine*, vol. 4, no. 1, 10 Oct. 1914.

Cambridge Magazine, vol. 4, no. 2, 17 Oct. 1914.

Bertrand Russell, 'Fear as the Ultimate Cause of War', *Cambridge Magazine*, vol. 4, no. 3, 24 Oct. 1914.

T.L., 'What Norman Angell Thinks Now', *Cambridge Magazine*, vol. 4, no. 3, 24 Oct. 1914.

'C.U.O.T.C. Progress – Parade Ground Prattle', *Cambridge Magazine*, vol. 4, no. 3, 24 Oct. 1914.

'An Illegal Proposal', *Cambridge Magazine*, vol. 4, no. 4, 31 Oct. 1914. (This article originally appeared in *The Sportsman*).

Cambridge Magazine, vol. 4, no. 4, 31 Oct. 1914.

N.P. Bagenal, letter to *Cambridge Magazine*, vol. 4, no. 4, 28 Nov. 1914.

Gilbert Cannan, 'Kept Alive', *Cambridge Magazine*, vol. 4, no. 8, 28 Nov. 1914.

Cambridge Magazine vol. 4, no. 10, 23 Jan. 1915.

Gilbert Cannan, 'Addenda and a Soft Answer', *Cambridge Magazine*, vol. 4, no. 10, 23 Jan. 1915.

Cambridge Magazine, vol. 5, no. 18, 29 April 1916.

B. Russell, 'Liberty of Conscience', *Cambridge Magazine*, vol. 5, no. 22, 27 May 1916.

Cambridge Magazine, vol. 6, no. 1, 14 Oct. 1916.

Cambridge Review

Bertrand Russell, 'Can Great Britain and Germany be Reconciled after the War?', *Cambridge Review*, 10 Feb. 1915.

Bertrand Russell, 'Mr. Russell's Reply to his Critics', *Cambridge Review*, 24 Feb. 1915.

Edinburgh Review

Edmund Gosse, 'War and Literature', *Edinburgh Review*, vol. 220, Oct. 1914.

English Review

'The Task of the Allies', *English Review*, Sept. 1914.

The Herald

'War's a Crime', *The Herald*, 19 Dec. 1914.

Hibbert Journal

Hibbert Journal, vol. 13, Oct. 1914.

International Journal of Ethics

Bertrand Russell, 'The Ethics of War', *International Journal of Ethics*, XXV, Jan. 1915.

International Review

Bertrand Russell, 'On Justice in War-Time. An Appeal to the Intellectuals of Europe', *International Review*, 1, 10 Aug. 1915 and 1 Sept. 1915.

Labour Leader

Bertrand Russell, 'Will this War End War?', *Labour Leader*, 10 Sept. 1914.

The Listener

Edmund Blunden, 'The Somme Still Flows', *The Listener*, 10 July 1929 (reprinted 18 Jan. 1979).

George Bernard Shaw, 'As I See It', *The Listener*, 10 Nov. 1937 (reprinted 18 Jan. 1979).

Manchester Guardian

Manchester Guardian, 1 Aug. 1914.

'On the Brink', *Manchester Guardian*, 3 Aug. 1914.

'Neutrality League Announcement', *Manchester Guardian*, 4 Aug. 1914.

'The Mental Attitude to War', *Manchester Guardian*, 6 Aug. 1914.

The Nation

Goldsworthy Lowes Dickinson, 'The Holy War', the *Nation*, vol. 15, no. 19, 8 Aug. 1914.

Bertrand Russell, 'The Rights of War', the *Nation*, vol. 15, no. 20, 15 Aug. 1914.

Edward Thomas, 'This England', the *Nation*, vol. 16, no. 6, 7 Nov. 1914.

'Life and Letters: The Herd Mind', the *Nation*, vol. 17, no. 15, 10 July 1915.

C.E. Playne, letter to the *Nation*, vol. 18. no. 5, 30 Oct. 1915.

Gilbert Cannan, letter to the *Nation*, vol. 19, no. 24, 9 Sept. 1916.

'A Peace of Conciliation', the *Nation*, vol. 21, no. 18, 4 Aug. 1917.

The *Nation*, vol. 22, no. 2, 13 Oct. 1917.

Edward G. Smith, letter to the *Nation*, vol. 22, no. 3, 20 Oct. 1917.

'The Havoc of the Mind', the *Nation*, vol., 23, no. 10, 8 June 1918.

The *Nation*, vol. 24, no. 10, 7 Dec. 1918.

'The Defeat of the Imagination', the *Nation*, vol. 24, no. 13, 28 Dec. 1918.

'The Nature of Civilization', the *Nation*, vol. 24, no. 14, 4 Jan. 1919.

'Back to the Muses', the *Nation*, vol. 25, no. 4, 26 April 1919.

The *Nation and Athenaeum*

Ottoline Morrell in the *Nation and Athenaeum*, vol. XLVI, no. 25, 22 March 1930.

New Statesman

'The Moral Outcast Theory', *New Statesman*, vol. 4, no. 84, 14 Nov. 1914.

George Bernard Shaw, 'Common Sense About the War', (an eighty page supplement) *New Statesman*, vol. 4, no. 84, 14 Nov. 1914.

Leonard Woolf, 'International Government' (a supplement) *New Statesman*, vol. 5, no. 118, 10 July 1915.

'A Sergeant in a Line Regiment in Flanders' [F.H. Keeling], 'A Soldier on Compulsion', *New Statesman*, vol. 5, no. 130, 2 Oct. 1915.

George Bernard Shaw, 'Wanted: A Coalition of the Intelligentsia', *New Statesman*, vol. 6, no. 149, 12 Feb. 1916.

'War and the Imagination', *New Statesman*, vol. 3, no. 70, 8 Aug. 1917.

The Open Court

The Open Court, no. 30 (Chicago, IL), March 1916.

Quarterly Review

'The First Two Months of War', *Quarterly Review*, vol. 221, no 441, Oct. 1914.

'The German Spirit', *Quarterly Review*, vol. 223, no. 442, Jan. 1915.

W.R. Inge, 'Patriotism', *Quarterly Review*, vol. 224, no. 444, July 1915.

Lascelles Abercrombie, 'The War and the Poets', *Quarterly Review*, vol. 224, no. 445, Oct. 1915.

Arthur Waugh, 'War Poetry 1914–1918', *Quarterly Review*, vol. 230, no. 457, Oct. 1918.

Spectator

'If War Comes' and 'Britain's Duty', *Spectator*, vol. 113, no. 4492, 1 Aug. 1914.

Times Literary Supplement

John Galsworthy, 'Our Literature and the War', *Times Literary Supplement*, no. 695, 13 May 1915.

Review of Edmund Blunden's *The Shepherd and Other Poems*, *Times Literary Supplement*, no. 1060, 11 May 1922.

War and Peace

Bertrand Russell, 'Why Nations Love War', *War and Peace*, Nov. 1914.

Secondary sources

Books

Beauman, Nicola, *Cynthia Asquith* (London, 1987).

Bell, Quentin, *Bloomsbury* (London, 1986). First published 1968.

Bergonzi, Bernard, *Hero's Twilight: a study of the Literature of the Great War* (London, 1965).

Berry, Paul and Bostridge, Mark, *Vera Brittain – A Life* (London, 1995).

Boulton, David, *Objection Overruled* (London, 1967).

Bracco, R.M., *Merchants of Hope – British Middlebrow Writers and the First World War 1919–39* (Oxford, 1993).

Brittain, Vera, *The Rebel Passion: a Short History of Some Pioneer Peace-makers* (London, 1964).

Buitenhuis, Peter, *The Great War of Words* (Vancouver, 1987).

Caesar, Adrian, *Taking it Like a Man: Suffering, Sexuality and the War Poets* (Manchester, 1993).

Carsten, F.L., *War Against War – British and German Radical Movements in the First World War* (London, 1982).

Ceadel, Martin, *Pacifism in Great Britain 1914–1945: The Defining of a Faith* (Oxford, 1980).

Cecil, Hugh, *The Flower of Battle* (London, 1995).

Cecil, Hugh and Liddle, Peter (eds), *Facing Armageddon – The First World War Experienced* (London, 1996).

Clark, Ronald W., *The Life of Bertrand Russell* (London, 1975).

Cohen, Joseph, *Journey to the Trenches – the Life of Isaac Rosenberg* (London, 1975).

Delany, Paul, *D.H. Lawrence's Nightmare* (Hassocks, Sussex, 1979).

Dillistone, F.W., *Charles Raven – Naturalist, Historian, Theologian* (London, 1975).

Doyle, Charles, *Richard Aldington* – A Biography (Hassocks, Sussex, 1989).

Edel, Leon, *Bloomsbury – A House of Lions* (London, 1979).

Edel, Leon, *Henry James – The Master 1901–1916* (Philadelphia and New York, 1972).

Eksteins, Modris, *The Rites of Spring – the Great War and the Birth of the Modern Age* (New York, 1990).

Farrar, Martin, *News from the Front – War Correspondents on the Western Front 1914–1918* (London, 1998).

Furbank, P.N., *E.M. Forster – A Life*, vol. 1 (London, 1977).

Furbank, P.N., *E.M. Forster – A Life*, vol. 2 (London, 1978).

Gathorne-Hardy, Jonathan, *The Interior Castle* (London, 1992).

Gilbert, Martin, *Plough My Own Furrow* (London, 1965).

Gindin, James, *John Galsworthy's Life and Art – An Alien's Fortress* (London, 1987).

Gittings, Robert, *The Older Hardy* (London, 1980).

Harrod, Roy F., *The Life of John Maynard Keynes* (London, 1951).

Hepburn, James (ed.), *Arnold Bennett: The Critical Heritage* (London, 1981).

Holroyd, Michael, *Bernard Shaw – Volume Two: The Pursuit of Power* (London, 1991).

Holroyd, Michael, *Lytton Strachey – the New Biography* (London, 1994).

Hurd, Michael, *The Ordeal of Ivor Gurney* (Oxford, 1978).

Hynes, Samuel, *Edwardian Occasions* (London, 1972).

Hynes, Samuel, *The Edwardian Turn of Mind* (Oxford, 1968).

Hynes, Samuel, *A War Imagined* (London, 1990).

Jarvis, Adrian, *Samuel Smiles and the Construction of Victorian Values* (Stroud, 1997).

King, James, *Virginia Woolf* (London, 1994).

Knightley, Philip, *The First Casualty – The War Correspondent as Hero, Propagandist and Myth Maker* (London, 1975).

Lee, Hermione, *Virginia Woolf* (London, 1996).

Levy, Paul, *The Case of Walter Pater* (London, 1978).

Levy, Paul, *G.E. Moore and the Cambridge Apostles* (Oxford, 1981).

MacCarthy, Fiona, *William Morris* (London, 1994).

MacKenzie, Norman and Jean (eds), *The Diary of Beatrice Webb – Volume Three: 1905–1924, The Power to Alter Things* (London, 1984).

Marsden, Gordon (ed.), *Victorian Values – Personalities and Perspectives in Nineteenth Century Society* (London, 1990).

Marwick, Arthur, *Clifford Allen – the open conspirator* (London, 1964).

Marwick, Arthur, *The Deluge: British Society and the First World War* (London, 1986). First published 1965.

Monk, Ray, *Bertrand Russell – The Spirit of Solitude* (London, 1996).

Moorehead, Caroline, *Bertrand Russell* (London, 1992).

Mosse, George L., *Fallen Soldiers: Reshaping the Memory of the World Wars* (Oxford, 1990).

Nehls, Edward (ed.), *D.H. Lawrence: A Composite Biography*, vol. 1(Madison, Wisconsin, 1957).

Newsome, David, *The Victorian World Picture* (London, 1997).

Pierson, R.R. (ed.), *Women and Peace – Theoretical, Historical and Practical Perspectives* (London, 1987).

Priestley, J.B., *The Edwardians* (London, 1970).

Rae, John, *Conscience and Politics* (Oxford, 1970).

Robbins, Keith, *The Abolition of War* (Cardiff, 1976).

Roby, Kinley, E., *A Writer at War* (Baton Rouge, LA, 1932).

Rosenbaum, S.P. (ed.), *The Bloomsbury Group* (London, 1975).

Ryan, Alan, *Bertrand Russell: A Political Life* (London, 1988).

Sanders, M.L. and Taylor, Philip M., *British Propaganda during the First World War, 1914–1918* (London, 1982).

Seymour, Miranda, *Ottoline Morrell – Life on the Grand Scale* (London, 1993).

Seymour-Jones, Carole, *Beatrice Webb – Woman of Conflict* (London, 1992).

Silkin, John, *Out of Battle: The Poetry of the Great War* (London, 1987).

Skidelsky, Robert, *John Maynard Keynes – Volume One: Hopes Betrayed* (London, 1983).

Spalding, Frances, *Duncan Grant* (London, 1997).

Spalding, Frances, *Vanessa Bell* (London, 1983).

Stallworthy, John, *Wilfred Owen* (Oxford, 1974).

Stephen, Martin, *The Price of Pity* (London, 1996).

Thomas, R. George, *Edward Thomas – A Portrait* (Oxford, 1985).

Tylee, Claire, *The Great War and Women's Consciousness* (London, 1990).

Vellacott, Jo, *Bertrand Russell and the Pacifists in the First World War* (Brighton, 1980).

Webb, Barry, *Edmund Blunden – A Biography* (London, 1990).

Weintraub, Stanley, *Journey to Heartbreak* (London, 1973).

West, Rebecca, *1900* (London, 1982).

Wilson, Jean Moorcroft, *Charles Hamilton Sorley* (London, 1985).

Wilson, Jean Moorcroft, *Siegfried Sassoon – the Making of a War Poet: a Biography (1886–1918)* (London, 1998).

Wilson, Trevor, *The Myriad Faces of War* (Cambridge, 1988).

Wilson, Trevor (ed.), *The Political Diaries of C.P. Scott, 1911–1928* (London, 1970).

Wiltsher, Anne, *'Most Dangerous Women': Feminist Peace Campaigners of the Great War* (London, 1985).

Wohl, Robert, *The Generation of 1914* (Cambridge, MA, 1979).

Articles and essays

Bell, Quentin, 'Recollections and Reflections on Maynard Keynes', Lecture 3, *Keynes and the Bloomsbury Group – the Fourth Keynes Seminar, University of Kent, 1978*, ed. D. Crabtree and A.P. Thirlwall (London, 1980).

Bennett, Yvonne A., 'Vera Brittain and the Peace Pledge Union', in *Women and Peace*, ed. R.R.

Pierson (London, 1987).

Bond, Brian, 'British 'Anti-War' Writers and their Critics', in *Facing Armageddon: The First World War Experienced*, ed. H. Cecil and P. Liddle (London, 1996).

Graham, Deborah, 'Vera Brittain, Flora Macdonald Denison and the Great War: The Failure of Non-Violence', in *Women and Peace*, ed. R.R. Pierson (London, 1987).

Himmelfarb, Gertrude, 'A Genealogy of Morals: From Clapham to Bloomsbury', in *Marriage and Morals Amongst the Victorians – Essays*, ed. G. Himmelfarb (London, 1986).

Johnson, Elizabeth, 'Keynes' Attitude to Compulsory Military Service – A Comment', *Economic Journal*, ed. R. Harrod and R.A.. Robinson, vol. LXX, no. 277, March 1960.

Jones, Stephen, 'Attic Attitudes – Leighton and Aesthetic Philosophy', in *Victorian Values – Personality and Perspectives in Nineteenth Century Society*, ed. Gordon Marsden (London, 1990).

Keynes, J.M., 'My Early Beliefs', *Collected Writings of John Maynard Keynes, Volume X – Essays in Biography*, ed. Elizabeth Johnson (London, 1972).

Robinson, Austin, 'A Personal View', in *Essays on Maynard Keynes*, ed. Milo Keynes (Cambridge, 1975).

Williams, Raymond, 'Bloomsbury as a Social and Cultural Group'. Lecture 2, *Keynes and the Bloomsbury Group – the Fourth Keynes Seminar, University of Kent, 1978*, ed. D. Crabtree and A.P. Thirlwall (London, 1980).

Yates, Nigel, 'Pugin and the Medieval Dream' in *Victorian Values – Personalities and Perspectives in Nineteenth Century Society*, ed. Gordon Marsden (London, 1990).

Theses and dissertations

Johnstone, J.K., 'The Philosophic Background and Works of Art of the Group known as Bloomsbury', PhD thesis (University of Leeds, 1952).

Pollock, M.R., 'British Pacifism during the First World War – the Cambridge-Bloomsbury contribution', PhD thesis (University of Columbia, 1971).

Weston, Sally, 'Bertrand Russell, Leonard Woolf and John Maynard Keynes – A Biographical Examination of the Influences Established Before 1914 which Dictated their Reactions to the First World War', MA (University of Kent, 1992).

Index